D0300750

Managing Employment Change

Managing Employment Change

The New Realities of Work

HUW BEYNON, DAMIAN GRIMSHAW,
JILL RUBERY, AND KEVIN WARD

OXFORD
UNIVERSITY PRESS

*This book has been printed digitally and produced in a standard specification
in order to ensure its continuing availability*

OXFORD
UNIVERSITY PRESS

Great Clarendon Street, Oxford OX2 6DP

Oxford University Press is a department of the University of Oxford.
It furthers the University's objective of excellence in research, scholarship,
and education by publishing worldwide in

Oxford New York

Auckland Cape Town Dar es Salaam Hong Kong Karachi
Kuala Lumpur Madrid Melbourne Mexico City Nairobi
New Delhi Shanghai Taipei Toronto
With offices in
Argentina Austria Brazil Chile Czech Republic France Greece
Guatemala Hungary Italy Japan South Korea Poland Portugal
Singapore Switzerland Thailand Turkey Ukraine Vietnam

ISBN 0-19-924870-2

ACKNOWLEDGEMENTS

This book arises out of a project funded by the Leverhulme Trust, held jointly by UMIST and the University of Manchester and located in two research centres, the European Work and Employment Research Centre (EWERC) at UMIST and the International Centre for Labour Studies at the University of Manchester. After Huw Beynon's move from the University of Manchester to the University of Cardiff in 1999 UMIST took full responsibility for managing the final year of the project. Damian Grimshaw and Kevin Ward were appointed as researchers on the project but both have subsequently moved on to lectureships, in the Manchester School of Management, UMIST and the School of Geography, University of Manchester, respectively. This book is very much the outcome of a collective effort by the four authors, as is reflected in the alphabetical listing of authors' names.

Our first acknowledgement is to the support of the Leverhulme Trust for enabling this research to be conducted. Equal thanks are due of course to the participants in the research project, the managers and the employees of the seven organizations and twenty-three workplaces at the centre of the empirical research, and to the trade-union officials associated with the organizations. Others have also helped at various stages either with the empirical research or with the preparation of the book. The former include Philip Almond and Marilyn Carroll, researchers at EWERC, who have carried out some follow-up studies on this project that are not reported on here, but on which we draw from time to time. The latter include Laura Turney, Mary O'Brien, and Helen Dean. And not to forget Rhona Newborn, who with due care transcribed all our interviews. Finally, we would like to thank David Musson of OUP for his support.

CONTENTS

LIST OF BOXES

LIST OF TABLES

LIST OF FIGURES

Introduction

Nowadays it seems that people have lost many of the certainties that once organized their working lives. For a growing number of politicians, academics and media commentators, the reason lies with a fundamental transformation in the essence of the economy and the structure of the labour market. For example, Stephen Byers, the then UK Minister for Trade and Industry, has claimed that the traditional forces which acted as steering mechanisms for the economy have gone:

We are witnessing a fundamental shift taking place in our economy and society. It is driven by globalization, knowledge, technology and innovation. It is changing the nature of work and of the workforce itself.... The old era of the industrial economy with its big unions and big government has gone.

(Byers 1999: 1)

And several international institutions involved in debates over economic change have also made far-reaching observations. For example, the New York-based *Council on Foreign Relations*, an important contributor to debates on global economic, political and social issues, has related changes in people's working lives to a break in the post-war bargain that was built around the Bretton Woods agreement:

Rapid technological change and heightening international competition are fraying the job markets of the major industrialised countries. At the same time systemic pressures are curtailing every government's ability to respond with new spending. Just when working people need the nation state as a buffer from the world economy, it is abandoning them.

(Kapstein 1996: 16)

In place of nation-states and powerful trade unions has emerged the large global corporation. Joe Rogaly, the columnist for the *Financial*

Times, notes that:

> In the old days, many employees could look to a union for help. [But] ...
> the lions have had their teeth drawn ... We are left alone with our new masters,
> the large corporations, the ones who will do you down if they can get away with
> it. (1998)

Other changes also appear to have made it more difficult for workers to organize into trade unions. The last two decades have seen the fragmentation of manufacturing (with greater use of outsourcing and international location of production), the growth of the contingent workforce and the reduced opportunities for workplace solidarity in many parts of the service economy. The International Labour Organization (ILO), a key institution involved in monitoring changes in employment conditions and workers' rights, has recently argued that:

> The era of concentrated mass production is ending, and in the future unions
> will have to operate in large numbers of much smaller units of employment,
> increasingly in the private service sector. Collective bargaining is likely to become
> more dispersed.
>
> (ILO 2001)

But the persistent message is of the need to be flexible and to change. If Mrs Thatcher introduced the idea of TINA ('There is No Alternative'), it has been carried forward with even greater force by successive governments. Each has reminded companies, trade unions, workers and managers that they must be more flexible and that they must compete in order to survive. Gordon Brown, as a Labour Chancellor of the Exchequer, put it like this in his 1998 Budget Speech:

> The impact of the global market in goods and services, and of rapidly advancing
> technology, is now being felt in every home and community in our country.
> New products, services and opportunities challenge us to change; old skills,
> jobs and industries have gone and will never return.[1]

In the midst of these seemingly inexorable changes, questioning voices have reflected on the ways in which organizations have come to be analysed as simply financial entities dominated by shareholder value and cut off from the social world in which they operate (Froud et al. 2000). Others have pointed to the ways in which these ideas (as political ideologies) circulate and squeeze out other (potentially powerful)

---

[1] Available at http://www.hm-treasury.gov.uk

accounts (Walker 1999). The economist Paul Krugman has commented on the importance of this process in the USA, pointing to the:

endless round of meetings, speeches, and exchanges of *communiqués* that occupy much of the time of the economic opinion leaders. Such interlocking social groupings tend at any given time to converge on a conventional wisdom, about economics amongst other things. People believe certain stories because everybody important tells them, and people tell these stories because everyone important believes them. Indeed when the conventional wisdom is at its fullest strength, one's agreement with that conventional wisdom becomes almost a litmus test of one's suitability to be taken seriously. (1998: 37)

However, there are reasons to think that there is a great need for other kinds of ideas, especially those informed by detailed empirical examination of the ways in which our economy and the society are changing and the impact that the changes are having upon people's working and family lives.

This, with due modesty, is the purpose of this book. In 1997 we obtained funding from the Leverhulme Trust to examine changes taking place within workplaces through a case-study approach. Working as an interdisciplinary team (two economists, a geographer and a sociologist), we determined to examine the process of change in seven large organizations operating in the North of England. These organizations were located in the public and private sectors, and were spread across service and manufacturing industries. In keeping with the changing pattern of employment in the UK, our emphasis was upon large service sector corporations and upon those at the leading edge of employment and technological change in the region. We spent two years visiting these organizations and their various workplaces. We talked with managers and workers and conducted formal and informal interviews. We carefully studied (via documents, official reports and corporate publications) the ways in which these organizations have developed strategies and reacted towards uncertainty and new pressures for change that have often taken them by surprise. We interviewed trade-union officials and listened to the problems they have faced during periods of membership 'squeeze' and rapidly changing patterns of employment relations and collective-bargaining arrangements.

This book is based upon our contact with these organizations during our fieldwork between the summers of 1997 and 1999. In it we have attempted to identify the pressures that managers were under, and to make sense of the kinds of decision that they made, and the basis upon which they made them. In examining their motives and reasoning, we have talked with them at length and attempted to present an account that they would find both understandable and fair. In addition, we have been concerned to examine the impact of these decisions and the employment practices that followed from them upon the lives of the thousands of people who worked in these large organizations. What became clear in our interviews with more than 250 employees was that these changes have been quite profound, with deep and lasting effects upon the ways that people have come to reassess their notions of work, time and ideas of fairness and justice. In the way we have written and presented these accounts and in our analysis and conclusions we have endeavoured to be faithful to their sincerity. We are grateful to all the people who contributed to this study, for the time and the trouble they have taken in answering our many questions and for the frank ways in which they have responded. In order to protect their identities, we have felt it necessary to anonymize the names of both their employers and their trade unions.

MANAGING EMPLOYMENT CHANGE IN A SHIFTING ENVIRONMENT

1

Understanding Change at Work

ACCOUNTS OF CHANGE

Over the past twenty years there has been a growing and persistent awareness that major changes are taking place in the nature of paid employment, in the UK and the other OECD states. A considerable literature has emphasized the shift towards a flexible post-industrial society. This has identified a number of key processes associated with the rapid decline of 'smoke-stack' industries in Western industrialized countries (see, for example, Gorz 1976; Lash and Urry 1994; Lipietz 1987; Piore and Sabel 1984). These changes affect the distribution of work throughout society, particularly between men and women, the hours we all work, the shape and intensity of that work and the ways in which these experiences fit into the rest of our lives.

In assessing these changes, social scientists and other commentators have often presented contrasting accounts. Many of the analyses have been optimistic, stressing the new kinds of job and the prospects for economic growth that will be produced by the adaptation of new technology to the service sector and the general rise in the skill level of jobs (Gallie *et al.* 1998). The shift towards service employment more generally has been identified as a profound and often positive development (Gershuny 1983; Kumar 1987) with important consequences for task skills, the organization of employment relations and the nature of work. Others have taken a less optimistic view, arguing that most employment in this sector can best be typed as 'Mac-Jobs', involving low wages and basic levels of skill. As Warhurst and Thompson put it:

Indeed, proponents of the knowledge economy should appreciate that most tertiary sector growth has occurred not in knowledge work but in the lower paid 'donkey work' of serving, guarding, cleaning, waiting and helping in the private health and care services, as well as hospitality industries. (1998: 5)

Similar disagreement surrounds discussion over the emergence of a more flexible economy. The growing flexibility of working hours is seen by some to facilitate flexible employment careers that allow women more easily to accommodate child-rearing. Men and women, it is argued, can develop a more varied working career through the creation of a portfolio of jobs (Arthur and Rousseau 1996). However, such a strategy (for the employee) may be thwarted by the employer's own requirements for the flexibility to involve irregular patterns of working time. These changes also impact on domestic arrangements for the many households dependent upon two incomes (Green 2001; Machin and Waldfogel 1994). Furthermore, the benefits that flow from flexibility may be outweighed by the increased levels of insecurity that such arrangements introduce into individuals' working careers (Heery and Salmon 2000a; Sennett 1998). Company failures, bankruptcies, takeovers and successive downsizing policies have strengthened this sense of insecurity. The downturn in employment in financial services in the early 1990s made clear that the new service economy was not immune from these instabilities either. This can be interpreted as the 'other side' of flexibility: one that can have negative effects upon the economy and society.

This sense of change that has accompanied the shifts in the structure of the economy and the operation of labour markets is a profound one. It has been exacerbated in the UK by the large-scale privatization of state-owned industries and public utilities. In this way the boundary line between the public and private sectors has shifted radically. This has had further ramifications as market principles and managerial practices adapted from the private sector have been introduced into what remains of the public sector. These new arrangements were, of course, also associated with the policies of the Thatcher government, which operated with a strong neo-liberal understanding of market economies and the role of the state. This view also extended towards trade unions, and the legislation enacted in the Thatcher period (combined with the structural changes in the economy) severely weakened the capacities for trade unions to organize resistance to change or to forcefully press for alternatives.

So—something has happened. What is less clear is why it has happened and how best the new situation can be understood.

IT'S THE ECONOMY, STUPID!

The changes that have affected the system of employment in the UK have taken place within a context of increasing internationalization of the major economies and the increasing importance of both manufacturing and service companies, which operate on a global basis (see Dicken 1998). Such companies, in the pursuit of their objectives, have come to understand the importance of locational decisions and the variable nature of the kinds of labour and infrastructural support available in different places.

In this context, employers have become more concerned with the quality of the people they recruit and their qualifications and aptitudes. As a consequence, they now show considerable interest in the nature of national educational and training systems. In the 1990s, the presence or absence of skills within local labour markets in the UK became a recurring topic. The question of a skills mismatch came to be seen as concern for companies and governments alike. In these accounts, the new technological revolution was creating a knowledge-based economy in which the critical jobs were highly skilled and carried with them the high levels of value-added needed by companies in an increasingly competitive economy (DTI 1999). However, many are sceptical of this view and suggest that part of the problem is the way that advances in technology and science assume 'mythical proportions' (Bradley *et al.* 2000: 108). Moreover, claims of an emerging knowledge economy in Britain have rarely been supported by detailed analyses of the kinds of job associated with the introduction of information technology into offices and factories. In a wide-ranging review, Freeman and Soete identify multiple problems:

Numerous case studies of diffusion of robots, CNC, lasers, CAD and so forth in manufacturing or use of computers and ATM in banks or of EDI in retail firms... testify to the systems integration problems and the site-specific problems which arose and still arise in a widening range of firms and industries. Operating and maintenance skills do not match the new equipment; management cannot cope with the interdepartmental problems, changes in structure and industrial relations; subcontractors cannot meet the new demands; the software does not run properly... (1996: 56)

In spite of exhortations to 'work smarter not harder' (Drucker 1970; Francis 1986), survey after survey has indicated that British workers were working both harder and longer (Green 2000, 2001). Just how they have interpreted the enthusiastic publicity devoted to the new ways of working is very much a matter of conjecture. However, case studies conducted in the 1990s give some indication. At Royal Ordnance, at the time a subsidiary of British Aerospace, management reorganized production around new CNC (Computerized Numerical Control) machines in the early 1990s in a bid to keep up with new technologies. But by the mid-1990s the company was collapsing, and across the defence industry there was a haemorrhage of skilled workers. The workers blamed an unimaginative and inflexible management: 'We'll never change.... There's no intention here for diversifying. It's like banging your head against a brick wall trying to get them [management] to change' (cited in Bradley *et al.* 2000: 99).

On the basis of these findings, some analysts have begun to take issue with the viability or appropriateness of the high skills strategy for the UK economy (see Keep 2000). In these views, historically low investment levels in research and development make a low skills strategy more important in many sectors. This sectoral question has been picked up by other accounts that have identified important levels of variation by sector in skill acquisition and organizational adaptation to the new deregulated economy. In the early 1990s, comparisons of low skilled work within the service sector (for example, between subcontracted cleaning and catering services; see Rees and Fielder 1992) indicated quite different managerial approaches to training and skills development in different industries. What such criticisms (Warhurst and Thompson 1998: 19) point to is the importance of moving away from abstract notions of 'the market' and 'market clearance' to more concrete analyses of what actually happens in different workplaces across the various sectors of the economy.

In spite of these doubts, pressures associated with ideas of international competitiveness have continued to persuade Western governments of their role in relation to the creation of the right conditions for economic change and development. This has been particularly acute in the UK where there has been a long-running debate over comparative productivity levels and the poor performance of UK-based firms in relation to their counterparts in mainland Europe. Viewed in this context, the institutional changes that have taken place can be seen as a response to powerful economic imperatives of the kind that fuelled the idea that 'There is No Alternative'—that is, the weakening of the trade unions and the associated deregulation of labour markets was a necessary and sufficient condition for increased productivity, profits and economic growth. Britain has, of course, gone a long way down this road. During the 1980s and early 1990s, as part of an attack against 'inflexible pay arrangements', successive Conservative governments abolished provisions of the Employment Protection Act (1975) and the Fair Wages Resolution Act (1946), which previously encouraged inter-firm wage comparisons, and in 1993 brought an end to the role of Wages Councils, which recommended minimum wage rates in various low-paying sectors. In the public sector, the government encouraged decentralized wage setting (Bailey 1993; Elliott 1995), and in the private sector, employers pulled out of long-standing multi-employer collective-bargaining agreements in favour of single-employer bargaining (Jackson *et al.* 1993; Millward *et al.* 2000). As levels of regulation and coordination in the labour market declined, union membership also fell dramatically; between 1990 and 1998 the share of all workers in unions dropped from one in three (33 per cent) to one in four workers (27 per cent) (*Labour Market Trends*, July 1999; see also Cully *et al.* 1999). Even more dramatic has been the strengthened hand of the employer in setting pay and other terms and conditions of employment: the proportion of all workplaces where collective bargaining was the dominant mode of pay determination was cut in half between 1984 and 1998, from a share of 60 per cent to 29 per cent (Millward *et al.* 2000).

With the change in government in 1997, certain policy changes were suggestive of a reversal in the direction of institutional change—that there is, perhaps, an alternative. In April 1999, the UK introduced a national minimum wage (NMW) for the first time, thus setting a floor to the wage structure. In the public sector, there was no longer a determination to replace centralized with local pay determination. And the encouragement of new partnership agreements with trade unions is seen by some as a welcome initiative underpinning union renewal. Nevertheless, the level of the NMW was soon criticized for being too low, with trade-union and local community action groups calling for employers to sign up to a 'Living Wage' (*Guardian*, 26 March 2001). In the public sector, there are increasing numbers of workers employed outside traditional coordinated wage-setting arrangements, with local terms and conditions for civil servants and health care assistants, and performance-related pay for teachers (Grimshaw 1999; IDS 1997; White 1999). Finally, some have raised doubts about the prospects for union renewal on the basis of new partnership-based agreements. In part, this is because the Labour government has been emphasizing workplace partnerships over and above national-level developments, but also because it has realized that a partnership approach could undermine union activities at well-organized sites founded on adversarial relations (Fisher 1997; Kelly 1998; McIlroy 1998; Waddington 2000).

There seems little doubt, therefore, that employment relations are going through a detailed process of change. Clearly, these changes will have an impact upon power relationships within the workplace, and this has come about at a time when there has been considerable pressure to reduce labour costs. For example, in the early 1990s, a MORI poll of senior personnel managers found that: 'More than half the managers believed that the desire to cut overheads by avoiding the legal terms and conditions due to full-time workers might influence decisions to introduce flexible working patterns' (*Financial Times*, 31 November 1993).

These processes are general ones and they have had a major impact upon the ways in which workers and managers directly experience work. Most dramatic, perhaps, has been the impact that they have had upon the organization of work and employment relations in the public sector. In the postwar period, the labour markets in many of Britain's industrial regions were dominated by state-sector employment (Beynon *et al.* 1994). Many lower-skilled men found employment in nationalized industries, public utilities, local or central government; or in schools, hospitals or the fire service or police force. The public sector was also the generator of jobs for women, primarily in schools, hospitals and administration. Between 1981 and the end of the twentieth century employment in the sector declined by over two million (Corby and White 1999: table 1.1). This was almost entirely due to privatization, which moved whole nationalized industries, or parts of them, into the private sector. Those corporations that were sold off completely experienced radical restructuring. Changes were most obvious in the privatized utilities, with water, gas and electricity each shedding over 25 per cent of their labour forces, while British Telecom cut its workforce by over half in the period between 1985 and 1998 (Darlington 1998; see also Froud *et al.* 1996).

However, privatization did not occur across the whole of the public sector. Employment in the sector still stood at over five million at the end of the 1990s and most of these workers (in schools, hospitals, local authorities, the BBC and the emergency services) saw their jobs and the conditions under which they worked change dramatically, not least in terms of a severely increased workload. Ever-tighter budgetary constraints, new measurements of 'output' and the generalized introduction of what is termed 'the new public management' (Dunleavy and Hood 1994) have constituted little less than a revolution in many of these state organizations. Since the 1980s we have witnessed a blurring of the public/private divide, a growth in the public sector in the use of flexible employment contracts, reduced opportunities for collectivism among workers and a potential decline in the public sector ethos (Corby and White 1999: 15–20). Through policies such as Compulsory Competitive Tendering (CCT), the Private Finance Initiative (PFI) and, most recently, Best Value, the traditional role of the state in delivering public services has been undermined. Workers have been increasingly subject to evaluation, inspection and often public humiliation through the constant auditing of individual and group performance. Although these pressures are experienced and acted out in different ways in different sectors of the state, there is compelling evidence of individuals being unhappy performing their work. In a survey of job satisfaction in the UK, Oswald and Gardner (2001) found that working in the public sector during the 1990s had become increasingly stressful and less enjoyable. Job satisfaction levels had dropped dramatically in the early 1990s, rising again in the run up to the 1997 general election, only to decline again after the election of a Labour goverment.

Within the National Health Service, the development of NHS Trusts and the introduction of management systems built around the internal market have produced considerable friction. The parallels here with some of the more rigid management systems introduced into private manufacturing are quite strong. Regularly, nurses say that they 'love the work but hate the job' (Cooke 2000). As with other areas of public services, nurses and doctors are expected to do more with fewer resources. Managerial goals have been reshaped around increasing patient throughput and reducing costs. This change has been dramatic and has involved a shift away from a public service ethos to an emphasis on business and turnover. In health services, this has been interpreted by some employees as similar to the difference between working in a church and working in a garage (Nottingham and O'Neill 1998, cited in Martinez Lucio and MacKenzie 1999).

Changes like these have led to the transfer of the *modus operandi* of business from the private to the public sector, which has also seen the adoption of some of the more brutal private sector management styles. As a result, industrial disputes in the 1980s and 1990s in the UK became increasingly concentrated in the public sector, with public sector unions increasingly dominating the politics of the Trades Union Congress. Regularly, these workers and their representatives drew attention to issues of work intensity and stress associated with the organizational changes.

All this is indicative of important shifts taking place within the state sector which relate to changes in state policy and the imposition of external budgetary constraints upon those activities which were previously delivered on the basis of service and need. They form an arena in which conflicts over purpose and the evaluation of work are fought out. That the conflict over values seems to be so acute in the state sector illustrates the extent to which these state workers and public service professions drew upon ideas of public service as a means of establishing their collective identities and developing their complex interests within society. It was these codes that were being contested and broken down by the managerialism of the 1980s and 1990s (Du Gay 2000). In turn, many professional people came to resent the increased demands placed upon them in a world where their service wasn't valued.

In his general reflections on similar changes in the USA, Richard Sennett has linked these new work regimes with a 'Corrosion of Character'. Character, he says, 'concerns personal traits which we value in ourselves and which we seek to be valued by others'. He asks:

How do we decide what is of lasting value in ourselves in a society which is impatient, which focuses on the immediate moment? How can long term goals be pursued in an economy devoted to the short term? How can mutual loyalties and commitments be sustained in institutions that are constantly breaking apart or continually being redesigned? (1998: 10)

THE CHANGING NATURE OF WORK

There has, of course, been considerable discussion of the changes that have taken place in the workplace since the 1970s. Much research flowed from discussion of Harry Braverman's (1974) critical text *Labor and Monopoly Capital*, elaborating the theme expressed in its subtitle: 'the degradation of work in the twentieth century'. It was his view that labour market demand in the future would be for increasing numbers of low-skilled workers capable of performing routine tasks on instruction; a view that was partly supported by a manager of a chemical plant who informed researchers in the early 1970s that the future was one in which there would be an increasing polarization between 'scientific work and donkey work' (see Nichols and Beynon 1978). To many, it seemed reasonable to agree with Braverman's view of deskilling as representing a general tendency throughout the twentieth century. Nevertheless, problems still remain when dealing with specific workplaces and occupations. This is particularly so in periods of rapid change associated with the decline of some industries and sectors and the rise of new kinds of workplace and product.

Attention to these kinds of problem has encouraged views that a major transformation has occurred in the nature of work itself. Some have stressed the shift from a Fordist to a post-Fordist society (see Aglietta 1979; Lipietz 1987). This process was associated with a major transformation in the nature of the industrial economy and society. Piore and Sabel, in their highly influential book, identified this as 'the second industrial divide'. They argued that as a consequence of a number of external shocks (for example, the oil price increases and the collapse of Bretton Woods) the system of mass production was put under increasing pressure. These authors contrasted this old (Fordist) system of production with the potential of a new form, which they identified as 'flexible specialization'. This had many similarities with those outlined as 'neo-Fordism' and 'post-Fordism'. In the view of Piore and Sabel, the 1980s and 1990s represented a period when industrial corporations and national governments faced strategic choices. 'Flexible specialization' was one such choice. This view mirrors other accounts of market flexibility and conveys an extremely positive and optimistic view of change in workplaces. In their view, the erosion of mass markets and the arrival of the flexible productive capacities of new technological systems provided the basis for a new kind of efficiency. In this vein, researchers have talked of the emergence of an 'innovation mediated' system in which 'intellectual and physical labour' becomes mutually integrated around a dynamic production process (Kenney and Florida 1993: 14). The contrast between accounts like these and the earlier Braverman-inspired commentaries is quite remarkable.

Empirical investigations of these changes have failed, however, to provide convincing support for changes in work practices that are mutually beneficial to all employees. Ruth Milkman's studies (1997) in the USA have indicated how practice falls far short of the raised expectations. Studies in the UK have come to similar conclusions. New technologies have been introduced, but there is no evidence to suggest that these changes have produced workplaces characterized by multi-skilled workers involved in rewarding and satisfying work; nor is there evidence of a sea-change in the attitudes of industrial workers (for an assessment, see Daniel 1987; Elger 1990, 1999). For example, Delbridge was concerned to investigate the extent to which the successful management of contemporary manufacturing organizations required: 'the integration of low buffered and tightly controlled technical systems with flexible, high commitment, team-based social systems that incorporate increased worker skills and involvement' (1998: 6). In order to consider this issue, he went to work as a manual worker in two factories. Although he expected the jobs to be boring and laborious, he found that working in a factory was: 'more mundane, more repetitive and harder than I had expected, more soul-destroying to work on a line in a dreary factory for hour after hour, day after day, than I can really articulate' (1999: vii).

The extent to which people's experiences have not conformed to the optimistic expectations of both theorists and politicians is quite striking. Generally, it seems that the jobs of employees have changed in a number of ways: they involve more tasks than hitherto, often they involve more responsibilities; equally, people seem to be working harder with fewer breaks, and experiencing greater levels of stress.

Redundancies have also been a key feature of recent changes in work organization, with talk of 'downsizing' and 'rightsizing' as companies attempt to adapt to new conditions. But, as Turnbull and Wass (2000) remind us, this is a particular form of adaptation that is encouraged under UK legislation. They argue that judicial interpretation of the law has resulted in very explicit support for managerial definitions of efficiency and the (financial) 'needs of the business' (Turnbull 1988: 209–10), not only with respect to who goes but also who stays: workers can be declared redundant because of new working methods and new techniques, and those who remain must adapt to higher work rates and improved standards of quality and efficiency. Workers who fail to meet these new standards may also be dismissed and some may not even qualify for redundancy pay (Turnball and Wass 2000: 65–6).

The empirical evidence demonstrates the problems associated with insecurity at work. A survey of 170 employees in financial services found decreased motivation and morale and higher levels of stress and feelings of bitterness—a condition the authors labelled 'survivor syndrome' (Horsted and Doherty 1995, cited in Nolan *et al.* 2000). Another survey of 1,300 managers carried out by the Institute of Management identified a similar condition—'recession survival strategy'—as the source of significant levels of stress:

Four out of five of the managers in the survey said that their work loads had increased in the past two years and the same numbers were worried about their future financial position. More than half the managers said that they were concerned about future career opportunities. As companies emerged from recession, however, the new management job structures were not offering improved job security, reduced stress levels or the easing of work loads.

(Institute of Management 1995)

Reflecting upon these accounts, employment theorists began to operate with more generic approaches to changes in the nature of work. In his major study, *The Work of Nations*, Reich chose to move away from systemic accounts of change. In his view, changes in the nature of work could best be understood though a recategorization of the *types* of work that constituted the US economy. Reich calculated that just 20 per cent of the jobs in the new economy were ones that were intrinsically satisfying and economically rewarding. He refers to these as the work of the *symbolic analysts* (the consultants, journalists, designers, architects, lecturers) whose work has creativity at its core as they communicate complex ideas to a broader audience (clients, customers, user groups). They represent his 'fortunate fifth' (Reich 1991) and they correspond with the 30 per cent identified by Will Hutton in the 30 : 30 : 40 society (Hutton 1994). Their working lives can be contrasted with a second group who regularly perform routine tasks and a third who are responsible for the daily delivery of a variety of mundane services. Clearly, views of this new world vary with your position within it. Ironically, of course, part of the function of the symbolic analysts is to perform such tasks as that of spin doctors or public relations experts. We live uneasily in *their* interpretive world. The labour activity in this world is dominated by Reich's two subordinate categories: *routine production and service workers* and *in-person service workers*. Both these groups of workers share things in common, i.e. they typically work in the company of many other people who do the same thing, usually within large enclosed spaces. In Reich's view:

They are guided on the job by standard procedures and codified rules, and even their overseers are overseen, in turn, by people who routinely monitor—often with the aid of computers—how much they do and how accurately they do it. Their wages are based on the amount of time they put in or the amount of work they do. (1991: 175)

This is the world of the routine worker. In-person service workers conform to a similar regime, but their jobs carry an additional requirement: 'they must also have a pleasant demeanour. They must smile and exude confidence and good cheer, even when they feel morose' (ibid.: 176).

In many ways this borrows from and extends the ideas of 'emotional labour' developed by Hochschild (1983) and draws upon earlier accounts of service activities (Wright Mills 1957). In the 1990s increasing attention was paid to the growing importance of the changing nature of 'interactive service work', where 'jobs require workers to interact directly with customers or clients' (Leidner 1993: 1; see also Fuller and Smith 1991; McCammon and Griffin 2000; Sturdy *et al.* 2001). Within the workplaces where this 'deep acting' work is performed (Hochschild 1983), managers now talk of 'customer-facing' work, where this facing is done through a computer screen and a telephone headset. In analysing these developments, social scientists have begun to use military analogies, such as 'front-line work', in a way that captures many of the tensions that emerged in the 1990s (Frenkel *et al.* 1999). Behind this most recent attempt to capture the nature of work performed in the service is the belief that:

At the core of the service worker–customer encounter is an interaction—the worker supplies a service and the customer consumes it; and there are myriad types of transactions, from the waitress who takes orders and serves food to the athlete who scores the winning basket to the stockbroker [or call centre operator] who gives online... advice.

(McCammon and Griffin 2000: 279)

Poynter (2000) has extended this emphasis. He argues that the relative decline of the manufacturing sector has seen increasing pressure being placed upon service sector jobs. In his view, insistent processes of restructuring and re-engineering have combined with experimentation in new forms of work organization to create a service labour process that contains many of the features of manufacturing. He sees the call centre as the most extreme example of this trend. In these workplaces, Poynter maintains that:

[E]mployees are subjected to performance measurement and forms of work monitoring that obtain a level of management control and authority over the conduct of work that even Henry Ford would have envied. Indeed close analysis of the interaction between the human/computer/customer interface typically reveals a level of manipulation of human relationships that places the exchanges, including the emotional signals, between worker and customer at the centre of the process of creation of surplus value. (2000: 152)

Reich's classification, and the subsequent discussion of service- and customer-facing work, has proved helpful. If we attempt to relate these changes back to the ways in which work and employment relations have altered, a number of complex processes become evident. Most clear is the fact that the stable superannuated labour force, which characterized the 1950s, has been severely eroded. The labour force of the early 2000s is made up of a number of different kinds of employee: part-time workers, temporary-workers, casual-, even self-employed, workers. As we enter the twenty-first century these *hyphenated workers* are becoming a more and more significant part of the economy (see Beynon 1997). This phenomenon has been described as one involving 'flexibility and the fragmentation of contractual statuses' (Gallie *et al.*

1998: 10–13). The old industrial economy of Britain was highly regulated; it employed large numbers of highly unionized workers employed on full-time contracts. Most of these workers were men, and they were paid what was recognized as a family wage, a form of payment that sustained the idea of the man as the breadwinner (Supiot 2001). In the UK, this family wage, like coal and steel production, is a thing of the past. Generally, however, the standard of living for families is sustained by more than one income. Women's wages (once dubbed as 'pin money') have become an essential part of household incomes, and with this has come an enormous change in the composition of the labour force and the culture and form of many of the new workplaces.

As manufacturing employment declined, new employment opportunities emerged in other expanding branches of an economy that was increasingly dominated by service sector employment. These developments were most obviously visible on our high streets as banks and building societies opened new offices. The rise of these financial services associated with the borrowing, investing and lending of money was a dramatic phenomenon. So powerful was it that by 1995, more than half the regions in Britain (including the famed industrial economy of Scotland) earned more from financial services than they did from manufacturing. To this can be added the revolutionary changes that have taken place in the retailing sectors. Here, the development of the superstore, located away from city centres, has done much to rearrange the shopping and leisure habits of large proportions of the population. It has also contributed significantly to the operation of local labour markets, because this shift away from manufacturing has also been a shift in favour of the employment of women. Between 1980 and 2000 employment in the service industries increased by almost 70 per cent, from just over thirteen million to over twenty-two million workers (*Employment Gazette* 1984: table 1.4; *Labour Market Trends* June 2001: table B.18). Despite this rapid increase in the size of the sector, the share of female employment has remained largely static at around 55 per cent. However, the ratio of women to men of 1.17 : 1 in the service sector still dwarfs that of 0.28 : 1 in the goods-producing sector (OECD 2000). In spite of this high number of women employed in the sector, they continue to be grouped at the bottom of the job ladder. Women are still over-represented as shop cashiers, call-centre operators or care assistants. In the UK it is increasingly the norm for married women—and those with children—to continue in employment, raising such issues as equality at the workplace and who performs domestic work, to name but two.

These changes are considerable and have combined in ways that have produced significant shifts in the pattern of work and employment. They have also had a deep and profound effect upon the sensibilities of our society, something that social scientists are beginning to reflect upon.

ENTER THE ORGANIZATION

Perhaps the worst consequence identified in Braverman's excellent text relates to the way that the labour process and deskilling became separated from other aspects of capitalist society. It has often seemed that the discussion of work placed the labour process in a space independent of capitalist firms or the operation of the capitalist market. In the labour process literature, details of jobs and technical changes are often discussed independently of the product or the company and its sectoral location. As a consequence, it became clear that there is a positive need to 'bring the organization back in' and, in doing so, to link the study of work with other branches of economics and sociology (Rubery and Wilkinson 1994).

In the UK context of decentralized regulation, it is clear that organizations play a key role in determining the terms under which people are employed. They choose which people enter their gates and which people are excluded. Organizations also design what kind of work is undertaken, for how long and for what level of pay. In making these decisions, they are obviously constrained by local circumstances and by external regulatory forces. However, in the last analysis these organizations have the capacity to decide. As Henry Ford II once put it: 'my name is on the building'. While this is an extreme case, it makes the point that if companies find the terms and conditions that they feel obliged to follow to be unacceptable, they can shut up shop. The power of the organization in structuring employment has to be recognized within any account of employment change. This is all the more significant in the context of large transnational corporations.

Companies have reacted to the uncertainties of this new situation in a number of ways. In some cases, they have favoured temporary and part-time contracts over the creation of new, full-time, permanent posts and have often turned to outside employment agencies as a source of temporary labour (Geary 1992; Neathey and Hurstfield 1995). One job advertisement in County Durham illustrates the extent to which this 'flexibility' can be stretched:

We are seeking people who are prepared to work on a casual basis, with extremely flexible hours. We can accommodate from 3 to 10 hour stints throughout the 24 when work is available. Applicants must have very nimble fingers to cope with the work involved, and be prepared to work at 24 hours notice.

(quoted in Wray 1993)

The reference to nimble fingers makes it clear that women predominate in these kinds of contract. Women make up over 75 per cent of the part-time workforce, and this category of employment grew by 40 per cent between 1980 and 2000. In this period the numbers of men who work part time also grew, up by 122 per cent since the 1980s (*Employment Gazette* 1988; table 1.1; *Labour Market Trends* May 2001: table B.11), and both men and women have increasingly been employed on temporary contracts. Although total temporary employment flattened off during the late 1990s, at just over 1.5 million, placement through temporary work agencies continues to be on the up (Forde and Slater 2001). These developments have given risen to accounts of an 'insecure workforce' (Elliott and Atkinson 1998; Heery and Salmon 2000b). Initially this insecurity was believed to be confined to the so-called periphery of an organization (Atkinson 1984), but subsequently the distinction between the core and periphery has become increasingly blurred. Not only does the insecure workforce often comprise a majority of the staff (Walsh 1990), but the insecurity is seen steadily to be spreading to the core (Burchell *et al.* 1999).

Similarly, the development of functional flexibility strategies has also not resulted in a simple core/periphery division. Rather, these have often had the effect of increasing work intensity, and have not involved a significant upskilling of the workforce (Elger 1990). Furthermore, employees on all types of contract are increasingly expected to be involved in a wider variety of tasks, often involving increased responsibility (Gallie *et al.* 1998).

At the same time, and seemingly in conflict with these trends, employees have become more and more recognized in the management literature and in the public statements of governments and large corporations as a highly valuable human resource. One of the features of employment is that it requires the active cooperation of the employee. For the employer, employment is created in order to contribute to production or service delivery. But this contribution does not automatically follow from the signing of an employment contract. As the labour process debate has made clear, labour power has to be turned into actual labour. Individuals are active agents in this process and they can influence the operation of the organization's employment system in a number of important ways. Individuals decide which organizations and which job opportunities to apply for, how long to stay with an organization (provided they are not forcibly ejected) and how actively they wish to participate in and respond to employer-based initiatives. Employees themselves can have a considerable influence over the shaping of the organization of work and the level and form of its activity. Many of these initiatives are unanticipated by management and arise out of the tendencies of workers to use both their human intelligence and their resistance to control in ways that shape their own activities and environment.

As a result, all large companies have become concerned with *human resource management* (see Storey 1995). To this end, they have developed policies that emphasize the recruitment, appraisal, retention and managed retirement of key employees. They have also been involved in the creation of forms of working which develop teamwork, cooperation and commitment to the company. Management texts emphasize the significance of the successful management of the internal labour market to the company's well-being (see Webb 1992).

These accounts are important, inasmuch as they draw attention to the organization and the management process as active agents in ordering relations within the workplace. As such, management is identified as a group capable of mediating market pressures and constructing forms of relationships (as with teams) that have an impact upon work that goes beyond the detailed operation of the job task. Many of these accounts provide insights into the nature of change taking place in the employment architecture and provide a rich vein of evidence on the tendency for employment change not to be driven solely by technological and market imperatives.

There is a danger, however, that in these organizational frameworks, managers are transformed from mere ciphers (as in some labour process accounts) into super-heroes. Here, there is always a 'best fit' between the human relations strategy and the overall business strategy for the company. Often, however, this is not the case. Changes in external conditions can create an environment in which 'best practice' is irrevocably undermined. This, of course, was the experience of Elton Mayo and his researchers as their successful experiments of work group behaviour were brought to an end by the slump and factory closures.

Markets and market competition do not always operate in ways that encourage creativity and good working relationships. There are moments when markets can be destructive forces, and some markets can be more destructive than others. For example, it is not clear that the City of London and the stock market have always functioned in ways that have encouraged fixed capital investment and the building of long-term team-working relationships within British industry (Hutton 1994).

In the context of a competitive economy that has displaced the site of production from the centre of the modern corporation, companies have to deal with the need to sell and to please their consumers. The market has taken an ascendancy that relegates the workings of offices and factory floors to subordinate status. Anthony (1994) has pointed out, with much perception, that management now claims the right not only to manage but also to manage the meaning of events. It is they who form the conduit between producer and consumer. But they are often not up to the task. In his research, Anthony detected a 'schizophrenic' tendency in British management: on the one hand, emphasizing team working and togetherness, while, on the other, being swamped by the onset of further downsizing as the market takes its toll. Much empirical research into management strategies in the UK suggests that, in practice, in contrast to adopting a strategic approach, managers' policies are driven by events. Far from being super-heroes, they are firefighters, compromisers and opportunists (Legge 1995a; Purcell 1987; Rubery 1994; Storey 1995). Even where new policies such as team working have been embraced by management, research (see, for example, Willmott 1993) has discerned evidence of 'confusion and emptiness' among the workers involved in these practices.

EMBEDDEDNESS AND INSTITUTED ECONOMIC PROCESSES

In each of the previous sections we have indicated how research has tended to isolate particular processes—markets, labour processes and organizational analysis—and study them apart from the others. Furthermore, it has become clear that it is often difficult to generalize from one sector to another and from the micro-level of the workplace to the macro-level of the economy and society. This relationship between the general and the particular was looked at more closely by Touraine who, in his early studies of technical change, emphasized the direct and personal effects of these changes. They involve, he said:

an appreciation of what is symbolized in terms of outside control and of the individual's activities and prospects. At all these levels, change will be judged according to the worker's total life experience, his social and economic environment, his commitments and aspirations, the picture he has formed of his employers and the value he puts on his working career. (1965: 12)

Ideas such as these contributed to a growing appreciation that comparative analyses of organizational structure and change need to consider the significance of the environment in which the organization is embedded in shaping responses and outcomes to apparently similar technological or market changes. Moreover, broader political, cultural and social conditions and norms interact with the dynamics of employer–employee relations in the workplace. These ideas have been developed by economic sociologists (see Granovetter 1974, 1985), who have emphasized the *embeddedness* of market and production relations within local social, political and cultural forms. This analysis builds on Karl Polanyi's (1944) classic historical analysis of UK industrialization. In this view, the commodificiation of labour associated with capitalist production systems is everywhere associated with regulatory forms developed by the state. These forms vary and will relate to and provide the underpinning of different degrees of commodification, but they are an essential feature of all capitalist production systems and are not merely epiphenomenal. Polanyi's work focused upon the historical development of industrial production in Britain, but it has been developed by others who have indicated its importance for a study of comparative capitalist forms (see Block 1986; Granovetter 1985) and of 'instituted economic processes' (Harvey 1999).

Whether the end product of this is 'one capitalism or many' is a moot point (see Albert 1993). What is clear, however, is that the complex interface between the economic organization and its external environment is of considerable importance. It has been, nonetheless, overlooked in many analyses of employment change.

For example, within sociological accounts of workplace change it became common in the UK and the USA to talk of the Japanization of workplaces associated with the location of Japanese transplants and the ways in which UK and US managers came to mimic the best practice of the Japanese. However, little consideration has been given to the ways in which local arrangements and understandings modified and altered the ways in which the Japanese system operated in a new context. By focusing on organization techniques alone (techniques, for example, such as 'Just in Time' and 'Quality Circles'), too little attention was paid to the ways in which the Japanese employment system relied upon and was embedded in the wider social and political contours of Japanese society. In this vein, the common uniforms worn by workers and managers in Nissan's Sunderland plant were often erroneously attributed to the Japanese system. Subsequent re-examination of what was meant by Japanese practices in Japan, the UK and the USA revealed significant and surprising variations. More generally, studies observed how Japanese techniques—as practised by Japanese transplant and local producers—were constituted in quite different forms of work and employment relations (Delbridge 1998; Elger and Smith 1994; Graham 1994; Jain 1990; Smith and Elger 2000). Similarly, the long tradition of institutional analysis within economics has paid careful attention to the ways in which social institutions coordinate economic activity. However, these approaches have operated with a formalized dichotomy between the influence of institutions and the operation of the market. As a consequence, they have also been remiss in not analysing either the embeddedness of organizations in the external environment or the impact of institutions on the operation of the market. The following two contrasting examples will illustrate this problem.

Doeringer and Piore's (1971) analysis of the internal labour market located it within a set of internal conditions and imperatives. In this account, the external labour market was seen as influencing only the entry level wage rate (Grimshaw and Rubery 1998). This can appear feasible in the context of a single workplace, but comparative analyses have indicated that the external environment exerts a more detailed influence (Maurice *et al.* 1986; Sorge and Maurice 2000). The ways in which corporations are embedded in broader social and economic institutions have a deep effect upon the very form of their internal labour markets.

An alternative example is provided by Cappelli *et al.*'s (1997) account of the ways in which changes in external market conditions have led to the destruction of established internal labour market structures in the USA. In this view, the reshaping of employment towards more short-term and perhaps even more spot contracting is synonymous with the collapse of institutional influences. While Doeringer and Piore emphasize the inviolate nature of internal hierarchies, Cappelli *et al.* see the market as entirely determinant in shaping employment patterns. This view is also flawed. It sees the market as an uncontrollable force over which corporations have little influence. While external (market) changes are clearly important, only rarely (as in catastrophic slumps or wild inflationary excesses) can they overwhelm the institutions that operate within economic organizations. This approach shares something of the methodology of transaction costs economics. In these schemas the transformation from bureaucratic systems to flexible or networked ones is seen to represent a long-term adjustment to new market imperatives and new structures of transaction costs.

These accounts share an approach that produces an elision between the organization and the market. However, organizations always play a major role in shaping and creating employment systems. In all economies and employment systems there is a dynamic between the organization and the environment in which it operates. Employment has a macroeconomic, social and organizational dynamic and the understanding of employment change has to address and interpret these different dynamics and their interrelationships. To treat them either as separate or as simply reflections of the same phenomena underplays the complexity of forces shaping employment change.

TOWARD AN INTEGRATED APPROACH

Analyses of employment change which are focused at only one level, on either macro-social and economic developments or on organizational level change, have been seen to be inadequate for understanding the processes of employment transformation. What is required is an integrated and iterative analysis between the macro and the micro and the external and the internal labour market systems.

Building upon the idea of embeddedness, it seems clear that an approach to organizational analysis should begin with an assumption that organizations always play a major role in shaping and creating employment systems and that they are always involved in a dynamic tension with their social and political environment. Such a dynamic is clearly very complex and could give rise to vacuous statements in which everything relates to everything else. In order to avoid this, it is sensible to structure the account around a number of different dimensions. Figure 1.1 represents an attempt to do this, and it presents the framework we propose to adopt here. This framework has previously been developed from an approach first suggested by Osterman (1994; see also Grimshaw and Rubery 1998).

Fig. 1.1. A dynamic framework for analysing employment change

Osterman proposed analysing this organizational–society dynamic according to three rings of influence: the first ring related to performance considerations at the organizational level; the second ring related to organizational culture and power relations, reflecting internal custom and practice or the past history of the organization; and the third ring related to external market conditions and regulatory institutions. For Osterman, the main tension lay in the interaction between the performance-led imperatives for change and the restraining or constraining influence of organizational custom and practice. External labour market considerations were only likely to influence change from time to time, for example when there was a rise in the minimum wage, but, for most of the time, these could be considered a constant factor. The extension of this framework by Grimshaw and Rubery took issue with two aspects of Osterman's analysis. First, the influence of external conditions seemed to be underplayed and, second, the mutual, two-way link between the external and the internal was undertheorized. If the framework were to be used to explore change across societies, there would be a particular need to understand the interplay between the first two rings as conditioned by the third ring—the external conditions. Even within national economies the external conditions are likely to have a continuous rather than an intermittent influence in shaping the options or the social space for change determined by the interactions of rings 1 and 2. This extension of the framework adds to its complexity but, in line with analyses of *embeddedness*, it emphasizes the interrelationships between the rings as well as the existence of separable influences. A detailed consideration of each of the *rings of influence* will reinforce the significance of this analysis.

Ring 1: performance pressures

Pressures on organizational performance arise out of product market, stock market, budgetary, regulatory and reputational considerations. These pressures are mediated through the actions of managers and, as such, may be felt more or less keenly by different holders of managerial positions. Thus, change related to performance criteria is not necessarily related to change in the external environment. It may also reflect changes in the characteristics and holders of senior management positions in the organization, or indeed changes in internal political and organizational considerations, including, for example, changes to how a manager's own performance is perceived and monitored.

Performance pressures lead to changes in what the organization does and how it chooses to carry out those tasks. Change may be a response to market, regulatory or technological change within the organization's established product/service area. It may also reflect a response to opportunities in new areas, possibly because of changing synergies or spin-off opportunities from existing areas of expertise. Diversification may also be a precursor to a move out of the organization's traditional tasks and markets. Organizations respond differently to pressures on performance in part as a consequence of their past position in the sector or market. Competitive strategies may vary from the defensive to the proactive and organizations may position themselves in markets and segments as innovators, close followers of leading companies or reluctant implementers of change, preferring ad hoc and opportunistic patterns of change rather than a planned competitive strategy. Moreover, some organizations may be committed to one market and set of tasks, while others operate across a range of markets and may select between alternative opportunities for expansion and downsizing.

Because organizations position themselves in different parts of the market, a programme of change which one organization regards as essential for its competitive strategy may not be seen in the same light by another. Similarly, some organizations will prioritize, for example, short-term shareholder value and will take all actions required by the City; others may be more sheltered from the City or may be outside direct City control in the public sector. Internal governance factors will also play a part. In this way, where governance structures allow for parts of the organizations to pursue their own interests of survival, the pressures for change may be interpreted differently than when competitive strategy is more centrally controlled and directed.

Individual organizations may be ambivalent as to whether the pressure for change comes from a fundamental advance in technological or organizational knowledge, or from increased competition induced, for example, by the deregulation of product or labour markets. For the organization, the main message is the need to adapt or face potential extinction. At a societal level, however, recognition of the particular source of the pressure for change is important and a distinction between pressures does need to be made. One set of changes may be interpreted as pushing forward the activity of industrial and service delivery, while another set may be pushing in the opposite direction. For example, some forms of deregulation may discourage research and development and deter the implementation of productivity-enhancing innovation (Lazonick 1991). Similar conflicting pressures may also appear in public services. Some fundamental and often irreversible changes are taking place in the organization and structure of society to which the public sector needs to respond; such as, for example, the ageing of the population or the greater demands for education. Other pressures, exerted in different ways through government budgetary restrictions, are aimed at taking cost and possibly quality out of public service provision.

Often employment change can be considered a consequence (direct or indirect) of policies designed to respond to these competitive pressures. However, in some cases change in employment may be sought for its own sake, particularly where management performance is measured according to the adoption of human resource management practices; here the motivation may be to retain or establish a position or reputation as a leader in human resource management. Such a reputation may be for either 'hard' or 'soft' human resource policies, to use common phraseology (Legge 1995b). It is less likely that an organization will gain a strong reputation for an in-between position or for following a mixture of the two. Reputational concerns may apply to whole organizations or to individual managers within an organization. Organizations or managers may, in focusing on image or reputation, seek to mimic or imitate other organizations. They may do this in the hope that such policies will enhance performance, even if they have little hard evidence to support this expectation. Alternatively, they may be simply seeking to meet internal management performance targets with respect to employment change and innovation.

Ring 2: organizational culture and power relations

Organizations are necessarily constrained in their strategies for employment change by their own history and culture, and, in particular, by their established system of employee relations and workplace norms and values. Organizations are not able or willing to scrap all previous investment in their workforces and their organizational arrangements, except under exceptional and isolated occasions when they decide to close plants and reopen under greenfield conditions. These occasions tend to coincide with fundamental changes in the way of operating within a given market, and the impact of recent technological, market and regulatory change has perhaps induced a higher incidence of radical transformations, involving a complete change of workforce and organizational structures. Nevertheless, once these transformations have been made, organizations often start again, having to cope with an existing structure and set of expectations and adapt them to new conditions. Where organizations are aware that their radical transformation is only the first stage in further technological and service/product delivery transformation, they may try to avoid these problems by making less investment in the new forms, for example through the employment of temporary staff.

For the most part, however, prior organizational choices and paths of development close off some options to organizations while pointing them in particular development directions. These paths should be consistent (or at least not in direct conflict) with their current human and organizational capital, broadly defined. In the original formulation of Osterman's three rings model, ring 2 was interpreted as only providing a constraint on change. However, a more general interpretation requires an exploration and understanding of the conditions under which the internal systems may not be considered a binding constraint. To some extent this may depend upon the pressures under ring 1, to use the traditional economists' interpretation that institutional structures survive until market pressures become too great (Hicks 1955; Marshall 1920). A more sophisticated interpretation identifies the internal power relations as embedded in organizational, production and external structures (Wilkinson 1983). Changes in these broader sets of interrelationships may provide chinks in the internal structures that can be exploited in the process of change and transformation.

Thus, whether the organizational structures act as a strong constraint on the pursuit of performance enhancement, as defined under ring 1, will depend on how far management is reliant on internal cooperation in the implementation of changes. For example, if the key group of employees within the organizational industrial relations system is also critical for the implementation of technological change, then the tradition of industrial relations may indeed act as a binding constraint on the mode of implementation of change. If, however, the changes may reduce the significance of this group for the overall performance and productivity of the organization, managers may be more willing to challenge the status quo and status hierarchy. Similarly, if key groups inside the organization derive their power from a strong external labour market position, management may face a more binding constraint on its room for manoeuvre than if the key group inside is losing power in the outside labour market. The increasing possibility of redrawing the boundaries of the firm and entering into partnership and subcontract relations with other providers of services certainly also expands the scope for organizations to break their dependence on specific internal groups, even though they in turn become dependent on external partners and suppliers.

Ring 3: external market and regulatory conditions

Changes in external conditions may force organizations to respond to new constraints. For example, governments may enact new regulations, such as the national minimum wage, which requires internal changes in pay policy. Equally, changes in external conditions may create new opportunities for organizations to exploit.

Managers may be more likely to respond to new external opportunities in two situations: first, when they are under pressure to improve performance (ring 1) and second, when they are keen to change the internal organizational culture and industrial relations system (ring 2). In these conditions the organization may be an active exploiter of new opportunities. Where external conditions throw up new constraints, the impact will again be contingent on internal conditions. In some organizations the adjustment may simply result in marginal adjustments to current practice, but in others the need to make even a small change may initiate a more radical process of innovation.

Changes in external conditions are not always fully understood by organizations. For example, organizations may observe changes in labour supply conditions but they may be unclear whether they need to respond to short-term, cyclical factors or to a more long-term trend related to changes in labour supply composition, attitudes and expectations (including, for example, class structures, educational levels, ethnic composition and gender roles). Moreover, external trends are not independent of organizational policies. Again, labour supply trends can illustrate this point. While labour shortages or surpluses may reflect more general macroeconomic trends, they may also reflect specific organizational policies and practices. For example, widespread downsizing may create temporary gluts of surplus skilled labour, which in turn may induce organizations to cut back on training, leading in the longer term to increased labour shortages (Cappelli *et al.* 1997). Similarly, labour shortages may be a response to organizational cutbacks in training provision or to organizational changes to career ladders that reduce the supply of willing entrants.

Changes in external conditions often interact with and reinforce the same pressures for change as have been identified under rings 1 and 2. For example, general trends towards competition based around service delivery may put pressure on those organizations and sectors that have not yet adopted these types of practice to consider changing their mode of operation. This is particularly evident in the public sector where pressure to imitate so-called 'best practice' in the private sector is particularly strong. Thus, processes of mimicry and adoption of best practice may spread across dissimilar sectors and markets, fuelled by ideological ideas relating to the new or appropriate ways of organizing delivery and employment (see also DiMaggio and Powell 1983).

Commentators, politicians and academics discuss notions such as delayering, downsizing, networking, partnerships, flexible working and concentration on core competencies as general trends independent of specific institutional and market contexts. The pressure on management to consider these options, even prior to any consideration that these policies might be appropriate or relevant for their operation, is clearly strong.

Perhaps an even stronger influence from the external environment in the UK comes from the actual material change in power relations between management and labour as a consequence of two decades of labour market liberalization and attacks on union power. These changes exist both at the level of ideology and in the real power of unions to resist change. As such, organizations that wish to introduce changes to improve performance but have in the past felt inhibited by internal considerations of industrial relations may take encouragement from the general change in power relations. They may feel strong enough to tear up their implicit or explicit contracts with their staff and introduce changes that would, in the past, have been fiercely resisted. Indeed, management may introduce change for change's sake, deciding to reinforce the external change in power relations by reasserting managerial prerogative at the workplace, not to meet any specific performance target, but to legitimate and strengthen their position in the company. Of course, not all changes will be in this direction. The change in power relations does not mean the ending of the opportunity for labour to resist managerial change. Individual or collective negative responses to employment policies and practices may lead to changes in the other direction, for example, towards the renewal of the industrial relations framework through partnership agreements. Again, however, the form of renewal may reflect external influences on what are considered best practice forms of industrial relations.

To summarize, management-induced change in employment policies and practices can be related to these three sets of pressure or influence. For the purposes of analysis, it is useful to identify these as separate forces. However, these three rings not only interact in both competing and complementary fashions, but are also mutually constitutive. Performance imperatives perceived by managers derive not only from their examination of the organization's balance sheet but also from their perceptions of what organizations ought to be doing to keep pace with competitors and best practice. The extent to which internal custom and practice act as a binding constraint will depend, inter alia, on how far internal power relations are supported by wider power relations in the external market. Nor is there any suggestion here that the responses to these pressures are predetermined or automatic. Responses depend on the behaviour of actors, and pressures for change are filtered through the perceptions of actors. Moreover, actors are also subject to a range of potentially conflicting motivations. In particular, managers face at least three conflicting motivations: to pursue the interests of the organization as a whole; to promote the interests of the specific managerial group or subsidiary of the organization in which he or she is employed; or to pursue their own individual and immediate career interests. The relative importance of these objectives and how they are perceived to relate to performance pressures will be specific to the individual and the context. Thus in focusing on the range of performance pressures, we are explicitly not reverting to a contingency form of analysis. Indeed, we are assuming that the role both of structural factors and of human agency must be given serious consideration.

A TOUCH OF REALISM

An integrated analysis also requires the adoption of a common methodology. Thus, in order to develop a social analysis of the internal and external labour markets we need to conceive of the constitution of the external labour market as the outcome of social processes and not as the outcome of forces beyond human and social control. For the individual organization the external market conditions may appear to be exogenous givens, but, at the sector, the national and indeed the international level, the social constitution of the market becomes clear. It is political decision-making, influenced by the lobbying of multinationals, which has liberalized the free movement of capital. What is more, even within this globalized world economy the policies and practices of nation-states and large organizations continue to shape the form and nature of competition in product markets on the one hand and the organization of labour markets and the structure of labour supply on the other.

In arguing for a common or seamless methodology for understanding organizational-level and macro-level change, we need, however, to differentiate our approach both from the mutually constitutive approach of the postmodern, post-structuralist school and from the infinitely flexible transaction costs approach to the analysis of market structure. Starting from very different standpoints, both schools of thought have denied the existence of structures and institutions as having independent impacts on the organization of society. For the post-structuralists/ postmodernists, social structures are not analytically separable from the agents who interpret and give meaning to the structures (see, for example, Rorty 1980). This theoretical approach is built on a critique of earlier approaches that stressed the determinacy of structures and (at worst) created a society without humans. This critique has revealed the asocial nature of these accounts and the ways in which human beings (their ideas and emotions) were theorized as merely the vessels through which social structures interact. However, in developing this critique, and denying any separation between the individual actors and the world they inhabit, postmodern writers come close to denying any coherent role for a social science as a source of explanation for social phenomena (Ackroyd and Fleetwood 2001). In commenting on this elisionist approach, Archer (1998) has noted the consequences of retreating from any attempt at explanation that involves reference to causality. She argues for the veracity of a social science that analyses change from the assumption that 'structure necessarily predates the actions which transform it and that structural elaboration necessarily post-dates these actions' (ibid.: 202). In developing this critical realist perspective, Bhaskar (1989) has written of the need to 'distinguish sharply between the genesis of human actions, lying in the reasons, intentions and plans of human beings on the one hand; and the structures governing the reproduction and transformation of social activities, on the other hand' (quoted in Archer: 203).

This approach fits well with our analyses of organizational dynamics. Here, the elaboration of the notion of three rings of influence allows us to identify particular structures that are external and internal to the organization. From this, we consider carefully the ways in which they iterate and interact with the 'intentions and plans of human beings' (managers and workers) in workplaces.

The problem of separability also arises within the study of economics through the literature on transactions costs. In contrast to the traditional approach to industrial structure, where the structure of organizations was treated if not as an independent, at least as a separable variable in the analysis of the system of competition, literature on transaction costs treats governance and institutional structures as the outcome of market conditions (Williamson 1975, 1985). Trends towards either greater concentration, on the one hand, or towards more fragmentation and networked organizations, on the other, are assumed to be manifestations of a process of transaction cost minimization. The assumption that the economy always moves towards transaction cost minimization allows advocates of this approach to ignore the need for separate identification of transaction costs as an independent check on the hypothesis and also allows all developments to be rationalized ex post facto, even if not foreseen. Thus, the break-up of the large bureaucratic internal labour market is rationalized as a response to changing systems of transaction costs and as necessarily efficient, simply on the grounds that it is happening.

In contrast to these approaches, in this text we maintain a separation between structure and agency and evaluate trends and developments empirically without assuming a necessary tendency towards efficient or equilibrium outcomes. Within this framework, however, we do accord a more active role to human agency than was allowed for in the institutionalist economics texts of the 1960s and 1970s. Indeed, the current trend towards the decentralization of decision-making in the UK employment system has necessarily allowed for a greater role for human agency at the individual organizational level in shaping the development of new social structures and labour market organization. Because this decision-making is taking place within an uncoordinated, fragmented and often inherently inconsistent structural environment, there is the potential for this process to result in inconsistent and unsustainable policies, which reinforce the chaotic nature of the structural environment. Structuralists have been happy to allow for a considerable amount of random noise around a central tendency, while still aiming to explain the central tendency with respect to rational measurable variables. However, the reliance in the UK on individual organizations to chart the new territory, without the provision of strong coordinating signals, increases the potential range of variance and indeed calls into question the notion of a central tendency, except in so far as this is maintained by notions of best practice. Moreover, as we will argue, analysis of the implementation of best practice must also allow for the role of agency in the interpretation of best practice. Before applying this critical realist approach to our understanding of the roles of structure and agency in employment change, we must first introduce the case studies that provide the empirical basis for this book.

2

Seven Case Studies: An Introduction

INTRODUCTION

The research upon which this book is based draws on case studies of
seven large organizations in Britain. Between 1997 and 1999, we
explored in some detail the changes in work and employment in a bank,
a pharmaceuticals company, a newspaper company, a large city council,
a food retailer, an NHS Trust and a telecommunications firm.

This chapter introduces these organizations. It begins by explaining
the choice of sectors, from each of which one large organization for
case-study research was selected. The second section introduces each
case study in turn. These descriptions of the organizations are, in part,
designed to act as a reference section for use when reading subsequent
chapters. We outline their main areas of activities—in the form of
services provision or production—and assess the key features that
describe their systems of business and work organization. Chapter 3
provides a more visual guide to the workplaces we visited and the
nature of work carried out. Appendix 1 provides details of the number of
interviews conducted.

THE SEVEN SECTORS

Our choice of sectors was designed to reflect (approximately) the
employment mix of Britain, including manufacturing and services,
public and private sectors, as well as female-dominated and male-
dominated activities. In addition, we wanted a sufficiently diverse mix

of sectors to capture the range of pressures for change on employment, including, for example, the significance of technological change,
new product markets, pressures of internationalization and changing
government regulation. With these broad objectives, the following
sectors were eventually selected:

- banking;
- local government;
- healthcare;
- newspaper journalism and printing;
- pharmaceuticals;
- food retail;
- telecommunications.

The employment mix found across these sectors is approximately
representative of the composition of employment across Britain. Around
half of all British employees work in the private services sector (53 per
cent), one in four in public services (24 per cent) and fewer than one in
six in manufacturing (17 per cent).[1] Our selection includes three and a
half organizations in the private services sector (banking, retail, telecommunications, plus the journalism side of the media organization),
two in the public services (local government and healthcare) and one
and a half in manufacturing (pharmaceuticals and the printing arm of
the media organization).[2]

The seven sectors also illustrate more general trends in employment,
such as the shift towards more atypical forms of work (part-time and
temporary), the growing insecurity among workers, patterns of
upskilling, deskilling and work intensification, as well as the persistence
of low pay. For example, food retail is a major source of employment for women (more than one in ten women in the UK work
as sales assistants) with the bulk of jobs organized on a part-time

---

[1] Data for all employees in employment in Great Britain, *Labour Force Survey*, 1999 (SIC
categories, D (manufacturing), L–N (selected public services) and H–I (private services)).

[2] While the selection of an approximately representative sample of organizations from
different sectors may seem obvious, employment research has, until very recently, failed to
keep up with the changing fortunes of manufacturing and services. Of course, the collapse of
the manufacturing sector (from 30 per cent to 17 per cent of total employment between 1978
and 1999) was in itself an important focus of study in order to appreciate the consequences of
industrial restructuring and 'hollowing out'. Nevertheless, the rise of the service sector has not
been accompanied by a similar growth in research interest. Our research thus contributes to a
broader effort which seeks to offset the previous research bias towards manufacturing and the
associated neglect of the nature of work and employment in the service sector—both public
and private.

basis.[3] Moreover, it has pioneered the use of flexible, or zero-hour, contracts (Neathey and Hurstfield 1995). More general use of contingent employment forms—either temporary employment contracts or use of temporary workers supplied by an agency—has been associated with the development of call centres (in banking and telecommunications). It is in these sectors that there has been the most notable transformation in expectations of a job for life. In banking, in particular, a sense of job insecurity among workers exploded during the 1980s and 1990s as large numbers of workers were hit by downsizing and rationalization (Cressey and Scott 1992; Pratt 1998; Tickell 1997).

Job insecurity has been associated with work intensification (Heery and Salmon 2000b) and our choice of sectors reflects an attempt to contribute to an understanding of such contemporary patterns of changes in job tasks (whether through upskilling, deskilling, job enlargement or work intensification) by considering a broad range of forms of work organization. More generally, the sectors are representative of different forms of change in a context of broad pressures and opportunities for adaptation. For example, policies of deregulation and liberalization intensified the degree of competition in particular sectors in Britain during the 1980s and 1990s. As a result, sectors once dominated by monopolies or small numbers of large organizations witnessed the arrival of new competitors, leading to intensified pressures to develop new products, provide new services or 'grow' new markets. These trends are perhaps best captured in our choice of banking and telecommunications. Both sectors were forced to adjust to enormous changes in regulatory policies and in the scale and scope of competition. In banking, the deregulation of financial services in the 1980s transformed the nature of competition in the industry, leading to a number of new entrants into the markets for financial products (Leyshon and Thrift 1993).[4] Indeed, such was the scope of deregulation that some new entrants were able to cross sectoral boundaries, for example, moving into banking from a base in retail. More recently, however, a wave of consolidation across the sector, involving mergers and hostile takeovers (at a national and international level), appears to have reversed the trend leading to a new concentration of capital in the sector. In telecommunications, the privatization of British Telecom (BT) in 1984

[3] Use of part-time workers in this sector grew more among men than among women during the 1990s. By 1999 men were almost as likely to work part time as they were full time (48 per cent and 52 per cent, respectively), while among women, more than four in five worked part time, up from around three in five in the late 1980s.

[4] In particular, deregulation enabled many building societies to provide standard banking services (Gentle 1993).

opened the door to increased diversification in the industry (Beesley and Laidlaw 1997; Ferner and Colling 1991). A number of new UK and foreign-owned corporations have entered the market for telecommunications, reflecting small and large companies by market value. However, the pattern of employment in the sector is still dominated by BT. By the late 1990s, despite the presence of around thirty telecommunications companies in the UK, around three in four jobs in the industry were still with BT (Darlington 1998).

The two public services sectors on our list also reflect aspects of deregulatory pressures and privatization, albeit in different forms from those of telecommunications and banking. Public spending rules during most of the 1990s severely restricted expenditures in health, education and local government, and reforms to the delivery of public services continued the thrust of 1980s policies, which introduced private sector competition into areas of services delivery traditionally provided by the public sector (Corby and White 1999; Cutler and Waine 1994). The steady privatization of public services ranged from the outsourcing of cleaning and catering in NHS Trusts to invitiations to private firms to run prisons and 'failing' schools. In the NHS, the 1989 White Paper, *Working for Patients*, paved the way for greater competition (and collaboration) across public and private sector organizations by transforming the organizational structure of the NHS from a bureaucratic form to a market-based form, with purchaser and provider divisions (the so-called quasi-market which splits the purchase of healthcare from its provision). Moreover, the grouping together of NHS hospitals as Trusts—defined as non-profit corporations, rather than public sector organizations—meant that hospital managers were forced to act and respond more in a manner that was meant to imitate private sector pressures. Managers were free to introduce local employment contracts, for example, and a new system of capital charges made all Trusts accountable for interest and depreciation costs of all assets (Ranade 1994). Similar changes have occurred in local government. City councils have been transformed into cost centres through the introduction of quasi-markets, which force managers in departments defined as providers to bid for funds from local government purchasers in competition with private sector firms. The very rapid growth of business services in the private sector partly reflects this shift in the playing field, as low cost private sector firms providing school catering or home-care services have gained an increasing amount of business from public sector purchasers (Colling 2000).

Another major pressure for change in recent years concerns the increased internationalization of organizations and markets. In certain sectors, internationalization acts as a pressure on organizations both to diversify their operations across countries, and to adapt to the increased uncertainty and instability of international competition. In different ways, the pharmaceuticals and food retail sectors face these pressures. The pharmaceuticals industry is strongly global in character. It is dominated by a small number of global corporations, which have linked manufacturing, sales, and research and development operations across the world. While multinational corporations (MNCs) may be able to carve out a relatively stable niche for particular products, subsidiaries within different countries face an artificially strong degree of competition where MNCs seek to maximize returns by imposing competition across subsidiaries in a bid to drive down production costs. Changes in the structure of the food retail industry, towards greater internationalization, are a more recent trend. The entry of the US giant Wal-Mart into the UK market brought pressures on domestic companies to expand their volume of products (Wal-Mart has around 100,000 different lines, compared to around 40,000 at one of the leading UK firms, Tesco) and to reduce product prices. The British retail sector has also expanded abroad. Around half of all mergers in retail in 1998 were cross-national (worth around $6 billion), perhaps reflecting speculation that future retailing will polarize around global mass-market retailers (such as Wal-Mart) and niche market companies. Also, however, British government regulations which restrict use of greenfield sites may encourage UK-owned firms to expand market opportunities abroad.

A third pressure for change concerns the impact of new technologies on systems of production and the organization of work. Interest in this area intensified during the 1990s with the rapid developments in information and communication technologies (ICT). Developments in ICT were associated with the innovation of new products, as well as new forms of manufacturing and ways of delivering services. Each of the seven sectors selected for research has transformed considerably in the context of technological change, although in some the changes have been more far-reaching than in others.

In the newspaper industry, new technologies abolished the traditional crafts of printing. In the past, compositors made decisions on lines of text and spacing based on their knowledge of print layout. Now, these decisions are made automatically on computers in the editorial offices, as journalists write up their own stories. The finished page is faxed, in negative format, to the printers, making the traditional work of the compositor redundant (Gennard 1990; Goodhart and Wintour 1986; Littleton 1992; Noon 1993). The ability to relay information in a codified form also weakens the traditional vertical linkages between editorial and printing arms of a newspaper, and is associated with a geographical dislocation between offices and printing outlets, as well as a growing tendency for outsourcing of newspaper products to different printing outlets. Advances in IT have also generated a growth in Internet sites for newspaper products, leading to pressures throughout the media sector to devote resources to IT products in the absence of clearly defined returns to these investments.

In banking and telecommunications, the most obvious expression of adoption of new technologies is the use of call centres. Banks use call centres to deliver a range of services (from account details to loans) and to provide information to customers regarding new products ('cold calls'). However, recent developments in Internet banking and 'armchair banking', which relies on the television as the interactive medium, are expected to supersede telephone banking in the near future. The tele-communications sector has also witnessed a massive expansion in the market for a new ICT product—the mobile phone. This has been an important factor in encouraging a more diversified and competitive industry, with the traditional large players, such as BT, slipping down the ranking of companies (ordered by asset valuation) as niche-based mobile phone companies expanded their share of the international market at a more rapid pace.

In pharmaceuticals, developments in biotechnology have brought a new tool in drug design to the industry, involving the manufacture of therapeutic proteins produced by the body's immune system via genetic engineering and cell culture. Early developments were thought to be associated with a growing role of small biotech firms in the industry, since it was the small firms that tended to make the most important contributions to new research (Sharp 1994). The wave of mergers and take-overs at the end of the 1990s, however, suggest that the large players have been able to consolidate their position. Finally, developments in ICT have also transformed the organization of food retail services. ICT facilitated a major innovation in stock management systems, for example the 'electronic-point-of-sale' (EPOS), where products are tagged with computer-readable bar codes and sales assistants no longer have to key in price details. EPOS also reduces stockholding through the principle of 'just-in-time' delivery, and allows managers to anticipate fluctuations and local variations in sales patterns through detailed information of customer purchases (Burke and Shackleton 1996).[5]

A final area of change concerns the weakening of trade unions, or what we might refer to as the shifting balance of power between capital and labour. As we set out in Chapter 1, the relative bargaining strength of workers in the UK was eroded considerably during the 1980s and 1990s by a collapse in the number of union members and a restriction of the scope of union activities, the retrenchment of collective bargaining, the weakening and eventual abolition of the Wages Councils[6] and further fragmentation of wage-setting arrangements in the public sector. By the end of the 1990s, there were some signs of recovery. The national minimum wage was introduced in 1999, and the Employment Relations Act (1999) extended rights to trade-union recognition. Because of the timing of our research (1997–9), these more recent changes do not figure in our story.

Perhaps the most extreme example of change in industrial relations is the newspaper industry. Until the mid-1980s, printing unions had hung on to relatively attractive terms and conditions. But the Employment Acts (1980, 1982) and the Trade Union Act (1984) implemented under Thatcher paved the way for proprietors such as Eddie Shah and Rupert Murdoch to win influential battles with the trade unions. In particular, Murdoch's victory at Wapping was seen by many as the catalyst to a dramatic shift in power from the unions to management (Littleton 1992). During this period, the large printing firms withdrew from long-standing multi-employer collective-bargaining agreements in a bid for greater local autonomy (Jackson *et al.* 1993). This new-found autonomy provided an opportunity for employers to challenge job demarcations and pay differentials between craft and non-craft jobs, which had traditionally been regulated by strong unions.

Overall, the seven sectors that we have selected for research provide a potentially rich and diverse source of evidence for mapping changes in the nature of work and employment in the context of transformations in the nature of competition, extended liberalization, privatization and internationalization of markets, advances in technologies, and changes in the balance of power between capital and labour. Now that we have

[5] In addition, the main food retail outlets in the UK introduced loyalty or brand cards for customers. Given that around 80 per cent of food sales at any given supermarket chain is said to come from just 20 per cent of its customer base (*Financial Times*, 16 March 1999), these loyalty cards provide an effective tool in matching consumption preferences with product distribution.
[6] Wages Councils set minimum wage levels in a range of sectors associated with low pay, including retail, clothing, catering and hairdressing.

set out the motivations for our choice of sectors, we turn to a detailed introduction and overview of our case study organizations.

THE SEVEN CASE STUDY ORGANIZATIONS

Throughout this book, our analysis of changes in the way work is managed, and the implications for changes in the nature of work and broader transformations in the British employment systems, draw primarily on case study research carried out in seven large organizations: Bankco, Councilco, Healthco, Mediaco, Pharmco, Retailco and Telecomco. Box 2.1 provides an overview of each organization. The chapter proceeds with a brief overview of each organization. The aim here is to document key characteristics across four interrelated areas: corporate structure, management structure, employment structure and payment structure. In subsequent chapters, our discussion and analysis assumes a certain familiarity with each of the organizations. Thus, the following outlines also act as a point of reference for the reader.

BANKCO

Bankco is a major clearing bank in Britain. It is the banking arm of a large national corporation, which is the sole equity shareholder and owns a number of subsidiaries operating outside and inside the banking and financial services industry. During the late 1990s, Bankco was the best performing subsidiary of the group. This was not always the case. During the recession of the late 1980s and early 1990s, Bankco was struggling; it suffered from a high level of bad debts and was forced to withdraw from the mortgage market. However, a number of senior managers claimed that the severe downturn in business conditions acted as a catalyst to the implementation of radical new business strategies that have successfully generated a turnaround in business performance. As one manager told us, 'there probably was a sort of, right now we need a "big thing" feeling among managers'. Underpinning the changes was the belief that Bankco ought to identify niche markets for competition, given its inability to compete with the major banks in all areas. Bankco has since become a market leader in various new banking products, as well as in new forms of services provision through call centres and the internet.

Box 2.1. Introducing the seven case study organizations

- **Bankco** is a major clearing bank in the UK. It combines a relatively high ratio of infrastructural costs to income with a reputation for introducing new financial products in the sector. It has also been quick to exploit the new technologies in information and telecommunications systems.

- **Councilco** is a large urban city council. Operations stretch across a range of activities, including school and civic catering, community care, environmental health and indoor and outdoor leisure services.

- **Healthco** is a large city centre NHS Trust. It combines the provision of acute medical care with teaching and research activities and often acts as a tertiary referral site.

- **Mediaco** combines two companies in the newspaper industry—a local newspaper company and the nearby printworks which prints the newspaper. The newspaper company is wholly owned by a large national media group, which owns a range of media companies. The printworks company operates under joint ownership with this and another national media group.

- **Pharmco** is one of the leading global pharmaceutical firms. The bulk of its activities is split between the R+D and manufacturing of pharmaceuticals, with a mix of both carried out in the UK.

- **Retailco** is one of the leading food retail chains in the UK. It supplies a range of around 40,000 products across more than 600 stores. With a total workforce of around 155,000, predominantly part time, it is one of the largest private sector employers in the UK.

- **Telecomco** is one of the largest providers of telecommunications services in the UK. It delivers a range of business and customer services, in addition to maintenance of the telephone network. Development of mobile telephone services and the internet has recently contributed to high profit margins.

Note: organizations are labelled as 'sector + co' in order to identify the sector of the organization and to provide for confidentiality.

In the late 1990s, Bankco employed a workforce of around 3,700, distributed across a national network of branches and telephone banking centres. Through its rapid exploitation of new technologies and introduction of new financial products, it built up a reputation as a leader in the radical transformation of the sector and enjoyed a steady expansion of its business and personal customer base throughout the 1990s. In particular, Bankco was at the forefront of the expansion of telephone banking (and, by the late 1990s, Internet banking) with an accompanying shift in jobs from a much reduced branch network into a booming number of call centres. By 1998, the proportion of the Bankco workforce working in call centres was 38 per cent—a fourfold increase from just 9 per cent five years earlier. In this context of radical shifts in forms of services provision and the uncertainty surrounding the nature of work organization, Bankco managers negotiated a 'partnership' agreement with the major trade union, aimed at providing job security in exchange for various reforms of working practices (see box 2.2).

Bankco is structured across six divisions, with most of its workforce (87 per cent) employed in the two largest divisions—the Corporate and Commercial Division and the Personal Customer Services Division. These form the focus of our research. The contribution of personal banking, compared with corporate banking, to overall revenue has risen in recent years, representing a ratio of around 55 : 45 in the figures for 1998. In part, the relative success of the personal banking division is a direct result of the new banking initiatives which have generated an expansion of the customer base—at an annual growth rate of around 20 per cent during the mid-1990s.

When addressing the form of management structure, senior Bankco managers argued that it was the central vision that was important, rather than a centralized system of decision-making and control. Moreover, human resources (HR) managers play a key role in formulating the broader corporate vision. For example, the decision to outsource cash-handling activities was taken in conjunction with the human resources (HR) team. Also, the strength of the top-down HR vision was an important factor in the development of job security policies across the bank, following the uncertainty created by the closure of dozens of bank branches and the move into telephone banking. However, the difference between vision and control in guiding management decisions tends to become rather blurred. One senior manager explained to us, for example, that the ability to implement a centralized HR vision was assisted by the shift from branches to call centres, since it is far easier to manage the quality of services provision in a standardized fashion when these are delivered through a 'factory' environment as opposed to a hundred branches where work effort is less visible.

Despite the closure of many bank branches, Bankco experienced several years of employment growth during the 1990s. This was most pronounced in the Personal Customer Services Division, where Bankco expanded into new areas of telephone banking. The Corporate and

Box 2.2. The partnership agreement at Bankco

In 1997, Bankco and the major trade union signed a partnership agreement—the first of its kind in the British banking sector. The agreement covered an initial period from April 1998 to March 2000 and was intended to provide a framework for:

- effective use of change management;
- improved pay and rewards;
- new working practices and employee benefits.

In broad terms, it sets out a compromise between job security and worker adaptability to 'change management':

we have recognised that continued flexibility and commitment by the Bank's people is essential for successful management of change and business development. This enables us to agree that it is not currently anticipated that there will be any involuntary redundancies during the period of the Agreement.

(Partnership agreement)

Similarly, in union documents distributed to staff, it states:

The Bank and the Union do not anticipate involuntary redundancies throughout the three year partnership agreement. Job roles are certain to change. We must anticipate a rapid level of business change.

(Trade union bulletin)

The first stage of the partnership process involved setting up a 'partnership project team', made up of four HR staff and eight union representatives. One HR manager explained the novelty of the approach:

We began by exploring the idea of partnership and looking at the partnership agreement. We have always worked closely with the union, but in a conventional way. What is new about this is that we are starting out from scratch, at the project definition stage, with both partners involved.

Source: Bankco Partnership Agreement (1997)

Commercial Division also expanded through the successful marketing of new business accounts, again managed through call centre forms of work organization. By 1998, there were around 2,300 employees in personal banking—making up almost two-thirds of the bank's entire workforce. This division is not only the largest, but also has the highest representation of women working (around a 70 per cent share) and is thus a key area of job growth for women.

Although segmentation of the workforce by sex is clearly apparent, all workers appear to be increasingly divided by the walls between the

Box 2.3. New agreement on work and pay for Bankco call-centre staff

In 1998, Bankco and its trade-union partner agreed to a Service Centre Review which introduced new terms and conditions of employment for staff employed in call centres (including Business Customer Services and Personal Customer Services). The agreement was, in part, motivated by a recognition that job roles had changed within the call-centre environment, and that pay scales ought 'to recognize the distinct current market for staff in these areas and provide improved progression opportunities'. As well as changes in grading structure, the review involved a number of other changes, including pro-rata pay and benefits for part-time workers; the appointment of all staff on temporary contracts to permanent contract positions; and greater staff movement between call centres.

While the traditional structure consisted of four layers—senior management, middle managers, appointed staff and clerical staff—across a total of sixteen grades, the new system distinguishes between three broad call-centre jobs: customer service adviser (levels A–F); team manager (levels G–J); and service centre managers (number of levels not finalized).

Implementation of the new pay scale was accompanied by a guarantee that 'no existing employee, whether currently permanent or temporary, will be faced with any reduction of their current financial position' (with protection of the net difference until the new salary catches up with the old level, although scale rises will continue to be paid). Also, all temporary staff receive the same terms and conditions as 'normal Bank terms' (e.g. holiday entitlement), excluding pensions. And the agreement sets out new premium payments for work during non-core hours (outside of 8 a.m.–6 p.m., Monday–Friday) to reduce overall costs. Unlike the previous system premium payments are only paid for *actual hours worked* and are set at a lower rate (although higher than the levels previously set for a greenfield Customer Services Centre where core working hours used to include weekend working).

Source: Bankco 'Service Centre Agreement' 1998

different banking divisions. There is evidence of a growing divide between internal labour markets in the Corporate and Commercial Division and in the Personal Customer Services Division. In part, the weakened links between the personal and corporate arms of Bankco reflect the move away from bank branches and the fragmentation of telephone banking operations by geographical site. Also, however, there is a concern among managers that while cross-divisional transfers may benefit employees' all-round knowledge of banking, it may also disrupt the continuity of service provision to customers, especially with regard to the smooth management of business accounts.

Of greater concern to senior managers, however, is how the new call-centre environments of banking have changed the nature of banking work. The transformation led to a rethinking of traditional forms of pay and skills development. Following the 1997 partnership agreement, Bankco and the union agreed to a 'Service Centre Review' in 1998, which specifically addressed issues of pay, job insecurity and skills development among call centre staff through the redesign of the pay scale and grading structure and review of employment contracts (see box 2.3). As a result, around a third of the Bankco workforce moved to a new structure of pay and grading. Compared to the traditional structure, the new system potentially provided a more transparent indication of progression, coupled with greater opportunities for advancement through the different levels, as well as across the different job bands.

COUNCILCO

Councilco is a large urban city council under strong Labour Party control. It is one of 46 local authorities in the UK and provides services over a very wide range of activities, including school and civic catering, community care, environmental health and indoor and outdoor leisure services. As well as providing services to meet the needs of the local population, Councilco also has a political commitment to its elected members representing the interests of different communities. For example, it has political concerns to improve the quality of life in the city and to create jobs, and these are associated with various initiatives around inner-city regeneration, encouraging the 24-hour city, hosting national and international events, and use of local residency criteria in Councilco recruitment policy (in an aim to provide jobs for the city). Each of these policies, in turn, also shapes how and where services are provided.

At the same time, Councilco must also respond to national initiatives for change in local government. After 1997, the newly elected Labour government introduced a series of new policies aimed at modernizing local government one of which, Best Value, was of particular importance during the period we conducted our research (see box 2.4). In addition, Councilco had also to manage locally the Single Status agreement that had been agreed nationally between employer and employee unions (see box 2.4). At Councilco, the two big questions associated with Single

Box 2.4. Single Status and Best Value in local government

The Single Status policy was agreed nationally in April 1997 with the aim of harmonizing terms and conditions of employment between the blue-collar and white-collar workforces. Harmonization generally benefits blue-collar workers, who have traditionally enjoyed shorter holidays, a longer basic working week and weaker rights around sick pay arrangements. With a guideline framework agreed nationally, individual authorities were then charged with local implementation, with the flexibility to adapt the framework to meet specific requirements.

The policy of Best Value was announced in July 1997. Initially, it was designed to replace the existing regulatory framework of 'compulsory competitive tendering'. The aim was to balance the traditional market-led focus on cost with attention to the quality of services provision, and to remove the ideological preoccupation with privatization of public services. Unlike its predecessor, Best Value was not introduced on a contract-by-contract basis. Instead, local authorities could pursue an area or theme-based approach. In the case of Councilco, its Best Value bid centred on three local wards. Service delivery in each area was reconsidered, as traditional departmental differences were removed and the how, where and when of delivery was restructured (Boyne 1999; Martin 1999; Walker and Davis 1999).

Status concerned restructuring job grades in line with a new job evaluation and the cost implications of harmonization. On the one hand, managers claimed that job evaluation would impose a more regulated framework that would limit the arbitrary matching of jobs to grades by management. On the other hand, it was believed that the policy would represent a new level of bureaucracy that might remove the flexibility enjoyed by managers. In addition, the potential costs of Single Status ignited feelings of anxiety; a number of managers talked to us about their expected 'huge impact' on the delivery of services. The challenge for Councilco was how to absorb the costs potentially associated with a cut in weekly working hours of all manual workers from 39 to 37. Part of the problem involved how to ensure that, with no extra provision of funding, the quantity and quality of services would still be provided. However, the more challenging aspect of the problem involved the knock-on implications for the wage bill for manual workers in part-time jobs, for whom the hourly wage rate would be increased (since the hourly rate is calculated by dividing the weekly rate by the basic number of hours worked).

As part of the national formulation of the new policy of Best Value, Councilco won the right to act as one of 37 national pilot sites. Councilco aimed to test Best Value as a means to implement its goal of building sustainable communities in the city, with improvements to physical environments and education, as well as reduction in crime. In fact, during the period of research, little progress was made in this area of policy, although three areas of the city were designated as Best Value sites, reflecting different characteristics and levels of sustainability.

A number of internal pressures were also driving change at Councilco (in common with most local government organizations; see Cochrane 1993). The management structures across and within departments had been reshaped in line with principles of flatter structures and cross-functional working, and cost savings were made through integrating some of the administrative work among the different management teams. However, a stronger wave of change followed shortly after the arrival of a new chief executive in the early 1990s. The aim was to use a model of corporate planning in order to enhance coordination among departments (see box 2.5). Under this new model, heads of departments contribute to overall corporate policies and are responsible for drawing

Box 2.5. Corporate management at Councilco

During the 1990s, senior management at Councilco developed a model of corporate management that aimed to restructure and coordinate the activity of different departments in line with specific corporate aims. A Councilco document entitled 'Towards corporate management' explains the motivation:

The Council's capacity for achieving its aims in effective service delivery had been hindered by a lack of coordination between departments and the absence of a corporate vision. Until recently, the Council's departments were still largely functioning as separate organisations rather than as part of a cohesive whole.

The new 'vision' involved the following features:

- dissemination of corporate aims to the whole workforce;
- a culture of corporate working across departments;
- linked service planning to corporate aims and priority budgeting;
- improved services through internal and external benchmarking;
- implementation of a communications and staff involvement plan;
- introduction of human resources initiatives.

up annual departmental service delivery plans that must be seen to meet key corporate aims. Centralized governance is facilitated by the centralized decision-making around the distribution of the annual budget allocated by government. Nevertheless, senior managers, charged with implementing a more transparent corporate culture, experienced difficulties with what one manager referred to as 'crusty department-alism'. Departmental heads tend to identify more with the specific professional aims of delivering services than with the central aims of Councilco. Overall, therefore, there remains a relatively high level of departmental autonomy, which, in part, reflects the persistent difficulties of institutionalizing centralized systems of governance in an organiza-tion involving such an extraordinarily complex structure and mix of professional aims and ideals (see, also, Hoggett 1996).

One of the central corporate aims of Councilco was to protect jobs—a direct reflection of the political objectives underpinning the Council's strategies. This policy is loosely reflected in the employment data, which show that numbers employed were relatively stable, fluctuating around 27,000 from 1996 to 1998. More than half of this workforce (52 per cent) work in just one department—education. There are rela-tively few employees in the smaller departments, such as galleries and museums (69 staff) or architects (208 staff).

The pay structures at Councilco follow national agreements for the local government workforce. Traditionally, this has meant separate pay structures for manual workers (such as school caretakers) and non-manual staff (such as technical and clerical staff). With the new national single status agreement, this distinction was abandoned in favour of an integrated pay spine, although, at the time of research, the new local structure had yet to be implemented. Despite the fragmentation in pay structures by occupational group, there is a common application of the seniority-related principle of pay advancement, so that all employees advance up an incremental pay scale with years of service.

HEALTHCO

Our chosen case study organization in the health sector is a large inner-city NHS Trust with a workforce of more than 5,000. One of around 750 Trusts, it combines teaching and research activities with acute medical care and is a regional referral centre in many areas of specialization (such as obstetrics and gynaecology). During the 1990s, Healthco was forced to comply with a number of national initiatives for the NHS. It gained Trust status during the first wave of applications in April 1991 (following the 1989 White Paper). This involved bringing together the activities of several different hospitals and community health services under a common administrative umbrella. Later, it responded to the aims of the patient's charter (following the 1992 implementation of the Citizen's Charter)[7] by introducing a range of performance targets including patient throughput, waiting lists and mortality figures. Stringent controls on government public spending during the 1990s also meant that Healthco management had to find annual cost savings of 2.5 per cent.

A major long-term strategy at Healthco (in its preliminary stages during the time of research) involved the restructuring of the provision of health services around plans for new buildings. Government restrictions on the release of public expenditures to finance new infrastructure (following changes in the financing arrangements of public sector capital projects) forced Healthco managers to bid for private sector investment, following the guidelines of the Private Finance Initiative (PFI) (see box 2.6). Once completed, the new buildings will be owned by a private sector consortium which will also sell ancillary and estate maintenance services to Healthco. Hence, key to the construction project is the transfer of Healthco ancillary workers (porters, cleaners and caterers) to the private sector consortium charged with managing the new buildings.

In common with Councilco, the organizational structure of Healthco is relatively complex. Activities are organized across a range of clinical and non-clinical directorates, referred to by managers as 'business units' or 'cost centres'—no doubt in an effort to reinforce the commercial mindset of doing business. The directorates vary in size, with 824 staff employed in surgery, the largest clinical directorate (16 per cent of the total workforce) and 765 people working in facilities (which covers ancillary and estates maintenance services), the largest non-clinical directorate (15 per cent of the total workforce). Other directorates include the dental hospital, laboratories, maternity care, medicine, psychiatry, and opthalmology. Each directorate, or cost centre, must meet the centrally determined annual cost savings. For example, in 1998, in order to meet the budget, the medical directorate was hoping to cut £500,000 from the budget

---

[7] The Citizen's Charter (HMSO 1991) initially covered the Inland Revenue, prison service, police and education. It covered six key principles: to enforce standards; information and openness; choice and consultation; courtesy and helpfulness; putting things right; and value for money.

Box 2.6. The strategic outline case for PFI at Healthco

The Regional Health Authority assessed Healthco's bid for PFI and found that new buildings, funded by the private sector, would provide the following:

- better access to high-quality patient care;
- provision of tertiary children's services on single site;
- new models of care;
- critical mass in key specialities;
- a greater shift to care outside hospital setting;
- economies of scale in support services.

An additional major factor underpinning the decision was the need to eliminate the Trust's £54 million backlog maintenance costs, which could not be met under existing public spending rules. In an environmental assessment, it was found that:

- 'almost one half of the Trust's estate is not functionally suitable for the functions currently delivered from it';
- 'over 60% of [Healthco]'s estate requires major repair or replacement';
- 'only 8% of the estate complies with all current fire safety regulations';
- 'over half the estate demonstrates non-compliance with energy conservation measures'.

Source: Healthco document: *Strategic Outline Case* (1998)

and, at the same time, to treat 300 more patients. While cost savings are expected from all directorates, some are able to generate additional revenue from privately funded research, and others are known to be running on already tight staffing levels.

Overall, directorate managers enjoy a relatively high degree of control over decision-making. However, in common with Councilco, and perhaps in a similar effort to respond to the diffuse professional identities of separate directorates, Healthco managers have tried to consolidate and centralize activities across the Trust wherever possible. For example, in 1997 a new directorate—Rehabilitation—was created with the aim of bringing together all forms of therapy, rehabilitation and elderly care. Also, heads of directorates all mentioned a gradual shift in the organizational structure, from a relatively fragmented to a horizontally integrated structure, with the aims and objectives of separate directorates linked to an overarching corporate committee. Key to the strengthened

Box 2.7. Local terms and conditions for unqualified nurses

In 1997, Healthco introduced a new grade of unqualified nurse, the health care assistant, employed on local terms and conditions. The new post was designed to meet the following objectives:

- to train and develop unqualified staff to undertake duties presently performed by nursing and medical staff;
- to introduce flexible working practices across the workforce;
- to introduce remuneration packages which assist staff recruitment, retention and development;
- to encourage flexibility across historical job descriptions through assigning responsibility for a core set of tasks plus any other reasonable duties.

The new pay scale consisted of three levels: a trainee grade; a qualified grade (on completion of NVQ level 2); and a maximum grade (after one year of experience and dependent upon satisfactory performance).

Source: Healthco document

interlinkages between directorates was the shift towards the quasi-market principles introduced in the NHS in the late 1980s. For example, if portering services are required on a particular ward within the Directorate of Medicine, then a charge for services provision is passed from facilities to the medical directorate.

Within Healthco, there are also specific areas of centralized management decision-making, such as the attempt to strengthen the coordinated management of nursing services—covering areas of recruitment and selection, training and new policies of working time. Healthco managers have been very keen to communicate corporate aims to individual directorates through greater involvement of clinical practitioners, running half-day workshops designed to share the financial and operational concerns of managers with medical staff.

Terms and conditions of employment for the vast majority of Healthco employees are covered through national collective bargaining, within the occupational framework of the Whitley Council system. Annual pay settlements for the professional groups (doctors, nurses, midwives, health visitors and professions allied to medicine) are determined through the national process of independent pay review, and for most other groups pay is jointly regulated through collective bargaining. Thus, despite strongly centralized systems of pay determination, there is a high degree of fragmentation among different occupational groups with, for example, the payment system for nurses and midwives distinct to that for ancillary or for medical staff. While at Councilco there is a national agreement to harmonize occupational differences (between manual and non-manual groups), the degree of fragmentation at Healthco is exacerbated by the recruitment of new unqualified nurses (health care assistants; see box 2.7), with terms and conditions set outside the existing national framework. In common with many other NHS Trusts, the local management of Healthco has designed and implemented a local pay structure for this new group of staff.

MEDIACO

Mediaco consists of the editorial offices of a local newspaper company together with the nearby printworks where the newspaper is printed. Both come under the umbrella of a larger media group, which is the sole proprietor of the local newspaper and has a 50 per cent stake in the printing company (shared with another large media group).[8]

Mediaco bears all the hallmarks of the radical restructuring of the industry. The local newspaper company is characterized by strongly adversarial industrial relations, exacerbated by a business cost-cutting strategy that seeks to establish a competitive pay structure by freezing rates of pay for incumbent employees and hiring new recruits on to a lower entry wage rate. The printworks was established in 1986 in the midst of closures of a number of long-standing newspaper printing firms in the local area. At a greenfield site, the original workforce of 450 (now reduced to around 280) was drawn from the hundreds of redundant printworkers in the area, with a conscious effort by managers not to recruit union activists. Since its inception, the printworks has doubled the number of presses (from two to four), and has extended hours of production to seven nights and six days per week. The printworks has a range of contracts with different news organizations, including the two

[8] As a grouping of two somewhat separate companies, Mediaco is somewhat dissimilar to our other six case studies. We have chosen to study the newspaper company and printworks together, since, until 1990, the management of the local newspaper offices and a different printworks came under 100 per cent ownership of the corporate group. In 1990, there was a break-up between these two organizations, leading to the redundancy of all the printers and the transfer of production to the current printworks.

national media groups that share joint ownership of the company. Hence, in addition to printing the local evening newspapers of Mediaco, it also prints several national daily papers for distribution in the North of England, Scotland and Northern Ireland.

The newspaper offices of Mediaco operate as a subsidiary, wholly owned by a larger company, with activities concentrated in the sector of media and entertainment. The larger media group encompasses national newspapers, regional and local newspapers (of which Mediaco is the largest), magazines, book publishing, television and radio, as well as an expanding Internet business. As part of a larger conglomerate, Mediaco, like Bankco, potentially benefits from access to a larger capital base for expansionary investment, as well as from opportunities to reduce costs through economies of scale where subsidiary activities overlap. However, managers at the newspaper offices repeatedly pointed out that capital flows were decidedly one-way—from Mediaco to the larger group—in order to offset regular losses of one of the major national newspaper subsidiary companies. Moreover, there was little evidence of the media group exploiting economies of scale by sharing functional activities across subsidiary companies (such as in advertising or sharing information on news stories).[9]

The newspaper offices at Mediaco are split into three relatively autonomous departments: editorial, advertising and distribution. At the printworks, activities are structured across four broad areas of production: warehouse, printing, plate-making and packing. In each case, there are relatively strong horizontal demarcations between worker activities in the different departments, although the introduction of new grades of production assistants at the printworks is breaking down traditional craft boundaries between the divisions. At the Mediaco newspaper offices, managers enjoy considerable autonomy in decision-making. There are few instances of strategic decisions made by the parent media group. At the printworks, on the other hand, the reliance on capital investment as a means to boost production means that managers must look to the two parent companies for strategic decision-making. However, managers have been free to bid for work from other news companies and, given the high risks associated with capital investment in this sector, it is expected that the strategy of sub-contracting work is likely to continue. In terms of performance targets,

---

[9] There is, however, some evidence of integration of activities at the regional level. For example, there has been a consolidation of accounts departments for local newspapers within one region and there are plans to integrate the advertising sales activities of the various local newspaper offices to form a regional call centre that shares services and thus reduces costs.

one of the notable changes in the news industry is the relatively recent shift amongst the key drivers of company performance. In the past, the journalistic and editorial processes were considered inseparable from the successful print run of the newspaper. Today's uncertainties revolve around the volume of advertising sales generated, reflecting the loss of union strength in the industry, the growth of alternative forms of advertising media and the changes in printing technology.

The shift from multi-employer collective bargaining and the associated decline in union strength during the 1980s transformed both the printing and the editorial arms of the national newspaper industry. Payment structures in newspaper printing traditionally drew a strong distinction between 'craft' and 'non-craft' jobs, although this was coupled with a strong linkage between the two; at the printworks, for example, assistant printers traditionally earned 87.5 per cent of the basic rate of printers. More recently, however, trade unions were removed from the negotiation process and replaced by a Joint Staffing Committee (see box 2.8), paving the way for the introduction of new employer-designed pay scales for low-skilled staff (such as the production assistant mentioned above).

Box 2.8. System of staff representation at the printworks

Since its inception, the Medicao printworks have not cooperated with unions, despite an estimated union density in the plant of around 70 per cent (distributed between the two major unions, the Graphical, Paper and Media Union and Amalgamated, Electrical and Engineering Union). There is no collective bargaining with unions either on pay or non-pay issues, such as holidays, health and safety or working time. While pay settlements during the late 1990s were all slightly above inflation, the part of the pay rise above the level of inflation was not consolidated as part of the basic rate of pay.

As an alternative, managers set up a system of worker representation whereby staff elect representatives to the Joint Staffing Committee (JSC), which meets every two months with senior management. The JSC is chaired by the production manager and consists of twelve members—eight from the staff side and four from senior management. The eight staff members represent each of the departments (night-shift printers, day-shift printers, plate-makers, day-shift packers, night-shift packers, engineers, electricians and paper handlers). The JSC operates as a single-table forum for negotiation on many substantial HR issues, including pay settlements, disputes and grievances, for all groups of staff. Agreement requires a majority decision on both the staff and the management side.

At the local newspaper offices, where managers continue to negotiate with union representatives, a pay freeze has been in place since 1995, coupled with a major effort to reduce starting rates of pay in line with 'external rates'. For van drivers, for example, the change in pay structure in 1998 reduced the annual basic salary from £19,000 to £15,400, subject to buy-outs and protected rates. Among journalists, the policy has generated a great deal of acrimony, as well as a concern among unions that the company will suffer in the long term from an inability to recruit and retain high-quality journalists.

PHARMCO

Pharmco is one of the leading global pharmaceutical corporations and one of the top ten companies in Britain. The company rose to prominence during the 1970s through the development of three widely used drugs, which enabled it to carve out a niche for its business. Since then, it has merged with another leading transnational pharmaceuticals company in an effort to coordinate the enormous investment in research and development (R&D) spending and to combine specialist areas of expertise with the aim of capturing a greater share of the market. The new company generates the bulk of its revenue from the sales of just ten products.

The four different divisions of Pharmco had diverging rates of success during the period of research, with year-on-year sales growth in pharmaceuticals outperforming slower growth in agrochemicals. However, within the pharmaceuticals division there are also diverging trends across subsidiaries. Reliance on the export market means that the strong pound had a substantial impact on profit margins of UK subsidiaries. Managers told us that a major challenge for the company was to reduce the development time of new products—the period from the identification of a new compound to its launch in the product market. For example, where a typical patent lasts twenty years, and the development time is thirteen years, this only leaves seven years to recoup investment costs before competing generic drugs enter the market. One goal, therefore, was to cut development time by half. Also, R&D spending has been expanded as a result of forging joint alliances and outsourcing research, particularly with smaller companies.

In our research, we chose to focus on the pharmaceuticals division, the largest of the four divisions. This division is split between the manufacturing side and R&D, and it was in the former that we concentrated our investigation. Pharmco manufacturing involves a wide range of forms of production, generating a variety of different products. For example, there is 'bulk drug' processing, where raw chemical materials are transformed into bulk drug products, as well as the specialized production of products through adding materials to the bulk drugs. Among managers, there was a worry that the manufacturing arm of Pharmco was not being granted equal status or recognition with the sales and R&D side of the business. This contributed to a fear that manufacturing may, at some point, be redefined as outside the core business of the company and, perhaps, be subcontracted. During the period of research, there was no evidence of a general trend in this direction, although some activities were subcontracted, such as the bulk compounds and some of the more technically difficult tasks.

The main pressures on manufacturing plant managers were, in the words of one of them, 'impossible budget targets' (expected annual earnings growth of 15 per cent for 1998–9) imposed from central Pharmco headquarters. The pressure to meet these targets was such that expectations of 15 per cent annual growth may have forced some managers to postpone investment spending to meet the target. In part, Pharmco sets its different subsidiary units in competition with each other. As part of a worldwide network of manufacturing units, British Pharmco subsidiaries face relatively high pressures on costs (since capital and labour costs are typically lower in other countries) and a real threat of relocation of production jobs. In this context, the manufacturing site had committed itself to meeting a number of challenges, as part of its central aim of becoming 'the world's best manufacturer of pharmaceuticals' (see box 2.9). In the early 1990s, the site implemented a 'lean warehousing' scheme, also referred to as the 'four-week company', which aimed to cut costs and to improve throughput of products along the supply chain between different parts of the production process on the site. The result was a massive shedding of workers (by around 20 per cent). For a number of reasons, most managers we talked with agreed that this scheme had been a mistake; as one of the HR managers told us, 'It looks now as if it should never have happened.' The company had since struggled with meeting rising orders with a reduced workforce, leading to a growing use of temporary agency workers and efforts to reverse many of the lean warehousing scheme initiatives.

While the broad challenges for a restructured production strategy were centralized, managers of the different processing plants were

Box 2.9. Challenges for Pharmco in 2000

- Speed to market:
  ⇒ open all hours
  ⇒ on time, in full
  ⇒ four-week company

- People development:
  ⇒ skilled people
  ⇒ culture
  ⇒ empowered teams
  ⇒ performance management
  ⇒ business focused

- Right first time:
  ⇒ vendor assurance
  ⇒ reliable processes and equipment
  ⇒ simple, accurate information
  ⇒ 100% right first time for all

- Improve and innovate continuously:
  ⇒ customer focused
  ⇒ simple performance measures
  ⇒ cost improvement programme
  ⇒ best factory award

- New products on time:
  ⇒ positioning for new technology
  ⇒ total project management
  ⇒ design for manufacture
  ⇒ launch all new products to plan

- Total compliance:
  ⇒ change managed
  ⇒ clearly visible compliance data
  ⇒ develop the compliance culture
  ⇒ external audits welcomed

Source: adapted from Pharmco company documents

relatively free to design and implement employment policies and practices through negotiated local working arrangements. Moreover, across the different activities of any one site, there is a diversity of policies and practices. For example, at the site where we carried out our research one of the specialist product plants had introduced an annualized hours scheme, while others operated a traditional shift system. Rather than setting centralized policies and practices, the HR department sees itself as a form of in-house consultancy, although one HR manager recognized that a certain amount of top-down 'fire-fighting' was still required.

Across the ten Pharmco manufacturing plants in Britain, there is a strong division between manual and non-manual occupational groups. Manual workers are concentrated in the production plants of the site (working as process operators, packers or technicians) and non-manual workers are employed either in the administrative centres, or as managers and supervisors in the production plants. Manual workers may be employed as line coordinators in the production plants, and therefore do exercise some managerial authority; however, the status of managerial authority is not recognized at higher levels, as illustrated, for example, by their exclusion from management committees. The division between these two groups is sealed through the use of two distinct pay structures and systems of pay determination. Manual workers are strongly unionized and receive an annual pay rise negotiated with five trade unions. Unionization among non-manual workers, on the other hand, is low; Pharmco withdrew from the collective-bargaining framework in 1994–5 and, at the time of research, awarded pay increases on the basis of performance-related pay.[10]

The one feature that unites manual and non-manual workers is payment by monthly salary. A major staff agreement in 1991 (agreed between Pharmco and the trade unions) replaced the previous 1969 weekly staff agreement for manual workers and established a monthly salary. It also involved a review of the existing system of job evaluation and the introduction of a new grade at the top of the scale to allow for future development of jobs (see box 2.10). It is also worth noting that the two scales for manual and non-manual workers overlap. Standard rates of pay for the seven manual grades overlap with the rates paid to non-manual workers on the lowest four (out of twelve) grades.

RETAILCO

Our selected food retail company, Retailco, is one of the leading food retail chains in Britain. It supplies a steadily expanding range of products (around 40,000 at the time of research) from fresh fruit and vegetables to personal computers and financial services. During the late nineties, its workforce expanded considerably, both within Britain following the construction of new retail outlets (bringing the total to around 600 stores), and abroad following a series of acquisitions of major foreign retail chains.

In its early years, Retailco was one of the first British stores to emulate US retailing trends by introducing 'self-service' grocery stores. Early expansion was facilitated by stock-control arrangements that enabled

---

[10] Unions are only recognized for representation in grievance disputes.

Box 2.10. Staff agreement for manual workers at Pharmco

In 1991, agreement between Pharmco and trade unions established the following conditions for local implementation:

- improved salary scale;
- monthly salary payments;
- opportunities for training;
- reduced working hours;
- changes in holiday qualifying agreements.

A new pay scale was constructed around a new structure of job grades which, in turn, was the product of a revamped job evaluation system. In the words of the agreement: 'It is an essential feature of the scheme that the job is evaluated in terms of the characteristics required by the job.' Jobs were evaluated in terms of four factors:

- mental requirements (for example, memory, reasoning, speed of reaction, disparate attention);
- personality requirements (for example, even temperament, cooperativeness, initiative, leadership);
- physical requirements (muscular strength, stamina, agility, sensory accuracy);
- skills and knowledge requirements (education and training, experience, special skills).

Source: adapted from Pharmco document '1991 staff agreement'

goods to be sold before they had been paid for and by the production of own-brand products as a weapon to keep food manufacturers' prices low. More recent domestic expansion has been somewhat constrained by regulations on purchasing greenfield sites. But the adverse impact of government regulations has been offset by a number of new initiatives to expand market share: the expansion of city-centre stores; an expanded product range to include white goods; efforts to attract a loyal customer base through use of customer loyalty cards; and the provision of financial services, involving a joint venture with a major bank to offer an instant access savings account and visa card, as well as a programme of Retailco personal finances covering travel insurance and home insurance.

However, it is in the international realm that Retailco has really expanded, dispelling the idea that retail services are confined to a domestic market. During the 1990s, the company acquired several foreign-based retail companies, adding an overseas workforce of more than 10,000 employees. Its success in the area of international diversification accounts for a large part of the growth experienced during the mid- to late 1990s. At the same time, however, international expansion has generated pressures on filling senior management posts, as UK-based managers are circulated around an expanding number of international posts.

The activities of Retailco are organized through a combination of functional and regional divisionalization. Across the UK, the company consists of six divisions: retail, commercial, marketing, finance, support and distribution. The retail division is then organized across three regions, each of which is sub-divided into eight groups, which, in turn, each consists of around 27 retail outlets. In addition, all stores are categorized by size and a local 'health check', which is designed to classify the occupational class and ethnicity of the local customer population. Information collected in individual stores also covers relative performance in areas of finance, operations and staff management. This information is disseminated to local store management staff, with the aim of providing data on day-by-day, and even hour-by-hour, performance in comparison to other business units that share the same size, type of operations and volume of customers. For local managers, the information is seen as a vital tool in prioritizing strategies in order to meet set targets. Much of local management practice is therefore prescribed by a highly centralized information and monitoring system (see box 2.11).

Box 2.11. Corporate goals and values at Retailco

Documentation provided to all staff states the goals and values of Retailco. Importantly, the goals include a commitment to develop as a global retailer and to expand in non-food sales. In full, it is intended that Retailco will:

- be a growth business;
- become the business people value more than any other;
- have the most loyal and committed staff;
- be a global retailer;
- be as strong in non-food as in food.

Source: Retailco documents, 1998

An associated characteristic of Retailco's management structure is a relatively low degree of autonomy in local management to adapt or transform key principles and practices of the organization. For example, store managers typically enjoy few opportunities to influence the quantity and composition of products sold in a particular store. Stock is managed automatically through a centralized stock control system (within the separate purchasing division of Retailco), which assigns products to stores based upon its particular profile. Examples of management discretion are few, and include such instances as the management of promotions and one-off sales.

The divisions that structure the Retailco workforce most strongly are vertical rather than horizontal. In general, there are opportunities for staff mobility across the different stores, and within each store there are only weak lines drawn around different divisions (such as the warehouse, wine or fresh produce divisions). The few examples of horizontal demarcations include the bakery division and the work of file-maintenance operators (who process data on computers) where, in each case, patterns of mobility are relatively closed off from other groups of the workforce. Across all Retailco stores, there is a common vertical structure of four layers which distinguishes between store manager, senior managers (for example, personnel, customer services and sales), section managers (for example, cash-tills, bakery, stock control and night-shift) and general assistants (for example, trolley assistant, shelf-filler, cashier and baker).

These groups are also delineated by the type of payment system. General assistants, the group that makes up the vast majority of the workforce, are paid hourly, and annual increases for the six grades of staff are determined through collective bargaining with a trade union (see box 2.12). The agreed rates are applicable across all UK stores, with additions for the London weighting. Section managers are also covered by collective bargaining. The separate pay scale sets an annual salary structure and includes a pay supplement (around 4 per cent) for managers working in the larger superstores. For some reason, night managers do not benefit from this supplement. Finally, there is a unilateral system of pay determination for senior managers, which includes additions in the way of performance-related pay.

While the three main groups of staff appear relatively segmented, there are a number of Retailco schemes that seek to close the gaps. Since 1997, all staff (including part-timers who do not pay tax) have benefited from pro-rata payment of bonuses through an Inland Revenue profit-related pay scheme. In 1997–8, the amount payable varied between £50

Box 2.12. The partnership agreement at Retailco

In February 1998, Retailco signed a partnership agreement with a trade union. This was the first such agreement in the retail sector, although this was unsurprising given that Retailco has, for many years, been the only major retailer with a highly unionized workforce (more than 50 per cent). The aim was to consolidate a 'new era' of employee consultation and involvement, replacing the traditional union–employer bargaining arrangements (involving the rebranding of shop stewards as 'employee representatives', which would be broadened to include union and non-union representatives). In an interview with the group retail manager, we were told that the new deal would 'prevent the union culture being imposed on stewards' and would establish negotiations with all staff.

The general secretary of the union claimed that the partnership was a 'win–win' deal and would bring the union 'to the centre of business, rather than on the sidelines raising grievances'. On an equally optimistic note, the HR director of Retailco praised the opportunities for better 'two-way communication' to manage change.

(for staff with annual earnings of £2,000) and £518 (for staff earning £24,000). Inclusion of the 30 per cent or so of the Retailco workforce whose income is below the tax threshold is made possible by spreading the tax savings resulting from the scheme. In addition, employees with more than two years' service benefit from dividends paid out through the company's share options scheme, which, in 1997, enhanced earnings by an additional 4.15 per cent. While such schemes may foster some sense of loyalty or commitment to Retailco, it is worth noting that (as with other large corporations) the share of total profits that is distributed to employees is very small. In 1998, employees made up almost one in three of all shareholders, yet only held around 2 per cent of the total number of shares.

TELECOMCO

Our final case study organization is a leading international player in the world of telecommunications and one of the major providers of telecommunications services in the UK. During the period of our research, although the bulk of its revenue was generated through charges on telephone lines and calls, in a context of regulatory and competitive pressures for price reductions, the two major areas of revenue growth for Telecomco were in mobile communications and Internet services. Expansion strategies have focused on the international market. For example, Telecomco established a number of joint ventures and alliances with telecommunications and software companies across Europe, the USA and East Asia, largely with the aim of expanding services for business customers.

Telecomco is organized by function and by region. The four functional divisions, in order of size, are: Networks and Systems, Consumer, Business and Global Communications. The largest division, Networks and Systems, includes R&D and the operations of field engineers, and covers around half of the entire workforce. The Consumer Division, which encompasses around 120 call centres, covers a broad range of activities such as directory enquiries, operator assistance, repair services and 'cold-call' telemarketing services. The Business Division includes mobile phone services alongside sales, marketing and customer services for corporate clients. And, finally, the smallest division, Global Communications, provides services for customers requiring global services and oversees international joint ventures.

The management structure of the company is defined within an internal market (similar to the NHS) where individual trading units across the different divisions have delegated powers and commercial relationships to the rest of the group. The internal structure obliges managers to seek out the least costly supplier of services, in an aim to reduce internal prices to external market rates. In an effort to balance the discipline of the market with a notion of company loyalty (or unity) among trading units regardless of type of business, an associated strategy during the time of research was to encourage corporate citizenship among senior Telecomco managers by developing a brand of management that would maintain a corporate 'feel' across the company. Managers of individual 'units', such as call centres or network systems supply units, were aware of the need to compete against each other, since relative performance influenced the level of available resources. In response to a sophisticated, centralized system of performance monitoring across units, managers needed to respond quickly—for example, to arrest under-performance by disciplining staff for over-long rest breaks or average length of call times. Moreover, managers, particularly in the Networks and Systems division, were conscious that the internal market structure also continuously questioned what ought to be the core and support services provided by Telecomco, with the implication that certain activities would be outsourced.

Indeed, between 1991 and 1997, there was a rise from zero to 6,720 jobs outsourced, mainly in cleaning, catering and services.

Indeed, while companies like Retailco (and, in recent years, Bankco) have experienced steady job expansion, jobs in Telecomco fell rapidly in the period leading up to our research (the workforce was halved between 1985 and 1997; see box 2.13), and continued at a slower rate of descent during the period 1997–9. The largest workforce groups are still engineers (46 per cent of the total), followed by managers (25 per cent) and office grades (21 per cent). In line with the changing nature of the sector, however, which is becoming more customer-focused rather than network-focused, it is likely that there will be persistent pressure on engineering jobs concentrated in the networks and systems division of Telecomco.

Collective bargaining for the Telecomco workforce has traditionally been split between the managerial and non-managerial workforce, with a different trade union representing each group in negotiations. Levels

Box 2.13. Employment trends in Telecomco

During the late 1980s and 1990s, all groups of the Telecomco workforce experienced significant reductions in numbers. The greatest change was a reduction in numbers of engineers by 50 per cent. Other groups adversely affected included operators, although many of these were redeployed to office grades in the process of restructuring around new technologies. Examination of the distribution of occupational groups shows clearly that managers increased in importance, from a representation of one in seven employees to one in four between 1985 and 1997. And the 50 per cent reduction in engineers was in line with the overall reduction of the workforce so that their share of the total workforce remained approximately the same (from 47 to 46 per cent).

Occupational group	% distribution of occupational groups		% change in number of workers, 1985–97
	1985	1997	
Managers	15	25	− 13
Engineers	47	46	− 50
Operators	14	3	− 89
Office grades	14	21	− 21
Others	11	5	− 78
Total	100	100	− 49

Source: Telecomco document, 1998

of unionization and the negotiating role of unions weakened during the 1990s for two main reasons. First, collective-bargaining coverage was reduced by the growing use of temporary agency workers and workers contracted on a self-employed basis. For both groups, pay is negotiated on a local basis between the Telecomco manager and the individual contractor or agency (although many agency staff are union members). In 1997, for example, 14 per cent of the workforce providing Telecomco services were either employed by a job agency or were self-employed. Secondly, central management adopted a more critical view of the role of unions among the management grades during the 1990s (where levels of unionization were traditionally high). They were less willing to negotiate with unions and withdrew from a long-standing arbitration agreement. Also, while there were virtually no staff on individual employment contracts in the early 1980s, by the late 1990s for every twelve Telecomco employees covered by collective bargaining in Britain, one employee (typically mid- or senior management) had an individual contract.

CONCLUSION

Overall, then, the seven organizations selected for research broadly reflect the diversity of changes in work and employment witnessed across different sectors of the economy. Moreover, the selection captures important differences in types of business and work systems (see tables in Appendix 2). For example, there are differences in ownership structures, with the two public services organizations wholly state-owned and the private sector companies more likely to operate as a subsidiary, or wholly owned, by a much larger national, or transnational, corporation. There are also differences in management structure, with a stark contrast between those organizations with very sophisticated systems of centralized monitoring of business units and others where individual departments enjoy relatively high levels of management freedom.

In the next chapter we continue our introduction to the case study organizations. We provide a more visual assessment of the work carried out at the different workplaces we visited and a preview of the hopes and concerns of some of the workers and managers we talked with during the course of our research.

3

Patterns of Work and Labour

INTRODUCTION

During the closing years of the twentieth century, there were a number of debates concerning the degree of transformation in the nature of work in the British economy. The loudest voices belonged to those with the most optimistic message; advances in technologies would liberate the creative capabilities of individuals and, coupled with forward-thinking management practices, traditional boundaries between job tasks would be dissolved in the name of flexible innovation, opening the door to new areas for skills development and career opportunities (Champy 1995; Drucker 1993; Hammer 1996; Leadbeater 1999; Womack *et al.* 1990). However, evidence of new factory sweatshops, in the form of call centres (precisely in sectors at the heart of technological change, such as telecommunications and banking), along with the apparent persistence of traditional Taylorist production-line techniques in much of British manufacturing, jarred with the happy prospects identified by the futurologists (for similar arguments, see Bradley *et al.* 2000; Taylor and Bain 1999; Warhurst and Thompson 1998).

In the context of these debates (see also Chapter 1), it was decided at a very early stage in this project that an effective assessment of the changing nature of work and associated changes in employer policies and practices required detailed examination within different organizations. This involved around 50 interviews with senior managers and more than 250 interviews with workers and mid-level managers, as well as tours around the different places of work. It would not have been possible to construct an account of change at work simply by documenting changing employer policies and practices and assuming that these would have had a straightforward impact on the nature of work.

Equally, it would not have been possible to rely solely upon an understanding of broader changes in the particular sector of economic activity, since these cannot be assumed to trickle down to the workplace level. For example, in the world of pharmaceuticals—often claimed as the beacon of high-skill/high-productivity success in Britain—detailed interviews with workers in manufacturing plants reveal a scenario far removed from the stylized image of this sector. Similarly, recent changes in food retail have involved large-scale investment in new technologies; again, however, these have largely been aimed at speeding up, and making more efficient, point-of-sale transactions, and have had relatively little effect on the type of jobs carried out. Indeed, shelf-fillers were among the fastest growing occupations during the late 1990s. However, the nature of work has clearly not been static. Newspaper printers control enormous presses through computerized systems; face-to-face delivery of banking (and, increasingly, health) services has been replaced by telephone and Internet-service delivery; and workers in local authorities are increasingly encouraged to develop new skills in a bid to carve out a specialist niche to fend off competition from the private sector.

Building upon the previous chapter, here we draw upon our observations in the places where people work and the ways in which they describe their jobs to provide a graphic and more visual account of the organizations. Also, we draw upon interviews with different workers to illustrate the general degree of change in the nature of work in each organization.

BEHIND THE SCENES

The research for this book was carried out very much *inside* the organizations. A great deal of preliminary investigation relied on the usual sources: company reports, trade-union research, national statistics and archival research. But the real insights were gained from talking with management and employees behind the doors of the organization in question. After all, it is at the workplace where the central policies of an organization are implemented. It is here that relations between management and staff are most exposed; where customary patterns of working develop and change; where friendships and collective alliances are forged, or broken; and where most people spend the bulk of their working time.

Box 3.1. Introducing the workplaces visited

At each organization we selected key departmental groups or occupational groups, for detailed research. For each group we interviewed a number of employees, coded by number. In addition, at each organization we interviewed several senior managers, for which in the text we simply refer to their job title (see Appendix 1 for further details). The following is a list of the different organizations, indicating the respective code name for each departmental or occupational group and the number of employees interviewed:

Bankco
- business customer services (Bankco1, nos. 1–12)
- debt management centre (Bankco2, nos. 1–14)
- personal customer services, old site (Bankco3, nos. 1–10)
- personal customer services, new site (Bankco4, nos. 1–10)

Councilco
- civic and school catering (Councilco1, nos. 1–11)
- community care provision (Councilco2, nos. 1–19)
- environment and development (Councilco3, nos. 1–7)
- leisure (Councilco4, nos. 1–17)

Healthco
- ancillary staff (Healthco1, nos. 1–4)
- doctors (Healthco2, nos. 1–7)
- nurses (Healthco3, nos. 1–10)

Mediaco
- printworks (Mediaco1, nos. 1–14)
- editorial department (Mediaco2, nos. 1–13)
- advertising department (Mediaco3, nos. 1–11)

Pharmco
- processing (Pharmco1, nos. 1–16)
- packing (Pharmco2, nos. 1–10)

Retailco
- 24-hours out-of-town store (Retailco1, nos. 1–11)
- medium-size suburban store (Retalico2, nos. 1–12)
- inner-city store (Retailco3, nos. 1–13)

Box 3.1. *(cont.)*

Telecomco
- directory enquiries (Telecomco1, nos. 1–10)
- repair services centre (Telecomco2, nos. 1–7)
- telemarketing centre (Telecomco3, nos. 1–10)
- network engineers (Telecomco4, nos. 1–6)

In our visits to our case study organizations, we were keen to observe the work that people did and the ways in which they related to each other, to customers and to machines. In some cases (as in banking, retailing, printing and telecommunications) we observed a wide range of job activities and talked with people from a variety of occupational groups. In others, this was less possible. In the pharmaceutical company, it proved difficult to negotiate access to the laboratories where the scientific work was conducted. In the local authority and the hospital, the range and variety of activities were such that we concentrated our research in particular departments and divisions (see box 3.1). We begin our discussion with Bankco and our visit to four Bankco workplaces.

BANKCO

At Bankco, we visited four workplaces—two from the Corporate and Commercial Division and two from the Personal Customer Services Division (see box 3.1). We talked with staff at different levels in the organization, including the HR Director and other senior managers responsible for the operations of each subdivision (or service centre) and 46 staff employed as team managers or customer service advisors (see Appendix 1). The majority of interviewees were women (39 out of 53), reflecting the gender mix of Bankco as a whole, where around two in three workers are women. Also, among the 39 women we talked with, just 10 were in part-time work—again a reflection of the under-representation of part-time work among women as a whole at Bankco compared to the national average (see table 3.1).

We were struck, however, by the fact that most of the women we talked with were clustered on the lowest grades. Examination of the workforce data shows that this was no accident. Across Bankco, four in

Table 3.1. Workforce composition at Bankco

Division	Female		Male		Total no. of employees
	% full-time	% part-time	% full-time	% part-time	
Corporate and commercial	45	14	40	1	945
Personal banking	48	23	28	1	2,269
Group finance	32	6	61	1	170
Group resources	36	6	57	1	290
Central	47	0	53	0	17
Operating resources	36	0	64	0	11
Total	45	19	35	1	3,702

Table 3.2. Female employment shares and part-time working at Bankco

	Personal Banking Division		Total Bankco workforce	
	% female	% of women in part-time work	% female	% of women in part-time work
Low-grade staff	79	39	77	36
Medium-grade staff	63	5	58	6
High-grade staff	21	7	20	9
Total	71	33	66	30

Note: Low-, medium- and high-grade staff refer to 'clerical', 'appointed' and 'managerial' grades as used prior to the restructuring of grades in 1998.

five women work at the lowest clerical grades, compared to less than half of all men (79 per cent and 45 per cent, respectively). And, as table 3.2 demonstrates, among workers on the lowest grades, more than three-quarters of jobs are taken by women, whereas at the top of the job ladder this pattern is reversed. Where women have advanced into medium and higher grades (into supervisory and managerial positions), there are fewer part-time job posts, a pattern that is more marked at the Personal Customer Services Division where the majority of Bankco female workers are employed.

Our selection of workplaces to visit was made on the basis of representing those areas of work most subject to changing employment composition and working practices. In other smaller divisions, such as Group Finances and Group Resources, the traditional pattern of men working in full-time employment still defines the majority of the workforce (61 per cent and 57 per cent, respectively), perhaps because these divisions are closer to the corporate centre of Bankco.

Business customer services

Our research at the business customer services workplace involved visits to a large, grey warehouse at the edge of the city centre. We observed very little that brought to mind the 'normal' face of a bank. The centre was established in 1993 with the aim of physically separating out the administrative and services side of business relationships previously carried out within the central corporate division in the city centre. Inside, large open-plan offices cover two floors of space. Around 200 banking staff work on individually assigned desks, each with a computer and a telephone. At this workplace two in three workers are women, even though over 80 per cent of these work full time. Working hours at the centre stretch well beyond the 9 to 5 pattern. Shifts run from 8 am to 8 pm between Monday and Friday and between 8 am and 12 am on Saturdays. The shift rota is adjusted from time to time to meet the aim of providing sufficient staff to answer 90 per cent of calls over a four-hour period within twenty seconds.

Some workers we talked with are part of a small group of staff that provides typing support for the corporate division. For the majority, however, work involves managing the accounts for a number of dedicated corporate customers and, where requested, negotiating small loans (up to £25,000). Despite the responsibilities, most staff are employed on relatively low grades. However, unlike most call centres, work involves a mix of telephone and paper work, and, for many workers we spoke to, the centre is considered to be a first step in a career in the corporate division. One woman working twenty-four hours per week as a low-grade commercial officer told us she was relatively satisfied with the level of job variety:

Part of the day I still take phone calls and the other part of the day it's very varied. It can be anything really, ordering copy items, or doing status enquiries or anything really.... I'd rather do the work than be on the telephone. But that depends how many people are in and what the rota is for your team per week.
(Female, part time, no. 2, Bankco1)

However, as we discuss in later chapters, this experience was not true for all staff we interviewed. In particular, those with previous experience of branch banking found a reduced level of job variety, as well as a lack of responsibility for their work.

Debt management centre

Our second place of research was the debt management centre, which is located in Bankco's city-centre headquarters. Around 300 staff are responsible for analysing accounts, making contact with indebted customers and negotiating forms of debt collection. There is no weekend working; all staff work on shifts between 8.30 am and 8.30 pm, Monday to Friday. Unlike business customer services, work at the debt management centre can involve a great deal of emotional energy. One of the workers from the group known as 'collections' talked to us about the stress associated with her kind of work:

Since I have been here it [morale] has always been quite low. I think it's because... it's very stressful is debt collecting... and you have your family troubles as well and then you come to work and somebody says 'I can't pay because my husband has just died'. It is hard because you sympathize with them and there is a lot of hardship out there and the management says 'We need a minimum of this'. It's just a very hard job. I think that a lot of us feel that we don't get the support and encouragement and motivation from the management that we would expect.

(Female, part time, no. 4, Bankco2)

As the terms of competition changed in the banking sector, so the pressure on the bank to reduce its bad debts increased. The staff at this workplace were at the frontline of Bankco's corporate push to reduce the wastage incurred through having to write off bad debts.

Personal customer services

Finally, we visited two call centres, one relatively old and the other relatively new, which form part of Bankco's Personal Customer Services Division—by far the largest of its six divisions. Three in four of the people we talked with at the two centres were women, which closely reflects the gender composition of this division as a whole with 71 per cent women and two out of three women in full-time work. Operators at these two centres work in teams and spend their entire shift in front of monitors, answering telephone queries and processing paperwork. Many of them experience this as intensive work. For all of them, time away from the computer to do paper work is regarded as a treat. It is also closely regulated and controlled. The differences between this kind of work and the kind of work we witnessed at the two Corporate and Commercial Division workplaces was made clear in a discussion with one member of staff who had moved across from the 'debt management' workplace. The intensity of work in the new job was seen as critical. The worker explained:

[At the old debt management centre] you were on the telephones half a day and [paper] processing the rest of the day… so it was varied and interesting all the time. Your mind was active all the time.

(Female, full time, no. 10, Bankco4)

Experience of how technology had dramatically changed their work was most stark among workers at the older of the two workplaces. This site was opened in the late 1970s and many staff had remained there and had seen their work transform from paper-processing tasks to computer-based telephone work. Others had transferred to the centre during the 1980s when Bankco closed many of its bank branches. One of the customer services advisers summarized these changes:

The big change was the phone banking. When I first started [here] there was no phone banking at all. It was just basically processing and all you used to do was sit keying standing orders in all day…. There's a screen on every desk now. There obviously wasn't before and it's just completely different.

(Female, full time, no. 5, Bankco3)

Overall, across the four Bankco workplaces we visited we were struck both by the extent of the changes that had occurred and the speed at which they had been introduced. Interviews with management and staff underlined the depth of transformation, particularly among those who had experienced the shift from branch banking to telephone banking.

COUNCILCO

As with most areas of local government, Councilco is an extraordinarily complex organization. It provides a wide range of services and employs a mix of employees, from the low to the high skilled, manual and non-manual, full and part time, and male and female. We chose to focus our research on four divisions (see box 3.1) with the aim of capturing some of the changes in working life across the spectrum of different work-force groups. We talked with a number of senior managers (5 men and 4 women) and 54 staff working in a range of different occupations. The

Table 3.3. Workforce composition at Councilco

Division	Female		Male		Total no. of employees
	% full-time	% part-time	% full-time	% part-time	
Libraries and theatres	41	21	28	10	270
City works	5	0	95	0	1,385
Operational services	6	20	70	4	1,731
Treasurers	41	7	51	1	676
Housing	37	8	53	1	1,426
Environment and development	19	23	48	11	702
Chief executive	34	10	54	1	843
Galleries and museums	38	13	49	0	69
Architects	20	4	73	2	208
Social services	43	33	20	4	3,013
Education	32	47	14	7	12,784
Catering	7	86	4	3	1,651
Total	29	38	29	5	24,758

gender mix of different occupational groups varied considerably. Among our interviewees, women were over-represented among care workers (14 out of 19) and catering workers (9 out of 11). At the two other departments, men were in the majority: 12 of the 17 leisure staff were men and in environment and development we talked with 5 men and just 2 women.

This pattern reflects Councilco workforce data (see table 3.3). Overall, women hold two in three jobs, yet there is wide variation across departments, with female shares of 79 per cent and 76 per cent in the two largest departments of education and social services, and a share of just 5 per cent in the city works department (which covers refuse collection and street cleaning). Our research also documented changing patterns of work for a significant number of women in part-time work. Again, this reflects the general pattern at Councilco where around 60 per cent of women work part time.

Catering

Our research at Councilco began with discussions with senior management staff at the central Catering Department. This was then followed by visits to the town hall and three schools (one primary and two secondary) in order to explore management and work practices in more detail. The most striking feature of the council's Catering Department is that it is almost entirely made up of women working in part-time jobs—86 per cent out of a total of almost 1,700 staff (see table 3.3).

The bulk of jobs are in the school meals service. At the average secondary school, we were told that more than 900 meals are served by a team of female part-time workers consisting of one cook supervisor, one cook, one assistant cook and two or three general catering assistants. The number of contracted hours worked each week varied from around 10 to 35, with supervisors working longer hours. For example, at the primary school we visited, a team of six staff prepares around 350 meals each day. The supervisor was the only person on a full-time contract (seven hours a day). Her assistant worked five and a quarter hours a day and the other women, employed as general catering assistants, worked, respectively, four, four, three and two hours per day. At each of the three schools the women we interviewed spoke to us of their frustration with the way the catering element of the job had been diluted and, in turn, how their contracted number of hours had been whittled away over the years. Many of the women took the job because it provided an ideal working time pattern that fitted around their own children who attend school (because of the late morning start, the early afternoon finish and the school holidays):

And then I had two kids in between, and started here, because it was ideal because my eldest daughter was five years old and it was ideal really.

(Female, part time, no. 2, Councilco1)

I worked up until having my children . . . and then when they went to school I came here, so I've been here since they went to school.

(Female, part time, no. 6, Councilco1)

Q. So what made you take this sort of job?
Well really it was children at school and it fits in. You drop the children at school then on the way to work and you're there to pick them up—plus the school holidays.

(Female, part time, no. 8, Councilco1)

But, as many of the staff informed us, there was a marked difference between the initial contract of a long part-time working week and the gradual shift to very short part-time working. And the cut in hours went hand-in-hand with a removal of many of the fulfilling aspects of the job. One catering assistant who had been in the job eleven years had once harboured ambitions to 'run her own school' as a supervisor. Now, exasperated with the changes, she felt it wasn't worth it:

I've always wanted to come into catering anyway.... When I first started here the job was great. The job was brilliant. It was excellent and there were pro-spects.... Because I came here I actually started [another] catering course and did my three years and from there I was looking for my youngest to become ten, eleven years old and put in for my own school then. But now, it's gone out of the door now. I don't want to be in catering anymore. It's changed.... I'm not involved in the cooking any more like I used to be.... So because of that I lost my love for it really. There's not enough to do as far as I'm concerned.

(Female, part time, no. 2, Councilco1)

In contrast to the leaking roofs of inner-city schools, staff providing catering for civic and commercial functions enjoyed the rather grander interiors of the town hall. Again, however, there was evidence of cost-cutting. The catering manager we spoke to explained that the team of six managers had been cut back to three over the previous twelve months. The managers were responsible for taking bookings and or-ganizing civic banquets, as well as bringing in 'external' business functions, such as conference and party dinners. This meant that there were large fluctuations in the volume of business from week to week, which led to massive variations in staff rotas. The reduced numbers of core staff had generated excessive reliance on temporary agency workers and casual help, as well as undue demands on overtime working.

Community care

The second department we visited at Councilco was Community Care Services Provision. Work in the department covers a mix of activities, including home care, resource centres and mental health day centres. The division overlaps with NHS community health services and therefore involves continuous joint working with local NHS Trusts. For our research, we talked with three groups of staff: home-carers, who visited patients in their own homes; day-centre staff, who cared pri-marily for patients within the centres (but also often visited patients in their homes); and drivers, the only group largely made up of men, who transport patients between their homes and the centres. We visited three day centres to meet with day-centre staff and home-carers, for whom the centre served as their base, and a small workplace that serves as the base for drivers in the city.

Home-care staff are, typically, women in part-time positions working relatively long hours (around thirty per week). They consist mainly of a mix of long-serving staff and young women with children. For most of them, the work involves providing basic, non-medical care (washing, dressing and carrying out small chores) to patients (the elderly and disabled) in their homes, as part of the extended government programme of care in the community. For a small, but growing, number, care is provided as part of a four-week programme of rehabilitation and assessment for patients just out of hospital. These staff work in groups labelled STAR teams (short-term assessment and rehabilitation), and they are expected to work around a more varied set of hours and days. Staff working on the new teams transferred from traditional care posts and talked to us about the differences:

Like with home care, if you were helping someone to get dressed, you might do everything for them. Whereas once we'd been in—yes, they do need help—but they can manage to put their top on and it's just the buttons that they can't do.

(Female, full time, no. 1, Councilco2)

A second group of staff spend most of their working time within the day care centres and provide care for visiting elderly patients. The services provided vary between centres. In general, patients can have a bath, or they might be taken out to a local chiropodist. Then there might be regular activities; for example, at one of the centres there is a Thursday afternoon 'reminiscing' group, a Tuesday morning keep-fit class and an aromatherapy class on Fridays. For many of these day-centre staff, conversations about their work were tainted by their experience of recent upheavals caused by the decision by Councilco to switch from providing residential care to day care and to close care homes for the severely disabled. For many staff, these changes reflected badly on the council and on the way they felt towards their work:

I worked at the home for seven and a half years. . . . And then they just decided they were closing six of the homes down and they didn't seem to care what people thought, that the elderly were losing their homes, that we were having to be redeployed.

(Female, full time, no. 6, Councilco2)

I've seen quite a lot of changes. Like I say, when I first came here it was the residential and then it's been six years as the day centre for the elderly. So obviously the people that used to live here—it was quite an upsetting time because then they all had to move and went into the private sector.

(Female, part time, no. 13, Councilco2)

The district base for the community care drivers was an old, two-floor portakabin. The under-investment in this site may have been because there were proposals to redefine the jobs of drivers so that they would become support home-help workers. The new job activity would involve driving patients to a centre and then staying at the centre to provide care. In part, these plans were held up by the slow implementation of the Single Status agreement. However, the drivers, with union backing, had also reacted strongly against the plan. According to the transport manager we talked to, the plan had been imposed with no negotiation and as part of a wider strategy to repackage the driving division as a business that could then be sold off to the private sector.

The traditional work of drivers is split between providing transport services to patients who want to visit day-care centres and delivering a range of equipment (anything from a special mattress to a bath hoist) to the homes of patients due to leave hospital. In both areas, as the drivers were keen to point out, the work involved social interaction, as much as driving and delivery skills:

You're on your own all the time when you're a HGV driver. Whereas now you're dealing with people. Instead of boxes it's human beings.... It's different every day. Like somebody's poorly, or they're really upset, or somebody's had a break-in.... You find out different things about them. So I think it's a fulfilling job.

(Male, full time, no. 18, Councilco2)

Environment and development

The Department of Environment and Development was our third choice for research. It was formed at the end of 1997 through the merger of two and a half departments: environmental health, planning and engineering. The newly formed department covers five major areas: traffic and transportation, engineering design consultancy, planning, environmental health and management services. Reflecting this rather disparate set of functions, the department delivers a range of services, from providing school-crossing patrollers to operating an in-house engineering design consultancy.

Just over 700 people are employed in the department, although this number includes around 200 school-crossing patrollers working very few hours. Around two in three workers in this department are men, one in three are in part-time jobs and seven in ten are in non-manual jobs.

Unlike the other departments we have visited at Councilco, Environment and Development contains a number of professional occupations. These workers are located in the town hall in the city centre. The offices had been relatively unchanged since a refurbishment in the 1970s and were emblematic of the power relations at the time in the public sector. For example, managers still had large desks in spacious offices, and recent staff cuts had left some offices unused. As a result of budget pressures, an increasing amount of what was referred to as 'specialist work' was being performed by external consultants. One example was computer-aided design projects, where internal investment in training and technology was not considered possible by managers.

The department also contained groups of workers, including school-crossing patrollers, who had almost no direct contact with Councilco central offices. The combination of short working hours and a highly individualized place of work proved problematic for departmental managers. One manager, who had two years' experience, explained:

I am responsible for 4 supervisors... and 250 school-crossing patrol personnel who are based on individual sites through the city, which means a big problem in supervising them.... There's also a problem with the part-time staff, as they only work for an hour in the morning and an hour in the afternoon.

(Female, full time, no. 6, Councilco3)

Leisure

The fourth Councilco department we visited was Leisure. It delivers a number of services, including the running of city parks, indoor and outdoor leisure centres and youth services in the city. Tasks performed by staff range from feeding farm animals and teaching children how to sail boats, to maintaining the grounds of public parks. The department is split into five sections: indoor facilities, outdoor facilities, sports development, core engineering and contracts and development. It has a total workforce of around 420, with most staff spread around the different facilities and only a small number of managers resident at Councilco headquarters.

We talked with staff at both the indoor and outdoor facilities to assess a range of work performed across the department. We visited three indoor sports facilities and four outdoor facilities: city parks and water parks. Once again, we observed a strong segmentation of workers by gender between indoor and outdoor facilities: at the former, women typically made up around half the workforce, while at the latter it was rare to see a female employee.

Across the different places of work we visited, workers tended to have a relatively strong sense of job fulfilment. However, there was also a sense that things were changing for the worse, with evidence of buildings and grounds in disrepair and the perception that Councilco was not willing to fund the needed levels of staff. At one of the outdoor leisure centres, workers talked about the increasing trend towards employing casual labour. One male park warden, with more than seven years' experience at the centre, argued that this trend was reducing the skill base:

[When I joined Councilco], if I wanted to know anything about the gardens or the trees or anything I would go to [a more experienced worker] because he's been there and he has got a wealth of experience. [But now] they keep putting these 90-day temporary people on with him. Then they will take them off him and just have them sweeping paths. I know it needs to be done, but... they are not gaining anything.... They are not learning anything.

(Male, full time, no. 6, Councilco4)

At another leisure centre, we found evidence of low morale among workers, stemming from a combination of budget cuts and the sense that jobs were undervalued. A lifeguard explained his sense of frustration:

I have been in the job for 12 years and I know it inside out, back to front.... Years ago we had a lifeguard team... all trained up for doing lifesaving and now it's deteriorating. Now young kids do our jobs. It demeans our job.

(Male, full time, no. 11, Councilco4)

Overall, employment change at Councilco for most workers we spoke with has been a painful affair. The public sector ethos that often under-pinned people's reasons for joining the organization has been wea-kened by the combination of external pressures and their translation into new corporate policies and practices. While the work that people do at Councilco has not changed as dramatically as it has at other organizations, nevertheless, the wider context within which Councilco workers have to perform their tasks has been radically altered since the mid-1980s.

HEALTHCO

At the NHS Trust, we talked with a sample of workers from three of the main occupational groups: ancillary staff, doctors and nurses. Our aim was to understand the nature of work for both male- and female-dominated groups, as well as for high and low status groups. Nursing and midwifery makes up the largest occupational group at Healthco (1,901 workers, or 38 per cent of the total workforce), with more than 9 out of 10 jobs filled by women and around 2 in 3 being full time. The groups of ancillary staff and medical and dental staff are also significant. Ancillary workers are also predominantly women, but medical and dental staff are still more likely to be men (by a ratio of 2 to 3). It is within this group of medical and dental staff that men are the most likely to work part time for the NHS, largely due to the high share of part-time consultants (75 out of 170 male consultants work part time). This reflects the decision to split their work between the public and private sectors.

In our conversations with these different groups of workers, we talked about the kinds of job task that they typically performed. For all groups we talked to, this did not just amount to a set of technical tasks. Common to all jobs was a sense of duty to the patients and the exercise of social skills. For example, one woman in her thirties, working as a health care assistant (an ex-nursing auxiliary), described her typical round of duties as follows:

Basically, for me, it's making beds, giving anybody a wash that needs a wash, or giving them a hand if they do. Making sure that everybody's got breakfast and then basically just checking that everybody's okay in themselves. There's an awful lot of—I wouldn't say counselling skills—but you're there for people to talk to which is a very important part of the ward.

(Female, full time, no. 2, Healthco3)

And, in the words of one of the consultant physicians with nearly 20 years of experience:

As a consultant I've got a responsibility to my patients. I've got a responsibility to ensure that what I'm responsible for works as well as it can do. And I'm committed to making it do that. And so we work long hours. And we do work at home. And we're on-call at night. We come in at weekends. And we regard that as part of the job.

(Male, full time, no. 4, Healthco2)

The staff at Healthco also highlighted the increasing pressures of meeting service requirements and the problems of tight budgets and under-staffing. Ancillary staff seemed under the most strain. For example, porters had witnessed a massive reduction in numbers employed, following the amalgamation of three hospitals into one NHS Trust, despite having to provide a similar volume of services. Moreover, the different health departments no longer each had its own dedicated porter but, instead, had to bid for services from a pool. This forces porters to prioritize certain requests over others, increasing the pressure when complaints are received. One of the supervisors described the situation as follows:

With the Trust the way it is now, everybody's short staffed and everybody puts pressure on everybody else.... 95 per cent of my work is deflecting the flack that's aimed at my department and defending my power source, as it were. Departments are losing their staff and expecting the portering service to do more and more and that's what's happening.

(Male, full time, no. 1, Healthco1)

For porters, we identified little by way of change in what they do; rather, there was a change in the amount and organization of their work. This mirrors our findings at the Councilco departments. This was less true of nursing staff, who had experienced a widening of job tasks at all levels. At the same time, there were also problems of under-staffing, particularly among qualified nurses, related to the national shortage of nurses, which led to an over-reliance by managers on long working hours.

Most unqualified nurses had completed a programme of training that extended their job duties beyond making beds and changing bedpans to include checking blood pressure, or removing stitches. It also involved a change in contract, from the national grade of nurse auxiliary (or assistant nurse) to the local grade of health care assistant. As the new grade of unqualified nurses expanded their range of tasks, qualified nurses were encouraged to give up duties at the bottom end and take on new tasks that overlapped with the work of doctors. At the same time, however, a chronic shortage of staff and long working hours were draining goodwill, potentially undermining any managerial strategy to adapt the division of nursing duties. One of the qualified nurses explained:

Because we've got a problem with recruiting nurses, the banking agency has the same problem. So they're having problems filling in the shifts as well. The ward staff become tired because they have to work over to cover the ward and you rely on people's good nature really a lot of the time to work over.

(Female, full time, no. 6, Healthco3)

And where senior nurses running wards were relying on buying in extra temporary help to cover for unfilled vacancies, many found that the 'short-termism' of staff planning did not encourage a sense of loyalty to patients. In this scenario, all the additional, non-quantifiable elements of nurses' work, such as social skills and a sense of duty, were often not delivered. As one ward manager, a qualified nurse with 14 years of experience, told us:

They [agency nurses] are people who, at the end of the day, although they may be good people, they have no commitment to me and I have to be eternally grateful they have turned up—which is good, and we wouldn't be able to keep open and functioning without them basically. But it does mean that on a shift like today, there are actually two agency nurses on duty, so it makes it difficult for me because when I say that they have responsibility to the patients they really don't know the runnings of the set-up.

(Female, full time, no. 10, Healthco3)

Doctors were also struggling under the tight financial regime. Many were concerned about the increased intensity of work in conditions where the hours of junior doctors had been cut (following national legislation), but the numbers of medical staff had remained virtually the same due to lack of additional funds. The shortfall of qualified nurses at Healthco made matters worse. These pressures on work were exacerbated by a general sense that poor relations between the government and the medical profession were undermining morale. Pressures to meet performance targets, in the absence of additional funding, drove a wedge between a sense of professionalism and public service, on the one hand, and accountability to national government, on the other. One of the consultants talked to us at length about these problems:

We have a culture which is led by various governments, which says that all doctors are bastards, they're out at the golf course all day long. They're fat cats and they need cutting down a peg—which does wonders for morale.... We have lots of good ideas sent to us [by government] and we have lots of good ideas ourselves and we're in a sort of sheet-feeder system where we're beginning to feel—many of us—that we're actually simply a cog in a machine rather than a professional working within an organization.... I think the biggest change over the last fifteen years that I've seen actually is I've never seen morale go down so much and still be going. That is the biggest change. The commitment to say 'I'll work very hard and keep on working when I'm tired.' It's gradually going.

(Male, full time, no. 4, Healthco2)

Overall, there are clearly significant changes taking place at Healthco in the nature of work. For nursing staff there has been a radical change in the division of labour between qualified and unqualified workers, with new local qualifications administered to health care assistants in exchange for a widening of job tasks. For all groups, there is a sense of a leap into the unknown, where it is perhaps no longer possible to maintain a commitment to a notion of public service, or to be able and willing to spend social time with patients.

MEDIACO

At Mediaco we talked with people from almost all the different activities of work: workers who operate the printing presses and manage the giant paper warehouse, as well as reporters, sub-editors and advertising sales staff from the newspaper offices. The only group we were not able to talk to were the drivers who are responsible for distributing the newspapers. Negotiating access to this group proved difficult, as the period of research clashed with an industrial dispute over new rates of pay and working time. At the Mediaco printworks, we met with workers from each of the traditional craft groupings who worked within a particular production division (printing, plate-making and packing) as well as electricians and engineers who work across divisions. Printers make up the largest group, with 112 men in full-time work, split evenly between the fixed day and night shifts. The second largest category of electricians and engineers is also composed entirely of male full-time workers. At the newspaper offices, we talked with workers from both main divisions. At the editorial division, 5 of the 13 employees we spoke to were female, while at the advertising offices, 7 of the 11 employees were female.

The process of producing the newspaper begins in the newspaper offices, located in the city centre, and ends at the printworks, on the fringes of the city, where the newspapers are printed and delivered by van throughout the local region and beyond. Three editions are produced each day, in time for early afternoon, mid-afternoon and evening sales. For example, on most days, the first edition is faxed from the offices to the printworks at 10.25 am, the presses start running at 10.55 am and the vans are out on the road by 11.15 am. The exception is Friday, when, because of the large number of additional copies to print at a special reduced price, the finished pages must be faxed at 9 am. Normal daily sales are around 180,000, but special print runs may add up to 100,000 and thus require a finished product to be delivered to the printers earlier.

The manufacturing of the finished product thus exerts a direct pressure on the nature of work organization in the newspaper offices. The managing editor was acutely aware of the technological problems at the printworks that limited the degrees of freedom he enjoyed in putting together the paper, particularly on the days when a higher number of papers had to be printed. The printing arm was not, however, the focus of corporate attention—that was on the advertising division. With falling sales, Mediaco had come to rely more and more on generating revenue through advertising. Indeed, from our interviews with managers across the departments, there appeared to be greater support and commitment to investing in technologies and creating new job positions in advertising than in the other main areas directly involved in the production of the newspaper. Interviews with workers, however, revealed a great deal of evidence of working under high pressure, in a strict regime of daily performance targets and close monitoring of work.

Printworks

By far the greatest changes in technology have occurred in the printing side of the production process. The new printworks on the fringes of the city was purpose-built to house the enormous computer-controlled presses, as well as to incorporate automated distribution of the giant rolls of paper from the warehouse to the presses. Work is split over two floors. In the basement, directly below the giant presses above, is the area where the giant rolls of paper are set onto the presses. The process of transporting these rolls, from delivery by lorry to installation onto the press, is a mix of manual and automated work. The rolls are first brought into a warehouse from lorries that arrive every 45 minutes (delivering 2,000 tonnes of paper each week); they are then sorted, according to the type of paper, by men in forklift trucks. These men also bring the paper into the main area as and when requested by a computer-controlled queue system. From here, automated machines transport the rolls to the presses following a set of programmed tasks—for example, 'pick up roll three and take it to press five, then return and recharge'. Finally, the rolls are loaded on to the press with the help of manually controlled lifting equipment.

The plate room—or pre-press room—is on the ground floor behind the giant presses. Here, each page of the newspaper is faxed through in negative form from the newspaper offices. Once the aluminium plates have been produced, they are collected on to trolleys and the press men collect the trolleys and fix them on to the presses. The operations manager told us that the aim is to begin printing within 10 minutes of receiving the fax of the last page of the newspaper. The main area of the building houses the six giant presses, each capable of printing around

60,000 pages per hour. Each press prints a number of pages together on a sheet of paper, and the sheets come together to be cut and folded in a special machine, before flying out across the warehouse as folded complete newspapers on a roller-coaster conveyor belt which weaves through the air, taking them to the publishing room ready to be loaded on to the vans for delivery. The speed of the process, from the blank sheet of paper leaving the roll in the basement to the finished folded newspaper is just a matter of seconds.

Despite its greenfield status, the printworks is steeped in history that is carried in the memories of the large number of people working there who have spent many decades in the industry. The operations manager talked about his grandfather who had looked after the horses which delivered the Mediaco newspapers and his father who worked in the accounts department. On our several visits, he would often talk about the massive transformation of the industry. He conveyed some nostalgia for his lost skills as a compositor. But, rising through the ranks of management, he welcomed the decline of trade-unionism in the sector:

I was delighted for the change in the industry. In the past, I had no time to consider technology. I had to deal with unions all the time.

(Operations manager, Mediaco1)

It is difficult to disentangle the effects of these changes in technologies and the collapse of union strength on the nature of work at the printworks. Arguably, the very nature of the industry demands a fast pace of work to meet deadlines for the printed newspaper. The printers and plate-makers we talked to identified themselves as people who could think quickly and react effectively to problems that occur in the production process. Nevertheless, there were signs of stress associated with work intensity, particularly among the younger printers. One of the apprentices explained:

It is stressful at times. You are working to set deadlines and even today's newspaper is no good tomorrow.... It is quick, yes. And a lot of stress. You've got a lot of people stood over watching you and a lot of it has got to be right. It's got to be good. It's got to be quality. And it's got to be quick.

(Male, full time, no. 9, Mediaco1)

Editorial

As might be expected, there is more evidence of a sense of autonomy among people working in the editorial department. Work is split among journalists and sub-editors (the 'gatherers' and 'processors', as the managing editor called them) and is organized into sections, such as 'show-business' and 'sport', and, in the case of general news, into districts. Many of the journalists spend much of their time in the main office and produce articles on computers, which are then passed to sub-editors for editing and for integration into the main body of the newspaper. Others, the 'district reporters', work mostly 'in the field' and have little contact with other members of staff other than when they feed their news reports to the news desk. One of the women who had just joined Mediaco as a district journalist believed that the sense of isolation generated a strong sense of collective identity among district reporters:

We tend to talk [to each other] because we all have the same problems. We work in isolation and that's a bit strange sometimes.... It takes some getting used to, especially with the districts that border your own, you tend to chat and find out what's going on because it takes a while for things to drip through from the main office.

(Female, full time, no. 3, Mediaco2)

All the journalists spoke to us about the way new technology was changing the way they worked. Greater computerization of the writing process enabled more staff to work from home, and to submit stories to the news team without either visiting the workplace or dictating words over the telephone. One of the senior journalists argued that the changes brought productive benefits to the organization:

There are times when perhaps before you would get a story finished in the evening, which is obviously overtime, with telephone calls and looking-up information, and now you can type it up and it's done for the morning. Or you can bring it into work... and just press a button and it's done.... Whereas before you'd have perhaps waited for 15 or 20 minutes for a copy taker. So this has speeded up things I am sure for [Mediaco].

(Male, full time, no. 7, Mediaco2)

Computerization has thus gone hand-in-hand with a more individualized way of working, which, when combined with pressures to meet ever earlier deadlines, has transformed the working environment. Among the younger staff, these changes signalled autonomy and flexibility. Among the older staff, however, there was a nostalgia for the buzz of the old days:

The gathering system is much the same. We come in the morning like I did on previous papers and make the calls to the police, the fire, the ambulance—all the public services—make the calls to them.... It's just the technology in the office that's changed. It's quieter in newspaper offices. It used to be noisy—a lot of clatter. Not just typewriters, but people shouting and cracking and gagging and messenger shift this copy and da-da-da. Now they—everybody—sits around in silence. It's a strange atmosphere.

(Male, full time, no. 9, Mediaco2)

Advertising sales

Most of the 160 people in advertising work as canvassers and spend much of their working day on the telephone selling space. These workers are expected to establish a relationship with clients, by informing them regularly of new features. Each day workers are required to spend three hours on the telephone and make 60 calls. They are monitored daily by managers, who provide feedback to staff on a weekly basis. Meeting (or not) the six performance targets determines each worker's level of bonus payment, and also influences internal career prospects, since a prerequisite for being considered for promotion is to have met the targets for six consecutive months—36 targets in all. However, many of the people we talked to felt that the targets masked more than they revealed. As one canvasser told us:

Sometimes I look at [the performance sheets] and think, 'is that all?' Yet I could have made 60 calls and nobody has been in, I have only logged 1 hour and 42 minutes and I have slogged. When we are not 'on the phone' there are incoming calls too, there could be faxes. . . . If you have to make the advert for the client . . . you might have to design it there and then.

(Female, full time, no. 8, Mediaco3)

By reducing the substance of each call to a single indicator, it was felt that managers failed to appreciate the diversity of tasks demanded by customers. This led staff to be disappointed by the way their performance was translated into outcomes.

The experiences of work among the different people we talked to reflect differences in their job role and, crucially it seems in this case, their length of time working in the media industry. For example, while staff in the advertising offices were subject to strict monitoring and control as part of the process of earning pay bonuses, newly recruited printers expressed satisfaction with a deal that granted regular pay rises in line with training to give them up to £26,000 p.a. Yet, for older printers, the difference with the past arrangements reflected a marked erosion of benefits won through trade-union regulation. And journalists, while faced with few threats as a result of replacement of work by new technologies, had to put up with a pay freeze and experimentation with working time arrangements.

PHARMCO

At Pharmco, our visits to one of the large manufacturing sites were the only times during this research that we had to enter an industrial complex rather than simply a single building, warehouse or office block. The complex included offices, manufacturing plants, packing warehouses, dining halls and sports centres. Unsurprisingly, security at the site entrance was tight. The site itself was a maze of roads. The corporate flag flew at different points around the site giving the impression that you had entered a foreign country. More than 2,000 staff are employed at this site, comprising around two women to every three men, with men more likely to be working in the higher-paid jobs. For example, the data we collected show that there are just 6 women on the highest grades for manual workers (grades 7 and 8) compared to 166 men. Part-time work is used very little, with just 14 women working part time out of a total of 805 manual workers.

There are three areas of work: production, manufacturing and packing. For our research, we focused on two: a manufacturing/processing plant (Pharmco1) and a packing warehouse (Pharmco2). To enter the processing plant we had to don caps, long white coats and cover our shoes. Here, workers manufacture tablets through a series of different processes, which are divided up as 'granulation' and 'compression'. One of the operators explained these processes to us:

Granulation is basically mixing the ingredients together, making granules, just dried granules in a big container and then the container's taken to compression, put over a press and the granules are compressed under punches.

(Male, full time, no. 16, Pharmco1)

The tablets then move on to be packed. Here, people worked in a large open space, with packing organized along different lines, each following the rhythms of recently installed machinery (worth over £2 million on the newest line). Around three-quarters of this workforce are operators, with the remaining working as line coordinators, technicians and front-line managers. A packing operator, who had only recently joined Pharmco, outlined some of the similarities and differences in the work with other jobs in the area:

I think when you've worked in a company a lot of the jobs are similar [in terms of] packing. Although we were packing cigarettes and now we're packing pills . . . it is more that you get everything right. They've had mix-ups with cigarettes. It's not as crucial as having a mix-up with tablets!

(Female, full time, no. 7, Pharmco2)

When we first visited the Pharmco site, we discussed the nature of the production process and the selection of workers with several of the managers and supervisors. They were clear that in many instances the regulated nature of the industry made it impossible for the manual workers to be involved in any innovation-mediated activities. The labour process was fixed and, as such, it must not be tampered with. In the view of one of the HR managers: 'What we require are workers who are as near to being robots as possible whilst remaining human.' In this plant, Pharmco did not require intelligence. Forty years earlier, personnel managers at Ford's Halewood factory had insisted on the need to avoid intelligence at all costs: 'Anyone who puts an intelligent man on the sort of job that we've got here is asking for trouble. We've had it as well. . . . Intelligent blokes are bound to get militant if you stick them on the trim line' (cited in Beynon 1973: 90).

At Pharmco there was no fear of militancy. Instead, the worry was associated with the possibility that workers might have unrealistic ambitions or, worse, that they might try to improve things by interfering with the way the jobs were done. The managers were clearly of the opinion that young married women with children, who depended on having paid work, would best fill their requirements, especially those who had roots in the locality. But this meant that managers were not always able to find enough workers who fitted their specification. In light of this, management at Pharmco were constantly concerned to develop ways in which their workforce could be retained and involved in the work process. This was more possible in the production and manufacturing ends than in packing, but across the plant there had been a concerted attempt to increase the workers' sense of 'ownership' of the work process. To some extent this had been successful. For example, a process operator in the granulation plant, who had been with the company for 25 years, commented in this way:

You seem to have more ownership of the job . . . in the past it used to be sort of like you'd get a particular job given to you and that was it. . . . Whereas now you take more of an ownership really.

(Male, full time, no. 6, Pharmco1)

And this ownership involved more responsibility for managing yourself:

In the old days we used to have the quality control people, inspection section it was. And [now] we do all the QC work ourselves... we have a small lab at the end of the cubicles now and we do all the quality control processes in there.

(Male, full time, no. 6, Pharmco1)

These sentiments were general ones. When new technology was introduced in the tablets-packing plant, an operator told us how they were involved in the installation design:

Every line has emergency stops, which are the big red buttons, and if... there is an accident or you need to stop the machine then you quickly hit one of these. We [the team on the line] decided where they went because normally the electricians come in and stick them where they want.

(Female, full time, no. 8, Pharmco2)

In fact, it seems that this extension of the job, through the accumulation of additional tasks and responsibilities, was emerging as a central aspect of management's strategy—similar to the extension of the work of unqualified nursing staff at Healthco. One front-line manager outlined to us how the organization was seeking to redistribute tasks from one group of workers to another:

There are procedures at the moment going through so that maybe they [the operators] can start doing things like their own calibrations on machines... so [they] are not hanging around waiting for the electricians. So we're becoming a little bit more technically involved with the machines.... It's one of those things that you have to introduce carefully before the unions jump on your back, or the electricians get upset.

(Female, full time, no. 14, Pharmco1)

For some of the operators (as with some of the unqualified nurses at Healthco), these changes were welcomed, as they felt it put them in a better position to carry out their job. As one of them explained:

They [the electricians] are not quite probably as customer-minded as we are. We know we have got to get it [the product] out of the door for customers. They sort of, like, take things a lot easier than we do, and it gets to you that they've got time to chat.

(Female, full time, no. 8, Pharmco1)

However, a tension prevailed between attempts to instil in operators a greater sense of 'ownership' of machinery and the need for the technical know-how of trained electricians:

If we are getting a lot of machine breakdowns, and we're not hitting the targets then we get it in the neck from the managers and it can be really frustrating because we're there to do a job and if the machine won't allow it then it's a big knock-on effect.

(Male, full time, no. 2, Pharmco2)

Overall, managers at Pharmco were seeking to involve workers in their own self-management, while also ensuring that they stuck to the task in hand. Managers were quite frank about the dehumanizing nature of much of the work, but sought to remedy this by instilling a sense of ownership of the process and a level of understanding of how the particular job task, however monotonous, played a key role in the grander production process.

RETAILCO

Retailco has a range of stores across Britain, varying in size, opening hours and product mix to reflect regional differences. Our choice of three stores represents some of these variations: a large 24-hour store, a medium-sized suburban store and a small city-centre store. In all of them, work for the vast majority of the workforce consists of routine tasks: monitoring stock, filling shelves, checking products through the EPOS system (electronic point of sale) and helping customers with their bags. The jobs share many of the properties of those at Pharmco. Here, however, they also have to deal directly with the customers. This can make the job more interesting, but it is also a source of pressure when the store is busy: keeping eye contact, being polite and checking the length of the queue.

The 24-hour store and the city-centre store are both relatively new (opened in the mid-1990s) and both experienced massive sales growth in their first few years. At the 24-hour store, annual sales rocketed from £700,000 to £1.2 million, accompanied by an expansion in the workforce from 380 to around 500 staff over the 18 months prior to our first visit. During the same period at the city-centre store, the workforce almost doubled in size from around 120 to around 210 and revenue increased by 50 per cent. Here, the workforce is distinctive for its high proportion of young people, reflecting the attraction of city-centre jobs among the surrounding student population.

In all three stores, more than nine in ten staff work as low-paid general assistants and the largest group consists of women in part-time employment. Slightly more men work full time at the 24-hour store, perhaps reflecting their greater willingness to work night shifts. But, overall, the workforce is dominated by part timers. For example, at the medium-sized store 184 general assistants work part time, out of a total of 207. At the 24-hour store, there are 335 part-time general assistants out of a total of 449. Finally, at the city-centre store there are 184 part-time general assistants out of a workforce of 201. In all cases, male general assistants are as likely to work part time as full time, but women are almost five times more likely to work part time. Among managerial posts, we found no evidence of part-time working.

Many of the people we talked to said that their work was laborious; moreover, the fast physical routines carried out by the checkout operators were difficult to adapt to. In an early pilot interview, we asked one of the operators whether the 'beep' of the barcode reader was disturbing:

It was when I came here first. I could hear it in my sleep. But I've got used to it now and I don't even notice. The big problem is the pain in my arms—you know, with moving things across all the time.

The pace of work seemed particularly high at the city-centre store where, although the average expenditure per customer is relatively low (just £6.30)—limited, according to the store manager, by the fact that each customer can only carry two bags—the volume of customers is high. In addition to swiping goods, operators must check loyalty cards, weigh fresh produce and swipe credit and switch cards. In contrast, work in the bakery seemed less intense and regulated, although the bakers we talked to were not so sanguine about their work. A skilled baker with 17 years of experience at Retailco explained how the changes in the nature of the job influenced recruitment:

They [bakers today] don't seem as 'get up and go'. It's just laborious. People who come in just see it as a job. They've got no finesse and no pride in what they do. So they've ended up in the bakery, but it could have been any job.

(Male, full time, no. 3, Retailco2)

These changes in attitude are not simply the result of new technologies. Nor are they the result of direct customer pressures. One clue as to their origins lies in the corridors and staff rooms hidden away behind the corporate façade. There, in each store, we were struck by the overriding presence of the 'steering wheel' (see box 3.2). A giant-sized version of this wheel is displayed for all staff to see and was used by managers as a key reference point when they talked to us about the challenges and successes experienced at the store. However, it is far more than a visual aid. Each week, managers meet to assess the store's performance as measured by the wheel and use it as a guide to set and

Box 3.2. The steering wheel at Retailco

First introduced in 1997, the wheel includes a range of performance measures and shows, at a glance, how well the store is performing with respect to certain targets. The wheel is divided into four quadrants, within each of which there are different areas of performance. For each area, target levels are generated at central Retailco headquarters and disseminated to the stores. For each target there is a coloured circle to show whether the store is performing well (green), close to the required level (amber) or performing poorly (red). Certain targets, particularly those in the finance and operations quadrants, are 'scientifically' determined. This involves 'cluster grouping', which averages out financial statistics for stores of comparable size. These averages must then be met by each store, leading to an in-built process that generates higher and higher averages.

For example, 'cost control' is a limit on the wage bill as a share of total costs (typically between 7 and 9 per cent); 'stock management' limits turnaround of stock to eight weeks; 'morale' is measured quarterly by asking staff to complete 'smiley cards' which include questions on job satisfaction; 'recruitment' measures the number of weeks each vacancy is unfilled; and 'one-in-front' limits the time when customer queues exceed one person to less than 2 per cent of daily operating hours.

prioritize strategies. In addition, the store performance was broken down by management, so that individual workers were made to feel that they could be held accountable for poor results. Managers explained to us that the great advantage of this new system was the way it emphasized the interrelationship between policies. For example, a green light for wages ('cost control') may be the reason for a red light on 'morale' or 'absenteeism'. In particular cases, store managers said they were able to renegotiate target levels with central headquarters (for example, if the store faces the arrival of new competition in the area).

It was quite clear, however, that local store managers, on the whole, enjoy very little autonomy in the management of operations. When we talked to them about the way the job of the baker had changed, for example, most were concerned that these changes made it difficult to recruit and retain committed staff, keen to apply their skills in a creative fashion. Nevertheless, they were obliged to follow central Retailco business policy, which dictated new practices of food supplies and stock management.

In fact, store managers were concerned about a number of central Retailco policies and the impact they had on staff. In a bid to carve out a greater slice of the food retail market, Retailco was attempting to beat its competitors through 'non-price competition', in particular by expanding services to customers to include banking, as well as to speed up services provision by reducing queue lengths. Managers at each of the three stores we visited explained that these two policies were actually in conflict with each other in practice. When general assistants were asked to process large deposits, as part of a new financial services package for customers, they found it difficult to maintain short queue lengths. Also, store managers were under pressure to restrict the use of overtime and to ensure job tasks were completed within the contracted hours of work. However, to maintain short queues store managers had been forced to retrain shelf-fillers so that they could step in as and when required to work on the checkouts. This meant that managers either paid overtime to ensure the shelves were filled, and faced the penalty of a red light on 'cost control', or encouraged a greater intensity of working.

For many workers, the pressure and monotony of much of the work was partly balanced by the satisfaction from dealing with people. For some, Retailco provided a relatively friendly working atmosphere, with many tasks carried out in twos or threes with other colleagues. Others were happy with the contact with customers, and gained a certain satisfaction from providing information, selling a product, or helping them pack their bags. Indeed, a number of workers suggested that the retail sector was the ideal sector to develop 'people skills', which would provide a foundation for a number of different careers.

The sector was also characterized as low paying. One general assistant working in an office above the store in stock control felt that her pay reflected the pay of the sector, rather than the job:

Some friends do secretarial jobs and I think I'm doing that type of thing up here. But they are on quite a few grand more than me. So that sickens you. But compared to other supermarkets and things...

(Female, part time, no. 4, Retailco2)

Another told us:

I have spent my life being underpaid, so I guess I am not going to change now.

(Female, full time, no. 2, Retailco3)

Unlike the other organizations we visited, work at Retailco appears relatively straightforward. Across the three workplaces, there is a high degree of commonality of tasks carried out by workers. In common with Pharmco, jobs are relatively routinized and we found, again, that management is keen to convey to workers their place within the grand scheme of things—whether they work on the checkout tills, fill shelves, or collect trolleys from the car park. The giant 'steering wheel' picture set out for all to see in the staff corridors provides managers with a tool to assess relative performance of the store, but also, crucially, a new technique for engineering changes in the organization of work.

TELECOMCO

At Telecomco we selected four areas for research: three in the Consumer Division and one, the network engineers, in the Network Division (see box 3.1 on p. 72). At each of the Consumer Division workplaces, work for the bulk of staff involves sitting at individual desks with telephone headsets and computers, organized into small teams monitored by a team manager. Around 320 workers are employed in the regional area of directory enquiries, with work split across two sites within five miles of each other. At the repairs centre, 217 workers are employed to deal with fault repairs. Around half of the calls are settled on-line, and the rest are re-routed to the network division where engineers become involved. The third area in this division is the telemarketing centre, which employs around 2,000 workers. The work here involves 'cold-calling' customers in a bid to sell Telecomco products and services. At each of the workplaces the majority of workers (about 60 per cent) are women. More unusually, however, there is a very high use of temporary workers hired through local agencies. At the directory enquiries and repairs centres temporary workers make up around two-fifths of the workforce, and at the telemarketing centre there are nine temporary workers for each permanent worker.

Directory enquiries and repairs

At the different call centres we visited, the organization of work had been subjected to enormous change. This related to the process of privatization and to the ongoing introduction of new technologies alongside new forms of working practices. Managers also played a key role in shaping the experience of work. At one of the two directory enquiries workplaces we visited, we soon discovered that managers were determined to instil a team atmosphere. When we first visited the centre, we were convinced we had walked into a children's playgroup by accident. All around were flags on desks, stickers and hand-coloured drawings on the walls, and mobiles hanging from the low ceiling. We were told that this was the normal state of things and that during one day each month staff were invited to participate in a theme day, in an effort to encourage a sense of fun and team spirit. However, cultivating a team spirit was difficult for workers whose jobs involved them in another reality—connected by headset to the customer and by a computer to the data required to make a decision. In this way the contradictions between the restructuring of work into teams and the solitary nature of the computer-based labour process were highlighted:

We are supposed to be working in teams but team working is really difficult because you work with yourself. You're on a computer, you're talking to the customer. I think teamwork with us is a little bit difficult.

(Female, full time, no. 3, Telecomco1)

Telemarketing

The telemarketing call centre was different from the other call centres, both in its sheer scale and in the nature of work. Built at the end of 1996, this centre resembles an aircraft hanger—large enough to house a foot-ball pitch. Three-quarters of the 2,000 staff are commercial or clerical officers; they are organized either in early or late afternoon rotating shifts and work in one enormous area which houses 648 workstations. These workstations (or desks) are organized into cells of 12, with each cell separated from the next by a movable partition wall. As we walked around we noted the use of flipcharts within each cell—used by each of the 114 sales team managers to communicate the main performance message of the day, or notes on the latest product. Also, high up on the main walls in each corner of the vast space there were huge screens (far bigger than anything we had seen at the Bankco call centres), which displayed sales targets as well as details of best per-former of the day.

Managers at the telemarketing centre were keen to emphasize the advanced technological characteristics of the workplace. In contrast to the other two customer services centres, staff at this centre make out-going calls in order to market and sell Telecomco products. As with the other call centres, the technology facilitates the work of staff. However, as managers openly admitted, it also enables a sophisticated system of monitoring and control of work from the central management team at Telecomco headquarters.

They give us a script sometimes and what they used to do was more of a core guide as opposed to a script. That's become more scripted now. So now what they're saying is you've got to sell these products in that order, whereas we think in some cases, 'no, we shouldn't be selling them in that order, we'd be far more productive and consumer friendly if we sold them in this order'.

(Male, full time, no. 2, Telecomco3)

Among the operators, it was not only the order of the script, but also the frequency and intensity of 'cold-calling' that was seen to be problem-atic. One woman who had been at the centre for four and a half months felt uncomfortable with the way they were expected to hassle customers:

They call customers once or twice a quarter. They send them a mailer. Now obviously I would say 80 per cent of those customers are aware of what products we sell and perhaps they should only ring them perhaps once every six months. But I personally think we give them too much. We contact them too much. Some of them are being called two and three times a quarter and we're going over the same products and services.

(Female, full time, no. 6, Telecomco3)

And another felt 'guilty' about having to press a sale on certain customers:

I just don't like selling. I have a conscience and I can't sell to old people or foreign people who don't understand what I'm saying. I just couldn't do it—although some people could and not have a guilty conscience and I couldn't do that. I was going home suffering and worrying about it.

(Female, full time, no. 10, Telecomco3)

The pressure to sell is reinforced at the beginning of each shift with a macho-style sales push by team coaches. A central element to this is talking through different kinds of 'moments of truth', where the operator is expected to intercede with the customer on behalf of the organization. In fact, many of the operators we talked to enjoyed the challenge of selling and felt that the competitive spirit offset the routine nature of the scripts. One young woman with two years' experience explained:

I see it as a challenge really when I'm on the phone just trying to make the customer say 'yes'.... You get your stats [statistical results] every day and that tells you how you're doing and you're constantly trying to beat yourself.

(Female, part time, no. 9, Telecomco3)

For one of the team managers an important driver was the regular change in script (every three months) and accompanying change in products. This added a sense of change and freshness to the nature of the job:

The job itself, I suppose, could be the similar sort of environment as a factory where you're maybe putting something into a box. You're saying the same thing over and over again for maybe a quarter. So when new products do come along and maybe changes in what we have to sell it is good because it makes people think again, and they have to readdress their selling skills and things like that.

(Male, full time, no. 7, Telecomco3)

Network engineers

When we talked with managers and workers at the Network Division, we found a different set of concerns and anxieties. Here, the problems were not so much how to make up for the low-skill nature of the job as how to prevent a downgrading of the high skills and experience widely regarded as essential to do the job well. Each of the five engineers we met talked to us about the complex and fulfilling nature of their work.

But there was a strong view that Telecomco management was refusing to invest in training for new recruits, which would lead, in their view, to a downgrading of their job in the future. Two engineers, each with more than ten years at Telecomco, spoke of their frustration:

For me, who's been in Telecomco a while, I find it difficult. I'm not saying I'm slow, but what I'm saying is I think it's generally hard … and they expect these new starters within eight weeks to go out and do the job. They get pressurized and do so much and they drop clangers, let's say. Problems arise and we mop up after them. And then that gets us [annoyed] because we think they're on the same wage as us and they're looking good because they're doing a lot of clears [completed jobs] per day. But they're leaving a lot of muck behind which we mop up.

(Male, full time, no. 2, Telecomco4)

They take someone off the street and they will give him a brief training course, maybe a couple of weeks and then send him out shadowing. Go out with another engineer for maybe four to six weeks and then there's your van, there's your stuff, go out and do the job. And it's not easy to do. And they're making so many cock-ups. And we're going round and sorting it out after them.

(Male, full time, no. 3, Telecomco4)

For these engineers, the much reduced training programme signalled less of a commitment to the skill base of the engineering workforce. Another engineer explained to us how in the past the apprenticeship involved shadowing a senior colleague for more than a year, but this was now reduced to a matter of weeks. And there was no evidence that technology had made the engineering side of the job any less complex. Rather, the changes witnessed over recent years involved changes in the way the work was coordinated and distributed among engineers, often not for the better.

What we do physically has changed very little—what we do out in the field. The way it's run by management and the way we sort of pick up our work has changed tremendously and unfortunately it isn't for the better. It was far better run ten years ago.… We now have a hand-held modem where we pick work up from, which is totally inefficient. Nobody in the world likes it. It's a rubbish system… things are far more time consuming.… If you come across a problem… where you want something a bit special or specific doing, the rigmarole to go through is phenomenal and you get passed from pillar to post.

(Male, full time, no. 3, Telecomco4)

The paradox of offering a greater semblance of autonomy with the hand-held modems and the reduction in real control over their work was not lost on the engineers we talked to. In the past, engineers said they had more independence to make decisions over the length and nature of a particular job, whereas under the current regime all jobs were quantified in units of time and costs. However, far from establishing a sense of order in the system of work organization, engineers spoke of an increasing sense of chaos. And they were uncertain of the capacity of Telecomco management to adapt to providing services for the new digital products. Nevertheless, compared with other companies in telecommunications the engineers still believed that Telecomco offered some job security—all the more significant given the massive extent of downsizing of engineers in the company over the late 1980s and 1990s (see Chapter 2). And most were optimistic of their futures within what they perceived to be a rapidly expanding sector.

Overall, the sense of change and innovation visible at the sector-wide level of telecommunications was not a universal experience among workers across the different Telecomco workplaces we visited. In particular, at the directory enquiries call centres and the telemarketing centre, team managers (referred to as 'coaches') are forced to appeal to the competitive animal instincts of operators to drive up performance ratings and offset the demoralizing effect of job monotony. Among network engineers, in contrast, the sense of change and innovation is striking. The engineers we talked to had survived successive waves of downsizing and yet were still optimistic about their future—as long as they could keep up with the rapidly developing digital technologies.

CONCLUSION

Over and over again in our visits and conversations in these seven organizations, we found evidence of change. These changes affected what the people did and the context within which they did it. Clearly, a pharmaceutical plant is, in many respects, different from a large grocery store—as is a hospital and a print works. But there are similar themes, and we found this when we invited managers from these different places to discuss the changes with each other. What we also found in our visits was that the people we met there were not simply passive, non-reflective observers of this process. All those to whom we talked had something to say and many of them had a point of view about what was going on—whether it was for better or for worse. What also became clear (to these people and to us) was that these changes were not simply a product of new technology or of bad management. They were the product of a complex set of changes within workplaces and within British society generally. It is to these wider forces, and their manner of operation, that we now turn.

II

INNOVATION IN EMPLOYMENT PRACTICES

4

Dimensions of Employment Change

INTRODUCTION

A satisfactory and convincing account of employment change must recognize that the concept of employment itself has multiple and inter-related dimensions, including those of skill levels, job security, remuneration, time patterns, representation and employee involvement and career structures. Changes in supply and demand, following Adam Smith's 'invisible hand' argument, provide an inadequate or over-simplified explanation for employment change across these various dimensions. Such accounts are still, however, the norm, whether in explanations of changes in wage structure, workforce skills or job security. As we argued in Chapter 1, we take issue with the way these analyses give primacy to the workings of the labour market and neglect the role of the organization in actively constructing patterns of supply and demand in ways that go beyond simply responding to wage/price signals.

In our alternative account, we begin with the assertion that organizations play a major role in shaping employment. Moreover, we recognize the market simply as one institution of many which make up the dynamic social and economic environment within which the organization operates. In accordance with our primary emphasis on the organization, we designed our empirical fieldwork around three aspects of employment where organizations play a critical role:

- staffing policies and practices;
- training and skill development;
- working time.

Staffing policies and practices shape employment in a number of ways. They affect entry into employment, the numbers of people employed within organizations and the mode and rate of exit from employment. This first area focuses on policies related to numerical forms of flexibility and the associated issues of employment security and contract.

Organizations also have responsibilities for the development of the skills of the workforce, through both the design of systems of work organization and the development of the skills of their employees. Here we address the 'up-skilling' versus 'deskilling' debate that has been prominent in recent national employment surveys (Crouch 1997; Gallie *et al.* 1998; Green *et al.* 1999, 2000; Keep 2000). In contrast to other survey-based approaches, we view skill development and deployment in this analysis from a case study perspective and focus primarily on lower-skilled employees.

Thirdly, organizations play a strong role in shaping the pattern and organization of working time. This has become an increasingly contested area of employment change over recent years (Bosch 1999; Lehndorff 1998; O'Reilly and Fagan 1998; Rubery 1998a). The structuring of the time dimension to work has implications not only for the patterns of hours worked and the division between work and personal time, but for a whole range of aspects of the employment relationship, including the wage-effort bargain.

While each of these areas is taken up separately in the following three chapters, the overall aim of this book is to identify the interlinkages between areas of employment policy and employment change. The objective is to highlight both the internal coherence of employment policies and the scope for internal contradictions. Before moving on to our empirical findings, we briefly outline the issues of intrinsic interest in each of the areas of employment policy selected for study. We set out how each of the dimensions of employment change contributes to a more general understanding of the current dynamics of employment change.

STAFFING POLICIES

Under the traditional internal labour market model, entry into an organization is confined to a limited number of ports of entry and is subject to strong external competition. Once entry is gained, however, the employee becomes a privileged worker, enjoying job security, protected pay rates and access to a structured job and career ladder (Doeringer and Piore 1971; Williamson 1985). While these types of internal labour market may seldom have existed in their pure form, such an approach to staffing policies nevertheless provides a model against which actual policies and practices can be assessed. Nowadays large organizations are not expected to follow an ideal type policy or to set standards as good employers, as expectations of internalized protected employment have declined. As Cappelli puts it:

The circumstances that helped create formal arrangements for managing employees in large firms, often referred to as internal labour markets, are changing. Internalized employment arrangements that buffered jobs from market pressures are giving way to arrangements that rely much more heavily on outside market forces to manage employees. (1995: 563)

Downsizing and redundancies have become associated as much with large as with small organizations. Stable patterns of recruitment and promotion along well-defined career ladders have broken down (Applebaum and Batt 1994; Cappelli 1999; Cappelli et al. 1997; Osterman 1996). In their place, large organizations may make use of a range of recruitment strategies. These may include, for example, direct-hire temporary contracts and/or the use of temporary work agencies instead of open-ended secure employment contracts (Arthur and Rousseau 1996; Barker and Christensen 1998; Cappelli et al. 1997; Vosko 2000). In addition, large organizations may now change their staffing and recruitment policies to take advantage of changes in so-called 'market wage rates', for example using external over internal recruits when the former are available at cheaper rates.

Staffing policies also have implications for the more qualitative aspects of employment change. As Felstead and Jewson argue, the continuous and to some extent circular debate over the significance and role of flexible labour needs to be recast through defining 'non-standard forms of employment in terms of the social relations of production. This principle seeks their common denominator in the relationship between the seller and purchaser of labour power' (1999: 5). For example, switching from the use of permanent to temporary employment contracts may not be simply a means of reducing employment overhead costs, but may also involve the introduction of new systems of work organization or new working time requirements, or indeed the promotion of change in organizational culture (Drago 1998; Ward et al. 2001). Also, decisions to recruit new people and/or to downsize existing staff, rather than redeploy and retrain existing staff, may be used as part of a more general policy to change the employment relations climate within the organization. Changes in staffing policy are also linked to changes in the form and nature of labour supply, with the use of part-time and temporary jobs related both to change in the organization of work and to the rising share of job seekers with constraints on their economic activity, such as mothers and students.

Thus, the staffing policies of organizations are key to an understanding of employment change. In analysing the way these staffing policies change and impact upon employment we draw upon our 'three ring' framework set out in Chapter 1. Figure 4.1 provides a schematic analysis of how pressures for change under the three rings of performance imperatives, internal constraints and external conditions interrelate with key staffing policy decisions with respect to recruitment, downsizing and retention. As the figure outlines, the same pressure may lead to a variety of staffing policy responses. Similarly, reading the figure downwards, we can see that different rings push towards the same form of staffing policy response, although the mode of implementation may, of course, be shaped by the dominant pressure for change.

Performance pressures on staffing policies, to minimize staff levels or headcount levels, may emanate from the City in the case of private sector organizations and from public sector budget requirements for public organizations. These performance pressures become even more salient when they are included in the system of monitoring or evaluating individual manager's performances within organizations. The policy responses may include declaring redundancies, minimizing permanent staff or directly employed staff, while employing large numbers of temporary or agency staff, outsourcing activities or maintaining unfilled vacancies. Where these changes are not justified by declines in activity, the impact may be greater work intensity, more overtime or lower quality standards. Similar policies may be adopted where the organization is less certain of its future and prefers to limit its staffing commitments. Here, use of different types of temporary contract or holding vacancies empty or even subcontracting may increase the room for manoeuvre to adjust to a demand downturn, in comparison to taking on new recruits on permanent contracts. Even though new recruits can be easily made redundant under UK law, senior managers may prefer not to take this option if it is felt to increase feelings of job insecurity for their key staff.

Performance pressures may also be an indirect cause of change in staffing levels. For example, a decision to resort to new hires may reflect an organization's preference for new staff. This may stem from a desire to save on training costs, or to reduce resistance to new ways of working or even to enable the organization to bring in the new staff on different terms and conditions.

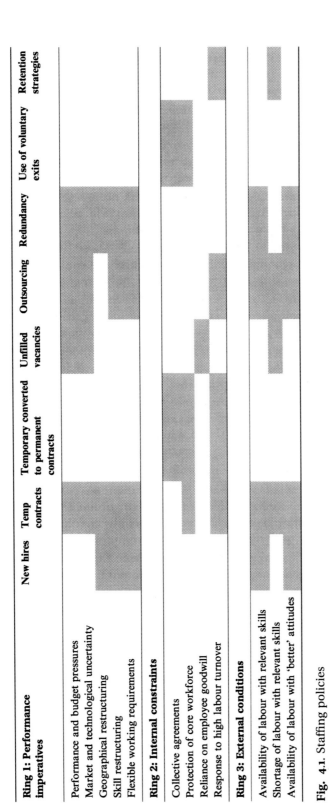

Fig. 4.1. Staffing policies

The second ring, that of internal organizational factors and power relations, also affects the adoption of staffing policies and practices. Perhaps the most obvious examples of this are found in the policies adopted to facilitate downsizing and redundancy. Organizations may opt to downsize through voluntary rather than compulsory redundancies in order not to lower morale and motivation among remaining staff (Casey and Wood 1993). This strong social norm seems to exist independently of trade-union organization, but will be reinforced where specific agreements are made with unions over non-compulsory redundancies and/or redeployment policies. These formal or informal agreements may either reduce the incidence of downsizing and redundancy or raise the cost of these policies by increasing the pay-off to existing staff.

Internal employee relations will also influence the extent to which organizations can rely on the goodwill and extra efforts of staff to cover unfilled vacancies or to cooperate in longer overtime hours, particularly unpaid hours. Organizations are not necessarily able to control their staffing policies, either because they have difficulty recruiting, or, more commonly, because they are unable to achieve their desired retention rates. Higher retention rates can normally be accommodated through changes in recruitment rates but may still raise labour costs, for example if the pay structure rewards staff according to experience or seniority. Lower retention or higher than anticipated turnover can cause more serious problems. Higher rates of recruitment may bring about more turbulence and instability in the organization, producing yet higher rates of demoralization and turnover and possibly creating difficulties for future recruitment if the reputation of the employer suffers. High labour turnover may lead to policies to improve security, through, for example, the offering of permanent contracts to temporary staff. However, pressure to meet staffing needs in the short term could lead to increased use of temporary agency workers as organizations seek an easy way of raising recruitment rates.

External market conditions, the third ring of influence, also impact on staffing policies. Where there is a relatively plentiful external supply of appropriately skilled labour, organizations may be more likely to move away from the provision of internal labour market privilege, even if this leads to higher labour turnover among skilled groups. Labour market tightness will also influence organizations' decisions to use temporary employment or agency workers instead of permanent recruits, although, as we have already explained, this influence does not always work in predictable directions. Other external factors may influence the use of temporary agency workers, particularly the availability of certain types of labour (for example, students) for temporary contracts. Where some skilled groups are in short supply, organizations may be more likely to adopt policies designed to retain and develop their own staff. However, in the short term the skill shortage may lead not only to unfilled vacancies but also to attempts by senior managers to use temporary work agencies or even outsourcing to pass the burden of filling the shortage on to other organizations.

Finally, restructuring decisions will also be subject to influence by the external market. Whether to outsource, relocate, redeploy or hire new staff after downsizing will depend, directly or indirectly, on the cost, reliability and skills of external labour supplies (Rubery 1994; Rubery and Wilkinson 1994). External labour market conditions will also affect employers' perceptions of whether or not their current terms and conditions of employment are generous or competitive. Awareness that other organizations are able to recruit at lower terms and conditions may lead to the introduction of staffing policies designed to reduce labour costs. Perceptions of the availability of an external labour force with more compliant attitudes and lower expectations of rewards than internal staff could encourage organizations to use external recruitment as a way of delivering internal culture change.

TRAINING AND SKILL DEVELOPMENT

The role of organizational policies in training and skill development has been at the centre of recent UK debates on employment change (Cappelli et al. 1997; Cully et al. 1999; Gilroth 1998; Green et al. 2000; Millward et al. 2000). Pressures on organizations with respect to these issues can be identified as pulling in different directions. In the USA, Cappelli et al. (1997) have made the argument that the nature of competition may be increasing organizations' reliance on the skills of their workforces—both the absolute level of skill and the development of company-specific skill—but, at the same time, the preconditions which allow organizations to invest in in-house training and skill development have been eroded. Organizations, it is argued, have moved away from the provision of long-term job security and have changed the nature of work organization, from long skill-based job ladders to flatter hierarchies requiring more even levels of skill among the groups or teams of workers (Applebaum and Batt 1994). Both factors reduce the likelihood of organizations offering training: first, because of the increased risk of 'quits' and, secondly, because of the disappearance of basic entry-level jobs. While some of these changes stem from the introduction of new technology and heightened competition, the fragmentation of the internal labour market is also seen, in part, as a consequence of the policies of deregulation in the US labour market. These may be having negative impacts on the ability of US organizations to generate the skill levels required in some sectors.

Something similar may be happening in the UK, where there has also been a policy emphasis to deregulate the labour market. However, there are two reasons why the story of Cappelli *et al.* (1997) may not apply to our research findings. The first is a problem with their analytical framework; a problem that is rooted in the work of Doeringer and Piore (1971) on internal labour markets. This approach identified internal labour markets as an employer-induced innovation to overcome the problem of market failure in the area of training provision. In the 1990s the problem of market failure still persisted, but, according to Cappelli and colleagues (1997) the stable product market conditions which allowed the establishment of internal labour markets were no longer present.

We wish to offer an alternative explanation for the increased divergence between market structures and employer needs. We question the assumption that the establishment of sheltered internal labour markets arose out of organizations recognizing the benefits of moving away from competitive labour market systems. It may be more appropriate and historically accurate to argue that internal labour market systems were, to a large extent, enforced upon employers, either directly through workers' organization or because of the perceived threat of unionization if better conditions were not provided (Jacoby 1984; Rubery 1978). It was only after the stabilization of markets that organizations came to see the benefits of these arrangements. Developing this argument suggests that some of the contradictions identified by Cappelli and colleagues in the current situation may be the result of the absence of a strong union presence to provide a counterweight to the destructive tendencies of unfettered competition. Now that power relations, and not simply universal market and technological requirements, are brought into the analysis, the picture painted of the USA by Cappelli *et al.* becomes only one of a range of possible outcomes and situations and is not necessarily a universal model.

This brings us to the second reason we cannot simply re-tell Cappelli *et al.*'s story in the UK case. Under our alternative approach to understanding shifting internal labour market structures, the external environment and the internal pressures for change are analysed as an integrated whole. This particularly applies to Continental Europe, where the stronger training traditions and the commitment to a less deregulated labour market may significantly affect the conclusions derived from a US study (Crouch *et al.* 1999; Sorge and Maurice 2000). Even in the deregulated UK, there is more evidence of government or state action in shaping the training system and provision than is the case in the USA. Moreover, social and political conditions may affect the range of basic skills available, without recourse to organization-specific training.

This more general framework allows us to develop an analysis of the pressures on skill development and training provision using the three rings of influence as described above (see figure 4.2). Training and skill policies can be considered, first, according to the direction of skill development (up-skilling, multi-skilling and deskilling); secondly, for skilling or training purposes (for team working, company branding, or external employability, or for other reasons such as regulatory requirements); and thirdly, according the decision over whether to 'make' or 'buy' skills, that is to train in-house or seek ready-trained workers outside.

Within the first ring—performance pressures—we find contradictory tendencies. Technological change is placing pressure on companies to upgrade and renew skills through training. However, this general focus on up-skilling, associated with the increased focus on knowledge-based competition and the apparent increased need for organizations to become 'learning organizations', coexists with pressures in the opposite direction also stemming from technological change. An increased rate of technological change makes organizations potentially less willing to invest in skills which may become rapidly obsolete. These concerns may favour a dual policy of buying skills where necessary and simultaneously taking skill out of the production process through the mobilization of new technological capacities. The rapid change in technologies may indeed reduce the willingness of organizations to make their own in-house investment in training facilities and trainers because of the constant need for updating. The increasing use of flexible employment forms could also reduce employers' willingness to invest in training, as these jobs may be specifically organized with the idea of relatively high turnover in mind.

Budget and cost pressures are also likely to favour these policies, since the alternative approach—up-skilling and enhanced training

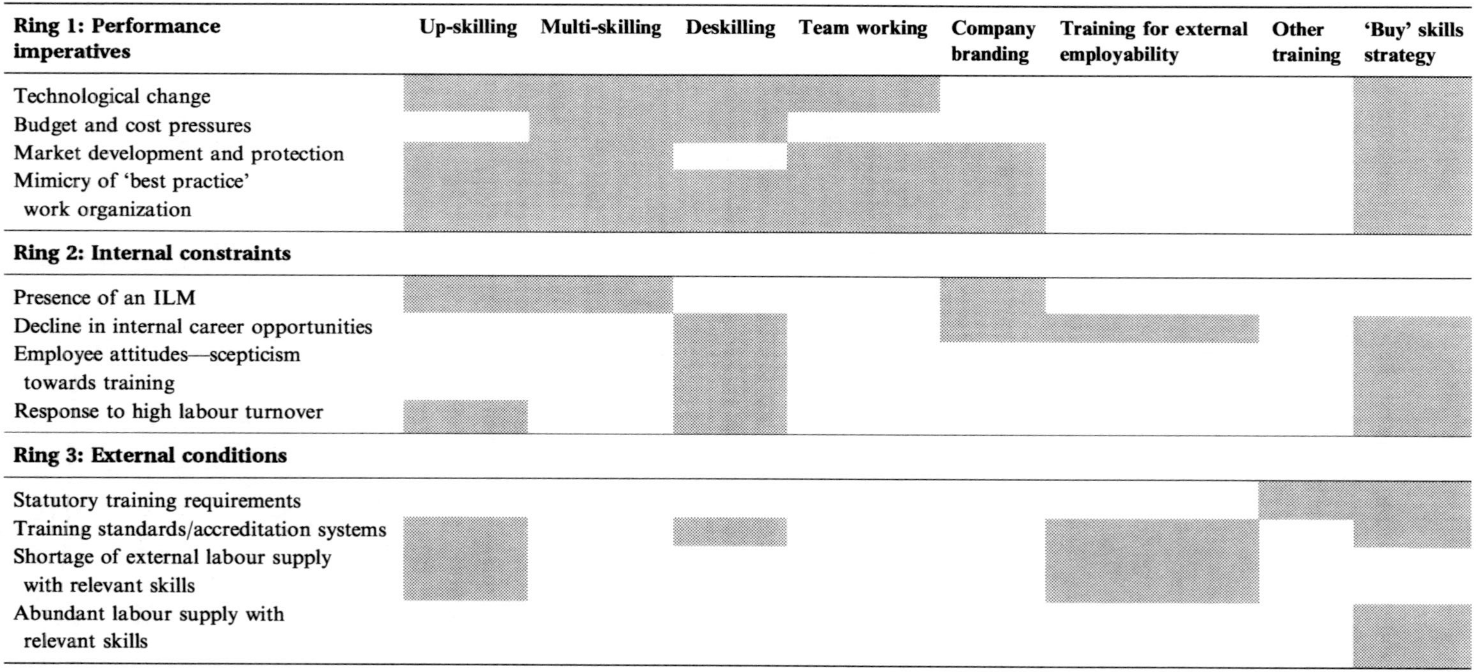

	Up-skilling	Multi-skilling	Deskilling	Team working	Company branding	Training for external employability	Other training	'Buy' skills strategy
Ring 1: Performance imperatives								
Technological change	■	■		■				■
Budget and cost pressures		■						■
Market development and protection			■		■			■
Mimicry of 'best practice' work organization	■	■						■
Ring 2: Internal constraints								
Presence of an ILM	■		■		■	■		■
Decline in internal career opportunities			■			■		
Employee attitudes—scepticism towards training								
Response to high labour turnover	■							
Ring 3: External conditions								
Statutory training requirements	■		■				■	■
Training standards/accreditation systems							■	
Shortage of external labour supply with relevant skills	■					■		
Abundant labour supply with relevant skills								

Fig. 4.2. Skill and training policies

provision—involves a long-term investment which is not compatible with an increased emphasis on short-term shareholder value. Other indirect effects of technological change stem from the new opportunities created for team-working arrangements and for working across traditional occupational boundaries or borders. Multi-skilling may provide a means of utilizing these opportunities, but equally may provide a means of cost reduction if it facilitates a new division of labour or a reduction in the share of skilled staff employed. As Green notes, 'multi-skilling may be a process of raising skill levels and reducing idle work time while (for example) waiting for other skilled workers to mend broken-down machines, a process of work intensification' (2001: 57).

Market position is increasingly expected, however, to depend not solely on cost minimization, but on the development of company-specific market niches based on company comparative advantage. The correlate of this form of competition is an emphasis on the development of company-specific skills (Crouch 1997). These product market pressures are reinforced by the focus in human resource literature on employee development as the basis for company competition. It is argued that employee development programmes serve both to improve quality and to induce greater company commitment and loyalty. From these developments one may expect moves towards up-skilling and/or multi-skilling, an increased focus on company-based skills and the use of training to develop identification with the company.

Here one identifies the contradictions in current ideology regarding employment policy 'best practice'; the notion of greater company loyalty and higher skill levels to meet new market needs sits side by side with notions of increasing employment flexibility and downsizing as strategies designed to reassure the City (Crouch 1997).

Performance pressures are also likely to influence the content and nature of training and skill development; greater emphasis on company and brand loyalty may lead to more attention to induction training, on how the organization does things. This is in contrast to more technical task-related training. An organization focus is particularly likely to be adopted where staff turnover is high and there is a need for staff to be regularly reminded of the organization's ethos. More generally, the change in competitive strategies towards 'customer focus' may lead to more 'soft skills' or customer service training, particularly amongst what are termed 'front-line workers' (Frenkel *et al.* 1999; Sturdy *et al.* 2001). Changes in work organization designed to meet new technological and market challenges or to demonstrate awareness of best practice will have considerable consequences for training provision. For example, policies such as team-working or outsourcing may all change the internal composition of skills, although often in contradictory directions. Team-working may require more multi-skilling, while outsourcing may lead to either the higher or the lower-level skill tasks being removed from an activity area. Both strategies have repercussions for skill development and training (Cooke 2002). Changes to the skill mix may be an indirect and even unintended consequence of organizational policies. However, in other cases, changing the skill mix may constitute a policy objective in its own right, particularly in those organizations concerned to reduce the wage bill through taking out high-skill labour costs.

While the outcomes of the contradictory performance pressures on training and skill development are unclear, the picture is further complicated by the influence of past conditions within the organization— ring 2—and by external conditions—ring 3. The past history of the organization is likely to have a particularly strong impact on both the form of, and the response to, new initiatives in the area of skill development and training. Skill-enhancement policies can only be effective if the employee is convinced of the usefulness of the training and development received. Organizations may only be willing to train if they expect their employees to remain loyal to the company. This behaviour will depend on internal beliefs concerning the expected stability of the organization and the ability of the organization to deliver better employment prospects than those that exist outside. Organizations may try to develop company loyalty but may be frustrated if employees are sceptical about the organization's ability to deliver. It is here that some of the contradictions of policies may become most evident. For example, organizations that have downsized and delayered may meet cynicism among their retained employees if they are offered new training and career development opportunities. Training policies for one group of workers will not necessarily be judged in isolation from their implications for the whole workforce. For example, policies to up-skill one set of workers in order to change the system of work organization, and ultimately to reduce the overall proportion of high-skilled workers, may be met with hostility or scepticism. Even the workers who stand to benefit may be hostile if they are aware of the broader consequences for overall workloads, work intensity or industrial relations. The effectiveness of training to include brand and company loyalty is perhaps the most dependent of all on the past history of the organization. Where past policies have created feelings of distrust, the workforce may be less willing to embrace the notion of brand or company loyalty.

External conditions impact on internal training and skill development in three main ways. First of all, sector-wide or national training regulations are likely to influence internal policy and practice for a variety of reasons. Training policy may need to be changed in line with compulsory requirements, for example, in the area of health and safety and other forms of regulation. Secondly, even when new regulations remain voluntary, organizations may feel under pressure to adopt new government or industry-level training systems of qualifications, both to maintain their attractiveness to recruits and/or to foster an image as a 'good employer'. Even if they wish to maintain their own systems, they may still seek to demonstrate that these are better than the industry standard. Conversely, they may stop providing some forms of training where the national or sectoral systems change, disappear or become ineffective.

The third external form of influence comes from the changing labour supply. Prior levels of education, work experience and skills will influence the extent to which employees receive further training. Where specific qualifications and skills are required, the size of the pool of externally qualified recruits will again inform the commitment to internal training. Large organizations may wish to go further and try to influence the overall pool of skilled workers through initiatives to change the wider training and skill development infrastructure.

The influence of the external labour supply depends not only on its perceived quality but also on the extent and nature of external career opportunities. Organizations may find that providing training to their employees results in considerable enhancement of their external market power, just at a time when internal opportunities may be declining. Thus, an organization's need to improve training may conflict with the equally important need to keep hold of their labour force. Other paradoxical situations may develop; for example, organizations may feel the need to compensate employees for the lack of internal promotion prospects by offering opportunities to develop 'employability' as a recruitment strategy, even though this policy explicitly helps the individuals to leave the organization and find employment elsewhere. Here we need to recognize that organizations are not always able to use the external labour market to further their own interests; if they wish to recruit and retain staff, they also have to meet workforce expectations and needs. Again, this challenges the argument of Cappelli *et al.* (1997) that organizations will only provide training if they are able to guarantee the stability of the workforce. Training may be a factor in trying to recruit and retain high-quality staff who are

aware of the problems of entering an organization which either provides little opportunity for career development or focuses all training
on company-specific needs, thereby inhibiting the future mobility of
their employees. Integrating the internal and the external again provides a way of understanding potentially contradictory pressures and
policies in this area.

WORKING TIME

The time dimension to employment has moved to centre stage in the
restructuring of employment relationships (Sennett 1998; Supiot 2001).
The focus on time arises out of a set of different and not always directly
interrelated dynamics apparent in both the production system and the
social system. The new system of competition has been described as
focusing on the economics of time; the time taken to process and deliver
goods, to innovate and to market new products and services (Best 1990;
Rubery and Horrell 1993). The 'just-in-time' production and service
system has implications for rhythms of work and thus for working time
schedules and practices.

Changes in the structure and nature of jobs also have implications
for the scheduling and regulation of time. As we outlined in Chapter 1,
Reich (1991) categorizes jobs into three types: routine production and
service workers, in-person service workers, and symbolic analysts. The
first set of jobs can be carried out according to time schedules which
are not directly driven by the provision of services. Nevertheless,
the rise of the 'just-in-time' competitive strategy even in services has
reduced, to some extent, the opportunity for production or service
delivery to follow regular schedules and patterns. These pressures
may lead to the extension of operating and opening hours and
increases in the flexibility of scheduling within them. Workers within
these routinized sectors include those who are likely to remain on
time-based contracts, lower skilled production and service workers,
and those who are required to provide supervision, often on the basis of
a non-time-based contract; for this last group, extended operating
and opening hours may lead to longer working times without pay
compensation.

For 'in-person service workers' there is even more pressure for flexible scheduling; here, the client and the provider of the service must
be present for the service to be delivered. Examples include catering

services, personal services and healthcare services. The need for the recipient of the service to be actively involved in its provision leads to pressures to ensure that the availability of labour supply is closely matched to the structure and pattern of client demand. These pressures move the employment relationship away from continuous contracts based around standard working days and instead favour the development of contingent time-based contracts.

For the final set of jobs—symbolic analysts—there is a different set of pressures at work. 'Symbolic analysts' are those workers whose tasks are related both to the use and to the application of specialist knowledge and to the development and maintenance of new markets and activities. It is in this group that the new employment relationship is characterized by a growing similarity with the role of the independent entrepreneur who not only has to undertake work but has also to create the demand for the work. This group also faces conflicting time pressures at work. On the one hand the reliance of organizations on their skills and creativity confers bargaining power and allows the analysts to claim some autonomy to shape their own work and working time patterns. At the same time they face pressure to work as much and for as long as is necessary both to create the demand for the work and to complete the tasks demanded.

In practice, most of the occupational groups examined within our case studies fall into either the routinized worker categories, including the attached supervisory and managerial staff, or involve in-person services. We have included relatively few jobs that fall into the symbolic analyst group. While this limits the scope of our empirical findings, it also serves to redress the rather exaggerated attention paid to the Silicon Valley engineer or their equivalent in debates and accounts of the future of work.

Pressures from the production side to intensify the time-based management of employment coexist with pressures from the changing social environment for new forms and patterns of working time. For example, the integration into employment of women with childcare responsibilities has facilitated the development of non-standard or atypical time contracts, particularly part-time work. The development of atypical employment can be considered in part the result of a mutual interaction of demand and supply side factors. Other labour supply groups for whom part-time work is a feasible option have also increased: for example, students, those on early retirement or those claiming Family Credit or Working Families Tax Credit. Part-time work is effectively only available to those with access to alternative sources of income, but these alternative sources now include the state as well as family support for mothers and students.

It is not only the number of hours but also the scheduling of hours that may be facilitated by the more diverse labour supply composition; women with very young children are known to be more likely to work during evenings so that childcare responsibilities can be shared with their partners. This situation changes, however, when children reach school age. Similarly, students may have a positive preference for evening and weekend work. Further social pressures on time schedules arise from changing lifestyles that impact upon the pattern of demand for services. The growth in dual earner households, the increased interest in evening and late-night leisure and entertainment facilities, the expansion of the elderly population requiring 24-hour care, and so on—all impact on the pattern of provision of services.

We can again adopt the 'three ring' framework for analysing pressures for change in working time. Figure 4.3 outlines some of the working time policies that may be introduced. These include those related to the scheduling of hours (flexible scheduling and increased unsocial hours working), the use of different forms of employment contract to facilitate flexible working time (use of part-time contracts and temporary contracts) and the development of policies which affect the cost of flexible or long hours of working (the provision or withdrawal of premiums for unsocial working hours; the use of paid or unpaid overtime and policies to cut paid overtime hours).

A number of performance pressures may be associated with changes in working time arrangements. The first is the need to provide services or products according to different schedules to meet changing customer requirements—interpreted here in the broad sense to include recipients of public as well as private services. These pressures may require longer opening hours for customer services or the adoption of 'just-in-time' production or service delivery. Secondly, organizations may seek to use working time change as a means of increasing productivity, through changing operating hours to increase capital productivity, cutting out slack labour hours to increase labour productivity and through more flexible scheduling to reduce throughput time to lower costs of overheads and work in progress. Thirdly, new technologies and new ways of operating may provide fresh opportunities for working time schedules and arrangements. For example, new information and communication technologies may allow for a more flexible location of work, with working time implications, or they may facilitate more detailed planning of work schedules through new monitoring facilities.

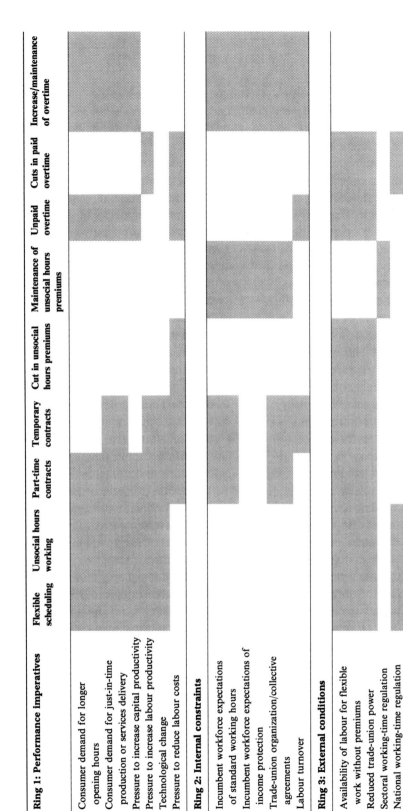

Fig. 4.3. Working-time policies

Finally, new working time systems may be designed to meet budgetary constraints by reducing the cost of providing similar services, by using new arrangements with less emphasis on premium payments or which allow a different skill mix.

Past working time practices in the organization—ring 2—will influence the acceptability of new working time arrangements. On the one hand, it is possible to argue that there is a wide range of working time arrangements that may be acceptable to some segments of the workforce—as is evident in the diversity of working time patterns across occupations and organizations. On the other hand, this working time flexibility preference does not necessarily extend to the incumbent workforce. Organizations with standard and regular working time regimes may attract employees for whom such arrangements are very important in their job choice (Horrell and Rubery 1991). Moreover, where overtime working has been offered on a regular basis, these opportunities may either have influenced the initial job choices of those employed, or at the very least the rewards from overtime may have been incorporated into their expected living standards. Thus, although similar organizations may be able to operate without overtime or with flexible scheduling, these options may not be open to an organization that has recruited workers on the basis of alternative working time arrangements, or where the alternative arrangements have become a major factor in employee income expectations and job satisfaction.

These constraints may not be sufficient to prevent organizations adopting new working time arrangements in line with competitive and performance pressures, but overcoming these constraints may require more dramatic action on the part of employers. Some organizations, faced with strong internal constraints, may find it easier to seek new recruits, new hires for the non-standard schedules, either in addition to or in place of the incumbent workforce, or to use non-standard workers, such as part-timers or temporary agency workers to fill the gaps in the schedules. Others may offer to 'buy out' the overtime earnings, thereby raising the cost of moves to more flexible schedules. These constraints are likely to be stronger if backed by trade-union organization and collective agreements that provide protection for overtime rates and unsocial hours premiums or even protection for standard working hours. However, some organizations may decide it is necessary to resist the opposition from trade unions and insist on the changes. Shifts in the relative power of the unions, both inside and outside the workplace, may influence the willingness of the employer to risk employee opposition to these changes. As Bosch (1997) argues, the impact of specific working time changes, such as annualized hours schemes, depends critically on the strength of regulation in and outside the workplace. While these schemes in principle could be used to create more standard jobs and cut the use of peripheral or contingent labour, 'in many plants where trade union representation is weak... the abandonment of standard daily and weekly hours will have only negative consequences for employees' (ibid.: 34).

However, whatever strategy is adopted, if working time changes conflict with the needs and preferences of staff, then organizations may face potential employee dissatisfaction and low morale. Dissatisfaction with working time may lead to higher rates of job turnover. This, in turn, may exacerbate problems of poor morale by leading to greater use of non-standard workers or to increased reliance on core workers for either unpaid overtime or for long hours of paid overtime—even in organizations where the espoused policy is to reduce overtime or to make less use of temporary staff.

Internal organizational considerations are not the only factors driving the decisions over whether to proceed with the change and then how to implement it. The changing composition of the external labour supply may, for example, provide organizations with greater flexibility in recruiting workers who want to work non-standard hours. Furthermore, employers may anticipate less resistance to new working time arrangements if they perceive that there has been radical and widespread culture change within the wider employment system. Employers may now believe the predominant culture to be based on compliant or non-existent trade unions and on the general acceptance of flexible working hours as the norm. If all similar organizations are thought to be moving down the same path, or if employees increasingly consider that the cost of seeking any position of responsibility is an acceptance of long and flexible hours, employee resistance to change may be likely to diminish.

Internal change will also be shaped by external regulation. Sector-level regulation, especially in the public services, still sets standard working hours (Arrowsmith and Sisson 1999). Yet even here there is evidence of change. New agreements on working hours, some of which involve reductions in standard hours, come with options that allow for more local flexibility in the scheduling of hours, provisions that increase local discretion, perhaps allowing for new initiatives to meet performance pressures. The working time directive is also likely to have divergent effects. On the one hand, restrictions on the working week may lead to cuts in overtime hours, but, on the other, the opportunities to calculate working hours over a longer time period than one week may encourage the adoption of more flexible scheduling systems, including annualized hours systems which combine a work schedule that includes fewer regular hours with more unsocial hours.

CONCLUSIONS

In this chapter we have outlined the rationale for exploring change in employment policy using the three-ring framework of analysis. In adopting this 'pressures for change' approach we are not confining the analysis to those very direct or immediate pressures where a failure to respond might lead to significant and direct consequences. Examples of such direct pressures could include the imminent loss of a major contract or the need to meet a statutory deadline to balance a budget. Many of the pressures for employment change are more indirect and stem from what managers believe is the appropriate path of action and from the likely effects of reacting in a particular way. There may, in fact, be nothing dramatically new about many of the performance imperatives we are currently witnessing. These may have been present in the past but ignored or downplayed by management because of their perceptions that to change established employment policies and practices would be too risky, invoking negative and adverse reactions inside and outside the organization. Under alternative conditions, however, management may welcome the opportunity to challenge internal power relations and the status quo. They may be encouraged in this endeavour by examples of other organizations following similar courses of action or by the evidence of increasing compliance with management wishes within the labour market as a whole.

In focusing on the factors shaping managerial policy, we must be clear that we are not adopting a crude or deterministic approach to managerial behaviour or motivation. As we discussed earlier in this book, the opportunity to increase profits or to reassert managerial prerogative is not sufficient to predict action, in contrast to more deterministic accounts of the role and functioning of organizations and the managerial class in society. Managerial response to opportunities is likely to be influenced by a range of factors, not only or mainly their perception of opportunities to further the interest of the organization. Other factors may include, amongst others, what they believe to be the likely impact of this line of action on their own future work environment and career opportunities. Perceptions of potential resistance by the work-force, individually or through group or trade-union action, may still provide powerful restraints on the pace and the form of proposed employment policy change. It is, in fact, through the experiences of the employees, as recounted to us in interviews, that the actual impact of the policies on workplace practices and experiences can be assessed. These accounts also reveal the conflicts and tension surrounding the implementation of new employment policies and provide insights into their likely viability.

In the next three chapters we turn to our empirical findings and explore how these possibilities are reflected in the evidence we have collected from both managers and employees. Each chapter describes employment change around one of the three selected areas of employment policy. In each, we build on the analysis set out in this chapter in order to explore how employment policy and practice has changed in a context of both mutual reinforcing and conflicting pressures for change emanating from the three rings of influence. We also highlight areas of potential interaction between one employment policy and another, which could lead to contradictory policies or unintended outcomes.

5

Staffing the Organization:
New Patterns of Entry and Exit

INTRODUCTION

In the postwar period the large bureaucratic organization came to be identified with stable recruitment and employment policies, most often based upon collective-bargaining agreements. Trade unions tended to be actively involved in the discussion and implementation of these policies and this had clear implications for individual careers and the opportunities available in particular places. By the end of the twentieth century, however, it seemed that these arrangements had changed. The position of trade unions had been weakened over a 20-year period as a consequence of new employment legislation and a more vulnerable labour market. Moreover, the organization of employment had altered considerably (see Beynon 1999; Millward *et al.* 2000). In this context a new 'employment system' seemed to be emerging which involved a move away from permanent to one type of temporary contract or another, declining job security and career opportunities, increased outsourcing and the use of redundancy schemes. Taken together, there is no doubt that these practices contributed to a general reduction in staffing levels within large organizations, a process that became referred to as 'downsizing' in the USA. These changes were seen to have had a considerable impact both within and beyond the organization.

The seven organizations selected for study here therefore provide ideal cases for investigating the extent to which these anticipated changes have been (or are being) implemented. They also provide a basis for considering the implications of these changes both for the viability of organizations' employment systems and for what they are likely to mean for present and for future employment opportunity and security.

The chapter is organized as follows: first, we summarize the main changes that have affected the ways in which people join the organizations: their employment contracts, the overall staffing levels, and company policies relating to 'downsizing', redeployment and outsourcing or relocation. Secondly, we analyse the various pressures that lie behind these changes in staffing policies, focusing on performance imperatives, internal constraints and external labour market conditions. Thirdly, we consider the effects of these policies on employees' experience of work and on managers' experience of managing.

CHANGES IN STAFFING POLICIES

Each of the organizations has made significant changes to the ways in which they staffed their various workplaces in the 1990s. However, the methods used and the kinds of policy that have been developed differed one from another.

Ports of entry and employment contracts

All seven organizations have offered stable employment careers in the past, although the opportunities for internal mobility varied by organization and by sector. As such, obtaining a job with any of these organizations provided an important level of employment security and protection for those in the lower and middle rungs of the labour market. All the organizations had in the past followed a common practice of recruiting to these grades on permanent contracts. Three of them (Bankco, Pharmco and Telecomco) have moved away from this policy to one that hires people on direct-hire temporary contracts or through temporary work agencies (TWAs) (see table 5.1). The remaining four organizations have retained a policy of recruitment onto permanent contracts. Indeed, Retailco, after experimenting with the use of direct-hire temps to cope with fluctuations in demand, abandoned the policy. Instead, it employs permanent workers on an arrangement that sees them varying the length of their working day and week. Mediaco has also not generally resorted to the use of temporary staff or temporary

Table 5.1. Changes in ports of entry and employment contracts

Change	Bankco	Councilco	Healthco	Mediaco	Pharmco	Retailco	Telecomco
Use of temporary direct-hire contracts or TWA workers	Main mode of lower-level entry (TWA workers)	Used because of freeze on permanent posts (casual workers and some direct hire temps)	Used because of freeze on permanent posts and for overtime (TWA workers from the bank)	Not used except for some freelance journalists	Main mode of lower-level entry (TWA workers)	Not used	Main mode of lower-level entry (TWA workers)
Recruitment policy change used to adjust skill or attitude mix or to change terms and conditions	Change in skill mix and working-time practices	Introduction of private sector ethos and attitude	Introduction of private sector ethos and attitude, change to skill mix	Change to wage structure, staffing levels and multi-skilling	Change to skill mix	Increased use of permanent staff to ensure quality standards	Change to skill mix, wage structure, and working-time practices

contracts, although the sports section did use freelance staff to provide extra flexibility and to ensure cover for illness or other absence. In the two public sector organizations, Councilco and Healthco, the situation is more complex. Both have retained a principled commitment to recruitment on permanent contracts, but budget constraints have meant that, in practice, they have not been allowed to fill vacancies on this basis. Permanent positions have been frozen and both organizations have had to use a variety of temporary arrangements for essential appointments and temporary cover. In Councilco this has involved the use of its own list of casual workers, while in Healthco temporary cover is provided through the 'bank'. This is an external private nursing agency that provides cover for a range of trusts. It has an office on the Healthco site and many Healthco employees are registered with the bank to work additional hours through the agency.

The organizations have also taken different approaches to the management of those on temporary contracts. Bankco and Pharmco, while using direct-hire and agency temps for initial recruitment and, indeed, to provide some flexibility in relation to demand, have a corporate policy to offer a permanent contract whenever possible to 'suitable' temporary staff. Telecomco is much more committed in principle to maintaining a high share of agency temps and has made much less effort to move long-term temporary staff onto permanent contracts. The result of these different policies is that Telecomco has by far the highest proportion of agency staff, with figures ranging from 40 per cent up to 80 per cent in the workplaces we visited. These high figures reflect an explicit policy of keeping the official employment headcount at low levels to satisfy the City. This policy operates throughout the telecommunications sector and it has become a major source of irritation for the trade unions, which see this as a dramatic departure from previous employment practice. Bankco and Pharmco both have lower shares of agency temps and the managers expressed more mixed views on the desirability of a high temp ratio. Pharmco, in part, had been using agency temps to solve a short-term need to increase staffing levels, while Bankco recruited direct-hire and agency temps to protect its commitment not to make permanent staff redundant. As a consequence of these different motivations, the overall ratios of agency temps to directly employed staff and temporary to permanent staff varied significantly, even between those organizations using non-permanent contracts as the main route of entry. In Councilco and Healthco, the other two organizations with significant numbers of direct-hire and agency temps, their share in practice is a function of the number of frozen vacancies. Budget constraints have prevented managers from hiring permanent staff and, as such, they have reverted to direct-hire or agency temps as stopgaps.

The changes in recruitment strategy all involved the use of one form or another of temporary contract. However, the strategic issues involved were often different and were rarely informed by a policy directly aimed at reducing job security per se. Certainly, the use of the agency temp or recruiting onto direct-hire temporary contracts have been convenient adjuncts to general employment policy. At Pharmco, for example, managers talk of simply being able to 'pick up the phone' and obtain an agency temp the next day. The ease of this operation, and the lack of commitment involved, was clearly attractive to managers involved in unstable and unpredictable product markets. At Pharmco this policy was made easier by the tediously repetitive nature of most of the production work and the lack of requirement for significant social or technical skills. The managers we talked to were keen to recruit people without career ambitions into these positions. However, it was not a policy that was viewed sympathetically by the trade unions and the local shop stewards. The question of agency temps became an agenda item in all union–management meetings. Managers recognized this as a problem. They also knew that their policy was likely to generate problems of motivation and retention across the labour force.

Even in those organizations where the temporary contract had become a central feature of policy, it often blended in with other strategic issues. Bankco and Telecomco provide interesting examples of this process. In both of these organizations the change in the nature of work (associated with the development of call centres) meant that they needed to recruit workers who differed considerably from their existing staff. The use of agency temps allowed for the rapid introduction of staff who were selected for their customer service skills and who, unlike redeployed staff, had no expectation of using their knowledge and experience of either banking or telecommunications. Moreover, both organizations used agency temps to facilitate the move away from standard working hours. As a result, the new recruits were required to be both temporary *and* flexible. Agency temps also allowed organizations to save on fixed employment costs such as holidays, sick pay and pensions. Telecomco sought additional benefits by linking the contract to local rather than national pay scales.

While the use of temporary contracts was the most common way in which hiring practices had changed and were changing organizations, it was not the only one. In places where permanent contracts remained the principal form of employment, recruitment policy was still an important part of management's armoury. This was most clearly expressed in Mediaco's newspaper office. Here, where particularly strong trade-union organization was linked closely with occupational norms, new recruits were brought in on terms and conditions that were significantly worse that those already in operation in the office. These workers were introduced as part of a systematic attempt, by management, to alter the ways in which the jobs were performed and organized. One journalist with several years' experience at other local newspapers, had been working at Mediaco for twelve months:

I was brought in to do an all round job which was unusual. It was like a mould-breaking exercise.... Historically, in a sports desk... you're either a writer, you just wrote for a sub-editor or you drew pages and I was brought in... I was the first one who came in who does all those jobs, so some days I write, some days I scheme pages, other days I sub-edit. Some days I do all the three in one.

(Male, full time, no. 4, Mediaco2)

This change in corporate culture at Mediaco was eased by its ability to recruit new senior staff from those made redundant by the closure of regional offices of national newspapers at the end of the 1980s and in the early 1990s. This collapse broke the established link between the pay scales of the local and national newspapers. Freed from this constraint, Mediaco was able rapidly to change its pay and reward structures by recruiting new (experienced) staff on radically different terms and conditions. The organization recognized that this was a short-term, one-off policy. However, it was a policy that had provided it with the opportunity to use external recruitment as a means of obtaining rapid organizational change. In the future it would have to 'grow its own' editorial and managerial staff, and it established a new graduate-training programme for this purpose. In this scheme the trainees would be inculcated into the new Mediaco ethos.

New recruits can be significant in other ways too. Healthco faced a national shortage of qualified nursing staff, which made the recruitment of personnel difficult. In this context it was decided to employ a different kind of worker, termed health care assistants (HCAs). This innovation in recruiting policy had significant effects upon the organization of the hospital's wards and the overall operation of the organization. The ratio of qualified staff in the hospital was reduced, thereby both resolving the problems of shortages and cutting costs at a stroke. Furthermore, it was possible for the organization to recruit this new grade of worker on local terms and conditions (see Chapter 8). Through this arrangement, therefore, Healthco has obtained a more flexible labour force while, at the same time, lowering its overall wages bill.

This change was also associated with a shift in the corporate ethos at Healthco. Here, as in Councilco, the government's modernizing agenda has been embraced and equated with the need to emulate key features of the private sector. The recruitment of managerial staff with experience in private businesses was central to this strategy of introducing a positive appreciation of the market into their organizational cultures. This concern to reconceptualize patients as customers, in turn, influenced the recruitment of other staff (see Chapter 9). As one male manager of porters commented about recruitment:

I look for someone that's got a pleasant attitude.... Because of the way we now work with the patient's charter, the patients have got a lot more freedom to complain. They expect a lot more from the portering staff and we don't want people that have got surly attitudes, things like that. We're not looking for brain surgeons, we're just looking for people that are pleasant.... Know what we expect of them and realize that 'customer care' is a big plus in our job.

(Male, full time, no. 1, Healthco1)

What becomes clear in these accounts is the important role that the recruitment of new staff (from the external labour market) can play in changing the internal operations of the organizations and the structuring of the work process. In the context of the stable economic conditions of the postwar period, companies came to establish large quasi-permanent work forces. They came to rely upon their older and more experienced workers who are more integrated into the established corporate culture. This pattern lies at the root of analyses of the 'internal labour market' that gave weight to its capacity to organize labour forces around internal promotional ladders and patterns of training and retraining. However, in the context of rapid market changes and increased uncertainty, these qualities have become less important in the eyes of managers. In fact, given the objective of transforming company culture, a permanent workforce with its long memories and established expectations and work practices can become, to management, a positive encumbrance. In this context, the organization has turned to the new recruits who are seen to have the necessary adaptability and willingness to 'go the extra mile'; and the significance of recruitment was not restricted to the lower end of the job ladder. Most of the organizations have made greater use of external recruitment into managerial and other higher-level jobs than in the past. One consequence of this, of course, has been that internal promotional opportunities have become more scarce—another feature of organizational change.

Staffing levels

Each organization adopted, or tried to adopt, a policy of reducing staffing levels relative to workloads. In Bankco and Telecomco the application of new technologies facilitated a major increase in productivity per worker employed. In Bankco this involved a change from branch to telephone banking, and in Telecomco new communications technology enabled a rapid increase in the number of calls dealt with per person employed. Mediaco also made major reductions to staffing levels relative to workloads, particularly in the printworks. These reductions in unit staffing levels were combined with a major expansion in output and in plant operating hours so that numbers employed remained relatively stable. Retailco cut labour relative to output by reducing layers of management (see Chapter 6) and increasing labour productivity through the tighter control of performance as sales rose (see Chapter 9). Employment numbers nevertheless continued to expand. Pharmco introduced a 'just-in-time' warehousing system in response to advice from consultants, to reduce both staffing requirements and stock levels. Here, however, shortly after the downsizing policy had been implemented, problems in guaranteeing supply led to a reversal of this policy and to a rise in staffing levels, achieved initially through the use of agency temps (see table 5.2).

In Councilco and Healthco there were both planned and unplanned reductions in staffing levels relative to workloads. General budget cuts have been met by planned workforce reductions, particularly in areas subject to compulsory competitive tendering (CCT), where the hours of work, as well as the numbers employed, have been reduced prior to the competition. In some areas, however, staffing levels have been reduced further (as in the case of nursing) because the organization found it difficult to recruit suitable staff. There was also a more general systematic freezing of vacancies. This was often the result of budget overruns, but such freezes were also introduced in anticipation of future budget cuts and redeployment exercises. As a consequence, many work teams were required to operate without supervisory staff. In these circumstances, the organization relied upon staff accepting supervisory or managerial responsibilities on a temporary or 'acting-up' basis.

Table 5.2. Changes in staffing levels

Change	Bankco	Councilco	Healthco	Mediaco	Pharmco	Retailco	Telecomco
Method of achieving reduction in staffing relative to workloads	New communications technology	Planned and unplanned (frozen vacancies) reductions in numbers employed and volumes of hours	Planned and unplanned (frozen vacancies) reductions in numbers employed and volumes of hours	New industrial relations regime; dramatic reduction in manning levels per machine	New just-in-time warehousing system and just-in-time packaging and processing system	Expansion of demand; removal of supervisory layers	New communications technology; removal of supervisory layers
Policies to affect retention rates	Movement away from temporary to permanent contracts; new partnership agreement with union and move to re-establish career structures	Few policies to encourage retention; main focus is on cost cutting; relies on public service ethos etc.	Problem of nurse recruitment and retention increasing; more recruitment of healthcare assistants to compensate	In-house apprenticeship and graduate traineeships; training opportunities for telesales staff; pay still high for printers despite cuts	Converting temporary to permanent contracts; good terms and conditions even if limited promotion opportunities	Use of 'golden handcuffs' to encourage retention despite loss of career opportunities	Reducing skill levels to reduce costs of high turnover
Use of 'acting-up' for filling senior/supervisory positions	No	Yes	Yes	No	No	Yes	Yes

In some places, people who took on the responsibilities were not paid at a commensurate rate; instead, they were paid a weekly lump sum. Even after 'acting-up' for two or three years, these workers could be returned to the lower grade.

While aiming to reduce staffing levels, it was somewhat paradoxical to find that so many of the organizations were also concerned with their retention rates. Retailco and Bankco were the most proactive in trying to improve retention rates in a context where career opportunities appeared to be curtailed. To compete on quality, Retailco decided that a stable workforce was essential and used financial incentives in the form of share options and in-house discounts on purchases, as part of what management called the 'golden handcuffs'. As we set out in Chapter 2, Bankco was in the process of implementing a new policy developed through its partnership agreement with the trade unions. This involved both the offer of permanent contracts to current agency temps and the harmonization of grades across its various call centres. The policy was seen as a precondition for establishing the kinds of horizontal career mobility that might allow the bank to retain staff and to develop a more skilled and experienced workforce.

Pharmco was also in the process of converting many agency temps on to permanent contracts, again with a view to improving retention as well as internal human resource policies. Although there were more than 200 agency temps on site, 120 had been offered permanent contracts over the previous twelve months and an offer to a further 20 was planned. The main stumbling block was the concern of the chief executive that an increase in headcount figures could lead to a fall in the share price. Mediaco, as we have already noted, was more than happy for many of the more senior staff on the reporting and editing side to leave. In the advertising department the story was very different; this was considered the key area for profitability, and management was concerned not to lose staff to competing call centres. They succeeded in reducing turnover from a high of 50 per cent down to 20 per cent. One strategy was to exploit the greater opportunities for promotion in a newspaper telesales centre than were available in some competing sales centres. Some telesales people were allowed to train to become sales representatives even before vacancies became available.

Four out of the five private sector organizations had taken steps to encourage retention or secure future recruitment that, to some extent, modified the policy of destabilizing internal labour markets. Telecomco was also concerned about high levels of turnover and considered introducing loyalty bonuses. However, its main reaction to higher-than-planned-for levels of labour turnover has been to reinforce its policy of deskilling and casualization by further reducing skill content, thereby reducing the cost of labour replacement and training. As we described in Chapter 3, these policies were combined with local-level policies designed to make the deskilled work more interesting by introducing competitions or theme days to provide variety and novelty.

The public sector organizations also faced problems with retention. However, they seemed less able to reduce turnover levels or to overcome problems of labour shortage. This lack of action stemmed from both budget problems and the constraints of national collective-bargaining systems, which restricted the room for manoeuvre available to local management. Some specific retention policies were adopted; for example, Healthco managers always placed qualified nurses in psychiatry on a grade above the normal entry grade in order to overcome problems of labour shortage. Yet problems of retention were more often sacrificed to the more immediate problem of delivering services, cutting costs or even recruiting new staff. One of the major reasons for low retention rates among nursing staff lay with the intensive nature of the work. Nevertheless, and despite the shortage of recruits, the policy of unfilled vacancies was pursued in order to meet budget objectives. Even the policy of offering more flexible working time packages to new recruits to help resolve recruitment problems was likely to have some negative impacts on retention, if the result was more pressure on existing staff. Healthco, however, lacked both the budget resources and a sufficiently coherent and centralized management function to effect overall change, and instead relied on piecemeal and ad hoc responses to problems at the individual ward level, coupled with a generalized vacancy freeze.

Downsizing and redeployment

The implementation of staffing level changes relative to workloads depended not only on trends in demand but also on policies with respect to downsizing and redeployment. In five of the organizations we looked at there has been significant downsizing involving voluntary or compulsory redundancy (see table 5.3). Retailco has not been involved in any major downsizing but has been able to contain staffing level costs through expansion of business. Redundancies at Bankco and Telecomco were explained to us in terms of a consequence of a process

Table 5.3. Changes in downsizing, redeployment, outsourcing and relocation policies

Change	Bankco	Councilco	Healthco	Mediaco	Pharmco	Retailco	Teleomco
Examples of major downsizing exercises	1992 branch restructuring and opening of first call centre; voluntary redundancy but geographical relocation was required for redeployment	Voluntary redundancy and early retirement in selected areas; unfilled vacancies as further means of downsizing	No major redundancy programmes as yet but PFI scheme will involve significant workforce reductions; unfilled vacancies main method of downsizing	Closure of printworks and compulsory redundancy for all printers 1990; staff reduction in newspaper division on an annual basis based on targeted early retirement	Voluntary redundancy, early retirement and redeployment following introduction of just-in-time warehouse system	None—steady expansion during the 1990s	Major reduction in staff levels in 1990s; voluntary redundancy, early retirement or redeployment often to new location and lower grade; downsizing resulted in too high a loss of skills, particularly in engineering
Redeployment policy	Policy in place and activated	Active redeployment policy which involves redeployment across areas of the council	Redeployment policy but number of vacancies makes this easy to achieve; only problem in ancillary areas because of PFI	None	Redeployment used as part of adjustment to new warehouse system	Some examples of redeployment, for example after closure of a store, but not a major issue due to expansion	Redeployment but pay only protected for four years
Current/potential outsourcing and relocation issues	Cheque processing, IT currently outsourced; other areas under consideration	Best value leading to consideration of outsourcing and public/private partnerships; CCT led to changes in contractual hours and other terms and conditions	PFI to build new hospital which will involve transfer of staff to private sector organization	Current printing undertaken as joint venture; could pull out from printing when machines need renewal; outsourcing presented as alternative to pay cuts and pay freezes in negotiations	Competition for production between other sites owned outside UK	Some maintenance work outsourced; no major threat of outsourcing or relocation, only of merger/competition from other retailers	Constant process of reorganizing and restructuring call centres; geographical rationalization is facilitated by new technology

of geographical restructuring and the centralization of service provision. Redeployment opportunities were offered but were not feasible for many staff. In addition, Telecomco was under pressure from the City to reduce the level of its permanent staff. Staff had this pressure communicated to them. As a male clerical assistant with almost 20 years' experience in the job explained when talking about the closure of a nearby workplace:

It depends on how we [Telecomco] go on in the markets, I think the shares will go, we have had a good battering... if it gets worse then they will no doubt be led by accountants and they will look at the baseline and say 'we've got to get rid of so many men'.... That's what happened before and so it could happen again.
(Male, full time, no. 1, Telecomco4)

Telecomco initially allowed for too high a level of voluntary redundancy and early retirement, leaving it with a major skills shortage. This problem was particularly acute among the engineering staff, as the above employee sets out, where the reduction in workload as a consequence of new technology was greatly overestimated. As a faultsman joiner explained:

The offer was that good everyone went for it and all of a sudden they thought— we've got no engineers left... overtime went through the roof!
(Male, full time, no. 3, Telecomco4)

Bankco, a more regionally concentrated organization, minimized the rate of redundancy through redeployment of branch staff to its first call centre. Nevertheless, those branch staff unable or unwilling to move were offered voluntary severance or early retirement. Pharmco's experience of downsizing was explicitly related to its ill-thought-out 'just-in-time' exercise. As with Telecomco and Bankco, Pharmco used a policy of voluntary severance, early retirement and redeployment to reduce numbers. However, in contrast to Telecomco, it was selective in its decisions on which volunteers to accept for early retirement and redundancy, thereby minimizing skill outflow.

Mediaco provides the main example of a case study organization using compulsory redundancy. In 1990 Mediaco closed its own printworks and made all its printers redundant, following the withdrawal of a major client. It then transferred its printing operations to another printworks, operated as a joint venture between Mediaco and the original owners. Mediaco also pursued a policy of downsizing within its newspaper division, but here the policy was targeted at early retirement rather than compulsory redundancy.

Councilco has had more experience of downsizing and redundancy than Healthco. These initiatives were introduced in the context of its agreed policy of no compulsory redundancy and a right to redeployment. In part, as a consequence of this policy, Councilco has the highest use of the local government early retirement scheme of all councils, as well as facing many problems of redeployment. The downsizing has been driven by specific budget decisions, reflecting changes to needs or business flows. In some instances, the downsizing has been found to be unwarranted, at least on the scale undertaken. This happened in the direct works department, which was downsized by some 400 staff, 50 of whom were still waiting to be redeployed when a new recruitment drive took place as the direct works department won new contracts for maintenance work. These problems point to the complexities of determining staffing levels in public sector organizations increasingly reliant on winning external contracts, many of which are only short term and precarious. Healthco has not yet been involved in a large-scale redundancy exercise, but instead achieved staffing reductions mainly through not filling vacancies. An impending private finance initiative (PFI) scheme, however, did raise the prospect of enforced redundancies and this was the topic of aggravated discussions with the trade unions.

Five of the organizations operated no compulsory redundancy policies and six had commitments to redeployment (see table 5.3). Mediaco was the exception under both headings, while Telecomco had no explicit compulsory redundancy policy although it continued to offer redeployment to staff. The redeployment policy has had particular consequences in Bankco, where managers are reluctant to fill vacancies in case some are required for redeployment, and in Councilco where the diversity of activities covered by the council creates problems of retraining and matching staff to vacancies. In Healthco the level of unfilled vacancies was such that redeployment does not pose major problems. Pharmco used redeployment as part of its adjustment to the new warehousing scheme. The net result of redeployment plus the new hiring policy after the collapse of the scheme was that more than half of the workforce were either new to the organization or were in different jobs from their position one year earlier, with new supervisors. Telecomco has a policy of redeployment but only protects pay for up to four years, which has caused problems. As a result of the trend towards reducing the number of skilled jobs, many people have been redeployed onto lower grades.

Staffing levels are not only affected by changes in productivity and demand, but also by decisions over whether to maintain particular activities within the organization or within the particular workplace. In all the organizations, with the possible exception of Retailco, there was a real likelihood of either further outsourcing or relocation in the future. Bankco had already outsourced its cheque-processing activities and its IT facilities. These moves caused consternation amongst the remaining workforce, as they appeared to contradict the no compulsory redundancy policy. However, the management was clearly considering further outsourcing options.

Telecomco was in a constant process of rationalizing and reorganizing its call centre operations, such that any centre was, at any time, at risk from closure and restructuring. Mediaco had already demonstrated its willingness to withdraw from activities when it closed its print works and entered into a joint venture. The possibility that it would withdraw altogether from printing if the current plant became outdated was widely recognized by management and the workforce. Indeed the likelihood of outsourcing was an explicit option on the table when the management forced through pay freezes and the introduction of market rates as the only way to avoid the complete outsourcing of the operation. Pharmco is part of a multinational organization that maintains multiple manufacturing capabilities in different countries, in part to guarantee supply when production problems are encountered in the location. The strategy also maintains a constant possibility of moving production from one location to another.

Private sector organizations appear to use the threat of outsourcing or relocation as a means of controlling labour costs or labour militancy. Similar strategies are now being forced onto public sector organizations as part of government policy. In order for Healthco to build a new hospital, it entered into a PFI arrangement that involved the transfer of ancillary staff to private sector organizations. Similarly, Councilco faced pressure to outsource many of its activities under the Best Value initiative. Paradoxically both organizations had successfully resisted outsourcing under CCT, but with a change in government, Councilco in particular was less able (or willing) to maintain its opposition. It was explained to us on several occasions that it was now committed to supporting the government. Healthco was an even more willing participant in this process. Having been slow to introduce changes due to strong trade-union organization, Healthco had subsequently adopted a more bullish stance, embracing the so-called modernization agenda and welcoming the PFI terms as an opportunity to weaken trade-union control.

PRESSURES FOR CHANGE

The scale and nature of the changes in staffing policy provide immediate support for many of the predicted changes in employment arrangements arising from a decline and destabilization of internal labour market systems. However, it is also clear from the description of the main policy changes that the transformation has not been complete. Moreover, as would be expected, the transformation and restructuring of internal labour market systems is taking different forms within different organizations. To understand the processes and forms of change under way, we need to apply the 'three rings of influence' system of analysis to our seven case study organizations.

In table 5.4 we have provided a brief synopsis of the various pressures on the organizations to change staffing policies. We have examined the pressures to meet new performance imperatives, the problems posed by internal constraints (either experienced by the organizations in changing staffing policies or which had to be overcome before changes could be implemented) and the external conditions which influenced the form that the changes took. This 'three ring' analysis, as set out in Chapter 1, provides a framework through which we can map an iterative process of change. In many cases the new performance imperatives interact with and are reinforced by changes or opportunities in the external labour market. These changes have enabled organizations to adopt a more radical response to performance pressures than would have been possible earlier. In some cases these responses have been *too* radical and have begun to create new problems of their own for management. We have mentioned the restrictions on promotion opportunities in this regard. In others, the changes were not fully implemented because managers became aware of potential problems and were therefore more cautious. In a minority of cases managers were spurred on by the change in external conditions to introduce extremely radical changes. This was the case at Mediaco where, in the context of a substantial technological change, it (like others in the newsprint sector) set itself on an extremely radical course aimed at weakening internal constraints and neutralizing the power of the trade union. This was achieved though mass compulsory redundancies and the imposition of new terms and conditions for new starters combined with a wages freeze. What this analysis indicates is that there is no optimal managerial form that is appropriate to all circumstances. Rather, the organizational form is the product of a set of complex responses to a number of

Table 5.4. Pressures for change in staffing policies

	Performance imperatives	Internal constraints	External conditions
Bankco	Telephone banking provided opportunity to become a national player; needed to reassure the City after poor results; market niche dependent on quality standards	High turnover and low morale among temporary staff; new partnership agreement with trade union	Availability of non-bank staff for call centre work
Councilco	Achieve budget reductions in context of rising demands for services	Constrained by no redundancy and redeployment guarantee; new government provides new momentum for internal change	Encouraged by government to take private sector and flexible employment policies as a model for public sector modernization
Healthco	Achieve budget reductions in context of rising demands for services; change to skill mix and improve hospital bed utilization rates	Internal conflicts between medical and managerial staff; Private Finance Initiative provides opportunity to bypass conflictual industrial relations	Private sector seen by the management team as model for service delivery and labour market organization
Mediaco	Reduce cost of printing; emphasize advertising over journalism	Able to undermine strong trade-union controls in printing and journalism; focus on keeping advertising staff happy	Murdoch victory over print unions at national level provided a blueprint for action at regional level; closure of national newspapers provided supply of labour for new market rate terms and conditions
Pharmco	Compete for production against other plants in multinational; maintain quality and level of supply	Need to maintain good employer image to protect quality	Widespread adoption of best practice, just-in-time systems in other sectors/companies one factor leading to hiring of consultants to advise on 'just-in-time' for warehouse arrangements
Retailco	Need to compete through service, cost control and expanding market share, beyond national boundaries	Stable staff numbers, motivated staff needed to ensure quality service delivery	Students provide additional flexible but stable labour supply provided though married women
Telecomco	Satisfy the City expectations on headcount; exploit new communications technology	Maintain morale of permanent staff by using temporary staff for flexibility and for least popular working times	Availability of temporary staff for call centre work; opportunity to vary wage levels according to region

separate processes. This can be demonstrated more fully by a closer examination of our cases.

If we consider the private sector organizations first, we find a set of rather diverse stories. Retailco and Pharmco had perhaps made the least radical changes in their employment models over recent years. The high use of agency temps at Pharmco was, in part, the consequence of a failed attempt to re-engineer the production, packaging and warehousing process. This scheme appeared to have come out of the company's concern to introduce so-called 'best practice' techniques. They were spurred on in this direction by consultants who, in their recommendations, had failed to take account of particular features of drugs production and marketing. In pharmaceuticals there had been a growing trend towards a more customized packaging of drugs. More importantly, there was a clear imperative that the company should be able to supply quantities of its drugs on demand. Both of these features (which relate to the particular 'life and death' features of its product lines) meant that the company was obliged to keep higher levels of stock than imagined in a 'lean production' system. As a result, a large redundancy exercise was followed by a period of rehiring. It was at this point that the company made extensive use of a temporary work agency. The subsequent decision to convert most agency temps to permanent contracts signals a continuing commitment to the internal labour market system, albeit with limited rungs on the career ladder. This suggests that those internal factors behind downsizing did not necessarily form a major internal goal for the organization. It could operate effectively enough with higher levels of employment, as the subsequent modification of the project suggests.

Changes at Retailco have largely concentrated on the design of job and career structures, with employment policy reinforcing a commitment to stable contracts. The main objective has been to secure labour force stability. Even when taking advantage of the increasing supplies of student labour, Retailco's response has been to try to stabilize this essentially unstable labour supply source. By requiring students at school to work on a regular basis and by offering a transfer to a store close to the student's university, Retailco has effectively internalized (ostensibly casual) student labour for an extended period.

More radical change is found in both Mediaco and Telecomco. Both organizations had more complex internal labour market systems and stronger trade unions than were ever present at Retailco and even Pharmco, when focusing on the pharmaceuticals production division. The ability of both Mediaco and Telecomco to change their employment systems had been constrained by a long history of powerful trade unions. The change in industrial relations systems in the printing industry and the deregulation of the telecommunications sector were critical factors in allowing management at each organization the scope to dismantle the internal constraints through radical policies. These policies varied in form, with Telecomco mainly focusing on the recruitment of agency temps as a means of bypassing collective agreements, while Mediaco closed plants and imposed so-called market rates of pay and conditions, together with wage freezes.

Bankco, in contrast, started to go down the route of radical transformation but was initially more cautious than either Mediaco or Telecomco, and, more recently, has even undertaken a partial U-turn. Instead of seeking to remove union influence, it chose to change the nature of its involvement with the union and develop a broader partnership agreement. In part, this change of tack stemmed from the particular history of the organization and its long-standing involvement with the union. It also reflects concerns that the radical dismantling of the banking internal labour market system was not delivering the motivated and knowledgeable workforce it required to maintain its market position, based on quality of service and distinctive products.

It is in the public sector, however, that we perhaps find the most complex and contradictory pressures. Councilco and Healthco both face increasing problems in meeting budgetary squeezes and responding to rising demands for services. To resolve these dilemmas, they are urged to look to the private sector for models of employment change and of service delivery. Yet opportunities to make radical changes, even assuming that the private sector model makes sense for public service delivery, remain constrained by internal factors. Councilco has to answer to a political body that is committed to a no compulsory redundancy and a redeployment policy. Healthco is still facing the problem common to many NHS trusts, namely rivalry between managerial and medical hierarchies, which effectively prevents constructive discussion and the planned implementation of policy. These internal contradictions and problems have led to the adoption of more radical solutions, including the establishment of a PFI hospital. The issue remains whether these radical solutions are being sought to provide the route out of the impasse and to impress political decision-makers, without full consideration of their long-term consequences for service delivery and public employment.

THE IMPACT OF STAFFING POLICIES IN PRACTICE: HOW MANAGERS AND EMPLOYEES PERCEIVE THE CHANGES

The evidence from our seven case study organizations provides immediate support for the hypothesis that the 1990s was a period of relatively dramatic change in employment policy and practice. However, there is no generic pattern of change emerging from the case studies in relation to recruitment and staffing policies. They all started with different histories and backgrounds with respect to the establishment of stable institutionalized internal labour markets and the presence of trade union power. Moreover, each has faced a different set of interlocking conditions, affecting the extent and pace of the retreat from stable internal labour market systems. Nevertheless, the overall verdict must be that the already implemented changes, taken together with the changes in the pipeline and actively discussed by management, adds up to a rapid and extensive process of change. Yet it is clear that these policies do not necessarily constitute a coherent and convincing new model of employment arrangements. It is unlikely that they will provide solutions to the problems of managing employment under decentralized systems of governance and under increasingly competitive conditions. It is not necessarily the case that we can identify future directions of change without a closer analysis of the experience of the current policies and practices. While most of the changes have been introduced in a context of reduced collective employee power, organizations often remain increasingly dependent upon the loyalty, motivation and skills of the workforce, even under conditions of apparent deskilling and casualization. Individual employee accounts and perceptions of the changes may not only illuminate our understanding of the experience of work under these changing conditions; they may also indicate some of the problems and contradictions that these policies may throw up for managers. Similarly, managers' own accounts of these changes, particularly line managers, provide a different perspective from the often more upbeat accounts provided by higher-level and human resource managers on how these changes work out in practice. Here, therefore, we draw upon our interviews with employees— both non-managerial and managerial staff—to explore in greater detail the experience of change in staffing policies in these organizations.

It is worth noting before we begin to draw out these accounts that we had expected, at the beginning of our research, to find the processes of changes in staffing policies to be highly gendered and that there would be clear gender differences in the experience of change and flexibilization. As the majority of our workplaces were female-dominated, there was to some extent an inevitability about that finding. Many of the organizations were using high numbers of part-time and temporary contracts in which women tend to be over-represented relative to other employment arrangements. However, perhaps the more surprising and notable finding was that where men were employed in the workplaces and job categories covered by our research, they were as likely, and sometimes more likely, to have been affected by radical change in staffing policies than the women we encountered. When we interviewed men placed through TWAs and on temporary or flexible contracts, we found that their experiences resonated with those of the women employed. Where we included male-dominated occupations—for example, the porters at Healthco or the printers at Mediaco—we found these jobs to be as subject to as much radical change in staffing policies as any of the female-dominated occupations. The male porters were awaiting transfer to a new employer under the PFI agreement and, in the meantime, were subject to increased requirements to be customer-focused in line with the demand made of the more traditional female caring jobs. At Mediaco, not only had printers been stripped of their union recognition but they also faced the radical restructuring of internal labour markets, with new male recruits brought into the organization on much lower wage rates (see Chapter 8).

The similarities in the plight of male and female workers within the case studies are undoubtedly, in part, a function of the occupational groups studied. Women do predominate amongst the routine and lower-skilled workers in service sectors, and thus, to a great extent, the story revealed here is that of the typical female employee. Nevertheless, it is clear that men are having more difficulty in maintaining protected enclaves within female-dominated sectors and have faced very severe declines in pay, status and job security in traditionally well-unionized and protected sectors. Thus, in analysing the impact of flexibilization on the workforces in the case study organizations, we are, by and large, recounting a process that relates to both male and female employees. The effect may be to reduce the gender gap in employment equality, but it is a process that is levelling down the conditions faced by male employees rather than levelling up women's conditions of employment to those traditionally enjoyed by men.

There are three main changes that are found within these seven organizations that relate to the general debate on the flexibilization of labour markets and the dismantling of internal labour markets. These include, first, the move towards more segmented entry systems, involving both the use of direct-hire and agency temps as the main mode of entry, and the development of new terms and conditions for new entrants, based on the notion of market rates. Both systems serve to undermine the protections typically associated with entry into internal labour markets. The second set of changes relate to shifts in staffing or resource levels relative to demand; flexible labour markets are associated with tighter manning levels, reduced overheads and removal of built-in slack in the system, and a reliance on flexible and ad hoc methods to meet demands. The change in staffing levels interrelates with our two other areas of investigation—change in skill levels (see Chapter 6) and change in working time arrangements (see Chapter 7). Here, therefore, we explore mainly one aspect of change in staffing and resource policies, namely the practice of maintaining unfilled vacancies at senior or supervisory levels and the use of 'acting-up' rather than permanent promotion as a means of 'getting by'. The third change relates to the experience of downsizing and the associated methods of downsizing, including early retirement, redundancy and redeployment.

SEGMENTING WORK: THE USE OF TEMPORARY CONTRACTS AND 'MARKET RATES'

In the majority of the organizations we looked at, in some cases by design and in others by force of circumstance, there has been an increasing move towards the use of non-standard terms and conditions for new entrants. This involved the use of temporary agency staff or direct hires on temporary contracts. Additionally, some of the companies were imposing market rate conditions on their new contracts. This begs the question, how far have these changes met corporate objectives and provided new and effective ways of managing their staffing policies? To answer this question, we first need to explore the various motivations involved.

If we look at the use of one type of temporary contract or another we find considerable evidence of coherence between this strategy and the organizations' changing market and technological environments. These contracts have also allowed them to respond more flexibly to a changing system of work organization. Not only can temporary contracts be used to provide a hedge against market and technological change, but these practices can also be used to lower costs and to manage the problem of monotony and lack of career prospects. However, it is not clear that this strategy solved management's problem entirely. At Telecomco the organization hoped that it could keep the turnover rate under control and hold on to its agency temps for eighteen months or so. In practice, this proved difficult to achieve. Managers talked of 'burn-out' and frequently expressed scepticism over whether anyone could effectively perform the job for an extended period. One senior manager who had been in the post for just over a year put it like this:

Retention is difficult because there's burn-out in this job, there's no doubt about it. It's... the way the industry is going.... We can't offer contracts and... one reason is—it's burn-out. If you are looking to give somebody a contract then they'd have to be with us for twelve months... by that time... they're twelve months nearer to burn-out so if you give loads of people contracts what are you going to do with those [staff] when they're burnt-out because there aren't any opportunities elsewhere?

(Male, full time, no. 2, Telecomco3)

In fact we found the highest turnover rate at this Telecomco work-place—the telemarketing call centre. During one of our visits, a senior manager told us that in the previous quarter 300 staff had quit, representing an annual turnover rate of around 130 per cent. The target figure (as recommended to Telecomco by external consultants with expertise in call centres) was 60 per cent, but with the extraordinarily high number of agency temps, at around 9 in 10 workers, management struggled to meet this target. Exiting staff at Telecomco cited as their reasons for leaving the organization unsocial working hours and the lack of opportunities to progress. The reference to 'progress' is a common one amongst temporary agency workers and can be taken as a proxy for 'a permanent contract'.

At Banckco turnover rates were lower—at around 30 per cent in the call centres—but even these caused problems, partly because they conflicted with the ethos of the bank. As one manager observed:

I think a lot of it is historic and perhaps there is no rationale to it in one sense, in that we are a bank and this is a call centre and they are two different cultures.... The executive within the bank are bankers and there was a lot of pressure on us to reduce our turnover because traditionally bank turnover would be 5–10 per cent.

(Male, full time, manager, Bankco4)

One objective behind the corporate decision at Bankco, Pharmco and Telecomco to recruit agency temps was to remove the recruitment function from workplace managers and to locate it instead in local TWAs. It seems to have been assumed that high turnover rates are a natural function of the established work process. In such conditions (or, as in the case of Pharmco, where there was a need for a quick increase in the number recruited) the TWAs were considered better able to fill vacancies in the short term. As such, this use of agencies for recruitment can be seen as a means of economizing on scarce management time, taking care of the management of hassle, as well as securing labour supply. Some evidence in support of this conclusion comes indirectly from organizations (such as Councilco) that were not using TWAs. Here, management staff reported increasing difficulties in managing the process of recruitment. In part, this was because of new unemployment benefit rules, which required all benefit recipients to make numerous job applications. This increased not only the volume of paper work, but also the proportion of applicants who failed to turn up for interviews. As a result, local managers often found themselves recruiting into permanent jobs staff who already had some experience in the organization. For example, Councilco used casual staff to cover for sickness or absence and it was from the list of casuals that most permanent staff were recruited. This tendency to recruit permanent staff from a pool of temporary workers increases the motivation for employees to take on these types of job, thereby reinforcing the tendency towards this new mode of entry into employment. At Pharmco and Telecomco entry through either direct-hire or agency temps was effectively the only lower-level port of entry available.

However, while use of direct-hire or agency temps reduced initial recruitment difficulties, they generated a further set of problems for management in dealing with the effects of the volume of staff entering the organizations. For example, at Telecomco the high number of temporary staff leaving the workplaces was attributed to the poor skills of lower-level 'coaches' and led existing management practices to be questioned. A sales manager argued:

At the moment, the main problem is that we have a lack of ... people skills, communication skills and development skills in the management structure that we have in our teams, and if we don't get that right it [attrition] will just continue to happen.

(Male, full time, no. 3, Telecomco3)

These problems were exacerbated in organizations where there was a higher premium placed on meeting quality standards and where these standards could not be met unless the agency temp was integrated into the complexities of the service provision. This applied obviously and particularly within Healthco, where ward managers had to balance the use of 'bank' staff with meeting quality targets in the delivery of care to patients.

Recruitment through TWAs was often used in preference to internal recruitment, as organizations believed this method would be more likely to supply staff. In practice, however, the TWAs themselves encountered many of the same constraints as the client organizations. A particular problem arose for Telecomco when a new call centre opened where the local labour market for the kind of workers required was already quite tight. Here, agency temps who had been placed at Telecomco were in a good position to leave and obtain new permanent jobs because of the in-post training and experience gained. Telecomco managers had tried to move to different TWAs. However, there was only a limited number available locally, and this operated as a severe and practical constraint on management's options.

The limited scope for manoeuvre frustrated local managers and led a number of them to take issue with the corporate policy of favouring the use of agency temps. In some cases, local managers were able to take action to minimize the problems, at least from their own perspective. For example, some managers renegotiated contracts with the TWA to ensure that it undertook more initial training. In some cases recruits had to pay a financial penalty if they quit too soon after training (£300 at TWAs used by Telecomco), and in other cases the management was experimenting with a loyalty bonus. One Telecomco manager had established an arrangement with a particular TWA to recruit local university students. This local initiative was based upon the belief that it would result in a relatively stable supply of articulate agency temps, willing to work unsocial, part-time hours. The organization then used the performance of this TWA as a benchmark against which to compare the performance of the others.

The surrender of the control of the recruitment process to TWAs was, in fact, renegotiated regularly by individual workplace managers. There was a constant need for intervention by the corporate clients to ensure a more proactive or appropriate recruitment strategy; according to one Telecomco manager, he spent most of his time telling the managers at TWAs how to do their job. This applied also in Pharmco, where there were concerns that the local TWA was too ready to recruit highly-qualified A-level students or even university graduates for very tedious and routinized jobs. One male manager in tablets manufacturing commented that the over-qualified workers suffered from boredom in the job, and as a consequence, they 'wind other people up'. Nevertheless, the room for manoeuvre for local managers was limited. They were unable to recruit onto permanent contracts and had little scope to make the jobs more interesting. Some of the problems had begun to be recognized by senior and corporate level management at Bankco and Pharmco, and there was a rethink of the policy that relied so extensively upon TWAs.

In addition to the problem of recruiting agency temps, the use of differentiated terms and conditions has clearly opened up divides within the workforce, which were recognized by staff, both permanent and temporary alike. For example, at one workplace (Telecomco2), a new team was formed using only agency temps. In this case, the sense of division that already existed in the workplace between permanent and agency temps deepened. As an acting coach explained:

When I came in as agency worker it was called 'Fast Response'. We were supposed to go in, sign in, log on and take calls.... They called us Fast Action Response, they called us FARTs and so there was a bit of a them [Telecomco] and us situation.

(Female, part time, no. 4, Telecomco2)

Permanent staff at this Telecomco workplace viewed the introduction of agency temps in this context as a means of introducing new ways of organizing work that they might have resisted. For the most part, they were right. Through Telecomco's separation of jobs into discrete tasks and the creation of a new, all-agency workforce at the workplace, permanent employees viewed themselves as quite separate from their temporary colleagues. The acting coach, who had since moved on to a permanent contract, was clearly happy to have left the world of agency work behind:

No disrespect to them, I could not do that job [anymore]! It's so boring.... They are agency workers probably because it is so mind numbingly boring.... Telecomco probably know they wouldn't be able to employ anybody on a permanent contract to do it.

(Female, part time, no. 4, Telecomco2)

Demarcation occurred by contract-type and by type of work. On the one hand, Telecomco managers noted the difference in commitment between agency temps and their own staff. It was generally felt that permanent staff were more committed to the organization. Indicators cited included their greater punctuality and the standard of their performance at work. On the other hand, managers felt that the new ways of working that accompanied the recruitment of agency temps were more readily accepted by the group. One manager who had been at the organization for almost twenty years thought agency temps were easier to involve in new developments:

[T]hey're [agency temps] not as motivated.... [O]n the other hand Telecomco contracts are a big problem because they [agency temps] just want a contract. But you find that the agency people are the ones that you can get on board. They are more adept at changing with the company rather than the old Telecomco that have been here a long time.

(Female, full time, no. 10, Telecomco1)

This echoes the views expressed by Mediaco managers, who saw the new recruits as more amenable to their objectives, despite being employed on inferior terms and conditions. Here, segmenting work was not based on contractual differences (between temporary and permanent) but between new and existing recruits. There was an explicit policy of exploiting the apparent willingness of the new recruits to work more flexibly and to accept inferior terms and conditions. The price of this cultural change, however, was a loss of motivation and a drop in morale among existing staff. One show-business correspondent at the editorial department voiced a concern about the effect the pay freeze of 1997 had on the motivation of staff:

It was shattering for everybody. Morale is still [low]. People, well, obviously initially anger, people were very angry that this [flat rate of pay] was being imposed on them.... With the greatest respect to my colleagues, there's a lot of young staff who are here now with very little experience... and they're coming here for one reason: because they're cheap. People are looking to move on from [Mediaco] now which they never did before.

(Male, full time, no. 2, Mediaco2)

Another senior journalist who had been at Mediaco since 1990 reinforced the sense that morale had been undermined by the decision to freeze wages by the use of market rates in setting entry levels:

The logic was... that people had been paid a lot of money in the past and the market rates were lower basically and it was felt perhaps that the 'gravy train' had ended, I guess, and now people are being taken on lower rates of pay and obviously are keen and very able people that are able to get the same job done at less cost to the employer.... But in terms of morale it had... a detrimental effect for the rest of the people.

(Male, full time, no. 7, Mediaco2)

Nevertheless, management at Mediaco clearly felt that these effects were less detrimental than the continuation of the old system.

In some cases the problems associated with use of temporary labour, in fact, resulted in a reduction in the use of such contracts. For example, Councilco had faced difficulties in using direct-hire temps to fill vacancies on unpopular shifts for home-care workers precisely because there had been an upgrading rather than a reduction of skills and responsibilities in the job. They felt unable to rely on temporary staff in this context as they had insufficient control both over their recruitment and the supervision of their work while on duty in clients' homes. Healthco also faced these problems in their use of 'bank' agency nursing staff. This led to a policy of preferring, where possible, to use existing permanent staff through the bank to fill temporary part-time jobs, effectively worked as overtime. Retailco decided on a policy of upgrading service levels for customers, which was not seen as compatible with the use of direct-hire temps who would not be sufficiently knowledgeable about how the store operated as a whole. In Pharmco the high use of external recruitment over recent years was felt by management to have served a useful purpose in changing internal culture—to make permanent workers understand 'how good they've got it'. However, the exercise of rapid downsizing combined with a substantial use of agency temps resulted in high levels of uncertainty in the plant. To counter these problems, a policy of conversion of temporary to permanent contracts was put in place. There was, therefore, a recognition that the destabilizing effects of temporary recruitment, welcome though it might be for management in some areas, where life was perceived as having become too cosy, could easily spiral out of control and have knock-on negative effects on morale throughout the plant. Similar concerns had prompted Bankco to reverse its policy of using direct-hire and agency temps and to convert temporary to permanent contracts. However, in the case of Bankco the union had played a more active role in persuading management to change its tactics in employment, through the negotiation of a new partnership approach, based on the notion of workers as stakeholders.

Overall, therefore, the verdict on the new approaches is a mixed one. There are limits to the benefits that organizations can gain, even in the most decasualized environments. They also face the possibility of TWAs failing to deliver and of the recruited workers generating new and difficult problems of their own. From a management perspective, segmentation based on contractual difference remains potentially more acceptable than wholesale changes in the terms and conditions for permanent workers as achieved at Mediaco in the specific context of the newsprint industry. At the other extreme, Councilco and Healthco, the two public sector organizations, remained committed to a policy that relied upon their established and skilled staff. However, they both operated within extremely tight financial and organizational constraints. In these circumstances they were often unable to adjust their policies in the face of declining staff morale.

CONTROLLING STAFFING LEVELS: THE EXPERIENCE OF 'ACTING-UP'

The changes in recruitment policy were, in many respects, only to be expected. However, another feature of employment policy—the use of 'acting-up'—proved to be far more extensive than we had realized. This practice hardly got a mention in employment policy documentation outside the public sector. We became aware of it through comments made in our interview discussions. The frequency with which we came across the phenomenon suggested that this practice demands further discussion and analysis. 'Acting-up' is an arrangement whereby an employee agrees to fill temporarily a vacant post at a higher grade. This benefits the organization by keeping costs down, both by not providing replacements for the lower-level job where someone is asked to 'act-up' in a senior's or supervisor's absence, and sometimes by not fully compensating the person taking on the extra duties. It has the additional advantage of allowing staffing decisions to be delayed in the context of uncertainty over future staffing or resourcing levels and targets. Where future downsizing or redeployment exercises are anticipated, managers appear unwilling to fill higher-level vacancies, either because of the cost of redundancy in these posts or because they wish to hold the posts vacant for redeployment of existing higher-level staff. In both cases the effect is to shift the risk of uncertainty and the burden of cost reduction onto the staff who are offered the opportunity to 'act-up'. However, there were no guarantees that the promotion would be made permanent. In some workplaces staff were rotated through the 'acting-up' positions. In the absence of real promotion opportunities, this was as good as it got for many staff.

   In the public sector organizations the policy of 'acting-up' followed from the general policy of not filling vacancies as a means of meeting short-term budget requirements. There was a clear reliance on the employees' sense of responsibility for the delivery of a public service. Pressure on budgets also led to cutbacks in managerial staff and the applying of moral and other pressures on employees to work ever-longer hours at relatively low levels of managerial or supervisory responsibility. At one Healthco unit, nurse managers were made redundant, leading to a broadening of responsibilities for ward sisters. This was not met with an increase in the sisters' pay or grade:

We don't have a junior sister and a senior sister even though it was identified as a need before, and the junior sister and I have been 'acting-up' for the last four years. So I've been doing my post and somebody else's for four years.

(Female, full time, no. 9, Healthco3)

At the community care department at Councilco the policy of 'acting-up' was also evident. Lower-level staff on non-managerial grades acted as managers on a temporary basis while the organization undertook a review of policy, which took more than three years. During this period there was no security attached to the temporary positions. At its completion all those 'acting-up' went back to their previous posts, resulting in a loss of up to a third of their salary. None was offered permanent progression. Instead, a policy of external recruitment was pursued, deepening staff anxiety and stress and leaving some to feel that their status within both the workplace and the organization had regressed. One woman who had joined as a clerk typist had been asked to 'act-up' as office manager. Three and a half years later, as a result of the review, she was asked to return to her original post and accept a pay cut from £13 to £10 per hour. One home-care organizer we talked to had a similar experience:

[The 'acting-up'] just goes on and on and on. There is no given time.... It's just that it's extended and extended as you do it.... [T]hey had the restructure which took like three and a half years to do and all the people who were 'acting-up' into the post... we all had to go back to what we were doing originally.

(Female, full time, no. 6, Councilco2)

This practice, therefore, went further than asking staff to cover for relatively short periods such as maternity leave, or while the formal process of recruitment was undertaken. It was an institutional form of work-intensification. One of the problems was that staff did not really know why the 'acting-up' was required on such a long-term basis, nor whether the additional experience would assist them in their further careers. 'Acting-up' in the public sector appeared to be more a form of crisis management which exploited staff's public service ethos.

The practice of 'acting-up' was not, however, confined to public sector organizations. At Bankco there was evidence of the practice amongst junior-level managers. Part of the rationale for these policies was the uncertainty over future skill and resourcing needs; telephone banking was often seen as an intermediate stage in the restructuring of financial services and caution was exercised in expanding the permanent commitment to supervisory and senior staff.

At Telecomco, while staff acknowledged the returns to performing the extra tasks involved in 'acting-up', they were unhappy about the length of time spent in this role. At the telemarketing centre a sales manager noted:

I understand why, as a business because we're growing so fast, its easier to have secondments, but to me a secondment is a three-month period when you go and develop some different skills and come back or then decide to apply for that job [but] not two years!

(Male, full time, no. 7, Telecomco3)

Staff did not receive an increase in salary, but instead were paid only a fixed sum per day for taking on extra responsibilities. For the extra responsibility, this particular employee received an extra £6 a day and was expected to work over the weekend in return. Staff worked alongside others in permanent posts that received financial and non-financial remuneration according to the position. At another Telecomco workplace there was a policy of reducing the size of the managerial workforce by developing a management support team consisting of thirty employees designated as advisers but who were able to cover for management when they were away. For every day they covered they received £5 on top of their normal salaries. In addition to saving on the size of the managerial staff, the support team was seen as delivering a 'short sharp shock' to its permanent managers:

The scheme also gives permanent managers 'a kick up the backside' with these new 'flexible' managers hovering.

(Male, full time, manager, Telecomco2)

However, the incentive effect of expanding the range of potential managerial recruits has to be balanced against the feelings of frustration experienced by those offered a temporary taste of a higher-level job but from whom this opportunity is then withdrawn or threatened to be withdrawn. A transaction team manager found the whole process distressing:

It's demoralizing isn't it? You do it ['act-up'] for two years, and then you're thrown back into your original job. Then six months later 'we're stuck, can you come back and act?' Then you do it for another two years; how many times do you take being kicked in the teeth?

(Female, full time, no. 2, Telecomco1)

A centre manager meanwhile highlighted how middle managers were caught between selling the policy to other employees and supporting their colleagues:

A lot of these people [the staff] are seconded managers and they've been messed about. I've got to keep my [Telecomco] head on and say 'look you've got to bear with us and you can't get there that quickly'. But... they seem to have an interview every, well it is every three months and they're going through agony.

(Male, full time, no. 2, Telecomco3)

In these examples we therefore found that the practice of internal promotion was not providing the kind of orderly and safe career progression that is suggested by classic models of internal labour markets. Instead, internal promotion systems are being used to increase competitive pressure on existing managers. They also have the advantage of avoiding the need for external recruitment and the associated long-term commitments. At a more basic level, they provide a cheap means of reducing the numbers of staff and associated wage costs. The majority of the people we found in this position of being asked to 'act-up' were women. This finding is not surprising given the high proportion of women employees in many of the organizations studied. Those asked to 'act-up' are all drawn from the lower ranks of the organization, the majority of whom are women. This finding of a frequent use of 'acting-up' policies emerged out of the interview material. It was not a focus of our initial research, and we are not therefore able to say with certainty whether there was any gender bias in the 'acting-up' policy within our case study organizations. Nevertheless, on the basis of the qualitative interview material, we suspect that there is a tendency for more women than men to be placed in the position of 'acting-up' for long periods of time, without the position being made permanent.

DOWNSIZING AND REDEPLOYMENT

Managing the process

Five of our organizations had been involved in significant downsizing at some time during the previous decade. This process of shedding labour was often taken to be the defining characteristic of the restructured, flexible labour markets of the 1980s and 1990s. Relatively little, however, has been written about either the processes involved or the consequent effects on the organization. Two questions seem to be particularly pertinent: to what extent does the process of downsizing meet management's needs and objectives or generate new problems or unexpected impacts? What problems does downsizing present for those employees who remain within the organization?

Most of the organizations had experienced some negative effects as a consequence of 'downsizing'. In some cases there was a feeling that new technologies and new market conditions had led to an overestimate of the change in skill requirements and, as a consequence, many experienced and highly-skilled employees opted for voluntary redundancy. We came across many examples of this. The most obvious was at Pharmco where the disastrous experience of restructuring had led to a massive haemorrhage of experience through voluntary redundancy and extensive redeployment exercises. As a result, one of its production plants was constantly failing to reach the 'world-class' benchmark standard expected for all of the company's sites. It seems that over its short life it had only been kept up to standard through the skills and capacities of the old workforce, which enabled the company to 'firefight' and to deal flexibly with unexpected, non-routine problems. Less dramatic but similar consequences were experienced in the other organizations. Managers at Bankco came to feel that the lack of need for banking knowledge had been exaggerated. On the engineering side at Telecomco it was widely held that the capacity of new technologies to reduce the need for traditional skills had been overestimated. Councilco discovered that it had exaggerated the likely decline in demand for direct maintenance staff and it found itself redeploying tradesmen while, at the same time, being forced to recruit new staff in order to fulfil new contracts. Only at Mediaco did we encounter a management content with its use of downsizing and redundancy policies. Here, managers were happy to have lost experienced unionized staff and to have replaced them, in a new context, with staff with more flexible attitudes and lower wage expectations. However, this contentment may have reflected a willingness to accept a lower standard of journalistic expertise in a context where improved information systems allow local newspapers to take less initiative in resourcing and generating news stories.

The problems generated by downsizing in part related to the policy adopted for reducing staffing levels. Pharmco had lessened its problems by insisting on retaining some skilled and experienced staff who otherwise would have left. In Telecomco the union had been influential in insisting that the early retirement offer should be open to all volunteers, a policy that led to downsizing in engineering at a rate two-thirds greater than the planned reduction. It was this policy—which was subsequently reversed—that was responsible for the loss of skilled staff in its engineering division. In its aftermath, staff with traditional cabling and digging skills were redefined as pivotal workers with key skills vital to the organization. Mediaco has used a policy of targeted early retirement to ensure that its scheme has the objective of culture change and does not result in the loss of any staff it wishes to retain. Councilco had recently been forced, because of cost, to reverse its policy of favouring early retirement and instead opted for a cheaper policy of favouring the younger volunteers for redundancy, even though this did not meet with the approval of the unions.

A great many of the problems that management experienced with downsizing stemmed directly from the kinds of (mis)calculation that inspired the policy in the first place. However, other problems emerged from the way in which the organizations implemented the strategy. A number of schemes were available, including redundancy (on a compulsory or voluntary basis), early retirement or redeployment. The commitment to non-compulsory modes of downsizing remained high among the organizations studied, even though this inspired the adoption of other policies such as the recruitment of agency workers so as to minimize the costs of these commitments in the future. However, while most of the organizations were adopting a redeployment policy, alongside a voluntary redundancy or retirement scheme, some organizations were experiencing significant difficulties in managing the redeployment process. This problem was particularly acute in Councilco, where redeployment, offering indefinite protection of grade levels, was an important element in the council's political programme, but conflicted potentially with some other objectives, including meeting budget constraints and delivering quality services. Redeployment at Councilco provided not only protection of basic wages, even if redeployed at a lower grade, but also protection of bonuses and other additions, thereby raising the cost of the exercise. The diversity of activities and staff within the council also militated against a simple process of redeployment across departments. Particular problems with the system occurred where managers became surplus to requirement and there were only junior posts vacant. In this case, redeployment was difficult for the organization and the employee. The manager views the move as detrimental to his or her career progression, while the recipient department is not keen to have an 'over-qualified' employee carrying out basic duties.

In the Environment and Development Department of Councilco no fewer than eleven supernumerary posts were being held, many of them photographers who were too specialized to redeploy. In the same department, a school crossing patrol manager was frustrated by the embargo placed on recruiting from the external labour market and the requirement to take redeployments from elsewhere in the organization:

When people leave you can get given somebody from the redeployment register.... [I]t affects you, you can't actually choose your own staff. I've got no hope of ever being able readily to interview and choose somebody from outside who might bring something new and an insight into what's going on out there.

(Female, full time, no. 6, Councilco3)

The issue of who decides on the suitability of redeployed staff for their new posts and the incompatibility of certain skills for particular posts was a major issue for one manager. She managed a large outside facility and wanted to recruit from the external labour market, and had been frustrated by feedback from senior managers:

If they're not suitable for that department they're not going to be suitable for mine.... I would rather they would interview like everybody else and if they come in through an interview that's fine ... but I resent ... having people pushed on me because they're supernumerary, because they're misplaced.... It's not a suitable system, it doesn't work, it never has worked from what I can see and it's not going to work.

(Female, full time, no. 14, Councilco4)

A project officer at the Leisure Department who had been at the organization for over a decade outlined some of the internal contradictions of redeployment. In this case it had taken place through:

a sort of pseudo recruitment selection process and an interface rather than an interview.... I actually think the interface approach is actually quite counter to the whole equal opportunities principles ... because it's not part of the official process and it isn't vetted in the same way.

(Male, full time, no. 4, Councilco4)

It was the receiving department that had to bear the extra cost of retraining, often at the expense of upgrading the skills of existing employees. As this worker went on to explain:

More training budget has to go on particular people which obviously creates feelings of unfairness when you're seen to be spending ... £500 or £600 in training up in the basic skills, when somebody came to you originally and had several of those skills and has since only had a few hundred pounds spent on refreshers and so on. So that has caused some internal friction and also unhappiness about the lack of fresh faces. The issue is that we're just getting old [Councilco] hands rather than getting people with real enthusiasm in.

(Male, full time, no. 4, Councilco4)

Bankco management had also been experiencing problems with its redeployment scheme. Not only had this been a major factor in the recruitment of agency temps, which had proved to be a mixed blessing for the organization, but the terms of the agreement allowed staff to take as long as they wished in waiting for suitable redeployment opportunities. Managerial staff were beginning to suggest that a time limit should be imposed to provide a push to encourage the staff to enter into a new job or take up a new opportunity, possibly outside the bank. A team leader explained:

The bank does make an effort to redeploy people and I think the bank is really almost too caring. People are in positions that really don't suit them, there's very few of these staff left now in reality, but most of them are sort of remnants of when we centralized really. The bank tried to accommodate everybody and people have ended up in environments that they are not suited to really, they don't match their skills and it's mainly people who are late on in years and it's difficult to re-educate.

(Male, full time, no. 10, Bankco2)

One business centre, which had been expanding, had not been allowed to recruit externally in order to preserve jobs for redeployment, but in the interim many posts had to be filled by agency temps who had a high turnover rate. One of the consequences of this policy was that permanent staff then became demoralized, as they were constantly training up staff only to see them leave.

Telecomco had a more limited commitment to redeployment than either Bankco or Councilco and only protected the grade for four years. This presented problems for redeployed staff as they were often placed in lower grade jobs. Promotion opportunities had declined and few were keen to stay on in their new jobs once the protection expired. Redeployment appeared to cause fewer problems in Healthco, as there were a relatively large number of unfilled vacancies due to a combination of labour shortage and budget restraints. Thus, most of the staff employed in three wards that were closed during the period of our research were relatively easily redeployed. The closure of a hospital around five miles away from the main site was presenting more problems, largely because of the reluctance of the mainly local staff to be transferred to a large inner-city site. Retailco also adopted a policy of redeployment where possible, but for this organization the continued expansion of the stores plus the similarities between workplaces made this a relatively unproblematic policy.

DOWNSIZING AND STAFF MORALE

At a number of the organizations, downsizing policies had affected staff morale and sense of job security. It was not only the actual implementation of redundancy, but also the heightened uncertainty over both future employment prospects and the stability of the current organizational and work arrangements that led to feelings of insecurity and low morale. Where redeployment schemes were in place, staff distinguished between job and employment security. However, what was evident across all of the organizations was how changes in the external labour market and wider employment environment had lowered new recruits' expectations of the level of job/employment security that could be guaranteed by organizations or by their trade unions.

At the Leisure Department at Councilco, regular budget reductions combined with cost pressure resulting from CCT-led restructuring elsewhere in the organization. One project manager who had been at the organization since 1988 told us:

The first round of budget cuts ripped through [Councilco], we just weren't expecting it. . . . First of all cuts then competitive tendering, even though it does not directly affect us at [the workplace] in that none of us were put out to tender . . . because of the nature of their work there are a lot of question marks, a lot of uncertainty.

(Male, full time, no. 4, Councilco4)

At the Community Care Department there was a clear recognition that Councilco would protect the employment status of their employees. Nevertheless, there were costs associated with the heightened job insecurity that came with the restructuring to meet budget deficits. Another member of staff who had joined Councilco in 1986 outlined the difference between job security and employment security, against the backdrop of the organization's redeployment scheme:

I think most Councilco jobs are quite secure. It's like the 'project officer' it's only a thirty-week job. If it finished at the end of it I would go back to the STAR team [see Chapter 3], so I am not going to be unemployed, so in that sense it's a secure job.

(Female, full time, no. 3, Councilco2)

Another member of the same department, with a couple more years' experience, reinforced this sentiment. Responding to a question about

the options available to staff when faced with residential home closures, she told us:

We were just told that it [the closure] was happening and that was it. It was a bit
of a shock to the system and everything when you're applying for jobs and of
course by then you've got attached to some people as well. But I applied for this
job and I got it [through redeployment] and I like the job here.

(Female, part time, no. 4, Councilco2)

Views differed on whether large organizations, such as Telecomco,
could or would continue to deliver employment security. For one
customer service adviser there was a general fear of future insecurity,
related to direct experience of changes in recruitment policies over
recent years:

The biggest change is people... you do get a lot of people drifting in and out.
When I first came here [in 1995] there was people who had been here a long
time. The last lot to go... [in 1995–6]... had been here an awful long time. Since
then it is more agency staff... [and]... people's confidence starts to waver. You
start thinking, 'what is it leading to?' They [the organization] don't seem to be
replacing people, they don't seem to be replacing people other than with agency.
And they come and go.

(Female, part time, no. 2, Telecomco2)

However, for one middle-grade manager, at another Telecomco workplace, the sheer size of the organization still provided some form of
protection, reducing his fear of employment loss even in a period of
rapid change:

I feel very secure in my job. The sheer size of it I suppose. If we had a competitor
come in with a massive new idea... [but then]... we have these tremendous...
I think of them as battleships... out there [which] could just click into gear.

(Female, full time, no. 1, Telecomco3)

While downsizing has clearly taken its toll on the morale and the
motivation of staff, organizations were sometimes exempt from individual blame, as the changes were identified as part of a general pattern
or tide, against which no individual employer could protect their staff.
In this sense, organizations had been successful in persuading their
staff that downsizing was not a deliberate corporate policy but part of a
preordained logic in the evolution of national employment policy, often
stemming from globalization. This even applied to some employees at
Mediaco's new printworks. As a plate-maker explained, the offer of a

job was seen as a great advantage, despite years of experience with the trade unions controlling and regulating access and exit to the industry:

I considered myself quite fortunate because that was a break up. That was beginning around about the period when the unions broke up and unions had very little power. There was new technology coming in. There was a lot of old printers and old stereotypers being made redundant, and they had no hope of getting a job.

(Male, full time, no. 7, Mediaco1)

At a local school in the Catering Department of Councilco, a member of staff with almost twenty years service at Councilco talked about the level of job security at the organization in terms of perceived wider levels of insecurity in the labour market:

There is always that fear, I mean everywhere you go now there is that fear. But at the end of the day you've got to do what you enjoy and stay there or go somewhere you're not going to enjoy it and the fear is still there anyway.

(Female, part time, no. 2, Councilco1)

To the extent that job and employment insecurity are seen as being 'everywhere', individual employers may be able to escape some of the opprobrium that has traditionally been associated with downsizing or restructuring. The development of an attitude that no job or employment contract is secure may well mean that individual employers do not suffer a major dip in loyalty and commitment relative to other employers if they engage in restructuring exercises. However, the overall effect could still be a general loss of commitment and motivation, based on acquiescence in an uncertain future in which loyalty from employees will certainly not be any guarantee of similar consideration from employers, whether in the public or the private sector.

CONCLUSION

Our case study evidence set out in this chapter both supports and contradicts the belief that internal labour markets are being dismantled and replaced with flexible and lean employment systems. Two organizations, Mediaco and Telecomco, have broken with their past policies and practices, including the long-established acceptance of union involvement in employment policy and practice. Even in these cases, the pattern of change differs, and in no sense could we rule out the possibility that, in the future, there would be some return to stable internal labour markets. Mediaco, however, had been concerned to achieve a once-and-for-all change in culture but, even here, there were signs that it may well need to pay more attention in the future to creating a stable, coherent and integrated workforce. At the time of our research, Telecomco was already experiencing problems of managing work-places dominated by agency temps. Future policy, including the eventual mix of Telecomco staff and agency temps, remains uncertain. Retreat from radical change in employment policy is already evident in the cases of Bankco and Pharmco, two organizations whose use of agency temps as the main means of recruitment may, with hindsight, be regarded as more expedient than strategic. Retailco has made fewer changes to its staffing policies than any of the other organizations, but started from an already flexible and relatively unstructured employ-ment system. Change within the public sector organizations is signifi-cant and ongoing, but is as much a reflection of the lack of opportunity for public sector employers to develop new strategic approaches to managing employment as it is evidence of a new management style modelled on best practice from the private sector.

Managers in all our organizations have tended to seize greater con-trol over staffing and resourcing policy, but this has not necessarily resulted in the identification of solutions to the problem of combining flexibility with motivation and high morale. Implicit, however, in the policies adopted in most of the organizations is a willingness to pursue short-term gains, induced through higher work intensity and cheaper labour costs, at the expense of the more nebulous long-term gains from establishing higher-trust employment relations.

6

Bridging the Skills Gap? New Training Provision and Work Organization

INTRODUCTION

During recent years, a consensus has emerged among policy-makers across the majority of OECD economies that up-skilling the workforce is critical to strengthening international competitiveness and improving the quality of working life. The problem facing Britain, however, is that a legacy of piecemeal intervention in the arena of vocational training (Ashton and Green 1996; Finegold and Soskice 1988; Glynn and Gospel 1993; Green 1994; Marsden 1995) means that policy-makers have had to rely on the active support and initiative of employers to implement a national programme of up-skilling. In the absence of joint regulation (with trade unions), legislation, or coordination (among employers), the major agent in the operationalization of an up-skilling policy is the individual employer. This then raises a number of problems, not least the so-called aggregation problem where individual organizations make decisions regarding investments in skills on the basis of a narrow set of interests, which may not reflect the broader interests of the economy or society as a whole (Crouch *et al.* 1999). For example, individual organizations may seek to reduce their responsibilities (and associated costs) for training by poaching from other organizations, generating the well-known vicious cycle of reduced investment in training as all organizations face greater disincentives to make rather than to buy skills.

A focus on the individual organization is thus particularly appropriate for an analysis of what happened to training provision in Britain during the late 1990s. This chapter begins by detailing the changes in policies of training and skills development in our seven case study

organizations. The discussion covers new systems of induction training, multi-skilling and training in generic skills. We then outline the
variety of pressures for change, including new external labour market
conditions, different government policies on training and the weakened
role of trade unions. We argue that the new managerial approaches to
skills and training are closely intertwined with other areas of employment organization. Changes in work organization (such as delayering
and team working), the recruitment of agency temps and changes in pay
scales are important factors in our explanation of the way new training
policies have been designed and implemented. Finally, we assess the
effectiveness of these new policies against employees' experience of
reconstructed patterns of skill development and training provision.

CHANGES IN THE PROVISION OF TRAINING

All seven case study organizations had carried out a great deal of
experimentation and change in the area of training. However, while it is
true that each organization had broken away from its traditional policies and practices, the nature and direction of change is not, at first sight,
reducible to a single set of characteristics. Indeed, while some organizations had withdrawn from traditional areas of training provision,
others had increased their training expenditure. Among those that had
increased their investment in new areas of training, there were further
differences in training content. For example, some organizations had
increased the firm-specific nature of in-house skills development, while
others had introduced training in generic skills, which potentially provided employees with more general and transferable expertise. Finally,
where organizations had withdrawn from training provision altogether,
in some cases this decision effectively ended the development of
employees' formal skills and in others skill development continued but
was delivered through an external agency or institution.

  Hence, there appears to be little evidence of a unified shift in the
provision of training, whether in the quantity of training, in the balance
between firm-specific and general skills, or in who delivers training.
However, the lack of uniformity in new policies of training provision
conceals important similarities in both the pressures for change in
training provision and the implications for skills development and
career progression among the workforce. In all organizations, changes
in training provision had been led by managers in an effort either to

link new paths of skills development with new forms of work organization, or to respond to the problems generated by past policies of job restructuring—including delayering, outsourcing and the use of agency temps. Hence, while all organizations faced a common set of internal and external pressures for change, the increased confidence and autonomy of managers generated a diverse mix of responses across organizations in the way training provision has been transformed. Perhaps it is because the new forms of training were designed and implemented by management (as opposed to some form of joint regulation) that we find the second similarity—that is, the high level of dissatisfaction among employees. Across all seven organizations, low-level employees, in particular, seemed frustrated at the failure of new training to translate into opportunities for career advancement. In some cases, the training did not equip the employee with the quantity or the quality of skills required for a higher-level post, and, in other cases, the opportunities for promotion for a trained employee were very limited. Each organization had, therefore, failed to construct readily accessible bridges across the gaps in job ladders, reflecting either the inability of training policies to enable workers to bridge the gap or the lack of promotion opportunities.

We begin the analysis of new training policies and practices by setting out the diversity of new forms of training provision. Subsequent sections then address the common pressures underpinning change and the close linkages, in all organizations, between new training provision and changes in work organization. In this section, the diverse characteristics of training systems are collected together around five themes: withdrawal from training provision; expansion of induction training; expansion of firm-specific training; introduction of apprenticeship-type schemes; and training in low level, 'generic' skills. As table 6.1 demonstrates, no single theme captures the characteristics of training systems across all seven organizations, reflecting the diversity of current arrangements.

A number of organizations had withdrawn from the provision of traditional areas of training or had shifted responsibility for the delivery of training. With the growth of telephone banking in the Business and Personal Consumer Divisions, new recruits into Bankco are no longer trained in general banking skills, such as through an NVQ in banking; the tradition has been maintained, however, within the corporate banking arm of the bank. At Retailco, vacant mid-level management posts are increasingly likely to be filled with external recruits, reflecting the diminishing proportion of low-level staff who are able to progress

Table 6.1. New policies of training and skills development

	Bankco	Councilco	Healthco	Mediaco	Pharmco	Retailco	Telecomco
Withdrawal from training	Shift away from training in banking skills	—	—	—	—	Growing reliance on external recruits into mid-management posts	Temporary workers receive initial training from job agencies
Expansion of induction training	2-week induction including Bankco 'cultural heritage' information	—	—	—	Emphasis on team-working and ownership of job task	Expanded and greater emphasis on Retailco brand	
Expansion of firm-specific training	—	Training for new STAR team care workers	Plans to adapt external programmes for qualified nurses	New graduate training scheme; some provision of specialist training for editorial staff	—	—	
New apprenticeship-type programmes	—	NVQ for catering staff, with links to external training centres	—	New apprenticeship for printers	—	—	
Training in low-level generic skills	NVQ in customer services for telephone banking staff	—	NVQ training for unqualified nurses	—	NVQ training for production line operators	All general assistants are trained and assessed in general skills	NVQ in customer services for operators

through the management training programmes. Finally, at Telecomco a large part of the initial training in basic customer operator skills is delivered by the agencies that supply temporary workers.

At two of these organizations, Bankco and Retailco, the withdrawal from areas of training provision went hand-in-hand with an expansion of the induction programme for new recruits with a focus on the 'cultural heritage', or the 'brand', of the company. At Bankco, the induction focuses on the history of the corporation, its mission statement and its relationship with partner organizations and interest groups, as well as its ethical marketing policy. At Retailco, induction training for low-level staff grew from eight to twenty-four hours over recent years and now covers a host of issues associated with the particular brand of the company. This includes, for example, a script to welcome customers, the benefits of the share options and savings schemes, the performance targets of the particular store and, as at Bankco, the mission statement of the corporation. Pharmco also strengthened its induction training with a new emphasis on the principles of team-working among operators, as well as a focus on the benefits of low-level workers taking 'ownership' of their particular job task and piece of machinery.

While such programmes of induction were designed to orientate new employees to the aims and objectives of the organization, at three other organizations there were clear efforts to change the balance of future training. Such programmes are identified here as expanding the firm-specific nature of training provision on the grounds that they either explicitly aimed to shift the balance away from general to firm-specific skills (Healthco), or that they did not involve external accreditation of the skills acquired (Councilco and Mediaco). Healthco is, perhaps, an extreme case, where managers aimed to establish a new training programme for nurses in place of that traditionally delivered by the external education partners (primarily involving the local university). With the removal of Regional Health Authorities, responsibility for training provision had been devolved to various districts. Healthco is part of a group of twenty NHS Trusts—an Education and Training Consortium— which commands a budget of £20 million. Healthco managers see the Consortium as a vehicle through which they can challenge the content of nursing education programmes and have greater input into what is taught, with the viable threat of being able to withdraw funding and go elsewhere. At Councilco and Mediaco, the expansion of firm-specific training was the result of investment in new in-house training programmes. In the Community Care Providers' Division at Councilco, a new group of home care workers was set up in 1997 to integrate the tasks of home-carers (home visits and patient care) with the new task of patient assessment in liaison with care managers from the Community Care Purchasers' Division. Incumbent home care assistants were selected for the new post of STAR team workers (see Chapter 3) and trained during a twelve-month, one-day release programme (organized and paid for by Councilco), which covered topics such as patient assessment, monitoring and how to write reports. At Mediaco, whereas in the past the editorial division only recruited skilled and experienced journalists (from other local or national newspapers), in 1998 a new graduate trainee journalist programme was introduced. New recruits now spend two years rotating between news, features and other related areas and receive a special trainee rate of pay. Further training is also provided through identifying the specific needs of journalists for specialist seminars on topics such as business finance.

Two organizations established training similar to the traditional apprenticeship-type schemes, in which trainees develop skills through a combination of formal education at an external institution and informal on-the-job training within the workplace. At Councilco, civic and schools catering staff are encouraged to complete NVQ training with paid day releases at external catering training centres, as well as formal training provided centrally by Councilco managers at a dedicated training centre. At Mediaco, an apprenticeship for printers was set up in 1991, involving a four-year programme with college education provided one day per week. On completion, apprentices gain an NVQ Level 3, a City and Guilds qualification and a BTEC diploma in printing.

Finally, while there is clearly a diversity of new areas of training provision, one new practice common to five of the seven case study organizations involves training in low-level, generic skills and competencies. At both Bankco and Telecomco, operators and advisers are trained in customer services. For Bankco, this reflects a clear shift away from technical training in banking skills; at Telecomco, it is representative of an increase in the proportion of the workforce that work in customer services. At Healthco, new recruits into the post of health care assistant—along with incumbent nurse auxiliaries who transfer into the post—receive training up to NVQ Level 2. At Pharmco, an NVQ programme of training was being rolled out during the period of our research. Large numbers of experienced operators take part in 'train to train' courses, with the aim of monitoring and assessing NVQ training (up to Level 2) for newly recruited operators. Finally, at Retailco, all general assistants are included in a two-year personal development plan, which is designed to train and assess all staff on the general skills required.

PRESSURES AND OPPORTUNITIES TO CHANGE SKILLS AND TRAINING POLICIES

New training provision, whether a withdrawal from skills development or a move towards new areas of training, is not driven solely by a management desire to transform the skills base of the workforce. New policies across all seven organizations reflect the combination of a set of competing pressures and new opportunities for change. These pressures and opportunities involve distinctive business and competitive conditions across each sector of economic activity, as well as potentially similar conditions related to a new industrial relations and external labour market environment, in the context of wide-ranging government policies. In this section, we explore the interrelationship between the three rings of pressures, as previously outlined in Chapters 1 and 4 (see table 6.2).

Turning to our first ring—performance imperatives—we find there are a number of pressures deriving from fast-changing technologies, new forms of competition and limits to spending imposed by the City or by central government. Rapid advances in information technologies and telecommunications systems have dramatically transformed the traditional skill requirements of firms in banking and telecommunications. The introduction of automated telling machines and the shift to telephone banking has accompanied a large-scale closure of bank branches at Bankco. Information regarding new products, bank account details and loans, which was traditionally delivered by staff working in bank branches, has now been reallocated to call centres. The use of sophisticated information technology systems in call centres reduces the incentive for the bank to invest in banking skills, since much of the required information and knowledge can be programmed into the computer operating systems used by bank advisers. Similarly, at Telecomco, computer systems for operators are designed to display scripts and prompts in order to reduce the technical knowledge demanded of employees, which would previously have been acquired through formal training.

Table 6.2. Pressures for change in training policies

	Ring 1: Performance imperatives	Ring 2: Internal constraints	Ring 3: External conditions
Bankco	Fast-changing technologies act as pressure to transform skills base	New training policies associated with partnership approach	New training in basic skills required for new labour pool of potential call-centre workers
Councilco	Increased private sector competition in some service areas; restricted public spending	Strong union resistance in many areas and strong professional norms	Use of skill development policies to attract quality job applicants
Healthco	Restricted public spending forces policies of skills mix	Management-led initiatives for some groups of staff	Tight labour market for qualified workers but large pool of unemployed for low-skill posts
Mediaco	Old crafts overtaken by new printing technologies	Weakened trade-union presence and 'hard' HRM approach	Less ability to poach printers due to diversification of technologies
Pharmco	New production-line technologies	Tradition of neglect of policies of skill development	Management perception of falling quality among job applicants
Retailco	Shift from price-based competition to emphasis on the brand	Weak partnership approach with union and 'soft' HRM policies of delayering and employee involvement	Management perception that job applicants from a shrinking labour pool require intensive induction training
Telecomco	New information and communication technologies reduce need for technical know-how; city pressures to reduce high-cost/high-skill workers	Less powerful unions with deregulation of sector	Diverse pool of available labour leads to greater use of agencies to screen new recruits

Developments in newspaper printing technology have also radically transformed the training policies and practices at Mediaco. The traditional craft of printing based on hot-metal typesetting has been replaced by the automatic transfer of text from journalists to the printers. However, the new technologies have also been associated with a need to invest in new training provision, such as the new apprenticeship scheme for printers at Mediaco. The scheme was introduced because managers recognized that changes in technology throughout the printing industry made it difficult to poach skilled printers from other parts of the industry since few print firms utilized the new 'offset' presses. The introduction of new technology at Pharmco challenged the existing range of training provided. New machinery on the production lines was introduced in a way that, on the one hand, took skill out of the production process, yet, on the other, encouraged a sense of ownership among operators. This sense of ownership was supported by expanding particular areas of training provision (see below).

In the food retail sector, while there have been major advances in technologies (see Chapter 2), it is the nature of competition in the sector that underpins much of the change in training provision. Alongside price competition and expansion into new products and services, such as financial, pharmacy and photographic services, food retail chains have been investing large sums of money in re-establishing their brands in an effort to attract a loyal and growing customer base. At Retailco, the expansion in induction training reflects this goal; the recent inclusion of a script for communicating with customers—'hello, can I help you, goodbye'—may also, in part, reflect the arrival in the UK of the US-owned Wal-Mart which is seen as the champion of standardized services delivery.

In the public services sectors, restrictions on government public spending act as an important performance imperative on organizations since they are required to find annual cost savings; one source of such savings is to change the skills mix. At Councilco the need to meet budget targets for school catering led to reduced working hours among staff (see Chapter 7) and, therefore, a pressure to buy in more ready-prepared produce and meals. Hence, despite efforts to train staff in general catering skills, in practice there is a diminishing role for the skills needed to prepare meals. Similarly, at Healthco the skills-mix policy implemented to reshape the composition of the nursing workforce was also, in part, driven by cost-cutting pressures to employ fewer expensive staff. According to the Deputy Director of Nursing Services, the policy of hiring more health care assistants than qualified nurses saved the Trust between £200,000 and £300,000 during the financial year 1996–7 alone. At both Healthco and Councilco, the inability to attract recruits by paying higher wages means that training provision plays an important role in the recruitment package. However, in the case of Councilco school catering, there is a danger that attractive training packages may become redundant as cost-minimizing changes in the production and delivery of meals reduce the catering skills required.

Against these diverse performance pressures, which tend to vary in degree and form across sectors, each organization also faced relatively similar pressures and opportunities for change arising from our second ring—internal constraints (see table 6.2). At all seven organizations, there is evidence of a transformed industrial relations context characterized by a much weakened trade-union movement and an associated boost in managers' confidence to design and implement new training policies. For example, at Mediaco the new graduate journalist training scheme was introduced soon after trade unions had failed to prevent the imposition of a pay freeze on all incumbent journalists in the editorial division. Human resources managers had thus been successful in reducing labour costs both by reducing the real wage rates of incumbent journalists and through recruiting and investing in graduates fresh from college on a relatively low trainee rate of pay. In the absence of a strong trade-union defence, Mediaco moved away from its position as a high-paying employer in the sector and achieved substantial cost savings. Of course, the danger is that the more experienced journalists would seek improvements in pay by moving to another newspaper company, and thus diminish the level of skills and experience required to produce a quality newspaper at Mediaco.

At Telecomco, unions were relatively powerless to prevent a number of new initiatives being implemented in the name of privatization and deregulation. Again, in the absence of significant resistance, Telecomco had been able to meet City expectations of headcount figures through the artificial recruitment of call-centre staff by temporary work agencies (TWAs). However, this policy generated escalating levels of staff turnover, leading to further costs through wasted training expenditure. This, in part, explains the policy of subcontracting part of the training provision to the job agency. In addition, Telecomco had reduced training in basic technical skills from two weeks to one, facilitated by the introduction of new information and communications technology systems.

New training initiatives for unqualified nurses at Healthco were unilaterally designed and implemented by managers—again, in a context of lessened trade-union involvement and changes in public policy that grants greater regulatory powers to local Trust managers. The terms and conditions of health care assistants are not covered by the national Whitley Council system, unlike all other professional and non-professional workers employed by the NHS. Consequently, unions do not have a role in the determination of new local pay scales, or annual increases. Similarly, they are excluded from the process of designing programmes of skills development, such as the NVQ scheme.

Finally, at Retailco and Bankco, the changing balance of training provision—from programmes that assist career advancement for staff at low levels of the job ladder to sophisticated packages of induction training—reflects, in part, the large costs of helping staff bridge the gap from low-level posts to middle-management positions. This gap, as we explore below, has widened in recent years as a result of delayering policies that removed mid-level tiers from the job hierarchy. Again, the restructuring of the job ladder has been possible in a context of weakened trade unions and strengthened managerial prerogative. Armed with a bundle of human resource management practices, managers have sought to foster a more direct, and even individualized, path of communication with employees. The goal of delayering is not only to increase opportunities for direct delegation of responsibilities and feedback on performance, but also to substitute for traditional union-regulated channels of communication.

Turning now to the third ring, that of external conditions (see table 6.2), we find that all seven organizations have had to respond to the changing skills composition of the external pool of available labour. In principle, when an organization can draw upon a large pool of potential job applicants, it is more likely to be successful in selecting candidates with relatively high skills and/or previous work experience. This diminishes the need to provide training. With a restricted pool of job applicants, the firm faces an incentive to provide training for two reasons: to enskill those new recruits with relatively few skills or limited work experience, and as part of a competitive recruitment package to attract high-quality applicants. The examples of subcontracting the initial training to the TWA by Telecomco and the expanded induction packages at Retailco and Bankco are thus, in part, a response to the perceived need to deliver basic skills to applicants with few skills and qualifications. Telecomco effectively relies on the TWAs not only to equip recruits with basic skills but also to screen out those deemed incapable of learning the skills once they enter the workplace. The need for general assistants at Retailco to learn a script in order to deal with customers reflects both a management aim to homogenize the quality and brand of customer service and a lack of confidence in workers' abilities and style of communication.

Plans to establish a new package of NVQ training at Pharmco also reflect a perceived deterioration in the quality of applicants for operator jobs and a need, therefore, to provide basic training. One of the plant managers explained to us that in the past Pharmco was successful in filling vacancies with people who had lost jobs from local manufacturing, textiles and engineering firms. But times had changed, and while there were still large numbers of applications for each advertised vacancy, there was a feeling among managers that standards had dropped, leading to a new policy of NVQ training coupled with rotation of operators from one task to another over their first twentyfour months in the job.

Changes in training provision at Healthco reflect, in part, the dual conditions of a tight labour market for qualified nurses and a relatively large pool of available labour for unqualified nursing positions. New recruitment packages for qualified nursing posts include the promise of opportunities for further training, as well as finances to attend conferences, as part of a competitive attempt to lure newly trained nurses into the Trust. Efforts to systematize training for unqualified nurses in the new management-defined post of health care assistant were partly a response to the failure of efforts to fill vacancies for qualified nursing posts and a need, therefore, to equip unqualified nurses with some of the basic skills to assist with nursing care on the ward. Trust managers claimed that the new training provision justified an expansion of the ratio of unqualified to qualified nursing staff on wards, on the one hand, and contributed towards reducing unemployment among the low skilled in the city centre, on the other.

Overall, while changes in training provision in our case study organizations reflect a range of distinct sectoral pressures and circumstances, there are also commonalities in industrial relations and labour market conditions (rings 2 and 3). The capacity for managers to design and implement new systems of training provision in a relatively unilateral fashion is an important similarity across all seven organizations. On closer inspection, it is also evident that changes in training provision had typically been implemented in association with other employer-led policies. The following section explores this relationship between new forms of training provision and other changes in employment organization—namely, new forms of work organization (delayering and skills mix), policies of temporary recruitment and new pay structures.

NEW TRAINING PROVISION AND EMPLOYMENT ORGANIZATION

Across the seven organizations, new training provision is intertwined with other changes in employment organization (see table 6.3). Changes in work organization play a particularly strong role in shaping the form of training. Two such changes are investigated here: delayering practices that have dismantled the traditional job ladder and skills-mix strategies that have broken down traditional lines of job demarcation. In both cases, training provision has been adapted either in response to, or in association with, the new form of work organization. The rather more indirect interlinkages with two additional areas of employment organization are also explored: the increasing use of agency temps and the introduction of new pay structures.

New training provision and delayering

At four organizations (Bankco, Councilco, Retailco and Telecomco), changes in training provision were, in part, a response to past policies that had flattened the job hierarchy by removing mid-level supervisory and management positions. While the initial intention of delayering policies may have been to improve communications between low-level and managerial employees, one further consequence has been the rupture of a natural skills progression for different groups of staff from one level of the internal job ladder to the next. Transformation in the job ladder at Bankco was associated with a shift from branch banking to call-centre banking; consequently, the internal labour market principle of steady acquisition of banking skills has been replaced by a relatively flat structure of clerical, supervisory and managerial positions. At Councilco, a broad range of job grades were removed across a number of departments, including community care and school catering. At Retailco, disbanded categories include general assistant supervisor, assistant department manager and department manager, and at Telecomco, restructuring of operator grades in 1988 removed the

Table 6.3. Links between training provision and employment organization

	Bankco	Councilco	Healthco	Mediaco	Pharmco	Retailco	Telecomco
Delayering	Shift from branch to telephone banking led to a flattened job hierarchy	Job levels removed in school catering and community-care provision	—	—	—	Delayering removed a range of job positions (e.g., supervisor and asst. manager posts); greater use of graduate recruits	Grade restructuring removed range of job positions
Skills mix	Teamwork and multi-task work encouraged; new technologies designed to maintain job variety among advisers	Retraining of home-carers for new teams of carers	Strategy to transform nursing skills mix (% of qualified nurses) across the Trust	New recruits into editorial offices and printworks encouraged to work across traditional job demarcations	Multi-skilling of operators; additional responsibilities for production lines	—	Job routinization pursued through new technologies and reduced training
Temporary work	High use of agency workers in telephone operations	—	High use of agency nurses in wards	—	Some use of agency workers	—	High use of agency workers in call centres
Pay structure	New pay structure links increments to skill acquisition and appraisal	Higher basic rate for multi-skilled carers, but abolishes unsocial hours premiums	—	Cash bonus to journalists for skills acquisition; at printworks, lower relative pay for new assistant posts	—	No skills-related pay advancement; instead, long-term service rewarded with share options and pension	—

positions of assistant supervisor and supervisor as intermediate ranks between operator and team manager.

In principle, delayering was implemented as a means of improving communication channels within the organizations. There was certainly some evidence of this, and with it the reporting of more job autonomy and the weakening of direct and intense supervisory surveillance. At Retailco, for example, one section manager explained:

It was all Mr and Mrs . . . Now it's all first name terms so it takes away the barriers and people are more comfortable and more ready to approach you if they need to.

(Female, full time, no. 1, Retailco1)

Another manager working nights at the same store told us that with the new arrangements:

It's a lot easier to speak to people because there are a lot less tiers up and down the line.

(Male, full time, no. 11, Retailco1)

In addition, at Telecomco, it seems that for some staff delayering represented a loosening of supervisory control and an increased autonomy. Those employed at the bottom end of the organization reported how they appreciated working with less monitoring from above:

When I first came, a lot of people seemed to just watch other people work, like the supervisors. They didn't have a proper job really; they just watched the operators working. But now, people are encouraged to think for themselves and not to need somebody looking over their shoulder.

(Female, full time, no. 1, Telecomco1)

A more striking finding, however, is of a general dissatisfaction with the way the flattening of the jobs ladder opened up a gulf between layers of managerial and non-managerial staff. What remains of the traditional finely divided job ladders is, in general, a three-tier structure consisting of low-skilled employees (assistants, operators, advisers), line management and senior management. Large gaps (of skill, responsibility, qualifications and salaries) exist between the low-skilled and managerial positions. A store manager at Retailco explained to us that in the new delayered store:

The promotional leap is too harsh for many general assistants . . . a lot of staff get frustrated with this leap . . . few staff feel they can do it.

(Female, full time, Retailco1)

At Bankco, 40 per cent of respondents in a staff survey considered 'lack of opportunities to progress' as the company's worst feature (Bankco staff survey 1998). The manager of one of the call centres acknowledged these sentiments:

[Bankco] now seeks to overcome retention problems by putting in place a clear career ladder through the centres. This should overcome the boredom problems of today, as well as keep hold of the managers of tomorrow.... [However,] one problem that persists is the gap between team leaders and team members.

(Female, full time, Bankco1)

These perceptions are supported by data collected on workforce composition at each of the workplaces visited as part of our research at these four organizations. As figure 6.1 demonstrates, the distribution of staff across the three bands is highly skewed, with a remarkably high proportion of the total workforce employed on the lower grades and few employed in line management and senior management positions.

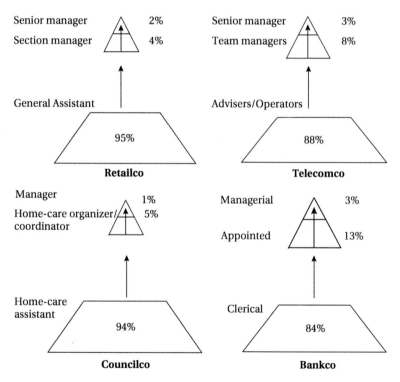

Fig. 6.1. Workforce structure in four case study organizations

Notes: Workforce composition represents an average of the workplaces visited for each of the four organizations where data were collected; the figure does not indicate horizontal delineations for the different groups (divided by occupation or by function or division) in order to emphasize the features that characterize the vertical segmentation of the workforce structure.

The distribution is particularly skewed at the three Retailco stores and the two Councilco community day-care centres (the only Councilco workplaces where sufficiently detailed workforce data were collected), where more than nine out of ten staff are employed on the lowest rung of the ladder. At Retailco an average of 95 per cent of staff across the three workplaces are general assistants and at Councilco an average of 94 per cent work as home-care assistants. For example, at the 24-hour Retailco store, just 23 employees are in supervisory or managerial positions compared to 439 employees who work as general assistants—with 412 employed on the bottom three of the five grades. The majority of general assistants work part time (335), with three in four of these jobs taken by women, whereas all managerial positions are full time, with an over-representation of men. At one of the Councilco community day-care centres we visited, there are 6 managers (working in a supervisory or coordinating role) and 108 staff employed as home-care assistants.

At the two Telecomco call centres where data were collected, 85 per cent and 92 per cent of employees work in non-supervisory or non-managerial positions as operators. At both workplaces this group is strongly female-dominated, despite differences in the relative importance of part-time work; 152 of the 184 operators at Telecomco1 work part time, compared to just 35 out of 176 operators at Telecomco2. Finally, the highest ratio of management to staff is found at Bankco, with an average of 84 per cent of the workforce employed on clerical grades across the three workplaces visited. At the workplaces in the Personal Banking Division, we found a similarity in gender composition of full-time workers across the three broad bands of job positions; here, the strongest lines of segmentation were between full-time and part-time workers.

The skewed distribution of staff generates an obvious limitation in promotion opportunities for lower-skilled staff. At the Retailco stores, where general assistants can progress from any of the five grades (A–E) to a section manager position, there is just one section manager for every twenty-six general assistants at the 24-hour store and at the medium-sized store, and a ratio of one to seventeen at the city-centre store. Opportunities appear less limited at Bankco workplaces where the ratio of middle-level ('appointed') managers to clerical staff is one to three in the Corporate Division workplace and one to eight at the two Personal Banking workplaces.

The recognition among managers that delayering had hindered possibilities for internal promotion was an important factor in stimulating the need for new training provision. At Retailco and Telecomco, managers had formalized pre-existing informal practices of on-the-job training with the apparent aim of enhancing employee motivation and commitment. However, these changes also carried the possibility of further frustrating low-level staff, since the training was not accompanied by new, codified job ladders. At Retailco, the range of job tasks carried out by general assistants had been carefully specified and set out in the form of 'workmate' instruction booklets for staff. These booklets include a general description of the role of the general assistant and details of the different tasks, divided into units and elements, with a small certificate corresponding to each unit. The idea is that each member of staff has their own booklet and works through it at their own pace. Experienced general assistants act as training sponsors; it is their role to train staff and to sign the small certificates. Hence, on-the-job training had been systematized and fully devolved to lower-level staff, lessening the need for mid-level managers to invest time in classroom training or at hands-on supervision.

However, Retailco general assistants seemed unconvinced of the need to formalize the learning process in this way. In our interviews, they emphasized that knowledge of these tasks had traditionally been passed on informally by staff with greater experience and that this system of task-based learning was still adequate. They stressed that the booklets themselves are pitched at a very low level and that their completion does not lead to an increase in pay, or bring them any closer to promotion. As such, in the views of the workers, the 'workmate' booklets do little to enhance skills or pay and career development within the organization.

Similarly, Telecomco operators said that skills that were traditionally picked up through informal on-the-job training had been reframed within a formalized system based on NVQ assessment. Again, the long-term aim was to devolve the positions of trainer and assessor to mid-level staff with several years of experience. However, the mid-level team managers we talked to were quick to point out the difficulties of assuming additional responsibilities:

To me, it is a bit of a hassle because I've got to fit it on top of everything else that I do. I find it hard to fit in.

(Female, full time, no. 2, Telecomco1)

This 'hassle' often meant that managers were unwilling or unable to prioritize time devoted to NVQ training. As a consequence, operators were often stuck in a drawn-out period of assessment. In one case, the planned six-month period of assessment took eighteen months to complete. The full-time operator explained:

Perhaps I am criticizing her [the team manager]. But she must be under pressure to do other things besides see to her team, because they have projects of their own to get through. Like NVQ is a good example. She started us off and then that was it. It was forgotten about.

(Female, full time, no. 5, Telecomco1)

At both organizations, strategies to codify the informal acquisition of skills appeared to be removed from efforts to plug the career gap between low-level and mid-level broad layers within the workplace. The requirement for low-level staff to acquire formal credentials as new tasks were learned may satisfy managers that low-level employees have a greater sense of job variety and progression, but, in practice, may do little to establish an effective platform for successful career advancement through up-skilling.

New training provision and skills mix

Management policies to adapt the skills mix of the workforce impact directly on the form and content of new systems of training provision. Six organizations had transformed the mix of skills associated with certain job functions, although this transformation reflects a widening of job tasks in some cases and a routinization of job tasks in others (see table 6.3). Policies of multi-skilling typically involve revised training programmes to extend the range of employee skills; policies of job routinization, in contrast, tend to reduce the quality and quantity of training provision.

Policies of multi-skilling, which were introduced at Bankco, Councilco and Pharmco, involve a genuine expansion of the range of job tasks. For example, within the Community Care Providers' Division at Councilco, incumbent home-care assistants were selected for the new post of STAR team workers and trained during a twelve-month, one-day release programme. Training covers a range of new areas of job responsibilities, including how to assess patients, how to monitor the stages of rehabilitation and how to write reports. This has expanded the range of job duties significantly. Also, at Pharmco, process and packing operators have been trained to work in self-empowered teams. Operators are involved in the layout of new production lines and are encouraged to rotate across job tasks on the line. This involves away-days, workshops and greater involvement of staff in project meetings with line managers.

At Bankco, multi-skilling involves integrating certain telephone operations with administrative work. At the business customer calls centre, advisers divide their time between answering telephone queries and dealing with related and additional paper work. Moreover, teams are organized to deal with telephone queries and administration on a geographical basis, rather than according to function, again enhancing the potential variety of job tasks encountered. In general, the principle of multi-skilling was welcomed among Bankco call centre advisers. As one commercial officer told us:

> Everyone's multi-skilled now rather than just being trained in one area, so that's the main difference.... I think it's a better thing really because people have had more training, more opportunities; people are more skilled at different things. You can say you know more so there's more opportunities.... They like people being mad on team-working and being able to rely on other people and not particularly knowing everything but knowing where to go for information if you don't know something.
>
> (Female, full time, no. 6, Bankco1)

There was also a general perception, however, that the investment in new training provision had not been complemented by sufficient change in employee discretion over how to vary and control the timing and division of tasks. Division of tasks between telephone and paperwork was predetermined by team managers. Among some of the advisers we talked to, it was felt that this created difficulties because of the uncertainties of length of telephone calls and the volume of associated paper work. As another adviser (in the same call centre) explained:

> People feel quite harassed in that they have the phone work to do and they have what they call 'the pap', which is paper work. And the paper work will build up and if you get say two hours on the phone and you have half an hour break where you could get some paper work done your last caller in a two-hour slot could take twenty minutes, twenty-five minutes of your half an hour when you're going to do your pap. And so you lose that time and then you're back on the phone again and so work builds up like that. I've noticed one or two people who seem to be quite stressed and I can recognize it because I was very stressed when I first came here.
>
> (Female, part time, no. 8, Bankco1)

At Telecomco, managers had decided against multi-skilling and expanding job tasks. Instead, new policies had been designed to simplify and to routinize jobs. For example, with the introduction of new communication technologies, managers separated out the job tasks carried out by operators according to the estimated level of skill required to answer a particular type of call. This simplified the nature of each operator's work and significantly reduced the need to provide new operators with costly programmes of job training. So, different groups of operators were trained in one particular area of services delivery only, reducing the costs and time associated with providing a training package covering a wide range of expertise in different types of query.

These policies of what is essentially job routinization led to problems of worker dissatisfaction and a deterioration in their commitment to work. Managers recognized these problems, but addressed them in a way that was quite separate from the issue of training provision. The approach adopted involved building a collaborative, team atmosphere in the call-centre workplaces—with the emphasis on the atmosphere, rather than the more substantive issues of multi-skilling or job rotation (which would, of course, have involved investment in costly training programmes, something Telecomco managers wanted to avoid). The atmosphere revolves around a monthly activity labelled 'the buzz'. Team managers at each of the call-centre workplaces became responsible for involving all staff in 'the buzz'. The chosen theme changes from month to month, ranging across such topics as the Country and Western day, or Caribbean day, each organized with food, fancy dress and quizzes. The idea is to encourage an informal working atmosphere that breaks the monotony of call-centre work, strengthens social ties between operators and team managers and reinforces the idea of a unity of purpose among the workforce.

New training provision and changes in skills mix at Healthco and Mediaco are less associated with multi-skilling or job routinization, per se, than with an organization-wide effort to dismantle traditional demarcations between occupational groups and to introduce new training provision that develops workforce skills in line with the changing needs of the organization. At Healthco, the new programme of NVQ training for health care assistants is interrelated with the strategy to reduce the high-skills composition among nursing staff. The training programme had been designed by management and sought to extend the duties of the traditional nurse auxiliary to overlap with qualified nursing staff duties; as the director of human resources put it, managers were busy 'chipping away at professional boundaries'. Each of the directorates had been charged with a policy target to reduce the ratio of qualified to unqualified nursing staff. For example, the largest department at the Trust, the Medical Directorate, was required to shift from an established ratio of 85 to 15 per cent of qualified to unqualified nursing staff to a target of 60 to 40 per cent.

At Mediaco, new training provision had also been implemented in a context of a skills-mix strategy that aimed both to dismantle traditional job demarcations and to reduce the proportion of relatively costly, high-skilled staff. New journalist recruits to the graduate training scheme were encouraged to work across previously demarcated job activities, such as sub-editing and page setting. At the printworks, printer assistants benefited from a new programme of training that enabled them to work alongside printers as part of a flexible team (for agreement to which printers were offered a lump-sum, non-consolidated payment). However, managers also established a new production assistant category, at a far lower rate of pay than the printer assistant, with the overall aim of generating long-term cost savings.

New training provision and temporary work

Formal and informal training provision at three of the seven organizations is directly shaped by the high use of agency temps (see Chapter 5). At Bankco and Telecomco, the high staff turnover rate associated with a high use of agency temps represented a major cost in terms of wasted training expenditures. At Bankco, the high staff turnover rate had adverse consequences for the informal nature of on-the-job training. Managers were concerned that permanent staff involved in the training of agency staff had become demoralized because they were unable to benefit from following the development of their trainees within the workplace. The problem was serious enough to raise concerns that there might be some link between the high use of agency staff and retention problems, even among senior staff in permanent posts.

At Telecomco, the use of agency temps was higher than at Bankco and was associated with a number of 'innovative' approaches to training provision. At one call centre, managers had a contract with an agency that imposed a training levy, so that if an agency worker quit Telecomco within a certain period he or she had to pay £300. At a second workplace, Telecomco managers arranged for an agency to provide workers with 'customer-focus' training prior to working at Telecomco. While this new arrangement may have reduced

Telecomco's expenditure on training, and thus reduced the need to recoup the investment through extended tenure of trained staff, it also raised problems of relying upon an external organization to provide the particular brand of customer service training that was a key feature of the company's competitive position.

The third example of a link between training and use of temporary staff is illustrated by the case of Healthco. As we have seen, Healthco covered unfilled nursing shifts by drawing on a pool of agency labour from 'the bank'. Sometimes, a particular ward encouraged nurses from its own team of staff to work overtime hours through 'the bank'. However, in many cases, each ward had to rely on agency nursing staff who were not familiar with the specific ward activities, or even had no experience of working within the Trust. In such cases, there was no provision of induction training, or otherwise, for the agency worker to acquire the basic information about the range of expected duties. Instead, more experienced nurses were expected to find time to teach agency workers the basic skills, despite the escalating demands on nurses' time and the rising levels of work intensity.

New training provision and pay structures

The development of new training provision is also often associated with new pay structures, or forms of payment systems. Indeed, from our evidence, it is clear that at three organizations (Bankco, Councilco and Mediaco) opportunities for new training provision are explicitly linked with new skills-related pay structures. There is also the case of Retailco, however, where the reverse trend is apparent—that is, a decoupling of the pay structure from skills development.

At Bankco, managers introduced a revised codification of tasks that links a finely divided structure of pay increments with acquisition of new skills. As new tasks are learned, a grade 4 adviser, for example, moves to the next increment within the grade 4 pay band. In part, the detailed codification of job tasks and pay increments at Bankco was a response to the radical restructuring of the banking career ladder, following the shift to call-centre operations. Training in generic competencies were substituted for technical skills in banking, and it was felt that there was a need for the new structure of pay and training to adapt to changes in IT systems and new product knowledge. However, the fine differentiation of the job-based pay profile met with mixed reactions concerning the equation between acquisition of skills and pay progression. One of the commercial officers put it like this:

Sometimes I feel I've worked harder than I needed to and that it should be more recognized than it is. You are recognized, but sometimes you feel like you're not recognized enough really. But they're bringing in the grades within your grades so within a grade 5 there'll be all sorts of different steps and your pay rise and your pay can go up as you learn new things.... But maybe that's just an excuse to say you don't know enough to give you a pay rise. Maybe that's just an excuse not to give you upgrades, just giving you extra levels within your grades so it takes you longer to get an extra grade in full. I don't know whether they're trying to rip us off or whether it's a good thing that. I'm a bit wary, a bit sceptical.

Q. It might slow down the period for promotion?

Yes. Say I'm a grade 5 now. If I do well and I apply for a grade 6 I've got a whole new grade. What they can keep saying is, 'You don't know this, you don't know that. Let's just give you one more level within your grade.' It might slow things down a bit. It might be a bit of a rip-off at the end of the day.

(Female, full time, no. 6, Bankco1)

In fact, despite the expanding number of job codes to encourage skills development, the overall pay range was fairly limited. At the time of our research, a newly recruited grade A adviser would earn £9,500, with increments of £250 subject to six-monthly appraisals, and advisers on grades B and C would receive pay within a range of £10,500 and £12,700 (again, with six-monthly increments subject to skills acquisition). While some Grade C advisers could potentially earn as much as £14,700, managers expected that most would remain on £12,700. The relatively low levels of pay may partly explain the negative reaction to the new job codification system among some of the employees we talked with.

The multi-skilling identified in the Community Care Provision Department at Councilco was also accompanied by an increase in the basic rate of pay. In practice, however, care workers who transferred to the new team-based work also experienced an indirect cost. Instead of the Monday to Friday work schedule, multi-skilled carers have the right to just one out of three weekends off, and are expected to rotate across early shifts (8 am–2 pm) and late shifts (4 pm–10 pm) (see Chapter 7 for more details). Crucially, all unsocial hours premium payments were abolished. Hence, despite the higher basic wage rate, a weekly wage calculated on the old lower rate plus premium payments for unsocial hours would have been substantially higher for many workers.

The printworks at Mediaco provides a third illustration of efforts to institutionalize a revised skills-related pay scale in line with new training provision. The new apprenticeship and pay scale for printers broke from the traditional single rate pay structure. New apprentices advanced up a relatively broad pay scale (from £12,869 to £29,277) during the period of apprenticeship (typically, four years from the age of 21 to 25 years old). In the past, printers would have been hired at the top rate. Managers explained to us that the old high-entry rate was required to poach printers from other firms; in contrast, the new arrangements represented a more practical solution to the classic internal labour market balance of reward to initial low levels of productivity among trainees and the need to retain staff on completion of training. Whatever the merits of this opinion, the exclusion of unions from the pay-bargaining process clearly facilitated the lowering of entry rates.

At Retailco, we found evidence of new training programmes that were entirely disconnected from the pay structure. For example, general assistants are encouraged to complete individual 'workmate' certificates, but this does not lead to an increase in pay. In fact, expectations of pay advancement among general assistants are more closely linked to a form of 'welfare provision', as Sanford Jacoby (1984) called it, rather than with a path of steady up-skilling. Retailco management appeared to have opted for a relatively effective policy of fostering the commitment and loyalty of staff through a long-term promise of income rewards. One general assistant told us:

To be honest, it's the benefits that have kept me here. When I was shelf-filling, I thought—god I can't go on doing this—and I did look round at other jobs. But when you think you get 10 per cent knocked off every shopping bill and the pension is quite good.... Things like, not just profit-related pay, but we get shares as well. You also get the save-as-you-earn schemes for shares. In the five years that we've had them we've doubled our money. Retailco shares have shot up in price.... When I say I'd like to move, my husband will just say—hang on, we've got this save-as-you-earn that's going to mature—and so on. It's like golden handcuffs really.

(Female, part time, no. 6, Retailco1)

Overall, we found the design and implementation of new policies of training provision at all seven organizations to be closely linked to other changes in employment organization, particularly changes in job hierarchies and skills mix, but also more indirectly linked with changes in the use of agency temps and the principles underpinning new pay structures. These links raise the possibility that employer-led training provision has been shaped by the need to respond to the problems, challenges and opportunities raised by a range of areas of employment organization, rather than the single objective of promoting skills development among the workforce, per se.

RESPONSES TO CHANGE

In our interviews with employees at the seven organizations, what was striking was the way in which the relevance and effectiveness of new policies of training provision were interpreted in two broad ways. First, new training provision was evaluated according to whether or not it had led to an up-skilling of the bulk of the workforce. For most of the people we talked to this involved a fairly straightforward evaluation. However, for older workers, who had a long work history, the issue was not around the particular net gains or losses of the latest training programme, but how recent changes measured up against a much longer period (typically, two to three decades) of changes in the skills required in the job. Secondly, employees assessed training policies as part of a broader context of change in employment policies and practices. So a person's views on the merits of a particular change in training provision were balanced against their views on other interrelated changes in the nature or terms and conditions of work. For example, many employees expressed concern as to whether new training provision would be able to bridge the gap between low-level and mid-level posts, following past policies of delayering. Also, there was a view among most people we talked to that new training provision ought to have some association with opportunities for career or pay advancement, which, as we described above, had been dismantled in many organizations.

Skills are not what they used to be

Despite positive reaction to new training and skills development programmes, employees in all seven organizations were keenly aware that the skills required for their present job were not of a comparable quality to those of previous times. For example, a Bankco call-centre adviser with eight years' prior experience at a building society had been ready for a new challenge in the changing world of financial services, but was disappointed by what she found:

I used to go into work at [local building society] and I would have particular work to deal with. I could organize my day... I could say I've got this, this, this, this and I could prioritize my work.... I found that coming here you're not responsible for anything in particular. You just come in and you're given pieces of work to do and you just get your work done and then go home at the end of the day.... I can't actually say I'm responsible for any particular thing.

(Female, full time, no. 1, Bankco1)

Another telephone banking adviser was convinced that technical knowledge was no longer needed in banking:

Q. Are you required to have any kind of detailed knowledge about banking and the technical skills involved in banking?

Not really, no. Because everything's—if you need—if a customer asks for a balance, it's on the screen. If a customer asks 'has a cheque gone through?', it's on the screen, kind of thing. I don't think you need any.

(Male, part time, no. 7, Bankco1)

At the Mediaco printworks, the changing nature of skills was directly linked to changing technologies. Advances in technology had eliminated the role of major traditional craft workers, such as engravers, compositors, copyreaders and stereotypers. In interviews, older workers were quick to identify a deskilling trend in the industry as a whole. Comparing the past with the present, a former copyreader, who then got a job as a paper handler in the warehouse, told us:

The jobs are all on the downward turn for me. I don't particularly like what I do. I was a copyreader which I enjoyed doing.... But now the journalists do it themselves on the computers. Of course, that dispensed with a lot of work.... And the saving must have been enormous in labour costs and jobs—very sadly, a lot of jobs.... I must confess there's not a lot of skills in here today. They tell you you're skilled, but I've worked on the machines.... The machines are a damn sight more complex.... You do need skills to a degree. But it's repetitious.... Basically you come in this job and you do the same thing every night, or every day, and really it is just like working at Ford's on the production line. It's no different. It's just the same thing. There's no variation.

(Male, full time, no. 12, Mediaco1)

Changes in the organization of local authority school catering met with similar reactions. For Councilco school catering assistants, the delivery of pre-prepared food removed many of the catering skills that initially attracted people to the job. One general catering assistant explained how when she first started the job in the late 1980s, she worked in a team (a 'kitchen brigade') made up of a head cook, a supervisor, two or three staff responsible for the vegetables and others responsible for the meat and fish. But, again, times had changed:

I don't enjoy myself and the work is different. I'm not involved in the cooking any more like I used to be and basically it's a lot of frozen stuff now. So of course, a lot of cutbacks on staff and where the frozen stuff has come in, basically like the food has replaced people because it's coming in pre-pack and things now.

(Female, part time, no. 2, Councilco1)

Moreover, a number of recently hired catering assistants felt that their City and Guilds qualifications in catering were wasted in the new environment of fast food preparation. Such clear frustration among staff raises the question of whether individual organizations can design and implement adequate training and skills development programmes in light of external pressures to adapt systems of production and work in a context of changing technologies and pressures to cut costs. These contradictory pressures were also evident at Bankco, where, despite a relatively high degree of multi-skilling, telephone advisers were tired of the intensive, production-line character of work:

You feel a bit like it's mass production.... Here it's just a case of a call, a call, and at the end of the day it's 'how many calls have you taken?'.

(Female, part time, no. 13, Bankco2)

We encountered these feelings of frustration and disappoint-ment most often at the Telecomco workplaces—which is perhaps unsurprising given the unwillingness, or inability, of Telecomco man-agers to invest time and money in policies of multi-skilling. The call-centre operators we talked to were concerned with both the lack of discretion in their work and the longer-term dilution of knowledge associated with the introduction of more sophisticated telecommu-nications systems:

Our daily job really consists of once you come in the morning, you log onto your computer, your calls just come in. So you just take whatever calls come to you. It's what the customers want. You've not got a set routine of things to go through. It's just what comes along. There's nothing specific I can tell you really about it.

(Female, full time, no. 3, Telecomco1)

Broadening the skill base—but at a cost

Clearly, then, a number of employees believed that their job and the associated level of skill it required were 'on the downward turn'. It is also notable that for these workforce groups, the perceived deskilling is associated with the introduction of new technologies—particularly, information and communications technologies. But this was not a general finding for all the people we talked to. Nor have all areas of work experienced significant change as a result of new technologies. At some of our organizations, there do appear to have been genuine efforts to enskill groups of staff who had traditionally fallen outside the net of policies of skills development and career advancement. At Healthco, for example, former nurse auxiliaries who transferred to the new grade of health care assistant welcomed the NVQ programme of training that accompanied it and interpreted the move as a positive change in status:

They're trying to upgrade everybody now.... Basically, as a health care assistant now, I basically do the same as a staff nurse [qualified nurse grade D and above] other than anything to do with drugs.

(Female, part time, no. 3, Healthco3)

New duties include patient observations, which involves taking blood pressure, temperature and heart rate, as well as the traditional duties of the nurse auxiliary, such as bed-bathing and stock-keeping. Another former nurse auxiliary told us:

We've got a lot more responsibility now than when we did when I first came here. You couldn't do anything.... All you did was change the beds and do the bedpans and that was your lot. You weren't allowed to do anything like blood pressures or anything like that.

(Female, full time, no. 4, Healthco3)

There is further evidence of policies to multi-skill or upgrade training provision at Councilco and Mediaco. But these came at a cost. Home-carers had to forgo unsocial hours payments and stable shifts to benefit from multi-skilling (see Chapter 7). And among printers, although the new apprenticeship scheme was welcomed for providing externally recognized credentials, this was weighed against the cost of losing the right to negotiate changes in skills and training provision. One printer with more than thirty years in the business put it like this:

Q. What about people coming into the industry today?
They have them trained and they've got to have an education standard. They have to go to college, which again is a good thing for them in my opinion. I have no objection. I think it's a good thing. They are creating something. But they have total control over this.

Q. Who's 'they'?
The management, of course. The unions are non-existent now.

(Male, full time, no. 12, Mediaco1)

Training policies are not always what they seem

We have already described how peoples' views on training provision typically reflected a broader judgement of several accompanying changes in employment policies. In addition, some of the people we talked to about new training provision were suspicious about the 'real' intentions of management.

For example, at the Mediaco printworks, the new apprenticeship positions for printers were generally understood as part of a broader management strategy to merge traditional craft and craft assistant positions and to introduce a new generic production assistant post. But for many printers, this new assistant post conflicted with the strong craft tradition of the industry, particularly as those taken on to fill the positions were expected to work across different departments and their tasks were designed to overlap with the traditional craft of plate-makers. One plate-maker was convinced that the overriding objective of management was in fact to cut costs:

You see what we're doing now we're not starting plate-makers, we're starting production assistants.... A production assistant is on half the salary of our pre-press operatives, our plate makers. [The company] realize because of the new technology and a lot of the machines and everything like this, the skill is actually going out of our job. So they are not having people on our salary. They are having people on half our salary to do our job. This causes a little bit of friction obviously. But eventually over a period of time the older people will retire and they'll have a new wage structure.

(Male, full time, no. 7, Mediaco1)

And at the editorial offices of Mediaco, the new graduate training scheme for journalists was also viewed with distrust concerning the real goals of management, for similar reasons. One senior reporter told us:

The face of the workforce here has changed considerably over the last three years or so. I know when I came here as a reporter... [Mediaco] was always considered, certainly in this city, the pinnacle of newspaper journalism and up there with the nationals. Staff were very well respected. Everyone knew that they were good writers. That perception of [Mediaco], certainly from inside, and I imagine to a certain extent from outside—because you can't fool the public all the time—has changed considerably. With the greatest respect to my colleagues, there's a lot of young staff who are here now with very little experience who wouldn't have had a cat in hell's chance of getting in before-hand. And they're coming here for one reason. Because they're cheap.

(Male, full time, no. 2, Mediaco2)

At Healthco, while health care assistants welcomed the new attention to job expansion and skills development, they were also aware of some resistance and suspicion from qualified nurses. In part, the suspicion was fuelled by knowledge of the broader management objective to dilute the skills mix among the nursing workforce. A nursing auxiliary, who had just transferred over to the new position of health care assistant, described the situation to us as follows:

They [qualified nurses on the ward] don't ask me to do things which I'm now trained to do.... They're frightened of change basically, because they've been here so long and that change is going to happen whether they like it or not. It's out of my hands. The only reason I wanted to do my NVQ at the time when I first came was because I wanted to help them as much as I could because I know they're short staffed.

(Female, full time, no. 2, Healthco3)

Hence, in organizations where new investment in skills development had been introduced as part of a wider, cost-reducing, skills-mix strategy there is some evidence of a weakening of cooperation between workforce groups and a decline in confidence and trust in managerial objectives. Together, these changes in work experience have a strong impression on people's overall assessment of new training provision.

Training and careers do and don't mix

A further issue that people considered important in their overall assessment of new training provision is the extent to which training provides opportunities for internal progression within the organization. For example, one health care assistant was quite pragmatic about the limitations to the new NVQ training programme in this respect:

You're not a threat to anyone that's qualified. But it makes you think, in my own little area I could go on and maybe do that if I had the right training. But you're never going to be a qualified nurse. It's just that it makes your role far more interesting and you feel as though you're contributing more.

(Female, full time, no. 7, Healthco3)

So although the overlap with qualified nursing duties represents a significant upskilling of the work of NVQ-trained health care assistants, the traditional boundaries between job ladders and job status appear firmly entrenched. At Bankco, the emphasis on multi-skilling, coupled with the shift to telephone banking, completely altered employee expectations of what was required to progress in a banking career. The shift from technical banking knowledge to generic customer care skills means that 'soft skills' are seen to be critical in guaranteeing promotion through the low-level grades. In one interchange with a commercial officer at a business call centre, the situation was illustrated as follows:

Q. And what kind of things do you think they were looking for in the promotion [from grade 4] to grade 5?

They like people being mad on team-working and being able to rely on other people, and not particularly knowing everything but knowing where to go for information if you don't know something. There's certain things that they like. They like you being keen on the phones and all this telephone banking and everything, things like that.

(Female, full time, no. 6, Bankco1)

Across all organizations, perhaps the most startling finding was the degree to which employees internalized their failure to progress up the job ladder. For low-level staff, knowledge of limited promotion opportunities was often accompanied by a conscious questioning of their ability, confidence, or suitability to make the leap to the next level. In some cases, this was linked with a deep sense of resignation, a feeling that there was no escape from the current job. Others questioned their own worth and capacities in the face of a changing set of job descriptions. A home-carer in the Community Care Division at Councilco felt that:

I haven't got a lot of ambition.... I'm not motivated enough to want to be a coordinator (the next level up).... I wouldn't like the responsibility, it's not suitable.

(Female, full time, no. 6, Councilco1)

For others, the expression of dissatisfaction was much more pointed. At Telecomco it was made clear to us that delayering had not been achieved without pain. The removal of layers involved disestablishing jobs and relocating their occupants—often to lower positions within the company. An operator who had been demoted from the abandoned supervisory post following delayering in 1988 told us:

I was very bitter at the time. It upset me a lot. It sort of knocks your self esteem and you think I'm not good enough. But then I used to think there's a purpose behind it.... I think [team managers] are under a lot more pressure than the old operator supervisor job was. There are more responsibilities. I'm thinking at my time of life, do I really need that? The money would be nice, but we can manage quite well on what I'm being paid.... I'm not bothered. We can manage quite well. Why should I have more grey hairs, there's no point. I've lost all that drive if you like that I used to have.

(Female, full time, no. 5, Telecomco1)

The failure to progress is clearly not simply a matter of individual acquisition of skills, since the changing nature of work conspires against career progression in a context where traditional job ladders have been delayered, opening up a form of promotion, or skills, gap within the organization. Moreover, in those organizations where informal on-the-job training had traditionally been passed on from senior to junior employees, new recruits who had to rely on new employer-designed formal training programmes sometimes experienced a lack of co-operation from disenfranchised, more experienced workers.

CONCLUSION

New policies of training provision are closely linked to other areas of employment reorganization. As such, their design and overall effects on the experience of work can not be expected solely to reflect the objectives of upskilling and career advancement no matter how important these may be to the particular organization. Mid-level managers with responsibility for the daily operations and decisions of individual workplaces or departments face the dilemma of implementing training against a backdrop of pressures to change the skills mix, to employ agency temps and to cut labour costs. For employees, the conflicting signals are only too apparent. The effectiveness of training provision is thus judged against both longer-term changes in the nature of work and management attempts to dilute the skills base in an effort to reduce the proportion of relatively expensive groups of staff.

7

The End of Standard Working Time?

INTRODUCTION

Many authors have drawn attention to the processes that are reshaping and reorganizing working time (Bosch 1999; Bosch *et al.* 1994; Golden 2001; Green 2001; Harvey 1999; Hochschild 1997; Kalleberg and Epstein 2001; Lehndorff 1998, 1999; OECD 1995). This has most often been understood quite narrowly as part of a general increase in time flexibility. However, these changes to time scheduling and the organization of work have potentially wider implications that go to the very heart of the 'employment relation'.

WORKING TIME: AN OVERVIEW

The changes to working time within our seven organizations are outlined in table 7.1. These need to be understood against a background of previous working-time patterns and the mode of regulation of working time that operated in each. A tradition of regulated working time was common at each organization, based around notions of standard working hours, premium payments for unsocial hours and, in most cases, voluntary rather than scheduled extra and unsocial hours working. The strength of the regulation and the extent to which overtime and unsocial working hours were voluntary varied from one organization to the next. Trade-union power at local and national levels has obviously been important here, as has the nature of the industry. For example, both Councilco and Healthco have traditionally been strongly unionized and regulated, but significant overtime and unsocial hours had only been worked at Healthco when the nature of the service makes particular

Table 7.1. Changes in working-time arrangements

	Bankco	Councilco	Healthco	Mediaco	Pharmco	Retailco	Telecomco
Extended opening or operating hours	Extended hours with shift from branch to telephone banking	Extended hours in leisure services; more weekend, evening and night working in community care	Extended hours in some departments bringing them into line with the majority already with 24 hours, 7 days working	Extended, 24 hours, 7 days per week operations at print works; late shift and compulsory Sunday working at newspaper	Extended 24 hours, 7 days per week operations at 'tablets' manufacturing	Extended late-night opening; open 24 hours in selected stores	Extended operating hours in telemarketing; lengthening of the standard working week for repair and maintenance workers
Increased 'productive' hours/reduced overtime		Reductions in core hours; flexible scheduling to eliminate unnecessary time on the job	Changes in rehabilitation to reduce in-patient stays; substitution of lower-paid for higher-paid staff in catering and medical divisions	Complex 39-week rota for print works day staff (37.5 hours p.w.) eliminates overtime	Complex shift patterns but overtime remains high in both packing and processing	All breaks are unpaid (full-timers required on-site for 39 hours but paid 36.5 hours)	Reduction in part-time shifts from 5 to 4 hours to reduce paid breaks; extended normal contractual hours for field engineers reduces overtime

Standardized unsocial or extra hours	Lower unsocial hours premiums in 'green-field' call centres; new harmonized agreement raises premiums in greenfield site but lowers them for rest of staff	New home care assistant teams introduced with lower unsocial hours premiums; use of casual staff to fill shifts, rather than pay overtime	Nurses' overtime organized through the 'bank' (paid at basic rates); high levels of unpaid overtime working; reduction in night premiums for health care assistants; no unsocial hours pay but higher basic pay on some new contracts in rehabilitation	Night-shift premium and day-shift rotation allowance abolished for printers; unsocial hours pay abolished for editorial staff; overtime to be taken as time off in lieu	Prospective introduction of 'annualized hours' in order to stop overtime and replace it with a 'disturbance allowance'	Saturday premium abolished (1995); reduced night shift premium from 33 per cent to flat-rate payments	Field engineers may be required to work additional flexible hours (up to 4 per week) paid at basic rate; extended flexible shift working for full-time operators without unsocial premiums

demands on time. Among the private sector service organizations, Mediaco and Telecomco traditionally had the strongest level of trade-union regulation of working time, but it was only at Telecomco that overtime and unsocial hours payments had been a significant part of the employment and rewards system, especially among the field engineers. There had been little overtime or unsocial working hours at the newspaper division of Mediaco, although any that did occur was remunerated with premium rates. Even in the printing division of Mediaco, there had been no tradition of continuous shift working. Some weekends and night shifts were worked on the basis of additional shift premiums or paid overtime. Bankco and Pharmco had less of a militant trade-union history, but these organizations had still worked around the notion of standard hours with overtime both voluntary and rewarded at premium rates. Retailco probably had the least developed tradition of standard or regulated working-time arrangements and in recent years had implemented a fairly continuous extension of both operating hours and working-time flexibility requirements.

Despite the different starting points, each organization had either experienced significant working-time change over the previous five years or was in the process of implementing changes (see table 7.1). These took three different forms: the extension of operating and opening hours; the rescheduling of work to increase productive hours and/or to reduce overtime; and the reduction in distinctions between standard and unsocial or standard and extra hours.

Bankco perhaps experienced the most dramatic change in working time culture. The organization had been traditionally organized around standard daytime, Monday to Friday, branch banking hours, with its opening hours and bank holidays an ingrained part of the culture of the workforce. In the 1990s the move to telephone banking involved staff working late nights and at weekends. In the other organizations the changes were more an intensification of flexible and unsocial working hours. This was particularly the case in Healthco, an organization well used to providing 24-hour cover, seven days a week in many departments. This policy of continuous cover was being introduced into all departments, instead of just those where patient needs made it necessary. The objective was to reduce costs by improving patient throughput. Retailco, which had been opening until 8 pm and on Sundays since the early 1990s, had recently extended late-night opening to 10 pm or midnight, and moved to 24-hour opening in some stores. Telecomco had also always provided 24-hour cover in some of its operations, but longer hours had been introduced into some other departments, including telemarketing and repair and maintenance, as a response to perceived customer needs. Pharmco had gradually been extending the amount of work its staff performed at the weekend. In both its processing and production plants, increased product demand had been met in the short term through the introduction of new shift patterns. In Councilco and Mediaco operating and opening hours continued to vary by department. Councilco's leisure department opened longer hours to meet consumer demand and social services was providing more weekend, evening and night cover in response to the greater dependency levels of the people for whom they provided care. At Mediaco, the printworks moved to a 24-hour working day in order to increase the use of machinery, while in the newspaper division late shifts and compulsory weekend working were introduced to improve the coverage of news events.

The desire to save costs and raise productivity also lay behind much of the rescheduling of working-time arrangements. The objectives of the rescheduling included, inter alia, reducing 'slack time', substituting lower-paid for higher-paid staff, reducing the number of hours paid at overtime rates and improving operational efficiency. Working-time changes in Healthco and the home-care sections of Councilco were part of both organizations' drive for greater operational efficiency and the pressure to reduce the length of patients' stay in hospitals. At Mediaco, increased plant utilization involved not only extended shift arrangements and the elimination of paid overtime but also very significant reductions in staffing levels. In other cases of cost saving, working-time changes had a more direct effect on labour efficiency. For example, within its call centres, Telecomco sought to minimize paid breaks and 'busy-time' breaks by moving from a 5-hour to a 4-hour shift for part-timers, thereby reducing paid breaks from 30 minutes per shift to 15. Field engineers were required to work weekends and evenings to match the patterns of consumer demand. At Councilco's school catering service, unnecessary hours (when schools were quiet as, for example, during examination periods) were eliminated. The tightened control over standard and extra working hours of manual workers often had indirect impacts on the working hours and wage–effort relationships of managerial supervisory staff. Without slack (spare time) in the system, the need to perform unscheduled work often left supervisory staff under pressure to work extra hours.

All seven organizations had also sought, or were seeking, to reduce distinctions between standard and unsocial hours working through either a reduction in premium rates or the consolidation of previous enhancements into the basic rate. In the public sector organizations, national collective agreements limited the scope to remove such payments. However, various strategies were deployed to overcome these constraints. At Healthco, for example, health care assistants were recruited on local terms that involved lower entitlements to night and overtime premiums. More generally, nursing staff were encouraged to sign on with 'the bank', to enable flexible overtime to be worked without premium rates. Bank nursing staff were also called upon to cover unsocial hours, and there was a general reliance on unpaid overtime among supervisory as well as managerial staff. Flexible scheduling without extra premiums was also introduced as part of new contracts for selected groups. Staff in the rehabilitation centre at Healthco were being offered new contracts on higher basic pay, but this involved work scheduled over seven days without additional premiums. At Councilco's Community Care Department, staff were being employed on new contracts devoid of any social/unsocial hours distinction. In these ways, therefore, national agreements were avoided and the organization of time payment radically altered in these public sector organizations.

There was even more evidence of change in the private sector. At Mediaco, Retailco and Telecomco compensation for working unsocial hours was reduced across the board. Telecomco extended the time period over which unsocial hours payments were not payable to 8 am to 8 pm, Monday to Saturday for clerical staff and Sunday premiums were reduced to time and a half from double time. This provided a framework for hiring temporary staff to fill most of the unsocial hours but on relatively low rates of pay. Retailco eliminated its Saturday premium for new staff in 1995 and converted its night-shift premium to a relatively low flat rate payment. However, it retained its Sunday premium at double time. Bankco initially retained premiums in its older sites and in its first call centre, but reduced the rates for unsocial and extended hours in its second call centre based on newly recruited staff. The operation of two different forms of time payments proved not to be sustainable, however, and in a major exercise in 1998 premium payments were harmonized across the company at below the traditional levels but above those that had operated in its new call centre. Finally, and in contrast to our other private sector organizations, Pharmco retained all its payments for working unsocial hours. While its move in the mid-1990s to a shift system in its manufacturing plants gave management greater flexibility around working-time schedules, staff still received premium payments for weekend work over the contracted hours. However, the new annualized hours system, which it was engaged in introducing at the time of our research, would again reduce the distinction between social and unsocial hours.

The main changes we have discussed so far have been for the most part one way, albeit with different levels of intensity. They have been towards the deregulation of working time. In their detail, they invite two critical questions. First, how are these changes to be explained? Secondly, how far do they represent a transformation in the ways in which time is understood and regulated at work? Does this represent a move towards a new form of employment relationship, and, if so, is this form sustainable over the medium to long term?

PRESSURES TOWARDS WORKING-TIME CHANGE: PERFORMANCE IMPERATIVES OR CHANGING POWER RELATIONS?

To what extent can the observed changes be explained by new performance imperatives or are they better understood as a response to either changes in internal power relations ('macho management') or changes in the pattern of external forces and conditions? Certainly, the pattern of causation is likely to be multi-layered and interactive, as our three-ring framework set out in Chapter 1 would suggest. Thus, restrictive performance pressures at the level of the organization may trigger management to make changes in employment conditions not otherwise on the agenda. Other studies have argued that management is often placed under such strong and complex levels of performance pressure that it has little alternative but to shift some of the burden onto labour by increasing flexibility and work intensification, even where this requires moving away from established work organization and working-time norms (see Burchell *et al.* 1999). The increasing discretion enjoyed by management in the UK to determine working-time arrangements at the corporate or even the workplace level makes it an attractive policy option. Moreover, many of the changes introduced may stem from management opportunism, taking advantage of changes in the internal balance of power or of perceived changes in external conditions and practices to reshape established norms and practices with respect to working-time arrangements and effort levels. Part of the process of change may be attributed to the exercise of increased managerial authority in the workplace, fuelled by broader political acceptance within society of flexible working-time and more commodified employment relations as a normal employment form. We thus need to explore not only the presence of, but also the interrelationships between, the three rings of influence: performance pressures, internal constraints and external conditions.

It is clear that performance pressures (expressed though changing competitive and technological conditions) help explain many of the changes in working-time arrangements. These pressures vary between organizations, of course. In Bankco, Pharmaco, Retailco and Telecomco changes to product markets increased the pressure to extend opening hours to match new customer demands. For example, the move in the banking sector towards telephone-based service delivery and the deregulation of the product market allowed the entry of new competitors and placed pressure on established banks to protect their market shares through the development of 24-hour banking facilities (Leyshon and Thrift 1993; Tickell 1997). Bankco management saw this as a new opportunity that would allow a primarily regional bank to increase its share of the national market. Deregulation of the product market was also an immediate factor at Telecomco. In addition to providing 24-hour cover for its essential telecommunications services, it also had to engage in telemarketing and other activities outside normal office hours to maintain or increase its market share.

Heightened global competition coupled with customer demand for differentiated products led Pharmco to alter its production runs, which necessitated (in the short term at least) an extension of plant opening hours. In Retailco, the moves towards more unsocial working hours arose out of inter-firm competition on length of opening hours, a process that started with late-night opening but which moved to Sunday opening (Gregory 1995) and more recently extended to very late-night opening, including 24-hour opening. Such opening hours are still relatively unusual in Britain and are not common on mainland Europe (Baret *et al.* 1999; Neathey and Hurstfield 1995). In part, it relates to the general change in work contracts and the need for shopping facilities at different times. It also suggests that other social or lifestyle factors are influencing these changes (Burke and Shackleton 1996). Performance pressures took a different form at Mediaco. Here, the main pressures for changing working hours were associated with drives to cut capital costs by spreading overheads and extending plant utilization. In fact, in each of the private sector cases, working-time change was an explicit part of new competitive strategies.

In the public sector organizations, on the other hand, working-time change was the indirect effect of attempts to cut costs in the context of both reducing budgets and changing demands for services (Cutler and Waine 1994; Ranade 1994). At Councilco these pressures saw labour costs being reduced as a result of a general attack on slack time. At Healthco there was less evidence of a successful and systematic response. In this organization managerial authority was still contested, between professional medical staff and general management (see Chapter 9). This contested terrain prevented the development of hospital-wide policies to use working-time reform as a means of dealing with staff shortages and also led to ad hoc, contradictory, and often self-defeating policies to deal with budget pressures. In only a few departments was working-time change being used as part of a strategic approach to improve patient throughput. In others, working-time change was more of an unplanned consequence of budget cuts. Unfilled staff vacancies resulted either in high levels of unplanned overtime working or high unplanned use of agency workers, as the need to provide basic services in the end took precedence over the impera-tive to cut costs. However, these conditions provide just a surface justification for the implementation of new forms of working-time. It is in the *method* of implementation of new working-time policies where we can perhaps trace the influence of both the second and the third rings of influence.

At one end of the spectrum is Mediaco, which explicitly took advantage of the changed labour-management relations in the print industry following the Wapping dispute in 1986 (Littleton 1992). The change in organizational and employment cultures at Mediaco was hastened by the closure of its printworks and the transfer of the busi-ness to a new site on the edge of town, where printers had been recruited externally and without the protection of union recognition. Within the newspaper offices the new working-time arrangements were imposed on reluctant journalists and sub-editors. Those who wished to take early retirement were encouraged to do so and replaced by new, often more junior (and hence cheaper) staff on more flexible terms and conditions.

Telecomco also took advantage of the uncertainties associated with product market deregulation to adopt a radical policy of downsizing followed by the extensive use of agency temps to achieve its new working-time patterns (Ward *et al.* 2001). This strategy was apparently adopted for two main reasons; first to satisfy stock market pressure that the organization was reducing its 'headcount' and hence its labour costs. Telecomco moved explicitly from a strategy of protecting its reputation in the labour market as a good employer to a policy of protecting its reputation in the City as a good investment. The second motivation was to limit its commitment to new staff under conditions of changing technology. The opportunity to reduce the wage costs of flexible working was probably a third but subsidiary motivation. Agency temps were hired to work the unsocial hours which many permanent Telecomco staff rejected, both because they preferred social hours and were unwilling to work unsocial hours for limited extra pay. Telecomco added to the cost advantage by using local pay rates for temps to reduce direct and indirect costs. Thus, restructuring induced by product market change was harnessed to bring radical changes to its employment relations strategy.

Bankco followed an altogether more cautious route. The rationalization of the branch network and the development of call centres was not immediately accompanied by any radical changes in terms and conditions. It became bolder when it opened a second call centre staffed by newly hired workers and significantly reduced the premium payments. However, the bank management soon recognized the drawbacks of this fragmented system. Concerned to attract and retain staff, the bank forged a series of partnership deals with one of the trade unions. A new harmonized pay structure was agreed upon that nevertheless established premium payments below the previous core terms and conditions but above the call-centre rates as the new norm for all staff.

At Retailco the changes represent an intensification of the previous practices of securing flexible working from employees rather than a major departure in employment relations. The ending of the Saturday premium and the replacement of the night rate percentage premium with a low flat rate was in line with what was happening in the rest of the industry. What is perhaps more surprising is that the Sunday double rate premium has been retained. In general, supermarkets have been both extending opening hours and reducing the costs of flexible working through changes to premiums and to contracts. Some further reduction of the cost of Sunday working might therefore be expected. A further consequence of the change in opening hours is that managers are required to provide cover for longer and on more flexible schedules. Flexibility requirements have also been institutionalized into a new contractual form at corporate level: staff contracted to work 15 hours were to be required to be available to work up to 31 hours (with holidays, sick pay and pensions linked to contractual hours). However, this intensification of flexible working continues a now long-established practice of flexible and variable working hours based around a high level of part-time working at Retailco.

Recent adjustments at Pharmco also reflect the extension of previous practice. A complex set of shifts ensures that staff cover long periods of the day and the weekend, but staff are only paid premium payments for those hours over and above their contracted hours, thereby reducing the incidence of additional costs. Overtime was traditionally used to manage product market change, but recently the level of overtime working reached what management considered to be unacceptable levels. It was thus no surprise that when we last visited the organization, management was in the process of introducing a form of annualized hours, although the fine print of the system had not yet been established.

In the two public sector organizations, the pattern of working time was subject to national collective-bargaining agreements which set standard or maximum working hours. In both cases there had been recent agreements, to reduce standard hours in the case of Councilco and maximum hours in the case of Healthco. These agreements left it up to local managers to decide exactly how to implement and pay for these. As a result, Councilco management was struggling to harmonize shifts for manual and non-manual staff around a 37-hour week, when current standard hours were 39 for manual and 35 for non-manual grades. The harmonization also had the impact of raising the hourly costs of part-time manual workers. For the unions this devolution of decision-making ran the risk of fragmenting negotiations. What became clear was the difficulty of introducing working-time change in an organization as complex as Councilco. At Healthco, management also had to adjust to the new regulations concerning maximum working hours of junior doctors—reduced from 80 to 56 (Audit Commission 1995).

Although these organizations remained constrained by the strong influence of national agreements, important changes were taking place in the established system of regulated working time. These changes were in part a response to the need to accommodate the new working-time standards but also reflected other changes in the funding and function of public sector organizations. In particular, Best Value in local government placed all service areas under threat of outsourcing unless labour costs were reduced. Specific strategies were developed to deal with the cost of harmonization and also to cope with new needs and modes of delivery. The home-care services management team, for example, insisted on care workers agreeing to new flexible working schedules, on the basis that their contracts contained an, as yet inactivated, flexibility clause. These changes for the regular staff were in addition to new contracts offered to the STAR teams that required flexible working without any extra pay for covering unsocial hours, in return for some upgrading of the basic salary. Management argued that these changes were needed to protect services against external competition, a threat that led to similar strategies emerging in other departments. In this way, the hours of school dinner workers were also cut. Other strategies deployed by Councilco to reduce costs included the use of short hours contracts to minimize the holiday and sick pay of workers who regularly worked longer than their contractual hours. In implementing these changes, and justifying them, management relied enormously upon the public service ethos; it drew extensively upon the goodwill of staff in all grades of work. Here, it seemed that the power of the local unions to resist these changes was limited. The national unions had passed the burden of finding ways of accommodating and funding the new national agreement down to the local level without providing firm guidelines on what would be considered acceptable or non-acceptable ways of implementing the changes. Additionally, the policy of Best Value in questioning the right of local authorities to provide all public services considerably weakened unions' bargaining power and their capacity to resist quite radical changes in the organization of public service employment.

Healthco faced similar budgetary constraints. It was, however, unable to adopt such an explicit and general policy of working-time change due to the delegation of actual working-time management to directorate and even ward level. The change in doctors' hours was the catalyst to the development of a more strategic approach. The redistribution of tasks from doctors to nurses and, in turn, from qualified to less-qualified nursing staff resulted in the recruitment of a new category of lower-skilled health care assistants on local terms and conditions with less generous premium payments. Such recruitment was seen by the local trade unions as the price that they had to pay for the maintenance of national terms and conditions of employment for the qualified staff. There was also a clear desire by management to avoid any new commitments to meet unsocial hours payments. New contracts were therefore used to introduce 7-day working without premium payments into departments such as psychiatry and rehabilitation. Other more limited changes to working time stopped short of any strategic changes in terms and conditions of employment or even to internal power relations, and were introduced ad hoc as ways of dealing with budget cuts. These measures largely consisted of not filling vacancies and, once again, relying on staff goodwill to maintain service delivery. When this failed, short-term solutions were adopted, such as the use of overtime and (with increasing regularity) the employment of staff through 'the bank'.

Generally, it seems that the public sector managers we talked to no longer believed that existing contractual arrangements had to be preserved and respected. In Councilco and Healthco new flexible working arrangements were introduced for selected groups of core staff (home-carers at Councilco or the rehabilitation workers at Healthco), which required them to forgo premiums for working unsocial hours in return for a new employment package, with only moderately enhanced salaries. Here, an explicit objective was to mirror practice in the private sector. Councilco explicitly justified its policy of changing working time in catering in these terms. Managerial catering staff were placed on contracts for long hours, with a requirement to provide whatever cover was required, while lower-skilled staff were kept on short contractual hours (which in practice were always exceeded) in order to reduce the costs of sick pay and holidays. These approaches would not have been adopted without both the increased pressure on budgets and the belief that notions of standard full-time working are outdated and outmoded. Mimicry of the private sector was even more evident in Healthco, where one senior manager insisted that if supermarkets 'provide a 24-hour service to sell baked beans to customers, then we ought to consider giving patients a 24-hour service'. Ironically, in this example, a wide number of services at Healthco had always, of course, been delivered over the whole day and across the whole week.

Further investigation of our case studies thus suggests that changing patterns of industrial relations both inside and outside the organization have played a major role in the transformation of working-time patterns. Of course, the increasing pressures on budgets and on product markets have also been important factors. However, the particular form this response takes is inseparable from the opportunities presented to management to change internal power relations. This, in turn, is often based upon changes in the external bargaining power of workers and unions. Thus, the attribution of changes to new competitive conditions is only part of the story and the factors that determine the particular response to competitive pressures depend both on the societal system and the internal power relations (Rubery and Horrell 1993).

WORKING-TIME CHANGE AND THE EMPLOYMENT RELATIONSHIP

Working-time change is associated with the search to change the system of production or service delivery and/or with the search to reduce operating costs. More specifically, changes to working time were motivated, as we have argued, by three main objectives: to extend operating and opening hours, to increase 'productive hours' and/or to reduce slack time and to reduce costs of flexible working. Each of these changes has clear implications for the organization and experience of employment, which extend beyond the mere change in the pattern or length of working hours. Changes designed to extend operating and service delivery hours may not only involve staff in more unsocial hours working, but may also lead to a more intensive pace of work if the restructuring is combined, for example, with tighter staffing levels. Extensions of hours may also have knock-on impacts on work volumes, if the same quota of supervisory or managerial staff are employed even though requirements for supervision and management extend over a longer portion of the week. The desire to increase productive hours or reduce slack hours has a direct relationship to processes of working-time intensification and indirect repercussions for the divisions between social and unsocial hours. One of the consequences of trade-union struggles to establish continuous stable working days was to reduce the opportunity for employers constantly to vary the employment offer according to the pattern and level of demand. In other words, the objective was to build some slack into the employment relationship, as part of a process of income and employment protection and as a means of managing the wage–effort relationship. New techniques of monitoring demand levels, on the one hand, and effort levels, on the other, are reopening these arrangements. They are laying staff open not only to processes of intensification but also to processes of fragmentation of working time, requiring extended availability for the same or lower levels of paid working hours.

Policies to cut the costs of flexible working through, for example, reductions in distinctions between social and unsocial working hours may not only affect the take-home pay of staff but may also lead to changes in employment contracts. For example, these strategies may affect choices between employing part-time or full-time staff or between using permanent or temporary contracts (Rubery 1998b). The objective of reducing the costs of flexible or extended working in these circumstances can have much wider implications for the nature of the employment relationship and people's experience of work. Staff on different forms of contract not only have different rights of access to premiums for unsocial hours; they also have differential access to other elements of the employment package, from employment security to sick pay and holiday pay. The extent to which these three motives for changes in working time—extending hours, increasing flexibility of hours and changes in the reward structure—lead to interrelated or separate changes in the employment relationship is dependent upon the bargaining power of the groups concerned.

In the past, relatively powerful workforce groups—for instance, well-organized and mainly male workforce groups—could obtain extra rewards in return for an agreement either to work longer hours or to accept more flexible arrangements. However, the weaker groups—for example, less well-organized female, part-time workers—might be required to accept both intensified flexibility and reductions in opportunities or pay enhancement. One of the features of the current situation is that groups that have traditionally been able to extract rewards for agreeing to changes may now also be subject to deteriorating employment conditions with respect to both time and material rewards. At least within low to medium job grades—including lower-level supervisory and management jobs—there seems to be evidence of an increasing powerlessness of workforce groups to be able to make new compromise agreements, let alone resist management changes to working time. What is more, within these workforce groups there is also some evidence of a greater gender mix. In our case study organizations, this involves not only some men accepting non-standard and often part-time contracts, but also the entry of women into supervisory and lower managerial jobs. The working-time arrangements associated with these jobs continue, however, to be made in accordance with a male breadwinner model, where employees are deemed to be free of personal and domestic commitments. Indeed, as we will see, current trends for supervisory and managerial staff have moved towards more flexible and longer hours, despite the increased rate of entry of women into these posts. Here we explore the experiences of staff affected by these various processes of working time change.

Extensions to operating and opening hours

An extension to operating and opening hours was a major cause of both more flexible working patterns and longer working hours. Two main groups of worker were involved in longer working hours: those on time-related contracts, scheduled to work shifts, and those on non-time-related contracts—mainly managerial and supervisory staff—who were required to provide more extended cover, often without any change to their contracts or remuneration.

At Mediaco the printing staff were required to accept complex rotating shifts designed not only to extend operating hours but also to eliminate paid overtime and reduce staffing levels per machine. This combination of objectives was achieved, but only at the cost of increasing fatigue:

We're running the presses with four men, five if you're lucky... stress and fatigue are beginning to creep in. Young men in their twenties are tired. I hear of people coming in at six and I say what are you going to do with the afternoon? I'm going to bed.... There used to be a lot of activity, there used to be football and God knows what else after. They haven't got the time.

(Male, full time, no. 4, Mediaco1)

[A]t night they [the engineers are] on a 10-hour night except for Saturday and Sunday, which are a 12- and a 14-hour [shift]. So for a 7-day period you are averaging nearly 80 hours which is when... you need a week of bed basically just to get back to being anything but a zombie!

(Male, full time, no. 2, Mediaco1)

The use of scheduled long shifts was specific to Mediaco. It should be noted that this was one of the few examples of a primarily male-dominated workforce and it might not have been possible to impose the very long hours of scheduled work on a more gender-mixed workforce. Each of the other organizations used a combination of flexible working arrangements for staff paid according to time, and long working hours for those on salaries. Staff paid on a fixed salary basis were often involved in unscheduled and unpaid overtime. Where they were allowed time off in lieu, they had limited opportunities in practice to claim the time owed. In these cases even women supervisory and management staff had to comply with the long and flexible hours as the price of promotion. For example, at Retailco, the reduction in management levels and numbers meant managers had to be prepared to work as and when required, outside of their contracted hours, and to cover extended opening hours. One of the section managers described the situation:

We do 5 days a week [but] some weeks we work 6 days a week.... I don't always get a dinner hour, I don't always get out on time. I would say, on the shop floor—10 hours unpaid overtime a week; sometimes on the shop floor we could do 13–14 hours day.

(Female, full time, no. 1, Retailco3)

Changes to more flexible schedules for all staff covering longer working days placed pressures on management time, even at relatively low levels. For example, one Councilco home care supervisor commented:

It's Monday to Friday at the moment. That's another thing that may be changing. The home-care staff are now going on to rotas which will be from 8 am till 8 pm. So the [home care] organizers are going to have to come on line as well to work sort of shadow.

(Female, part time, no. 7, Councilco1)

This increased commitment among supervisory and managerial staff was achieved largely through the promotion of a view that long hours went with the job:

Sometimes I take work home. Sometimes like last Friday I worked from about 8.10 am to about 8.40 pm because I needed to do that at the time. I needed to see some people ... it just goes with the territory.

(Female, full time, no. 1, Telecomco1)

Evidence of management and workers having to work longer hours was a matter of concern to both male and female managerial staff at all seven organizations. This was even the case at Pharmco, which had done less to move away from the traditional working-time model for time paid staff and had maintained paid overtime opportunities. Nevertheless, managers were under increasing pressure to work long hours. For example, one of the directors voiced his concern over the 'long hours culture'. And at Pharmco a technical officer with fifteen years' experience set out how he thought the distinction between contractual and non-contractual working-time obligations had been eroded:

I don't work weekends and I very rarely do any [paid] overtime, but having said that I work longer than the working week is and I think most people do now. I think there's been a deterioration of that boundary, if you like. People are trying to do more and they're in earlier.... But I'd say for me I try at the moment, anyway I'm here about 8.30 am something like that and if I'm not leaving by 6 pm I tend to get a little bit upset. Six o'clock is cut off. I have worked beyond that. I've worked till 9 pm in the past but not regularly.

(Male, full time, no. 11, Pharmco1)

Increasing productive hours and reducing slack time

A variety of different working-time strategies were used to increase productive hours and reduce slack time. These ranged from the straightforward reduction in paid breaks to the rescheduling of hours to meet demand patterns. These developments went alongside other organizational changes that involved a much tighter specification of job content and related levels of work intensity. Many workplaces, of course, had also adopted more flexible staffing policies, including the use of temporary contracts and short contractual hours to ensure no unnecessary slack time was paid for.

At Telecomco call-centre staff were unhappy about efforts to enhance individual productivity through the minimization of paid and busy-time breaks. This problem was also recognized by staff at Retailco, where the company only paid for productive time:

Wouldn't mind being paid for my breaks! On Saturday [when] I work a 9-hour shift, it is a one and a half-hour break. On the 4-hour shift it is just a 15-minute break. We are not paid for those.

(Male, part time, no. 12, Retailco3)

At Councilco budget pressures were forcing supervisors to cut staffing levels to the minimum, through ensuring that shift schedules did not include any time that was not absolutely essential. When asked about changes in his job, a duty manager at a leisure facility remarked:

It's more of a business... now we're looking at ways to make money all the time, or to save money. Like if I do the shifts, I'll look at them and say we don't need them for that half an hour or whatever and just cut half an hour off. We're penny pinching.

(Male, full time, no. 10, Councilco4)

Similarly, in the school catering service core working hours were reduced so that 'unnecessary hours' could be eliminated when schools were quiet:

In March we have the fifth years leaving so the hours get cut and things like that. We don't know until a Friday, whatever income we have taken on a Friday above the core hours gives me flexible time for the following week.... [The catering assistants] get paid at the same rate but they are not entitled to sick pay or holiday pay on it.

(Female, full time, no. 4, Councilco1)

The tighter time specifications for school meals staff also caused problems. Here, school meals supervisors felt under pressure to put in extra (unpaid) overtime hours each week, as in their experience the scheduled time to be spent at work proved too short for efficient management. In principle, these extra hours could be taken as time off in lieu, but most of the time this right was not exercised:

It's changed, because in September we started on breakfasts so my hours start now at 7.15 [in the morning] until officially 2.45 pm because that's seven hours, but I don't go home at that time because my work is not finished. So I can't go home before it's finished, plus the staff are normally still here.... I start to go about 4-ish.

(Female, part time, no. 3, Councilco1)

While this strategy of cutting guaranteed hours was primarily confined to part-time and therefore mainly female staff, organizations appear increasingly to disregard gender when it comes to providing income guarantees. In general, Councilco appeared reluctant to provide permanent contracts covering current working hours requirements and instead shifted the risk of variations in demand on to staff by offering permanent contracts at reduced hours, as this case related to a care worker reveals.

One of my colleagues now nearly left.... He had to reapply again to get a permanent job here after the eighteen months. He said, 'why do I need to reapply because I know my jobs, I've been here'.... He was on 36 hours. When he reapplied again the only job that they could offer for anybody, him and anybody else that applied was 30 hours.... So the only way he can bring up his money actually requires more hours... got to do that on a week-to-week basis that's why they've actually offered something that's called the bank where if there's more hours available they're flexi.

(Female, full time, no. 11, Councilco2)

At the Telecomco telemarketing centre there was also evidence of part-timers working full-time hours. For example, a clerical officer who had entered the organization as an agency temp but had secured a permanent position was contracted for 20.5 hours a week but regularly worked 37.5 hours a week.

In some cases, the organizations, while reducing core hours in practice, required an even greater time commitment from their staff. Staff were expected to make themselves available for work whenever they were needed. The flexible home-care (STAR) teams at Councilco were employed on 30-hour contracts but in practice were required to work for far longer.

They cannot recruit staff for it [the STAR team] because of the different hours, the different schedules. Because if you're only on a 30-hour contract you can't really fit anything in [another part-time job]. Because you're on lates one week and earlies the next.... And next meeting we are going to try, some of us, to get a 35-, 37-hour contract.

(Female, part time, no. 17, Councilco2)

Councilco also claimed that staff contracts specified that they had to be available to work between 8 am and 8 pm, Monday to Friday, even though management had only recently activated this clause. Part-timers working six hours a day might have to be ready to work the hours at any time in this period. This strategy belies the notion that part-time work is there to facilitate reconciliation between work and family life; instead part-time work can extend the hours during which work may intrude into family and personal life.

Reducing the cost of flexible working

The decision to offer short hours contracts is motivated by a range of factors, as we discussed in Chapter 5. Perhaps the primary motivation is the opportunity to reduce overhead employment costs and to maximize flexibility in the scheduling of hours. However, the incentive to use such contracts to reduce other elements of the pay package—for example, sick pay and holiday pay—was by no means lost on those employees at the receiving end of these policies. Although we found this policy most used in the public sector, it was also used at Retailco. It was quite normal, and even expected by managers, that general assistants, who made up the majority of the workforce at each of the three workplaces we visited, would work longer than their contracted hours. This meant some staff often working more than double the contracted hours on a relatively regular basis, for which they did not receive sick or holiday pay.

In Councilco a catering assistant felt she had been denied the full-time contract she had been promised:

She turned round and said there's no 35-hour contract going in the kitchen and there's no second chef (job). 'Assistant cook—25 hours' and it was 'are you taking it or are you leaving it?' ... It's hard to take time off because you've got to think to yourself I can work something like 50 (hours) for £170 ... to have a week off it's a £70 drop. And it's not really a decent wage when you look at it. I'm not even guaranteed £150 every week or something.

(Female, part time, no. 11, Councilco1)

For some staff, the consequences of reducing core hours was an increased reliance either on casual work or on assistance from the state, particularly when the traditional assistance from the family to low-paid married women was not forthcoming. A catering assistant at one of the schools we visited told us:

I used to do 25 hours and the hours are cut I'm down to 17.25 now.... Before, I could manage my family allowance, family credit and my wages, but now I can't. I'm struggling really.... When I started you had women here that did probably seventeen hours, they were quite happy with it because they had a husband, but it's no good if you haven't got a husband or partner. You're the breadwinner, I haven't got a partner so it's no good for me. [Family Credit] that's my husband.

(Female, part time, no. 2, Councilco1)

In some cases the means of reducing costs involved the opposite strategy—that of upgrading staff onto salaried contracts with limited or no provision for overtime. Portering managers at Healthco were, in principle, given contracts for 37 hours a week but received no extra pay for the regular overtime worked. This often meant they earned less than their juniors:

I could earn more as a 'portering supervisor' with the amount of overtime that the department's got, than I am earning now. In fact you will find that one of the 'portering supervisors' now, because of the vacancies we have got, is earning more than I am a week.

(Male, full time, no. 1, Healthco1)

Catering managers at Councilco were placed on contracts requiring them to work 45 hours; this provided guaranteed income but removed rights to overtime premia. Moreover, in practice these staff were working up to 60 hours per week, but without the possibility of claiming overtime pay. They also faced difficulties in claiming time off because of a relatively small number of staff having to provide cover for all catering events.

I was earning the same three or four years ago for a 35-hour week as what I'm earning now for a 45-hour week because I was getting paid overtime which was about £15–£16K a year. Whereas now I'll do 60 hours a week for the same salary.

(Female, full time, no. 10, Councilco1)

IMPACT ON THE EMPLOYMENT RELATIONSHIP AND THE SUSTAINABILITY OF THE NEW SYSTEMS

The changes to working time in our case study organizations were impacting on the nature of the employment relationship and on the personal and private lives of the employees, beyond the effects of the direct changes to working hours. The employment relationship was changing in three main ways: rights to private time in and out of work were being eroded; effort requirements were being intensified; and material rewards from working time were being reduced.

The loss of private time applied in three senses: pressure on private time at work, in the form of restricted entitlements to fixed meal breaks or rest periods and requirements to work as and when needed; pressure on family or personal life because of the flexible, unsocial and long working hours; and pressure on non-work time, related to stress, fatigue and requirements to remain available for work, which inhibit the enjoyment of leisure time.

The toll that working-time flexibility was taking on home lives was graphically described by a female manager at Telecomco, who faced the complications of trying to meet the flexibility demands both of her employer and of her husband's:

Working an evening shift causes me stress. I'm not really the most organized of people.... I've got two children and get them ready for school every day. But unfortunately my husband works shifts as well.... so I try and plan in advance as much as I can, a couple of weeks ahead. Like I've got two 5 pm to 1 am shifts and my husband might be on nights. I might try and swap or arrange for them to get to my mother's who lives in Liverpool, which means that I've got to get up early the next day even though I finish at 1 am to get them back to school.

(Female, part time, no. 2, Telecomco1)

Work intensity was being increased through both heightened effort levels and through longer hours of work. Some employees—those on time-related contracts—experienced, primarily, pressures towards harder work levels through the impact of more tightly scheduled working hours, coupled with increased performance-monitoring and leaner staffing levels. Others, on salary-based contracts, faced longer and more flexible working hours, sometimes also combined with higher effort levels related to increasing variety of tasks and reduced staffing levels.

While some of those on managerial and supervisory grades were paying the price of receiving higher material rewards, in the form of more extended and intensive working hours, most of the lower-level staff, together with many in lower supervisory or management grades, were being asked to forgo any specific material reward for participating in flexible and unsocial hours working. In all seven organizations, management was keenly aware of the advantages to be gained from treating each hour worked, whenever scheduled, as incurring the same costs. Collective agreements still provided some constraints on managers abolishing unsocial hours and overtime premiums, but in those organizations where premiums were retained, other strategies, such as the use of part-time or temporary labour, were increasingly being adopted to evade the regulations. For some employees these changes resulted in actual decreased earnings, while, for others, rising overall remuneration packages disguised a deteriorating wage–effort relationship, particularly once the personal costs of flexible and unsocial hours were taken into account. Male workers primarily experienced these changes in the context of longer hours combined with flexible scheduling, while female workers were more often affected by reductions in available hours combined with flexible scheduling. However, these gender divisions were by no means always observed. In particular, the very large number of women we found in supervisory and lower management jobs in our case study organizations had had to adjust to 'male' long hours and flexible schedules.

Taken together, these three sets of change represent a significant restructuring of the employment relationship. However, many of these changes had been relatively recently introduced or were still being implemented at the time of our research. It is interesting then to consider the future viability of these changes. In particular, is there evidence of resistance to them and can the new forms coexist with other management objectives?

In several cases we encountered explicit or implicit resistance to the implementation of new working-time arrangements. At Councilco the unions were opposing the activation of the flexible scheduling clause for home-care workers by lodging a large number of employment tribunal claims suggesting the change to the contract was illegal. In contrast, at Retailco, it was managers who appeared sensitive to the possibility of resistance by individual workers. The new flexible contracts designed by corporate headquarters had not been operated by store managers, who preferred to rely on voluntary overtime by part-timers than use a contractual requirement to work extra hours. At Bankco and Telecomco, staff management had shielded those with permanent contracts from requirements to work flexible hours except in managerial or supervisory posts, suggesting again that they anticipated resistance from core staff. Even in the printworks, where the closing of the old site and the refusal to recognize unions in the new could be expected to have considerably reduced the likelihood of resistance, any threat of protest was kept at bay by the payment of relatively high wages.

In the case of Pharmco, major changes in working-time arrangements are in the process of being introduced. In some ways an annualized hours system exemplifies the new employment relationship. In a pure, managerial-led form, the introduction of annualized hours reduces the divisions between work and non-work time and provides managers with increased power over their employees' lives. At Pharmco employees are to be asked to sign up for one of three options: low, medium or high overtime hours, which are paid in advance. Pharmco will then be able to call staff into work when it requires the extra hours to be worked. A woman who had been at the organization for more than ten years outlined where there might be some resistance to the policy if it was implemented in a way that gave direct control to management over people's private lives:

It seems a bit too good to be true to be honest with you. I think so long as you don't get called out because I've got two children and I can't afford to get called out silly hours, but with saying that, they're not going to call you out say at 6 am. Which is fair really. If they've got to call you out they've got to give you that four hours notice, which is fine.

(Female, full time, no. 8, Pharmco1)

Pharmco appeared to have resisted the temptation to take full control of time scheduling and was including some checks on management's control of employee time. Indeed, although managers in each of the organizations were better able to control and design working-time arrangements, there was still evidence that they recognized the limits on their ability to impose a new employment relationship. Caution in implementing changes in part reflected their awareness that a fully commodified system of labour exchange—that is, where the employer accepts no responsibility for maintaining a longer-term employment relationship based on income security—would not be compatible with their needs. This was most apparent in the public sector organizations, where, to a large extent, the policy of using work intensity and changing work schedules was not accompanied by a decreased reliance on the skills and the commitment of the staff. Instead, in both organizations, managers were relying increasingly on the goodwill, professionalism and responsibility of the staff, while, at the same time, reshaping the employment contract to involve the high work intensity, strict time scheduling and monitoring associated with low trust or commodified employment relationships. For example, in home care one of the factors that led to managers activating the controversial flexibility clause was dissatisfaction with the quality of non-permanent staff:

We've no control over their [the temporary work agency] staff and a lot of the time agency staff are not trained… all we can deal with is the complaints afterwards. It's a problem at the moment—people not turning up, a different person every night and all this sort of thing…. Hopefully if these rotas come on line we'll bring the work back in, in-house.

(Female, full time, no. 7, Councilco1)

Even where the work did not demand high skills and high trust, management also experienced limits to their ability to control the employment relationship. Bankco management introduced a harmonized working time and pay system to allow for more horizontal and vertical mobility to counter turnover of trained staff. It also sought to offset some of the stresses caused by flexible working by allowing staff to negotiate flexible hours to suit their own circumstances. These policies caused more administrative problems for management, but overcame some of the individualized resistance evident in high turnover rates. But whether evidence of resistance and of potential conflict across management objectives is sufficient to reverse this pattern of change is still unclear.

CONCLUSIONS

The evidence presented in this chapter supports the view that significant and ongoing changes are taking place in the way time is organized in large organizations. Our evidence is consistent with the emergence of a new approach to the employment relationship achieved through significant changes to the organization and regulation of the time dimension to the employment contract. In each of the organizations the direction of working-time change was similar. Furthermore, there was a clear indication from management that working-time changes were critical to employment change and restructuring. We found that very radical and far-reaching change had already been made, or was in the process of being introduced.

Yet, this apparent internal consistency should not be taken as evidence that these policies will deliver simple solutions to UK managers. We have noted that these changes are far from sustainable, particularly given the need for skilled and committed workers. Furthermore, the apparent strategic nature of the approach (involving major changes to the employment relationship) does not necessarily mean that it has been fully thought through. It may be yet another indication of British management's preference for opportunistic policies (Rubery and Wilkinson 1994; see also Chapter 1). Managers themselves were, in many cases, aware of the contradictions and conflicts within their own policies but considered themselves to have few options other than to adopt a policy of reducing costs and raising work intensity (Burchell et al. 1999; see also Chapter 9). However, there was no indication that this awareness would lead to a change in policy. The instant advantages were too great. The removal of restrictions on working-time schedules and reductions in the costs of flexible working provided managers with room for manoeuvre in the context of changed external conditions. As such, self-imposed constraints are not part of their agenda.

Most of the workers we talked to were trade-union members. Many of them were upset by the kinds of change that were taking place and several were contemplating other jobs. These individual responses—as expressed in dissatisfaction and high rates of turnover—could well provide trade unions with arguments and support for a more concerted strategy of resistance. Many of the trade-union officials and shop stewards we talked to were clear that the changes being implemented were eroding the very basis for the unions' traditional role in nego-tiating the dimensions of time in the workplace. However, they were uncertain as to their capacity to resist. In part, this relates to the fact that a small but significant proportion of their members (and our respondents) found the new systems acceptable. Some of the people we talked to even found them desirable because of particular domestic or life-cycle circumstances. Others regarded flexible working time as part of the package that 'went with the territory'—of managerial work on the one hand and service work on the other. On balance, however, the majority would vote to 'put back the clock'. This has contributed to the successful development of collective resistance in the organizations we studied. The partnership agreement negotiated at Bankco has had some impact, encouraging employee influence over working times, the development of the new harmonized pay structure and the policy of moving agency temps onto standard contracts. At Telecomco, unions have organized a series of strikes over the excessive use of agency temps, which they see to have undermined the effectiveness of their national agreements. It is in the public sector, where trade-union traditions were perhaps strongest, that the union response has been least effective. Here, negotiations over time at the national level have been traded against the incremental erosion of working-time guarantees at the local level. Undoubtedly, these trade unions have been caught in the vice of budget restrictions and privatization threats. Nevertheless, they have the scope to regulate more effectively the terms under which the national agreements are implemented locally.

Working-time regulation has in part been put back on the agenda by European-based legislation. However, so far the unions have been unable to use these new statutory conditions as the basis for re-regu-lating working-time arrangements. The decision to allow employers to exclude staff not on hours-based contracts from the monitoring of working hours associated with the Working Time Directive may in fact serve to reinforce the trends we observed in our case study organizations (Adnett and Hardy 2001). That is, towards, on the one hand, an increasing share of employees on contracts with no effective time specifications and, on the other, an increasing share of employees on short contractual hours where the possibility of 'on-the-job inactive time' (Supiot 2001) is no longer possible.

III

THE COSTS OF CHANGE

8

Drawing Together the Threads: A Question of Labour Costs and Work Intensification

INTRODUCTION

Changes in staffing policies, skill development and training provision, and working-time policies can be analysed with respect to their own separate dynamics of change, along the lines outlined in Part II. This approach, however, could serve to obscure the more fundamental changes taking place in the employment system and the employment relationship. In this and the following chapter we argue that the different employment policies and practices can be interpreted as a function of two interrelated factors—wage labour costs and work-intensity. In this way, the separate dynamics of change across dimensions of employment policy can be seen as a more interrelated set of transformations. These are linked, to a large extent, to the change in general power relations in the labour market, which have allowed a redefinition of the fundamental wage–effort relationship at the heart of the employment relationship.

If we begin with the interrelationships with the level of wage costs, we can analyse the three dimensions to employment change from a different perspective. New staffing policies, such as the use of temporary labour, may be linked to the reduction in wage costs, involving in some cases lower hourly wages but in other cases lower benefits and more limited progression up a salary scale. Similarly, while downsizing may increase immediate wage costs in the form of early retirement and redundancy packages, the policy has gained favour in part for the signal it provides to the City that an organization intends to reduce its long-term commitment to high overhead wage costs. Moreover, explicit polices to change wage structures in line with market rates may require change in the composition of the workforce, as incumbent staff are more likely to resist direct changes to wage rates. Thus, staffing policies and wage cost policies may prove to be strongly interrelated.

Policies of training and skill development may also be linked to wage cost objectives. In particular, application of what we describe below as the 'Babbage principle' involves reducing the share of skilled labour that commands high wages and increasing the share of low-skilled labour. The issue here is not so much whether policies of skill development encourage upskilling or deskilling of workforce groups, but how changes in the composition of low-, medium- and high-skilled workers (the so-called skill mix) are exploited to reduce the total average cost of labour (Babbage 1835). This principle may apply to the operation as a whole and not to an individual workplace, as the lower-skilled operations may be contracted out in order to save on wage costs. Such policies may even be pursued in a context where competition or changes in technology act as important pressures to upskill the workforce—pressures that run in the opposite direction to the reducing wage cost imperative. Nevertheless, the weakening role for trade unions and for custom and practice surrounding work organization may allow companies more scope to change the structure of the skill mix, by implementing the Babbage principle.

Working-time policies are even more focused on reducing labour costs. Examples of changes which reduce costs include reductions in overtime premiums and reductions in unsocial hours premiums through the use of part-time and temporary staff, or the introduction of new working arrangements for full-timers.

While action to reduce direct wage costs may be an important backdrop to the development of employment policies and practices in all three areas, the implications for work intensity may be even more significant. Policies to reduce the employment headcount and not to fill vacancies, in order to meet budgetary or City considerations, may be taken without regard to actual staffing requirements and workloads. Policies to extend the range of staff skills provide the opportunity for greater work intensity. Similarly, change to the skill mix may require the skilled workers to work more intensively at a higher level; these problems are particularly acute in management areas where extended operating hours coincide with reductions in numbers of managers to cover the longer hours. Working-time changes may be brought in directly to increase work intensity by more careful targeting of labour hours to service needs or demands. New contracts for full-timers may also involve more commitments to work as and when required, thereby facilitating increasing work intensity through extended unpaid overtime and more limited opportunities to take time off in lieu because of understaffing. All these problems may be accentuated if rising stress levels lead to more staff absences and greater difficulties in filling vacancies, even when there is permission to recruit. In short, policies to reduce costs through higher work intensity may spiral out of control if organizations are not able to manage stress and absence levels or to fill vacancies to meet increases in the volume of work.

Changes to the wage–effort relationship may thus lie at the heart of change to employment policies and practices, which appear to be geared towards other dynamics—such as, for example, changes in time and skill dimensions to service delivery. It is extremely difficult to disentangle the extent to which a change in policy is aimed at its explicit objective or has an underlying motive to redraw the wage–effort relationship. Organizations may attempt to pursue both objectives simultaneously; for example, they may seek to move to more flexible working-time schedules to meet the need for more flexible delivery given changing customer demand, but at the same time seek to reduce the cost of these working-time arrangements. Indeed, while many initiatives to change policies and practices may be associated with the new forms of competition, the process of change may be seen by organizations as an opportunity to redefine the employment relationship in more general terms. Thus, it is neither practicable nor intellectually possible to allocate the cause of changes to either new competitive conditions or change to the employment relationship. Instead, we intend to analyse the potential for interaction between the pressures for change and the general imperative of taking labour cost out and intensifying the pace of work.

There may be two reasons for anticipating that this general imperative has considerable importance in explaining change in employment policies and practices. First of all, the impact of two decades of change in industrial relations provides a framework in which it may be relatively easy for organizations to seize the initiative and to impose changes in the wage–effort relationship that previously would have been resisted. Thus, organizations may not feel it is worth making more marginal changes without reconsidering a wider range of employment policies and practices and challenging custom and practice.

The second factor that may bring such behaviour to the fore is the limited room for alternative forms of manoeuvre. Organizations claim to be under increasing pressure to implement changes to deal with technological, market and budgetary changes. Increasing global competition, on the one hand, and tightening public budgets, on the other, place both private and public sector organizations under rising pressure to reduce costs and expand services provision in order to survive. Under these conditions organizations have to identify areas where they can exercise the power to take cost out. Unable to exercise individual control over exchange rates, tax levels, business rates or even often materials cost, labour is seen as one area, in a period of deregulated labour markets, where the individual organization can seek to exercise some control over costs. This belief is evident in the City's concern over headcount figures as an indication of financial probity.

The temptation in decentralized employment systems, such as in the UK, is to move away from regarding some elements of labour cost as unchallengeable and to question the need to maintain premiums and bonus payments or even basic pay levels. Similarly, vacancies can be seen as a convenient way of saving on overhead cost, while premises, for example, tend to come in larger chunks and savings on space costs may be more difficult to achieve through the short-term manipulation of budgets and vacancy fill rates. These policies may be pursued even when organizations and their managers are fully aware of the longer-term costs of poor human resource management in terms of recruitment, retention and morale. But such actions may appear to be the only option on offer to satisfy ever-increasing pressures to meet short-term (or even long-term) budgetary or profit objectives. It is under these circumstances that some managers welcome constraints on labour cost-cutting strategies, such as minimum wage levels or established pay and grading scales, as these prevent them from having to justify not seeking yet further economies on labour costs.

We explore these interrelated changes to the wage–effort relationship in this and the following chapter. In this chapter, we begin with an analysis of the different ways in which managements have taken out labour costs in our seven case study organizations. First, managements have acted to reduce wage levels in an apparent effort to internalize the market through, for example, the introduction of market rates for new recruits. Second, they have relinquished part of their responsibility for the indirect costs of managing labour. Here, we explore examples of the reduced rights of agency temps to sickness benefits and holiday entitlements, as well as the reduction of wage premiums for working unsocial hours for a wide range of workforce groups. Third, we assess evidence of management policies designed to reduce total average wage costs by changing the skill mix. Examples include the design of new low-grade jobs, the widespread practice of 'acting-up', the outsourcing of job tasks and the introduction of new technology. In Chapter 9, we focus on changes in the effort side of the wage–effort relationship. We consider the different ways management practices have led to an intensification of work effort. Examples include the increasing attention to the needs of the customer, the broadening of worker responsibility and the use of new forms of control to monitor the pace of work and the quality of performance. Taken together, the evidence we present in these two chapters demonstrates the radical nature of change in labour costs and work intensification. Although we began our research with an explicit focus on broad dimensions of employment policies and practices— staffing, training and working time—the more profound changes have occurred right at the heart of the employment relationship, the exchange between wage and effort. These changes herald a major setback to the interests of labour, an issue we consider in the concluding chapter.

TAKING OUT LABOUR COSTS

Each of our seven organizations faced a bewildering array of pressures to adapt their employment policies and practices. In some cases, external pressures to meet standards of new competition demanded new work systems, or new investment in technologies and programmes of up-skilling. In other cases, changes in the principles of market competition required strategies to expand into new areas of services provision or the manufacture of a greater range of products. However, one pressure common to all seven organizations was the need to reduce costs. In the private sector organizations, the pressure often derived from the financial markets, where, throughout the 1990s, control of headcount was one of the main indicators of competitiveness. In the large multinational organizations, there was additional pressure from the forced competition among subsidiary business units. Here we saw workplace managers welcoming a greater devolution of managerial accountability, yet aware that their autonomy was framed within a greater concentration of power at the corporate level—what Bennett Harrison (1997) has described as 'concentration without centralization of power'. In the public sector, the 1990s were characterized by restrictive public spending policies. The nominal level of public sector spending was frozen under the Conservative government and this policy was continued during the first two years of the new Labour administration (1997–9). The real decline in expenditures imposed harsh cost constraints, which were clearly felt by managers at our two public sector case studies.

Faced with these pressures, management must then attempt to restructure the cost base of the organization. There may be a number of areas of attention, depending on the type of product or service associated with the organization, but in general these include the cost of purchasing goods and services from supplier organizations, the interest on capital stock (and depreciation costs), taxation liabilities, utility costs and, of course, labour costs. These costs are in some cases fixed, allowing little room for negotiation (for example, interest rates or taxation). In other areas, organizations may seek to influence costs through negotiations based on power relations. The two relationships where management has perhaps the most leverage are with supplier organizations and with labour. During the late 1990s, much was made in the British press of the ability of large retail groups to force down prices charged by suppliers—whether for agricultural produce from farms or manufactured foodstuffs from factories (see also Harvey 1998).[1] In other cases, organizations may integrate with suppliers in an effort to reduce costs—what is typically referred to as 'backward integration'.

Drawing on the evidence from our research, it is clear that the late 1990s presented management with considerable opportunities to reduce the cost of labour. In some cases, management imposed cuts by direct action, either by cutting wage rates or by making workers redundant. Cuts could also be made less directly. For example, workers on fixed-term contracts were 'released' from the organization; mid-level managers were asked to act-up in senior level positions without proper remuneration; the proportion of low-skill workers to high-skill workers was gradually increased and layers of management taken out and additional payments for working unsocial hours were reduced or abolished

---

[1] During the late 1990s, a number of media reports into the 'unbalanced partnership' between major supermarket chains and suppliers linked the existence of feudal-type gang-labour practices found in agricultural employment to the power of supermarkets to change orders on a day-to-day, or even hour-to-hour basis (see, for example, the *Guardian*, 9 June 1998). In 2000, the results of the biggest competition inquiry ever conducted in Britain found the 'big five' food retailers guilty on a number of counts, including 52 different types of practice in which they were exploiting their suppliers—such as charging for shelf space, coercing discounts and restricting dealings with other retailers. But the report commissioned by the Competition Commission in April 1999 did not advocate new legislation; instead, it only recommended provisions for a voluntary code of practice which would have OFT approval and for an independent party to resolve disputes (*Observer*, 1 October 2000).

altogether. While these policies were also intended to meet other management goals, it is clear from our research that in their design the issue of labour costs was central.

We can make sense of this broader conceptualization of how management seeks to cut labour costs by drawing on ideas from the tradition of political economy—in particular, ideas about commodity fetishism and skills mix—in the works of Karl Marx, Adam Smith, Charles Babbage and Karl Polanyi, among others. These contributions from political economy allow us to think about how management has cut labour costs in different ways. In particular, we consider three broad approaches: the reduction of wage rates, the reduction of indirect labour costs and the reduction of average wage costs. We consider how these different approaches interlink with the three dimensions of employment change and with contemporary concerns around problems of insecurity, polarization and the transformation of a work ethic.

REDUCTION OF WAGE RATES: INTERNALIZING THE MARKET?

One of the major insights in Marx's study of capitalism is that the portrayal of labour as a commodity, to be traded like any other, in fact masks the peculiar character of the labour market. In conventional accounts, the capitalist and the worker appear as simply the purchaser and seller of labour (or labour power as Marx called it); the wage rate reflects the value of workers' attributes as determined through the net effect of the market forces of supply and demand. However, Marx demonstrated that this vision of the labour market draws a veil over the capitalist nature of the economy, which is that the capitalist is the owner of capital, and the worker has nothing to sell but his or her labour. The associated notion of commodity fetishism thus refers to the way in which there is often a mistaken emphasis on the market in determining the terms of exchange, as if labour could be traded like apples and oranges. Instead, as Marx argued so forcefully, the value of labour traded exceeds the wage paid and, moreover, the wage paid reflects a range of factors other than market conditions, including the level of subsistence income, income to provide for dependants, social norms, wage-bargaining power and so on. This point was crucial for Marx, as it underpins the argument for the need to go behind the sphere of market exchange and to examine how profits are made in the process of production. In one of the more ironic, and well-known, passages from *Capital*, Marx caricatures the conventional vision:

This sphere [of market exchange] that we are deserting, within whose bound-aries the sale and purchase of labour-power goes on, is in fact a very Eden of the innate rights of man. There alone rule Freedom, Equality, Property and Bentham. Freedom, because both buyer and seller of a commodity, say of labour-power, are constrained only by their own free will.... Equality, because each enters into relation with the other, as with a simple owner of commodities, and they exchange equivalent for equivalent. Property, because each disposes only of what is his own. And Bentham because each looks only to himself.... Each looks to himself only, and no one troubles about the rest, and just because they do so, do they all, in accordance with the pre-established harmony of things, or under the auspices of an all-shrewd providence, work together to their mutual advantage, for the common weal and in the interest of all. On leaving this sphere of simple circulation... we think we can perceive a change in the physiognomy of our dramatis personae. He, who before was the money-owner, now strides in front as capitalist; the possessor of labour-power follows as his labourer. The one with an air of importance, smirking, intent on business; the other, timid and holding back, like one who is bringing his own hide to market and has nothing to expect but—a hiding. (1887: 172)

Marx's intention was to shift the emphasis—among academics, advo-cates and activists—from the workings of the labour market to the labour process at the heart of the production process; to open up the 'black box' of capitalist production. However, given the changes in work and employment that we have described in this book, it is difficult to resist the argument that, in fact, since the late 1980s we have witnessed a growing influence of the market—whether real or invented—in shaping the way employment is managed. Indeed, many contemporary accounts of employment change make just this argument. Peter Cappelli *et al.* (1997) suggest that, particularly in areas of pay and job security, there has been a shift to more market-mediated outcomes. And, more recently, work carried out for the Rowntree Foundation argues that the rise in job insecurity and work intensification is the result of (market) pressures for greater flexibility, which are imposed on all organizations by cus-tomers, competitors and dominant stakeholders (Burchell *et al.* 1999).

But emphasis on the increasing influence of the market and the way organizations are forced to respond to new, more intense competitive pressures may be misplaced. Recent changes are typically contrasted against the postwar golden age period, when employees benefited from the development of relatively protected employment conditions won through trade-union struggle and government reforms (Burawoy 1982; Jacoby 1984; Rubery 1978). Following this long period of 'market shelters', talk of the rise of the market is perhaps better understood as a euphemism for the collapse of these shelters, or the erosion of internal labour markets. The phrase 'internalizing the market' is often used as shorthand for the traumatic break-up of structured employment conditions that provided many workers with steady improvements in pay, status, skills and careers. What is needed is a critical account of the way the management of employment change is designed around the apparent need to meet market conditions; crucially, such an alternative account needs to ask the question: is a management strategy of removing costs a necessary condition for meeting market pressures?

In our seven organizations, there was a strong tendency for managers to emphasize the importance of meeting market conditions—over and above other concerns, such as, for example, setting out a long-term vision for human resource management. The type and intensity of market pressures varied from one organization to another, and included financial market pressures, government spending restrictions, labour market changes and product market demands. A concern to meet market pressures brought with it an acceptance among managers of the need to implement change and thus a willingness to break from many different aspects of the traditional employment relationship. In the accounts of Cappelli *et al.* (1997), Burchell *et al.* (1999) and others, the impression is that these market pressures present a series of threats to employer strategy—'adapt and respond or perish', they seem to be saying. It is also possible, however, that in the context of fast-changing and chaotic market conditions employers may enjoy greater freedom to engineer change on their own terms. Richard Sennett talks about the contemporary pattern of restructuring as one of 'discontinuous reinvention of institutions' (1998: 47–8). And, the more discontinuous and fragmented the context of change, the more opportunity there is for intervention; as Sennett puts it, 'its very incoherence invites your revisions' (ibid.: 48). This may explain why, in many cases, employer strategies to adjust to market pressures are not simply an adaptation of past practices; market pressures combined with greater opportunities to cut labour costs in a transformed industrial relations landscape mean that the new policies often rupture past norms and irreversibly alter traditional working arrangements. Here, we consider the case of Mediaco, since this provides a revealing illustration of how direct changes to wage levels were made in the name of introducing 'market rates'.

At Mediaco, the HR manager in the newspaper offices told us she was now known among staff as 'Miss Market Rates'. Management had taken the decision to revise the pay structure for journalists, clerical staff and drivers in line with market rates—as she put it, 'since there were large areas where we were clearly paying substantial sums'. The newspaper printed job advertisements for a high share of companies in the region, so they felt confident that they could construct a market rate for the different work groups. For each group, the new rate of pay represented a radical cut: for example, the basic salary of a driver was slashed from £19,000 to £14,000. Threats of strike action from drivers ultimately meant that while new recruits started on the market rate, incumbent drivers had their pay frozen rather than cut. Journalists and clerical staff suffered a similar fate and, when we looked at the company, had been on frozen rates of pay since 1995. In the case of journalists, the local union chapel advised members to sign the new agreement, since the alternative was the threat of dismissal and possible reinstatement on even worse conditions. Market testing for workers in advertising and sales showed that Mediaco was paying below the market rate. Curiously, however, in this case it was decided that Mediaco could recruit staff on the basis of more attractive working hours and the 'glamour' of working for the local newspaper company, rather than raise pay. For most groups, therefore, the market was 'internalized'; and in so doing, years of relatively attractive terms and conditions were discontinued.

The policy struck a blow to morale among staff, but for some it was seen as a pragmatic, albeit unwelcome, response to the reality of changing market conditions—a point reinforced by management through staff workshops organized by 'Miss Market Rates'. But the Mediaco manager's construction of the new market rates was, of course, at best partial. One of the major changes in pay structures in recent years had been their reduced transparency, as organizations shifted out of multi-employer wage-bargaining in favour of decentralized and individualized wage-setting arrangements. In many cases, rates are negotiated at the point of hiring and are likely to differ from rates advertised in the press. Also, increased use of incentive-based pay means that additions to the basic rate are increasingly important in distinguishing one organization's reward package from another—again, not transparent from a review of job vacancies. The idea of benchmarking pay structures against market rates is thus not only problematic, but also extraordinarily difficult to perform in practice.

Overall, Mediaco did achieve a radical cut in labour costs, a point not lost on many of the people we spoke with. One of the senior journalists put it like this:

The logic was that people had been paid a lot of money in the past and the market rates were lower basically, and it was felt perhaps that the gravy train had ended I guess. And now people are taken on at lower rates of pay . . . and are able to get the same job done for less employer's costs. In terms of morale . . . it has had a detrimental effect.

(Male, full time, no. 7, Mediaco2)

But management expressed no concern about the possibility that experienced staff on frozen pay might quit to work elsewhere. They were confident that new recruits were not only cheaper but could be required to work more flexibly, across a wider range of job tasks. While this was the general line among most Mediaco managers we spoke to, the managing editor at the editorial office was perhaps more astute. He spoke about the tension between the benefits of 'more versatile', younger staff who would be willing to 'go the extra mile' and older staff who, while less adaptable, may well be more reliable and better able to deliver quality news.

Compared with the other organizations, managers at Mediaco were among the most innovative in driving employment change. There were clearly pressures from the parent company to reduce the cost base. But we were struck by the way managers were quick to capitalize on this pressure to force through radical change in terms and conditions of employment for its highly unionized workforce.

REDUCTION OF INDIRECT LABOUR COSTS: COMMODIFYING WORK

A second management approach to reducing labour costs involves the rupture of societal norms around the extent to which employers take responsibility for the indirect costs of managing employment. These include paying for sickness absence and holiday entitlements, as well as the traditional additional payments for work carried out during unsocial working hours. Recruitment of agency temps, or casual workers, is often associated with reduced rights to these indirect pay benefits. However, many groups of workers with a non-temporary status have also experienced an erosion of benefits, as managers have sought to dismantle long-standing norms which couple the economy of work with some degree of societal responsibliity. This is particularly apparent with respect to the distinction between social and unsocial working hours. Here, the charge that work carried out during the night, or at the weekend, ought to be remunerated at a standard rate is a significant step down the road towards what Karl Polanyi would call the commodification of labour. Polanyi argued that where there is a growing disjuncture between the two spheres of society and economy, it is reasonable to expect damaging consequences in the long term:

To allow the market mechanism to be sole director of the fate of human beings and their natural environment... would result in the demolition of society. For the alleged 'commodity' cannot be shoved about, used indiscriminately, or even left unused, without affecting also the human individual who happens to be the bearer of this peculiar commodity. In disposing of a man's labour power the system would, incidentally, dispose of the physical, psychological, and moral entity 'man' attached to that tag. (1944: 73)

The strongest commitment to the use of agency temps was at Telecomco. In the Networks Division work had been outsourced to independent contractors, and in the Consumer Division managers made increasing use of temporary work agencies to supply workers. Among all operators and advisers working in the Consumer Division, there was (at the time of research) around one temp for every four workers on Telecomco contracts. However, at the workplaces we visited, we found much higher incidences of temps.

Workplace managers informed us that the practice of not recruiting staff on to Telecomco contracts was a corporate policy to keep the official headcount low and, by doing so, to maintain the confidence of City analysts. However, there were obvious cost advantages too. The company saves on sickness payments, holiday pay and other entitlements. In addition, whereas workers on Telecomco contracts enjoyed national rates of pay negotiated jointly with trade unions, agency workers received local rates of pay, which, particularly in call centres in the north of England, meant significantly lower rates. And the process of dismissal is both less costly and less time-consuming. One of the team managers on a Telecomco contract thought these benefits outweighed the costs of higher staff turnover and lower commitment:

We have obviously a higher turnover than we would if we gave [Telecomco] contracts out. Some of them [temps] aren't as committed.... But then from [Telecomco's] point of view it costs less. If the people aren't performing then it's not such a lengthy process; there is a process but it's not such a lengthy process.

(Female, full time, no. 2, Telecomco1)

But the contradictions and conflicts between the spheres of economy and society which Polanyi was so keen to illuminate are also evident at the micro-level of our organizations. The high use of agency temps at Telecomco generated a self-reinforcing circle. The greater the use of temps, the greater the immediate labour cost savings; and the higher the level of staff turnover, the greater the reductions in training investment, lessening the need for careful recruitment and selection procedures and increasing the usefulness of temporary work agencies. However, this picture of a virtuous cycle of cost efficiencies did not reflect the daily experiences of the Telecomco workers we talked to. Workers with Telecomco contracts were concerned about the deterioration of standards of services provision, and the more general collapse of a traditional work ethic. Temps, on the other hand, were fed up with working in the same job as Telecomco staff for less pay and fewer benefits. So, not only did we identify the obvious feelings of insecurity among workers, we also uncovered the potentially more damaging disintegration of mutual respect, solidarity and commitment between workers on 'the front line'. For the permanent workers, it was difficult to disentangle their personal relations from their belief that use of temps undermined their own future conditions:

You begin to wonder 'do they want all [Telecomco] staff out'. I know [agency workers] are a lot cheaper for them. They can hire and fire at will; they don't pay them for holidays—no sick leave or anything. I think that the longer you've been in [Telecomco] the more resentful you can get because you know what it was like originally when it was a good organization to work for.... There are good [agency] operators, but a lot of them are not paid to do the job. They're not paid enough to give commitment.... All these people want is a quick buck and they're out... they're loud, they're rude, they're not polite and I sit there and I cringe.

(Female, full time, no. 5, Telecomco1)

Equally, among temps, the level of acrimony was high:

I think it's off really. You sit at the side of someone doing exactly the same job and sometimes you're doing it better. Some of the [agency] operators in there are doing it a hell of a lot better than what the [Telecomco] staff are and they're getting paid twice as much as us.

(Female, full time, no. 7, Telecomco1)

So, while the cost reductions on the accounting balance sheet satisfied Telecomco managers at corporate headquarters, workers and mid-level managers were struggling with the less tangible costs associated with an erosion of trust, loyalty and commitment (Ward *et al.*

2001). A similar pattern of change was evident at other organizations, despite a somewhat less radical approach to the casualization of staffing. At Councilco, for example, several workers in the catering, leisure and community care departments all talked about the growing tendency for the council to use temporary workers and the way this seemed to represent management's reduced commitment to working conditions. A park warden with ten years' experience told us that at first he had been keen to follow his father's footsteps in working for Councilco, but times had since changed:

[The council] has treated my dad well and he got a promotion and everything like that. I've seen him go up a ladder and take charge and I thought it was quite a secure job ... so I actually applied for a job. The money was all right for the age I was. . . . When I first started for the council, there were quite a few people being taken on left, right and centre. But now there doesn't seem to be. If they are set on they are on like a 90-day scheme. Like a YTS but it's like a 90-day temporary contract.

(Male, full time, no. 6, Councilco4)

This affected morale among his team: '[Now] it's a case of getting the work done, do your seven hours, come away, get your pay and that's it.' New people coming through were not given the opportunities to go on training courses, and the overwhelming feeling, particularly among the more experienced workers, was one of a workforce group gradually being emptied of skill and experience. Overall, the pressure on Councilco to cut costs has radically altered the rules of the game. And, as we found at Telecomco, Councilco managers operating at the workplace level stressed their limited room for manoeuvre in meeting budget targets, in this case set by the Treasury Department. The manager of one of the indoor leisure centres we visited explained in some detail the way his budget had to be stretched to hold open vacancies to allow for staff redeployment from other departments:

Every year is a fresh challenge and every year you're constantly having to make savings. I get my budget on 1st April and then I'm having to make savings in the region of at least £8,000 just to make it break even ... on top of the [vacancy allowance] savings I'm already making. All departments run what they call a 5 per cent vacancy allowance. It doesn't always work because there's not that much employment out there now for people to keep swapping and changing jobs and lowering the scale especially. But we still have to carry a 5 per cent vacancy on each and every post that we have got. . . . And that's without any other savings.

(Male, full time, no. 9, Councilco4)

At both Councilco and Telecomco, workers used to permanent contracts with relatively decent conditions have watched these being whittled away through the recruitment of workers on temporary contracts, and, given these circumstances, it would seem unlikely that workers and managers will develop informal bonds of trust and commitment. This casualization of the workforce is perhaps the most extreme example of an employment strategy that reduces managers' commitment to rewarding labour above and beyond the pure economic value of work done. But, as we saw in Chapter 7, at all seven organizations many different groups of workers had faced a relentless assault on traditional premiums for working during unsocial hours, as employers sought to achieve further cuts in indirect labour costs. At Councilco, home-carers who had been promoted to the new STAR team worker posts were expected to work regular Saturdays and Sundays (two in three), and received no enhancements to their basic pay. Thus, while the basic rate was slightly higher, the overall weekly wage packet for most workers contained less. A project officer who had spent some time working as a STAR team worker told us:

That again was another bone of contention, because on home help you did get time and a half, or whatever, for weekends. But on the STAR team you didn't. So you could actually end up on less pay than you had as a home help. [The basic rate] was slightly [higher]. But it didn't always even itself out. If you did a lot of weekends, then you made up your money.

(Female, full time, no. 3, Councilco2)

At Mediaco, the extension of operating hours in 1990 to cover regular night-shift working was soon followed by the abandonment of the night-shift pay allowance. This break from traditional custom and practice was compounded by the random assignment of printers to work nights or days, with no rotation between the two. One of the printers remembered how it was when he finished his apprenticeship with colleagues:

It was four names and two got pulled out of the hat. Two went on days. Two went on nights.

(Male, full time, no. 14, Mediaco1)

And at Retailco, in line with trends across the whole retail sector, management abolished Saturday premium rates for new recruits in 1995 and converted the 20 per cent pay enhancement to a lump-sum payment to incumbent workers. In 1996 and 1997, premiums for night-time working were reduced. Instead of paying time and a third, management paid flat-rate payments of £1 per hour between 10 pm and midnight and £1.50 between 12am and 6am. Nevertheless, double time for Sunday working was still intact (for both full-timers and part-timers). And, for many workers we talked with, regular Sunday overtime working offered a much-needed opportunity to make up a decent weekly wage. But enhanced pay for overtime working during other times of the week only applied to full-time workers; as such, managers purposely restricted overtime during Monday to Saturday to part-timers. As the manager at the medium-sized store put it, 'we don't want to be paying £6 per hour if we can pay £4 per hour'.

In each case, traditional norms were being whittled away. Management appears to have been successful in its mission to transform the value of work done into a commodity value. In the past, the value of work reflected a range of societal, as well as purely economic, principles and conventions, so that payments were made for sickness or leave arrangements and working outside of standard hours was remunerated at a higher rate in order to compensate for the inconvenience imposed on the worker's private life. But these examples of the fusion of economy and society have weakened. Management has been able to respond to pressures to reduce the headcount and to extend working hours and, at the same time, has successfully cut labour costs. Workers, on the other hand, face increasing pressures on their working life and working-time arrangements and much-limited rights to claim compensating payments.

THE TRAP OF COMMODITY FETISHISM

In these two approaches to cutting labour costs—by reducing wage rates and cutting indirect labour costs—we find clear evidence of the way employers have taken the initiative in new policies of wage-setting, recruitment and working time. These new policies were implemented in a context of more intensive market pressures: strict monitoring of headcount by City analysts, pressures of privatization of public services and harsher market conditions for low-paid workers. With the vagaries of the market behind them, HR managers have sent a clear signal to workers that they are disposable and that previous employment terms do not count. Workers now find that their years within the organization do not have to be matched with steady rises in pay, their contract may or may not be renewed, and all times of the day and night are now considered 'standard' working time. However, this is not the end of the story. The problem for management is that although the uncertainties of the market may require disposable workers, designing employment policy and practice to suit plunges them into the trap of commodity fetishism. Unlike the consumption of other commodities, when an employer buys a worker's time the consumption of the commodity labour power involves adding value through the productive efforts of workers; and these efforts depend upon commitment and cooperation. As Marx showed, there is a central contradiction at the heart of the capitalist labour process—the need for workers to be both disposable and committed.

In our seven organizations, managers have exploited the rise of the market as a new organizing force in such a way as to bring to the surface this central contradiction. At Mediaco, editorial managers argued that new, younger recruits would accept lower pay and new flexible job arrangements, yet they were aware that they would probably not be as dependable as the older staff on higher, frozen rates of pay. And at Telecomco, extensive use of agency workers was meeting the criterion of disposability, but the corrosion of loyalty and commitment was clearly visible. Richard Hyman has suggested that part of the problem is that HR/personnel management has evolved as a function quite separate from the production process:

the structure of management itself insists on a dissociation between the sale of labour power and the performance of the labour process, between the worker as living individual and as instrument of production. While this division doubt- less helps obscure the exploitative basis of the capital–labour relation, it may also obstruct the formulation and implementation of a cohesive managerial strategy towards labour. (1987: 42)

Our research suggests that the intensification of market pressures coupled with a new-found confidence among employers, as the power of trade unions has waned, has exacerbated these contradictory ten- dencies. At each of the organizations, the rupturing of past wage struc- tures has tended to reinforce the commodity status of labour at the expense of establishing more secure, cohesive and cooperative relations at work. But the fundamental contradiction has not disappeared with the rise of the market. Rather, the new conditions have spurred employers to reduce both direct and indirect wage costs. Moreover, as we explore in the next section, evidence of a deterioration in opportu- nities for skilled labour and restricted programmes of skill development suggest that the search for a new productive set of relations in the British workplace will be an even more difficult and unlikely event.

REDUCTION OF AVERAGE WAGE COSTS:
UNBUNDLING SKILLS

A third way in which organizations seek to reduce costs is by cutting
the average wage cost across the workforce, or across an area of work
activity. This may be done by adapting the skill mix among the workforce. By increasing the share of low-skilled workers and reducing the
share of high-skilled workers who command high wages, organizations
can, in principle, reduce wage costs. But the strategy involves more than
a simple change in recruitment policy. It also requires a radical restructuring of the division of labour. To appreciate the importance of this
employment practice in the grander scheme of things, it is instructive
to return to the eighteenth- and nineteenth-century world of political
economy.

In *The Wealth of Nations*, Adam Smith famously argued that
employers could make more productive use of labour if they divided up
the work process into a number of smaller operations. Drawing on the
example of the trade of a pin-maker, Smith elaborated three reasons for
gains in efficiencies:

The great increase in the quantity of work... is owing to three different circumstances; first, to the increase of dexterity in every particular workman;
secondly, to the saving of the time which is commonly lost in passing from one
species of work to another; and lastly, to the invention of a great number of
machines which facilitate and abridge labour, and enable one man to do the
work of many. (1776: 112)

Of course, the division of a trade into narrow tasks, each carried out by
a separate person, also entails the simplification and the routinization
of work. Thus, while the dexterity of the worker may increase, the level
of job fulfilment is likely to decrease. Also, if workers (and indeed
generations of workers) spend the bulk of their time in a narrow job
operation, then there are fewer opportunities to understand the whole
work process and, as a result, less probability of suggesting fresh ideas
or new inventions. Indeed, while inventions in the eighteenth and
nineteenth centuries often derived from efforts by craftsmen and
engineers, this is no longer the case. So Smith's reasons do not seem to
withstand scrutiny. But if Smith's rationalization of the benefits of the
division of labour is inaccurate, then are there other reasons? Arguably,
a more plausible answer was provided by Charles Babbage (1835).

Babbage argued that the key feature of Smith's division of labour is that it involves a change in the skill mix among the workforce, which significantly reduces the total average cost of labour:

That the master manufacturer, by dividing the work to be executed into different processes, each requiring different degrees of skill or of force, can purchase exactly that precise quantity of both which is necessary for each process; whereas, if the whole work were executed by one workman, that person must possess sufficient skill to perform the most difficult, and sufficient strength to execute the most laborious, of the operations into which the art is divided. (1835: 175–6)

Returning to Smith's example of the pin-maker, Babbage shows that savings in average costs are made by replacing the well-paid and well-respected craftsmen, skilled in the trade of pin-making, with workers (men, women and children) who have fewer skills and command lower wages. Babbage describes the benefits as follows:

It appears that the wages earned by the persons employed vary from $4\frac{1}{2}d$. per day up to 6s., and consequently the skill which is required for their respective employments may be measured by those sums. Now it is evident, that if one person were required to make the whole pound of pins, he must have skill enough to earn about 5s. 3d. per day, whilst he is pointing the wires or cutting off the heads from the spiral coils—and 6s. when he is whitening the pins; ... It is also apparent, that during more than one half of his time he must be earning only 1s. 3d. per day, in putting on the heads; ... If, therefore, we were to employ, for all the processes, the man who whitens the pins, and who earns 6s. per day ... yet we must pay him for his time ... about 3s. 10d. *The pins would therefore cost, in making, three times and three quarters as much as they now do by the application of the division of labour.* (1835: 186; emphasis in original)

Across the seven organizations we researched, employers appear to have applied the Babbage principle in an effort to reduce average wage costs. A range of jobs traditionally associated with different occupational groups have been 'unbundled' through strategies of skill mix, allowing the employer to pay each separate labour task according to the capabilities required for such work. Examples of skill mix differ both by degree and by kind across the organizations. In some, the Babbage principle was applied by inventing a new post, which brought together some of the low-skill operations of pre-existing jobs, and recruiting new workers at a much reduced rate of pay. A second application of the Babbage principle involved the temporary allocation of lower-grade workers to higher-paid posts. These practices of 'acting-up' allowed organizations to fill mid-level management posts without incurring all the long-term wage costs. A third example involved the separation and outsourcing of low-skilled operations. In this case, costs are reduced first through the Babbage principle and second through the process of auctioning off work to the lowest bidder. Finally, some organizations have reduced skill requirements in favour of sophisticated machinery.[2] In this case, the potential for skill development of a job is limited by user-friendly technology, leading to a more superficial experience of work. The employer requires workers with limited skills, but with a sense of duty to the workings of the machine. We examine each of these issues in turn in the light of some of the findings from our research.

Creating new low-skill positions

At Mediaco and Healthco, managers talked to us with enthusiasm about the way they had designed a new low-grade post. We were told that this served two objectives: first, by separating out many of the low-skilled and routine aspects carried out by relatively qualified workers, it freed up time for them to devote to the core activity for which they were paid; and second, managers could develop the skills and careers of workers in the new post in ways that were restricted in traditional posts, because of the role of trade unions or the force of custom and practice. It also became clear that there were significant cost savings to be had, fol-lowing Babbage's principle of unbundling to reduce average wage costs.

At Mediaco, the production manager at the printworks explained that he had introduced a new post of production assistant in order to free up time for qualified craft workers. The new production assistant would also be required to be flexible—working across departments to develop a wide range of competencies in printing and plate-making, and working days and nights on a ten-week rota across seven days a week. However, as we described in Chapter 6, the new post was viewed with suspicion among some of the printers and plate-makers. They were concerned that as older plate-makers retired, they were being replaced

---

[2] In this case, the Babbage principle is modified by the insights of Andrew Ure (in his *Philosophy of Manufactures*, 1830) who argued that it was the introduction of machinery, as well as the division of labour, that ensured that workers were transformed into efficient 'factory hands'. He observed that: 'The principle of the factory system then is to substitute mechanical science for hand skill, and the partition of a process into its essential constituents... skilled labour gets progressively superseded, and will, eventually, be replaced by mere overlookers of machines.' (cited in Thompson 1983: 47).

by new workers recruited as production assistants who would eventually carry out the same work. This represented a threat to their craft tradition. Moreover, it represented an erosion of the tradition of the relatively high pay earned by craft and craft assistant workers following a history of strong regulation by trade unions. For example, assistant printers earned 87.5 per cent of the basic wage of skilled printers—£25,000 as opposed to £29,000 on the 1997–8 pay scale. Hence, because of the traditional strength of unions in the newspaper printing industry, relatively low-skilled workers were able to benefit from the relatively high-paying character of the industry. However, new recruits to the post of production assistant earned between just £13,000 and £18,000, with no additional bonus for shift rotation. The new pay differential between craft and assistant workers was thus somewhere between 47 per cent and 65 per cent, constituting a significant cut in average wage costs to the organization.

At Healthco, we found similar evidence of cost-cutting through skill mix. Managers had designed a new grade of unqualified nurse to replace the traditional nurse auxiliary and assistant nurse posts. However, the new position differed in two important ways from the traditional unqualified posts. First, the role of the new health care assistant (HCA) would overlap with the traditional job demarcation of the qualified nurse; managers were confident that qualified nurses would, over time, adjust their work upwards, enabling some substitution of HCAs in the lower grades (grades C and D). Secondly, the pay structure for HCAs was entirely designed by Healthco managers, whereas pay for the traditional posts was regulated at a national level and followed terms and conditions set out by the Whitley Council.

Managers at Healthco were quite explicit that this new grade would allow them to reduce the ratio of qualified to unqualified nursing staff and thus to reduce the average wage cost of providing nursing services—to employ 'fewer of the expensive people'. Managers of nursing services—a body that oversees the work of nurses across all directorates in the Trust—set out five-year targets for the appropriate mix of qualified and unqualified nurses within each directorate. At the time of our research (midway through their five-year target) the skill mix across the Trust had already been reduced from 85 per cent qualified, 15 per cent unqualified, to 75 per cent qualified, 25 per cent unqualified. The bulk of this change was achieved by halting the recruitment of qualified nursing staff and targeting the new HCA post. The shape and form of the new post is thus critical to the skill mix strategy and to the overall drive to reduce average costs. The design of a new local pay structure presented Healthco managers with an opportunity to recruit new HCAs at a rate of pay lower than the traditional nursing assistant, perhaps by appealing to the need to respond to market rates. However, this is not where the main savings were to be found. These were achieved by means of the Babbage principle. A director of one of the larger directorates told us that in setting up the new post, the Trust was very careful to present the jobs and responsibilities of HCAs and grade D qualified nurses as different, but admitted that it was expected that HCAs would eventually cover the tasks of grade C and D nurses, on substantially lower rates of pay.[3] The intention was to expand the work of HCAs as the work of qualified nurses was gradually broken down into separate components and distributed among lesser-skilled staff. On the one hand, this policy seemed to provide low-skilled recruits with a more clearly defined plan of skills development, matched with pay progression (see Chapter 6). But, on the other hand, it limits the volume of employment opportunities for people wishing to take up posts as clinically trained nurses, creates tension among nurses working at the boundaries of the new division of tasks and may even damage the quality of patient care.

In both the examples cited above, managers sought to reduce average wage costs by unbundling jobs into discrete skills. At Mediaco, derecognition of trade unions enabled management to sidestep many years of union control over the pay and task demarcations of craft and craft assistant roles. And at Healthco, management successfully made the first move in redrawing the boundaries between qualified and unqualified nursing tasks, with professional nursing associations slow to realize the importance of controlling broader 'bundles' of nursing labour to maintain higher average pay. Managers thus took the opportunity to recruit workers into new low-skill posts and, by recasting the traditional division of labour between high-skill and low-skill grades, were able to exploit the economic benefits illuminated by Babbage: substituting cheap labour for the more expensive, skilled and qualified workers.

'Acting-up' in higher-paid posts

One of the more surprising findings from our study—something we had not read about in other accounts of employment change—was the

---

[3] In 1998, new HCA recruits started on £9,400 and moved up to £10,100 on the completion of NVQ level 3 and to £10,700 after a further twelve months of satisfactory performance. In comparison, low-grade qualified nurses earned between £11,100 and £14,700 (grades C and D, 1998 rates).

quite extensive use of 'acting-up' (see Chapter 5). We talked with workers 'acting-up' at workplaces in Bankco, Retailco and Telecomco, as well as in the two public sector organizations. In general, the practice is used to cover a temporary absence or unfilled vacancy with a lower-paid and less-skilled member of the workforce. The person who is 'acting-up' is typically trained for the temporary post and may receive the higher rate of pay commensurate with the higher grade. Significantly, however, at the end of the temporary period the person returns to their original post and rate of pay, despite having achieved a higher level of qualifi- cation and skill. This unlocking of the linkage between pay and skill provides our second instance of Babbage's principle of skill mix. In this case, the need to pay higher-skilled workers to carry out a job is met on a temporary day-to-day, or month-to-month basis, redefining the status of each worker by the particular task carried out that day, or that month. Moreover, status can move backwards as well as forwards, in contrast to the usual expectations of steady upward advancement through the internal job ladder. Again, the link between a rate of pay and a broad bundle of job tasks of different skills has been unhinged as organiza- tions have acted to cut average wage costs.

At Councilco, a number of people we talked to had experience of 'acting-up' for periods stretching from six months to more than three years. At each of the three community care centres we talked to two or three people 'acting-up'. In Chapter 5 we documented the case of one woman who joined Councilco as a clerk typist in 1989, was promoted to office manager for three and half years and then had to return to her original post because the promotion was only on a temporary, 'acting- up' basis. At another care centre, one of the neighbourhood coord- inators was 'acting-up' from her permanent post as home-care organizer. The 'promotion' was worth around £1,500 extra each year, but, like the clerk typist, she had no idea how long this extra money would last. In each case, those we talked to made the point that Councilco was unwilling to invest in additional permanent posts because of the uncertainty of service provision and the need to keep wage costs under control. All residential care homes had recently been closed down; and the private sector was moving in on the day-care centre market. So, when senior managers were seconded to Councilco headquarters to participate in a long-term strategic review of services, Councilco did not secure permanent promotions.

There was a similar story at other organizations. At the telemarketing centre in Telecomco, one manager described his promotion as a 'secondment'. And he was not alone. Many of the level-one team manager positions were staffed by full-time and part-time telephone advisers in an 'acting-up' capacity, and many team managers were 'acting-up' in level-two management posts.[4] Like Councilco, the 'acting-up' posts did not have a clear start and end point leading to gradual upwards progression, such as one might expect with an apprenticeship or a probationary period. Managers at this particular centre were interviewed every three months; those who failed the interview returned to their lower job position, those who passed merely retained the 'acting-up' post. We found no evidence of managers moving into substantive posts. The centre manager provided us with the rationale for the policy:

You're not treated in any different way. You deliver against the results and targets that are set for you and there are no allowances made. So you earn your bonus. The benefit, I suppose, they don't have the salary to necessarily pay for all the substantive positions that are required. If you wanted to fill that centre with all substantive [posts] it would be a phenomenal bill.

(Female, full time, no. 1, Telecomco3)

The irony was that even the centre manager was 'acting-up'. She had been with Telecomco since 1996 as a level-two manager, but was 'seconded' to the level-four centre manager position. However, aside from the cost-based rationale, it was clear that the lack of certainty and stability in job posts was bad for morale and, as we reported in Chapter 5, many of the managers expressed strong feelings of frustration. So, ultimately, the potential for cost savings may be offset by the need to continually replenish the skill base among management staff because of the speed at which they were disappearing. A manager 'acting-up' in a level-two post illustrated the problem with a recent experience:

One of my managers actually resigned when she was supposed to be going [for an interview to retain her secondment]. She said 'I can't go through it again'. She gave me a resignation letter to finish in one month. Luckily enough I managed to talk her round.... She's a brilliant manager.

(Male, full time, no. 2, Telecomco3)

At Retailco, general assistants often 'acted-up' to cover mid-level section manager posts—typically, to fill in for a manager who was off sick, or to cover an unfilled vacancy. There was also the routine use of 'acting-up'—on a minute-by-minute basis—among shelf-fillers who worked on the cash-out desks during busy periods. All shelf-fillers at

---

[4] Level 1 team managers typically manage a team of around nineteen telephone advisers. Managers in a level 2 post have responsibility for six to eight team managers.

Retailco were trained to operate the cash registers, but were only paid the higher rate of pay for the exact time spent on that task (to the nearest fifteen-minute interval registered when each worker logs on and off). When they return to their job of filling shelves, their rate of pay drops, despite their increased level of skill.

In this case, Retailco management had incorporated a finely detailed version of the 'acting-up' practice. And it is this example that best illustrates the apparent ease with which organizations have applied Babbage's principle of skill mix, and perhaps even surpassed it. High-skill tasks can now be completed by workers who have the requisite training, but who no longer command the high wages commensurate with their level of skill. Instead of building up skills in line with pro-gressive pay rises, the long-term status of groups of workers remains fixed, subject to temporary fluctuations in pay, as they are called on to carry out high-level tasks or to fill high-grade job functions. While these changes signify a major break in traditional practices, there is evidence that there may be limits to management practices of unbundling skills through use of 'acting-up'. Most notably, at Retailco, when workers who were normally paid as cash-till operators were asked to fill shelves (what we might call 'acting-down'), they were not paid at a lower rate.

Outsourcing low-skill jobs

A third application of the Babbage principle involves a similar unbund-ling and separation of skills, but in this case the work at the low-skill end is outsourced. Cost advantages accrue both from the division of labour and from the process of auctioning off the work to the lowest bidder, through the process of market-led contracting.

At Bankco, managers outsourced a number of job activities in a bid to reduce average wage costs. For example, several areas of 'mass-production' type work, including cash-handling and cheque-processing activities, were outsourced in 1997. At Councilco, managers separated out the low-level job tasks traditionally carried out by home-carers in the Community Care Division, in recognition of the ability of a growing private sector that could compete successfully to win contracts for low-level services. Unlike Bankco, Councilco management was split between those operating in an invented 'purchaser' role and those operating in a 'provider' role—following the principles of the public services internal market. Thus, on the one side of the organization, managers were keen to outsource services to the lowest bidder, and on the other side, managers talked to us at great length of the difficulties of trying to hold on to a reasonable market share to protect jobs. In practice, these pressures led to a redesigned carer role that no longer included the low-skill tasks of cleaning and shopping. One woman carer with twelve years of experience at Councilco talked to us about the changes in her job:

Before it was, go in, do what you were told to do and leave. And now, it's more personal.... It's a more intense care package they put in. I originally went in just as a home help, did the shopping, did the housework and left. And it's sort of progressed in that they are looking more after the person and their needs.

(Female, full time, no. 3, Councilco2)

Thus, the strategy in the Community Care Department has been to redefine jobs as more skilled, but at the obvious cost of reducing overall employment opportunities as low-level work is outsourced. Again, albeit with a conflicting set of management strategies and objectives, this follows Babbage's principle of matching skill levels to wage levels. As Councilco was not able to reduce wage rates to those paid by private sector providers, it instead sought to raise the skill level, or value, of those tasks performed by inside labour.

New technology and limited skill development

In our final example of the Babbage principle, some organizations had restricted the growth of average wage costs through the introduction of user-friendly machinery that required few skills for its operation. The type of technologies of interest in this case include those that substitute for the use of high-skill labour by requiring operators of limited skill in a production process previously demanding a broader knowledge on the part of the worker. From our research, we found four prime examples: the introduction of more sophisticated printing machinery at Mediaco; the use of new communications technologies to separate out telephone queries at Telecomco; the replacement of traditional baking skills with computerized technologies at Retailco; and the use of machines on the assembly line at Pharmco.

At the printworks of Mediaco, many of the older printers talked to us about the 'downward turn' in their jobs accompanying the use of more sophisticated machinery. One printer nearing retirement age stressed to us the change in the nature of skill in the job:

It was a skill [the job of printer]. It was a skill and those skills have disappeared. I must confess there's not a lot of skills in here today. They tell you you're skilled... [and] the machines are complex in a way; the machines are a damn sight more complex and all it is is basically routine. You do need skills to a degree, but it's repetitive.... Basically, you come in this job and you do the same thing every night, or every day, and really it is just like working at Ford's on the production line. It's no different. It's just the same thing. There's no variation.

(Male, full time, no. 12, Mediaco1)

And at Telecomco, highly sophisticated information and telecommunications systems had been introduced with the explicit intention of separating out different types of incoming call according to the level of skill required. At the time of our research, management was intending to redesign the grade structure for operators around four levels—so-called 'call-handling grades'—with calls of different degrees of difficulty assigned to particular grades of staff. Managers claimed that staff would benefit from being able to handle an increased variety of calls, which at present are divided across operators by function (such as repairs, general enquiries, and so on). However, there was also some acknowledgement that the new grade structure may limit the potential for staff to develop their skills. But, for Telecomco, there were apparent net benefits, since, once implemented, it would enable managers to practise the Babbage principle of paying staff only for the exact level of skill demanded of the task carried out.

At Retailco, we talked to a baker in his early thirties who had worked full time with the organization since the summer of 1981. He came from a family of bakers and was proud of his bakery skills, but angry at the deskilling of his job. The application of new technology to the job of the baker was indirect. At each of the stores, small-scale equipment had been removed in favour of centralized production involving high-tech, computerized machinery and the delivery of almost finished foodstuffs to the local stores:

I am skilled, but I don't class this job as skilled.... It's so easy. It's completely different. We used to have to make the bread and cakes, etc. Now it's all brought in frozen for us. All we have to do is finish it... put a bit of apricot glaze on and a bit of piping—that's it. The doughnuts, we just roll them in sugar now. We used to make them ourselves.... We're like robots. Everything is speed. The tasks that used to break the monotony have gone.

(Male, full time, no. 3, Retailco2)

Finally, managers at Pharmco were perhaps the most explicit about the role of machinery in limiting the need for skilled workers. In a meeting with three senior HR managers, we were told that the type of machinery used in the production process required workers to be 'as close to robots as possible while still remaining human'. Elaborating on this, they explained that new recruits had to be responsible enough to be able to deal with instructions, but sufficiently under-educated and lacking in initiative as not to question instructions. As we discussed in Chapter 5, this typically meant that managers purposely selected the worst performers among interviewees for job posts.

In each case, with the application of more and more sophisticated technologies there seems to have been a shift in the perceptions of the nature of work, as well as in what managers believed were the appropriate personal characteristics to carry out the job. The changes we describe call to mind Sennett's (1998) description of 'illegibility'. Drawing on a description of workplace change in a Boston bakery, Sennett makes the argument that the user-friendly nature of new technologies limits the potential for skill development and leads to a more superficial experience of work: 'As a result of working in this way, the bakers now no longer actually know how to bake bread ... program-dependent labourers, they can have no hands-on knowledge. The work is no longer legible to them, in the sense of understanding what they are doing' (ibid.: 68).

From our research, we found that managers, keen to exploit cost savings from the use of new machinery, found themselves facing the paradox of wanting workers with limited skills, but also with a sense of duty (and identity) to the workings of the machine. However, if, as Sennett suggests, these new types of work environment reinforce a sense of 'detachment and confusion' among workers, then managers may struggle to rely on a sense of identity and commitment among deskilled workers.

CONCLUSION

In Part II of this book, we documented the enormity of change that has occurred at each of our seven case study organizations. It is now clear that the three dimensions of employment change share one thing in common: the drive to reduce labour costs. Importantly, this strategy extends as much to the two public sector organizations as it does to the five private sector organizations. This suggests that accounts of the British production system that bemoan the emphasis on cost reduction as the main long-term strategy of competitiveness apply equally to the process of reform of public sector services provision. In both sectors, it is difficult to envisage a positive transformation of the nature of work and employment without a commitment by management to invest in labour, rather than the persistent and widespread practice of taking labour costs out.

Reduced labour costs is only one half of the story. In the next chapter we show how workers have also lost out on the bargain over the level of work effort. Taken together, it seems we have moved to an era characterized by an unfair day's work for an unfair day's pay.

9

Work Intensification and
Forms of Control

INTRODUCTION

In this book we have explored the ways in which seven organizations responded to a variety of different pressures. In this chapter we focus on how the regulation of individual employee performance at the workplace has been tightened. As we saw in Chapter 8, the pressures faced by organizations have caused them to prioritize the reduction of labour costs. They have, however, also led to efforts by management to increase labour intensification. As a result, people are working harder and for longer hours and at less of a cost to the employer (Burchell *et al.* 1999; Green 2000, 2001).

We will focus specifically upon the labour process, the job tasks and the ways in which these changes have been associated with the emergence of new kinds of managerial control strategies within the workplace. The issue of 'control' has been central to studies of workplaces since the publication of Goodrich's classic work, *The Frontier of Control* (1920). In Goodrich's view, the site of the job, the immediate point of production where work is carried out, uncovers in its details critical aspects of power relations within the workplace. Analysis of these details, he argued, reveal aspects of the organization and the production process that are otherwise hidden. A considerable literature has developed in this tradition in which the question of control has been more carefully examined and with it the idea that these control mechanisms may vary between workplaces and over time. Friedman (1977), for example, argued that groups of workers critical to the survival of the organization could establish for themselves (or be encouraged to have) a degree of 'responsible autonomy'. Other groups would be subjected to more direct supervisory control through the regulated operation of the technology. The idea of 'control by machine' has been developed in interesting ways in the context of the introduction of new information technology and its operation in the expanding service sector occupations (Frenkel *et al.* 1999; Green 2000; Hage and Powers 1992; Poynter 2000a,b; Sturdy *et al.* 2001). Moreover, in the changed context of the 1980s, increasing attention has been paid to the ways in which workplace control has been achieved through other means. We have already examined how changes in the labour contract (relating to hours worked, payment, etc.) shape what happens in the workplace. Others have identified how the operation of tight financial budgets, supported by frequent audits, can have a similar controlling effect. In discussing these developments, Power (1997) has referred to the 'Audit Society', and examined how these budgetary pressures have been translated into patterns of control across the public and private sectors. Each of these pressures was evident at the different places of work we visited, although the outcomes varied from place to place.

PRESSURES TO CHANGE WHAT WORKERS DO AND HOW THEY DO IT

Building upon the analysis in Chapter 8 of the different labour cost-reducing strategies, we now consider the pressures behind the growing prominence attached to the customer in the delivery of services in the public and private sector. We then examine how these pressures have been interpreted by each of the organizations. Although it is twenty years since Peters and Waterman (1982) argued that successful organizations are those in which there is a high degree of consumer sovereignty, the implications of management adopting this strategy for their workforces is less well understood now than it was then. And, of course, there are a number of important differences in how organizations have overseen this change in the nature of work, particularly in those service sector companies where meeting the needs of the customer has always been an important part of what employees do—such as in retailing and in hospitals. However, it is possible to conceptualize the pressures crystallizing in two discrete ways. In tandem, these forces lie behind the transformation in the last two decades of what workers do across a range of different economic sectors (Albrecht and Zemke 1985; Frenkel *et al.* 1999: 2–6; Gutek 1995; Herzenberg *et al.* 1998; Macdonald and Sirianni 1996).

The first pressure is the push for increased product and service customization. As perhaps one example of what Bell (1973) meant when he pointed towards the emergence of the 'post-industrial society', the production and delivery of products and services has become increasingly differentiated. The how and the when of service delivery is more and more likely to reflect the personal preferences of consumers, or customers. While not quite the rupture with Fordist techniques that was once suggested (Hage and Powers 1992), it nevertheless means important things for what workers do, and the wider context within which they perform tasks. As table 9.1 sets out, this broad shift continues to mean different things for different organizations. Across our seven organizations the range of products and services delivered has fragmented. In the private sector, this takes a variety of forms: from shorter batch runs at Mediaco and Pharmco, to a widening of the range of products stocked at Retailco, to the massive increase in the range of financial and communication products and services on offer at Bankco and Telecomco, respectively. In the public sector, change is no less far-reaching and as equally varied. At both Councilco and Healthco we see evidence of the how and the when of service delivery being manipulated to fit with what customer feedback and focus groups reveal as customer wants.

The second pressure, and one that often accompanies the first, is the deregulation of product and service markets. This tendency is evident across both public and private sectors. Widespread deregulation through legislative reform in the 1980s and 1990s, in sectors as diverse as finance on the one hand, and local government on the other, challenged the market share of organizations. So, for example, in sectors such as banking and telecommunications, deregulation has in each case changed the terms of competition, and led to new firms entering the market, often better able to respond to these new terms. Deregulation sets the context in which workers perform their work at each of the seven organizations. At Councilco market conditions were created through state restructuring. This meant a de facto deregulation of service delivery. The provision of community care and the maintenance of the parks became subject to competitive pressures. At Bankco, Mediaco and Telecomco, changes in market conditions, largely brought about through deregulation, threatened existing market shares. Competition also came from outside of each sector. For example, Bankco found itself vying with large retailers, such as Retailco, to provide banking services to customers.

These twin pressures were enforced through the monitoring of each organization's performance. In the case of each of the private sector organizations, and as we have made clear throughout this book,

Table 9.1. Pressures to change what workers do and how they do it

	Bankco	Councilco	Healthco	Mediaco	Pharmco	Retailco	Telecomco
Product/service customization	Increase in the number of financial products and services	Limited: departments are changing the services they deliver and when they deliver them	The timing of healthcare delivery is matched more carefully to the profile of the patient	Shorter runs to reflect increasingly differentiated products	Differentiated demand for products requiring greater product customization	Increase in the number of food and non-food products	Increase in the number of products and services
Product/service market deregulation	New forms of competition inside and outside of the banking sector	Direct and indirect competition with private sector agencies for service provision contracts	—	Competition with other media types for advertising revenue	—	Competition in non-retail areas, e.g. finance	New entrants in the telecommunications market leads to increased competition with other service suppliers

performance was overseen and commented upon by the City. The health of the companies was monitored through various proxies, of which the headcount of numbers employed was the most common. In this way, the share value of the organizations fluctuated and with it questions of take-over, merger, strategic alliance and downsizing emerged as part of the daily discussion within the office. Managers found themselves pressured to introduce policies aimed at extracting greater effort from staff. This was an overt and consistent feature of each of the private sector workplaces.

On the face of it, the two public sector organizations—Councilco and Healthco—would appear to have been under different sets of pressure. Historically, these organizations have had to operate within an employment and performance context overseen by the state. This has usually meant significant differences between the public and the private sectors in the recruitment of staff, the job tasks performed by staff and the kinds of expectations staff had over their longer-term careers. In hospitals and town halls, public services have been organized and delivered through the activities of workers and professions imbued with some kind of public service ethos. While often criticized as being over-bureaucratized and inefficient, they nevertheless operated with sets of criterion that differed from those generated in the market. As we saw in the last chapter, however, the state has come to operate as stern a financial regime as the City. In both local government and health, quasi-market competition has been introduced in an effort to dismantle the traditional public–private divide. The reorganization of services delivery in the local authority and the hospital along the lines of the market informed how workers at both organizations talked about their work, and how their work was organized.

In the private sector, therefore, the performance pressures are reflected in the power exercised by the City and the importance attached to the share price; in the public sector, the state is the source of pressure, using indicators such as budgets and waiting lists to demonstrate its capacity to compete with the private sector. During the 1990s it seems that the state increasingly acted like the City, regulating local government and health sectors through ever-tighter financial and performance criteria. Throughout our research we were struck by the way managers at the two public sector organizations were often more concerned about performance pressures than were their private sector counterparts. Championing the role of 'captains of industry' in local government and health reform, the state continues to invoke the language of business—efficiency and competitiveness—and this has played its part in changing the employment relationship and the norms and values within which it is couched in each organization (Cabinet Office 1999).

The local managers to whom we talked at each of the seven organizations felt these pressures, often intensified not alleviated through corporate decisions. They all found themselves looking over their shoulder for the reaction of more senior managers, who in turn were looking over their shoulder for the reaction of central government and the City to the level of their performance. Their understanding of these pressures and the capacities available to them for manoeuvre varied from one to the other. Most frequently, their responses favoured short-term action—adjusting employment policies as quick fixes in the face of enormous pressures. These fixes were made easier by the changes that had taken place in the wider external environment. Frequently, managers referred back to the trade-union era, which had, in the 1990s, been transformed in some way into a period of partnership.

As a consequence of the changes in the external conditions experienced by our seven organizations, significant adjustments took place in the organization and representation of power relationships in the workplace. Here, managers in the private and the public sectors shared a common strategy of persuading, pressuring and cajoling their staff to change their working routines and do things differently. Often this involved people acquiescing to arrangements that they found distasteful and unjust. Frequently, we found that these managers were women, pointing to another significant aspect of cultural change in the workplace. Historically, women have performed much of what Leidner (1993) calls 'routinized service work'. In large service organizations such as banks, hospital and supermarkets, women have tended to do many of the routine jobs. However, the preponderance of women in service sector workplaces changed to some degree in the 1990s and men have found themselves employed in jobs that would once have been seen clearly as 'women's work'. This trend is seen most clearly at the check-out, on call-centre desks and in a variety of other 'production-line service work' (Bowen and Lawler 1992) that blossomed in the late 1980s. For example, UK employment data show that the proportion of jobs as sales assistants taken by men increased between 1990 and 1998 from 21 per cent to 26 per cent (Grimshaw et al. 2001).[1] Undoubtedly, this has involved an adjustment in expectations for both men and women.

[1] Here we refer to the category 'sales assistants' as defined by the Standard Occupational Classification (1990 definition), code number 72. Full-timers and part-timers are included in our calculations.

It has also involved quite complex alterations in the culture of work-places, with men and women working side by side.

In considering the ways in which these changes were introduced, we frame our analysis around three interrelated processes. The first is the increasing dominance of the customer and how the need to sell goods and services has reordered expectations of workers and the pattern of authority relationships within the organization. This is most acute for those workers who deal directly with customers (so called 'front-line workers'), but it also has a more general effect upon all jobs. Alongside these changes in the nature of work performed by a large number of staff, organizational restructuring has increased the number of staff dealing directly with customers (Frenkel *et al.* 1999; Herzenberg *et al.* 1998; Macdonald and Sirianni 1996; McCammon and Griffin 2000; Sturdy *et al.* 2001). This change has accompanied the wider turn towards the construction of the customer as a source of external control of workers' job performance. In these ways, by appealing to the needs of the customer, and by involving customers as de facto supervisors, we found that managers can successfully use a third party to secure gains in labour productivity.

The second process that has changed both the nature of work and the nature of control is the redesigning of job tasks. Generally, it seems that many of the jobs performed in the workplaces we studied involved increasing amounts of responsibility and increasing numbers of discrete tasks. Gallie *et al.* (1998) refer to this as 'up-skilling', in the sense that people take on additional responsibilities. In these ways, workers were increasingly expected to manage themselves. Building upon our earlier analysis in Chapter 6, where we set out how organizations had recast skills across levels, here we consider how responsibilities have been expanded for those at the lower end of the job ladder and how this is often experienced by individual workers as added pressure. This is especially the case when workers are working longer hours, when they (most commonly women) are juggling working time with domestic responsibilities in the home and when the satisfactory performance of extra tasks is tied to the possibility of future promotion.

Thirdly, organizations have developed new methods to control the pace of work and the quality of performance. This has been achieved though technological developments (computer-mediated in many respects) and a plethora of human relations techniques and complex output measurements. This third example is perhaps most directly related to the intensification of work. We draw upon Francis Green's (2000 and 2001) work, among others, on how the introduction of new technology at each of our workplaces increases work intensification in some occupations. This analysis adds a new dimension to our earlier discussion of delayering within the organizations and the removal of middle layers of management and supervision. What is suggested here is that this change in the organization of work is simply one aspect of the division of labour within the organization. Warhurst and Thompson (1998) have referred to this as a 'shadow division of labour'. What runs alongside it and monitors its operation is a hierarchical structure through which punishment and reward are orchestrated and work intensification levels pressured upwards.

CUSTOMER SATISFACTION

One of the major changes in the nature of work performed at our seven organizations is the growth in the number of jobs in which dealing with customers is a central task. Mirroring the trend in the USA, where employment in the service sector makes up 74 per cent of total employment, the UK service economy now employs 71 per cent of all workers (OECD 2000: table 3.2). In light of this growth, a series of recent studies have turned to examine what it is like to manage and to work in these new jobs. For example, Gallie and colleagues, in a study of the changing nature of the employment relationship, argued that: '[T]he last decade has seen the growth of more stringent criteria for "customer" satisfaction across a wide range of service industries and a greater emphasis on personal skills in the organization of work at all levels' (1998: 56). In their survey of UK workplaces they found that 46 per cent of staff were predominantly involved in what they refer to as 'people work'. Although the form taken by this type of work differs from one organization to the next, the trend was towards an increasing proportion of the workforce working directly with customers. Fuller and Smith (1991) seek to capture the diversity of forms through the term 'interactive service work'. This type of work is defined by the production of quality service work by staff and is accompanied, they argue, by the emergence of a form of 'management by customers' (ibid.: 1–2; see also Leidner 1993: 1). Du Gay (1996), among others, has further developed this theme through his work on the 'cult of the customer', in which the customer takes on an almost magical quality, and whose needs have to be met by the worker. This form of management can be seen to mark a departure from formal bureaucratic systems of control, of the sort set out by Edwards (1979), although it by no means necessarily implies a loosening of the managerial reins. At our case study organizations this development was most noticeable in the newly established call centres. This is a general phenomenon and Poynter has reflected that:

Call centres are the new front office or contact point for increasing numbers of customers in the service economy. The call centre labour process facilitates a twenty-four hour, seven-day a week provision of transactions and advice. Britain has become the call centre capital of Europe with over 250,000 workers employed, often on short shifts and flexible hours, in workplaces that share many of the characteristics and controlled environment of the assembly line. (2000a: 151)

But the trend is not restricted to call centres alone. Across our organizations there has been a general growth in the number of staff whose work involves interacting with and dealing with customers—face-to-face or via the telephone. This direct coupling of the employee with the customer has been accompanied by other, more subtle, changes. For example, at each organization we found that management used customer surveys and focus groups to gauge customer priorities and levels of satisfaction. This mirrors what others have found in studies of work in the service economy (Fuller and Smith 1991; Korczynski *et al.* 2000; McCammon and Griffin 2000). The 'customer call-back-system' at Telecomco is one clear example of this. Here, managers call customers after they have dealt with an operator, in order to quantify how satisfied they were with the service they received. Nor are these practices limited to the private sector. Measuring satisfaction in the public sector was also important, with managers at both Councilco and Healthco using customer-satisfaction surveys in order to judge service quality levels. Quite generally therefore, the notion of 'customer satisfaction' was used across both sectors to benchmark the performance of individual staff. As Fuller and Smith argue:

Managers now have formally designated accomplices in controlling workers, insofar as they exploit customers for their observations about how service is delivered. In sum, customers' reports broaden *managerial* power, augmenting it with *customer* power; conflicts between employers and employees may thus be reconstituted as conflicts between employees and customers. (1991: 11; original emphasis)

At all seven case-study organizations the place of 'the customer' in the logic of corporate management has changed quite significantly. As table 9.2 sets out, this shift is a general tendency across the organizations, although as one would expect, given the differences we have

Table 9.2. Customer satisfaction

	Bankco	Councilco	Healthco	Mediaco	Pharmco	Retailco	Telecomco
Importance of customers	Central: couched as more important due to the increasing number of financial products available	Relatively new: mix of mimicry of private sector and reaction to state restructuring	Relatively new: largely a reaction to state restructuring in the delivery of healthcare	Complex: need to maintain satisfaction amongst both buyers and advertisers	Growing; change in product markets behind increased demands of customers on all elements of product delivery	Central: in the face of growing market concentration, customer care is increasingly the driver of competition	Central: increased customer sovereignty in light of deregulation of UK telecommunications sector
Response by organization	Greater attention to product knowledge; taping of calls to ensure dialogue is routinized	Use of surveys to evaluate how and when services are delivered; production of a range of bench-marking statistics	Patients rebranded as customers and surveyed on their level of satisfaction with services; national production of waiting lists as proxies of customer satisfaction	Focus-group results feed into restructuring of product in order to meet customer demands	Change production runs and invest in new technology and machinery	Greater attention to product knowledge among general assistants; cashiers/packers expected to engage with customers using a script	Greater attention to product knowledge among operators; taping of phone calls to ensure dialogue is routinized; training for engineers in customer-friendly skills

outlined throughout this book, the form of this transformation differs markedly between each organization, and even between workplaces. Staff at Retailco have always been involved in direct contact with customers who come to shop in the stores. The same was the case at Bankco, where cashiers would deal face-to-face over the counter with customers. Patterns of organizational change have affected the intensity of this interaction and also its purpose. For example, at Retailco new loyalty cards were introduced in an attempt to increase the 'loyalty' of the customer to the company, at the same time allowing the company to monitor the nature and timing of consumption patterns. In some ways this was an attempt by the organization to invoke the same loyalty in customers that they used to show to local stores before the shift in UK retailing towards supermarkets in the 1980s. The cards are swiped at the checkout on the occasion of each visit. In this way the checkout comes to represent more that a simple cash transaction in exchange of groceries. It is understood by the organization as the front line of its customer servicing operations and as such is deeply affected by changes in retailing policy. For example, Retailco regularly alters its product line (especially in relation to fresh and chilled produce, bread, etc.) and this was explained to us in terms of the needs of customers. This has strong implications for the role of the checkout operatives who are pressed regularly to update and refresh their knowledge of all the products held in the store. Their capacity to identify different types of tomato, new kinds of exotic fruit, varieties of freshly baked bread, and so on, is seen to be critical to both the smooth running of the checkout operation and the ongoing relationship between the store and its customers. In the absence of real price competition between UK food retailers, management at Retailco argued that being attentive to the needs of customers was how a marginal increase in the domestic market would be gained.

This pattern runs right through the operation of the modern retailing store. A fast food section manager who had been with Retailco since 1972 indicated how this policy of customer care had permeated into the fabric of all the jobs in his section.

We have a Complaints Book in place, we have a Requests Book in place.... You know, if someone requests something, it could turn into a complaint.... The customer comes first at the end of the day.... At one time nobody could do a refund, [the customer] had to go to a supervisor. Now anybody can do a refund/exchange. We encourage everybody to deal with a customer rather than pack them from pillar to post.

(Female, full time, no. 3, Retailco3)

More generally, changes in product lines are associated with changes in the layout of the store and the location of particular products, especially those on special offer, and so on. As a result, customers often require guidance and employees involved in stacking shelves have found that their jobs have become more intensive as a result. A general assistant with two years' experience outlined how he perceived this shift towards customer-participation. He was clear that it now involved more work and that a great part of his job increasingly involved 'getting hassle off customers' (Male, part time, no. 12, Retailco3). At Retailco the quality of customer care is used as a means of differentiating its product from that of its competitors. This, in turn, raises the expectations of customers. Hence, customers expect more from staff who are made aware, through training and induction into corporate policies, of the need to satisfy the customer in order for the organization to remain competitive. In the general management of the store, devices such as the 'steering wheel' (see Chapter 3) directly link individual and team performance with the needs of the customer.

At Bankco the pattern of restructuring broke the direct link between the customer and the front-line employee. In closing its branches and centralizing many of its personal customer functions, Bankco gambled that it could recreate the 'customer-facing' element of its service provision through the use of new technologies. Under the new arrangements, existing customers with account queries and potential new customers interact with the bank though its call-centre operators. These operators (like those on the checkouts) are in the front line of relations with customers—'they are usually the only employees to deal directly with them' (McCammon and Griffin 2000: 279; see also Frenkel *et al.* 1999; Zemke and Schaaf 1989); but they 'faced' the customers along a telephone line, and as such did not have the visual clues and body language signs that are important in face-to-face interaction. In recognition of this, the bank equipped operators with verbal and emotional skills, about how to manage relationships with customers via the telephone. Managers believed that this would raise the quality of service that operators were able to deliver. As part of this new programme of training, Bankco also increased staff training in product knowledge. This allowed each newly trained operator to deal with a wider number of queries. Instead of dealing with a particular type of account or bankcard, each operator could now guide customers in their choice across a range of products. This change reduced the need for customers to be kept waiting as they were passed between operators. While this might be interpreted as an example of 'multi-skilling', in reality operators ended up performing the same labour process repeatedly, even when dealing with different product ranges. However, these changes did do something to make the job more interesting, as staff learned more about the operations of Bankco.

One important change that accompanied the widening of the product range at Bankco was the need for operators to sell products. This marked a shift away from the more passive role performed by operators, in responding to customer queries. However, the selling function increased the stress associated with the work of operators, as individuals were given selling targets. Work teams also had to meet targets, such as increasing the number of customers with Bankco creditcards, or saving accounts. Many of the people we interviewed, whether team managers or operators, were aware of how their own actions fitted within the wider performance of the workplace. A customer service adviser with over two decades of experience outlined:

> When I was first employed here... it was very much just dealing with enquiries for customers and sorting things out. The focus has gone more onto selling things now.... We don't have specific targets but we do have objectives within the team... you do feel that it is part and parcel of your job.
>
> (Female, full time, no. 3, Bankco3)

Mirroring the heightened sensitivity to the needs of the customer that shapes the changes at Bankco, Telecomco has increased the attention it pays to the quality of service it provides. Facing increased competition on a number of its product fronts from alternative providers, Telecomco has been forced to change how it delivers its services in order to meet profit and revenue targets and to maintain market share. Increasingly, Telecomco has begun to enter into an altogether different kind of relationship with its customers. It now regularly contacts them and asks about the quality of service:

> The customers are randomly rung and they have somebody's ID there and they ask how did such and such a person deal with you? Was the service good? Those are measured now.
>
> (Female, part time, no. 2, Telecomco2)

It says something about the insecurity and vulnerability of the workers at this organization that some of them were happy to be monitored, as if it acted as a safeguard from customer complaints. A part-time sales adviser explained:

> Every single one of our calls is taped, which I feel better about anyway. If there is any complaints off a customer who says 'I never ordered that, I never asked for that', they [the managers] have got a tape to go back now and check.
>
> (Female, part time, no. 8, Telecomco3)

The mantra of meeting customer needs was also evident in the work of engineering staff at Telecomco. In the context of traditionally very different methods of dealing with customers, this shift marked a new departure for this part of the organization. As a male engineer explained:

It's more customer-orientated now, a lot more information is taken from the customers on what we're doing right and wrong. [Work] is very much going towards the customer side of things.

(Male, full time, no. 5, Telecomco4)

At Mediaco, change has been just as radical. New objectives of increasing advertising revenues and gauging customers' needs represented a substantial shift away from the traditional goal of improving the production run of presses. To increase newspaper sales, Mediaco was exploring ways of increasing the customer base, and it made regular use of focus groups and customer surveys to help meet this objective. As these techniques have become more sophisticated, the organization's staff have been made more aware of the need to meet the demands of customers. Declining sales figures, interrupted only by episodic and short-lived increases, have highlighted the importance of the customer and their link to advertising revenues and corporate profits. In this intense atmosphere, journalists have become aware that although they write the news, they have become subordinate in the organization to the selling capacities of those employed in the advertising office.

At the manufacturing organization Pharmco, workers have no direct contact with customers as part of their day-to-day work. Nevertheless, changes in the nature of the market for Pharmco products place the customer centre stage; but here the customer is never a single individual. Unlike Retailco, for example, Pharmco customers are made up of corporations and national governments from around the world. Their increasingly differentiated requirements are influenced by consumer demand (patterns of ill health, etc.) and diverse patterns of state regulation. As such, Pharmco and its workforce are placed in a once-removed relationship with the direct consumer. But the customer appears to be no less of an influence. Workers in the packing area experience the impact of the external customer requirements routinely, as they are used to explain the features of particular production runs or the need for a new night shift. As the global market in tablets has become ever more differentiated, so production runs have shortened and the tasks of different workforce groups have changed. Even here, in the packing bays of an oligopolistic drug manufacturer, the needs and requirements of the customer have become an established part of management's efforts to introduce change.

Conventionally, of course, the customer is associated with the market and with the delivery of private goods and services. The public sector serviced more general and collective needs. These were delivered through bureaucratic forms of organization, where the delivery of services was regulated by formal rules and often sustained by a strong ethos of public service. This ethos commonly distinguished public service delivery from that provided through the operation of the market. Public service organizations operated as statutory monopolies that determined both the nature of needs and how they were to be serviced. By definition, they could not be benchmarked against other service providers. Since the 1980s this situation has changed dramatically (Martinez Lucio and MacKenzie 1999). State policies have deliberately eroded this monopoly status and subjected public sector providers to a variety of competitive pressures. These changes were clearly evident at Councilco and at Healthco. Through the fragmentation of community care, education, healthcare and housing services, the language of the customer has infiltrated the policies of both these organizations. In some cases this shift has been formalized, through initiatives such as CCT, Best Value and the PFI. In other examples the change has been less direct and achieved though the various customer charters introduced by the Conservative governments of the 1990s, the involvement of parents (and increasingly the private sector) in school governance and the regular surveying of users of each organization's facilities. In the Leisure Department at Councilco, for example, managers introduced customer cards. These were not only completed by users of facilities, but were also delivered by hand to local residents. They asked people (customers) for their views on issues such as opening times, the appearance of the physical infrastructure and, for those who had used the facility, the quality of the service they had experienced.

At Councilco and Healthco, the monitoring and the improvement of customer satisfaction was both a corporate objective and, as importantly, a political imperative. These pressures increased after the election of the Labour government in 1997. One of the clear goals of New Labour involved extending the influence of customers in the auditing of public sector organizations (Power 1997). At Councilco the 'democratic renewal' agenda was premised on making the organization more accountable to local customers (constituents). At Healthco, various pressures have been applied on the organization to improve the transparency of its decision-making in order to meet the concerns of customers (patients).

The impact of this turn to the customer has quite radical implications for the employment relationship in both organizations. At the Catering Department at Councilco, for example, schoolchildren were in the process of being rebranded as customers, in spirit if not by name. A supervisor with almost thirty years of experience with the organization outlined how the job had taken on board, in recent times, a PR component. This involved attempts to widen the customer base:

How do we convince them to get from that end of the dining room and come up and see what is actually on the hatch? Because if they come in with a lunch box and they sit down there they're just interested in what their mum's given them and cheerio I go home. But unless we actually get them to come up, that's why I think these theme days are good because sometimes you'll get them to come up to a school dinner those days.

(Female, full time, no. 1, Councilco1)

Another supervisor who had been employed at a different school for twenty-five years reinforced the point and stressed how the shift to thinking of children as customers was one part of the wider marketization of services:

I think it was a matter of them [Councilco] having to change because as things change in life, everything is changing, you have to move with the time and the diet, what children eat is different to the years gone by when the children had a meal then. We look at them as our customers now, they don't have to come to us they choose to come to us so we have to make it as appealing as we can for them. We want their custom, because if we don't have their custom we go down the road. Really we are geared up as an independent commercial unit, we are more cost efficient than we ever were and I would say that the children, you've got to do what they want and it is different altogether from years gone by.

(Female, full time, no. 3, Councilco1)

This general cultural shift had very direct implications for staff. Despite already behaving in some instances in a 'customer-facing' manner, some had to attend a corporate-wide training scheme. Councilco managers justified providing customer-service training in terms of the need to be competitive with other service providers. For example, in the civic area of the catering department encouraging staff to be more attentive to the needs of customers was essential if they were to be able to compete for contracts with private sector service providers. One manager who had only just joined the organization from the private sector argued that there were real problems in marrying the corporate drive to make departments and staff more aware of the needs of customers, while needing to work within tight budget constraints:

I really think it's going to be difficult for any improvements or major changes to take place.... Staff haven't got uniforms. Staff need training in customer care so when they pick the phone up they know what to say. And people have a conference here; you compare it to what they get in [Hotel A] or [Hotel B] we just can't compare, unless they [Councilco] are willing to spend money on equipment, training, uniforms, office refurbishment.

(Male, full time, Councilco1)

In the case of the Planning Department at Councilco, there had been a concerted effort by management in recent years to improve its profile both inside and outside of the organization. The nature of the work of this department made it easier for it to stress to staff the importance of satisfying the customers, whether they be other Councilco departments or other organizations. In this case, the corporate-led push to use 'the customer' as a means of monitoring performance took the form of a series of already introduced and proposed reorganizations:

The division is a consultancy with about 60 per cent of the work coming from [inside Councilco] ... and then another 40 per cent from outside [of it]. We're actually organized along professional expertise rather than customers, which is where I want to change it.

(Male, full time, no. 3, Councilco3)

In some cases the changes brought about by the introduction of the customer into the corporate vocabulary took a less striking form. Even here, however, there were a number of implications for staff. At the Leisure Department managers required staff to change how they looked. By wearing a uniform, managers argued that staff would look more professional and would be better able to relate to the customers. A sports development officer, who had been at the department since 1984, outlined how:

[The staff] used to be in tracksuits, but now we are in uniforms. That was my boss's idea because he said 'people see you in a track suit then automatically assume you're a coach', and we're not coaches but we're development officers. So we're trying to give this illusion that we're all development officers.

(Female, full time, no. 1, Councilco4)

At Healthco the changes have also centred on addressing the needs of the customer. Here, too, it would be foolish to imagine that health workers have never previously understood the needs of patients. In examining the elements of corporate strategy, it becomes clear that the new discourse around the customer supports a policy aimed at the restructuring of the employment relationship and the organization of work.

The evangelical way in which the customer has become a means by which management can secure extra effort from staff does, however, run the risk of providing a standardized, and thereby insensitive service to the individual needs of customers. A domestic assistant outlined how when she attended a recent training course, management made a science out of what appeared to be almost common sense. She took offence at the implication that she could not judge when to chat to patients and when to leave them alone. Sometimes, a fake smile would not be appreciated:

For a start off you had no patients, they were 'customers' and if you'd seen somebody upset in the corridor, you'd stop and ask them could you help them they were upset. Well to me that's a load of bull. Because it's obvious, you see a patient crying in a corridor or a visitor, it's obvious they've either received bad news, they're about to get bad news or they've just lost somebody and they're not going to thank me for stopping them and asking them if they're okay. What can I do to help them?

(Female, full time, no. 3, Healthco1)

The effects of these changes were not limited to non-medical staff. Nurses and doctors were also vocal in their concerns over how the expectation of patients had been raised through central government reforms. These expectations had, of course, to be managed alongside budget tightening.

The introduction of the language of the customer (and with it related terms such as 'throughput') into the public services is one of the most dramatic examples of the ways in which the ethos of public service work has been weakened by the discipline of the market. Naturally, in the private sector, the discourse of the customer has been a normal part of doing business. However, here too there have been important changes. Management has used the need to satisfy the customer as a means of introducing a third party in efforts either to make staff work harder and longer, or to take extra responsibilities. It is to the redistribution down the job ladder of job tasks in the context of this recalibration of the wage–effort relationship that we now turn.

WIDENING RESPONSIBILITIES

In each of the workplaces we visited increased work pressures have combined with other pressures associated with downsizing and changes in work contracts. In this process job tasks removed from the middle layers of management and supervision have been pushed both upwards and downwards. In Chapter 6 we examined the way delayering of job ladders has inhibited possibilities for upward mobility within the organization. Here, we explore the consequences for work intensification. Across the seven organizations, we found a variety of different ways in which new internal job structures have become associated with new kinds of job. Or, as a customer service engineer at Telecomco suggested to us: 'they keep adding bits on, or you're volunteered to do new bits' (Male, full time, no. 6, Telecomco4). Another employee who had been with Retailco since 1983 explained how job levels had been restructured:

The supervisory role was... more [a] case of supervising the operation and... the people side... all the training was managed by other people. Now a section manager is completely responsible for the personnel, the training, the budgets, the waste, the whole operation.... [Previously] there were seven levels of management [and] what they did was take away those levels that we didn't need.

(Female, full time, no. 1, Retailco1)

This finding is supported by other work in the retail sector. For example, Rosenthal *et al.* found evidence of 'the upgrading of supervisory work and reduction in their numbers... [which] created the space for enlarged jobs and more discretion for staff' (1997: 498). Changes such as these are often viewed positively, since people are assumed to welcome more information about their workplace and the additional responsibilities that they have taken on. However, often these arrangements have fostered a sense of unease and stress. At Bankco, for example, a customer service adviser emerged as a new position as part of a process of restructuring. We talked with some of these people and found that they took a positive view of their new work and the way it gave them the capacity 'to make a difference'. A customer service adviser who had recently joined Bankco told us:

I think you take a lot more responsibility for the accounts.... You actually advise people as well as dealing with their queries. You can look at it [the screen] ... and you can make a decision yourself and pass it on to the customer and see if it's acceptable to them. And you feel that you are actually doing something.

(Female, part time, no. 2, Bankco4)

Another customer service adviser who had worked at Bankco since 1979 reaffirmed the increased discretion open to lower-level staff:

We make decisions on whether to give customers refunds and things like that which we would have passed on to a supervisor previously and our discretionary limits have been raised slightly.

(Female, part time, no. 4, Bankco3)

We found similar evidence at Telecomco. A team manager with twenty-five years' experience outlined how the lower-level coordinating role had evolved:

When I first came [here] a lot of people seemed to just watch other people, like the supervisors. They didn't have a proper job really. They just watched operators working. But now people are encouraged to think for themselves and not to need somebody looking over their shoulder.

(Female, full time, no. 1, Telecomco1)

She also explained to us how staff dealing directly with customers regulated themselves. The logic of this, she claimed, was that 'the operators are not supposed to need supervision these days'. The fact that these changes are complicated ones was made clear to us at another Telecomco workplace, where a commercial officer who had been with the organization for more than twenty years questioned these interpretations of change and the variety of experiences currently open to staff. In her view, the present compared unfavourably with the past, when:

The work was more involved and we had more involvement. Now you're given a task to do and that's all you do.... Whereas a few years ago you could get involved in anything. You could perhaps be in one department one day and you'd be in another department another... and it was a lot more varied than it is now.

(Female, full time, no. 6, Telecomco3)

It is clear that the widening of responsibilities in the context of those changes in the employment relationship we have outlined throughout the book is a complex affair. Greater discretion often comes at a cost to the employee. It is a form of empowerment around which management set tight parameters. At the extreme, we found staff who had experienced new forms of job variety, involving, for example, dealing with different types of customer. Importantly, the variety came not from what staff did—that is, there was little evidence of enhanced task variety—but for whom they did it. More generally, across all organizations, while people discussed the changes in the levels of their responsibility, they also talked about increases in stress and the intensification in work that accompanied change. This was explained to us at Bankco by a customer service adviser:

I know a lot of people are off with stress. Because you get customers on the telephone and I have seen women sit there and cry because of the calls they are getting.... In this job women get sworn at and cry.

(Female, full time, no. 7, Bankco3)

A Telecomco customer service engineer drew our attention to the ambiguities for staff in the particular form of empowerment they experienced. We asked him whether he had more responsibilities in his job:

We do and we don't. [Management] give us more responsibility.... If a problem comes up you're supposed to be able to deal with it.... [But] if anything comes up you've got to go to your manager. And you've got to go through the control— 'what shall I do?' But they keep turning round saying we're going to put more responsibility, more onus on the engineers, and they say you're more free to do what you want. But you're not.

(Male, full time, no. 3, Telecomco4)

This was exacerbated in a number of our case study organizations where staff were required to 'act-up'. This often accompanied the widening of job responsibilities. Another Telecomco engineer, in this case 'acting-up' as a manager, explained what the impact had been on his work, and how the increase in job tasks spilled over into previously non-work time:

I probably work on average about eleven hours a day. As an engineer you work until whatever time, say six o'clock and that is it. I have [now] got to work until what I need to get done gets done, and make sure things are ready for the next day.

(Male, full time, no. 5, Telecomco4)

These processes were also evident at our manufacturing workplaces. At Pharmco, for example, a first line manager with sixteen years of experience outlined:

I should say there's far more responsibility taken now at low levels than there used to be. There's far more involvement with decisions, in other words, it isn't just telling, it's getting involved and agreeing a way forward.

(Male, full time, no. 1, Pharmco1)

This sentiment was supported by a line coordinator, who had been at Pharmco since 1988. She explained how she had taken over a number of tasks that were previously carried out by managers:

Whereas before we used to go and ask management, 'what do you think about this?'... [and]... 'what do you think about that?' But we make a lot more decisions ourselves now... we'll be taking more of the management role on. We also do more systems, like computers, than we used to.

(Female, full time, no. 8, Pharmco1)

This was also true for the management of the production line:

Our 'team' runs B7, the new line, which has been in place since April. [The managers] have tried to make it different to every other line in that aspect... instead of having the hierarchy of the line coordinator, a 'stand in' and operators, everybody is going to be doing the training to the same level. So basically we're more of a self-powered team.

(Female, full time, no. 8, Pharmco2)

This mixture of responses (and arguments) was also common in the two public sector organizations. At the Catering Department at Councilco, budget cuts had been the driving force behind 'delayering'. Here, there was no replacement of senior management and many of these responsibilities were pushed downward to mid-level management staff. One of the catering managers we talked to reflected on the ambiguities of this highly contradictory form of staff empowerment:

I enjoy the challenge and the responsibility is good, but there are days when you think this is crazy. You're just trying to fight the tide really. You're just managing to do the work without trying to stop. If you had to do the bulk of the work you can think this is where we are at the moment, this is where we want to go in twelve months time, this is how we can possibly achieve it. We haven't the opportunity to do that.

(Male, full time, no. 9, Councilco1)

But, while mid-level managers appeared to take most of the strain from previous delayering exercises, many of the low-level staff at Councilco and Healthco welcomed the increased task variety in their work. The creation of the STAR team worker at Councilco and the health care assistant (HCA) at Healthco are illustrative of this finding. One HCA outlined how:

I still do everything that an auxiliary did. The extras now are doing people's observations, temperatures, blood pressure and weight, any basic dressings that need doing.... It doesn't sound much but there's a lot more responsibility to doing it.

(Female full time, no. 2, Healthco3)

The HCAs we talked to enjoyed performing job tasks previously performed by qualified nurses and described their sense of personal satisfaction in being able to attend to more of the needs of patients. They identified themselves through their role in the care and recovery process. As another HCA explained:

As I say with this job, it's given us a lot more responsibility, you can do a lot more and you can get involved with the patient a lot more and get to know them a lot more.

(Female, full time, no. 3, Healthco3)

These changes, taken in the round, are clearly quite complex, within which management's attempts to reduce costs combine with aspects of the normative culture of the workplace. As we found, particularly at Councilco, Healthco and Pharmco, low-level workers once thought of as devalued can come to feel more integrated into, and important to, the organization. However, the expansion of responsibilities involved in low- and mid-level jobs can also leave people feeling over-stretched and even exploited. For these reasons, strategies such as 'delayering' which have largely been driven by the need to take out labour costs (Chapter 8), have also been accompanied by an enormous rhetorical outpouring that emphasizes 'empowerment' and 'involvement'. Often it seems that the level of normative integration achieved in these ways is far from complete—people break down in tears; people remember the past and argue about the rights and wrongs of change; and new people arrive who do not intend to stay for very long. In order to deal with these eventualities, many of the workplaces have introduced initiatives that aim to regulate the newly autonomous work groups.

SURVEILLANCE, REGULATION AND PERFORMANCE

Recent work in the UK has highlighted some of the changes that have taken place around the surveillance, regulation and monitoring of staff performance. In the words of Gallie *et al.*: '(T)he introduction of new technological systems appears to have acted as a stimulus for, and possibly as a facilitator of, the implementation of new philosophies of managerial control' (1998: 296). In our case study organizations it seems that three types of 'control' strategy had been developed through which work is intensified (see table 9.3). The spread of information and communication technologies is associated with a direct form of control of labour effort, recently labelled 'info-normative control' (Frenkel *et al.* 1999: 139; see also Baldry *et al.* 1998; Greenbaum 1998). Most obviously identified with the call-centre workplace, this technique enables the monitoring of labour productivity in parallel with the collection of data on the demand and supply of calls, which then feeds into workforce planning (Frenkel *et al.* 1999: 140–1).

The second form of control is more subtle and involves performance-management control through ex-post methods of appraisal, assessment and development plans. This form of control is an essential

Table 9.3. Surveillance, regulation and performance

	Bankco	Councilco	Healthco	Mediaco	Pharmco	Retailco	Telecomco
Info-normative control	■		■	■		■	■
Performance management control	■		■	■	■	■	■
Technical/machine control					■		

feature of the ways in which workplaces developed in the 1990s. In the classic model of Taylorism, outlined by Braverman more than twenty-five years ago, work is deskilled and managers and supervisors direct workers, persistently and continually. In the workplace today, workers are expected to manage themselves. This principle even applies to those occupational groups not yet subject to direct performance scrutiny, for whom managers rely instead on a sense of professional commitment to ensure the work is completed, regardless of workload. This approach is most obvious among groups such as doctors and nurses at Healthco, but also among journalists at Mediaco.

The third means of control involves the traditional, and still relevant, organization of work around the production line. At the manufacturing workplaces, the operation of the assembly line or the machines still provided the main means of regulating labour effort through what Richard Edwards (1979) called 'technical control'. Here, we also recognize that 'technical control' may be associated with a range of complementary management techniques to sustain, and increase, work effort. These include the practice of empowering workers and encouraging them to seek ownership of the work process, as well as the more brutal practice of threatening workers with outsourcing or plant closure if production targets are not met.

While analytically separable, we also recognize that there may be overlaps and interlinkages between these different control strategies, so that management practices may combine elements of info-normative, performance management and technical control (see also Callaghan and Thompson 2000). One way in which we might collectively conceptualize the three forms of control is around the notion of the assembly line. Alongside more traditional methods of control, such as process or assembly lines at Mediaco and Pharmco, we can also think of what Taylor and Bain (1999) term 'an assembly line in the head', where the employee internalizes the various mechanisms of control, such as sales or customer call targets. This is evident at a number of our case-study organizations, particularly at Bankco and Telecomco.

The impact of new information and communication technologies on the control of work can be seen in numerous examples, primarily in the private sector. At the Advertising Department at Mediaco a media administrator with fifteen years' experience at the organization argued:

The role I do isn't the same as it started out. Various tasks have changed. Reports [are now produced] on the PC. At one time we were setting adverts ourselves. A lot of our basic adverts get set on the computers ... at one time we could actually do [this]. The work has intensified.... New technology has not really allowed the pace of work to slow. The pace of work has quickened but other tasks stem from it.

(Female, full time, no. 4, Mediaco3)

Here, we find evidence of the different ways that new technology, and the means by which it is introduced into the workplace, can alter what workers do. Unlike in some of the more optimistic accounts of the 1970s, in which new technology would reduce the work of workers, we find instead 'technology-induced intensification' of work (Green 2000). For example, at Bankco, all incoming telephone calls were routinely monitored. As we outlined earlier in this chapter, one recent change in the organization of work was for operators to sell the bank's financial products through cold-calling existing customers. To manage this increase in the organization's sales work, each operator was issued with a script. This procedure was introduced while we were carrying out our research, and constituted an attempt by management to compensate for the inherent difficulties in ensuring that all customers received the same quality of customer care from the different operators. As one team manager outlined:

They [Bankco] have set up a group where they listen into calls and they're going to make [calls] ... more consistent so introductions to the customers [and] the way they [the staff] end the call are all the same.

(Female, full time, no. 1, Bankco4)

Similarly, operators at Telecomco also worked to a script. The parameters for this were set in part by government legislation. But Telecomco managers were responsible for the way these legal requirements were adapted into workplace practices. Operators with several years' experience at Telecomco argued that the script had become increasingly prescriptive, leading to more monotonous work experience. Moreover, they felt that Telecomco missed out on increased sales that might be achieved on the basis of a more personable and friendly style. Our discussion with a junior manager with three years' experience at Telecomco illustrates this point:

[Telecomco] gives us a script... and what they used to do—it was more of a core guide as opposed to a script. That has become more scripted now. So now what they are saying is 'you've got to sell these products in that order', whereas we think in some cases, 'no we shouldn't be selling them in that order we'd be far more productive and consumer friendly if we sold them in this order'. And we've tried that in the past and it has worked but now we just cannot do that.

(Male, full time, no. 2, Telecomco3)

In regulating what front-line workers said, it was then easier to check conversations to ensure they were achieving performance targets. At Bankco, some staff were uneasy about their telephone calls being taped. For example at the debt management workplace a team member in the Personal Collections Department outlined her concern over the taping of calls:

They [the management] tape your calls, which you are not notified about and they have a twenty-point checklist of points of things which you should be asking. Then they meet you and talk about it. As well as doing that, you might have six hundred accounts from one month to the next, they're going in and out because you are collecting on them. She [the manager] then goes through another checklist of things you should and shouldn't be doing. You don't get the support, they look at things very black and white, like you didn't ask for their [the customer's] work details at that time—that might have been your twentieth call of the day and they've got six accounts and it's not one of yours, it's another person's who is not in that day.

(Female, part time, no. 4, Bankco2)

Calls were also monitored in the Advertising Department at Mediaco. A telesales canvasser described the level at which their calls were monitored:

They monitor every minute. We have call sheets, every morning... they have the number of calls from each person. The average length of calls is printed out and [they can tell] if you have duplicated [calls] or phoned them before.

(Female, full time, no. 8, Mediaco3)

A similar situation was found at Retailco and at Telecomco. At the former, monitoring took the form of the surveillance of checkout throughput. This is monitored electronically and management can scrutinize the performance of the cashiers and the extent to which they are performing their main and secondary tasks efficiently. At Tele-comco all telephone calls are taped. While most staff were unhappy about this, for others it provided a safety check. At the workplace where selling is a large part of the work, staff do well not to forget that the customer rules.

In our conversations with management staff at several workplaces it was clear that regular monitoring of the performance of workers was seen as an essential part of their job. Unsurprisingly, this was most explicit at the call-centre workplaces at Bankco and Telecomco. For example, a senior team manager at Bankco outlined how important she saw performance-management control to the efficient running of the workplace:

It is important that I keep my eye on it [performance indicators] to make sure everybody on my team who should be on the telephones is actually on the telephones at core times because they can be off the telephones to do certain tasks and processes and obviously I've got to weigh up, 'well is it more important that this person goes on the telephone now that it's busy or should they stay here and do this paperwork?'.

(Female, full time, no. 7, Bankco4)

A Telecomco operator who had been at the organization since 1986 talked about the sense of compressed working routines:

Once you've got rid of a call, once you've connected a call, that call automatically goes off your screen. At the touch of that button that call goes off the screen and another call comes straight in because you're constantly in 'ready' unless you actually put yourself in 'not ready', which means you don't take a call.... The green man's for go, that means you're in 'ready', you get calls coming in. The little red man means you're 'not ready', so you don't get calls.

(Female, full time, no. 3, Telecomco1)

This sense of anxiety was replicated at the Bankco call centres, where the systems of surveillance mirrored those at Telecomco:

The major pressure is... the calls... and that is understandable because we work in a call-centre environment, and you also get the pressure... because you haven't got time to literally stand up and do what you need to do or take two minutes. You feel as though you're under pressure by taking the calls because it [the indicator] could be flashing 'there's eight minutes of calls waiting' which is quite regular in the evening.

(Female, full time, no. 10, Bankco4)

The pace and pressure of work appeared—at least in visual terms—to be more intensive at the newer of the two personal customer service call centres, where Bankco staff answer calls twenty-four hours a day, seven days a week. Large, one-metre screens are spread around the workplace. These display to management and to staff in real time how the workplace is performing (see box 9.1). During our visits to the call centre, the numbers on the screens changed regularly, and, depending on their size, they also changed colour. Red, amber and green reflect the volume of calls waiting to be answered by staff. These calls were differentiated by type, allowing management to switch easily the type of calls handled by each adviser.

This description of pressure and intensification of work being maintained by a system of flashing lights suggests comparisons with Fordist production systems and the assembly line. In Toyota's system, Andon

Box 9.1. Performance monitoring at a Bankco call centre

The following box is displayed in screens on walls around the workplace:

DOMLCW: 29	DOMNU: 3	VLCW: 19	VNUM: 2
IVRLCW: 0	NUM: 0	%ANS: 99	PORTS: 90

Each indicator represents a performance target that is traced to individual employees: DOMLCW refers to the longest time (in seconds) spent waiting by a domestic caller; DOMNU refers to the number of domestic calls waiting; VLCW is the longest time spent waiting by a visa call; VNUM represents the total number of visa calls waiting; IVRLCW is the longest time spent waiting by an interactive voice response call; NUM is the number of interactive voice response calls waiting; %ANS indicates the percentage of calls answered; and PORTS is the number of systems plugged in.

When we visited, the DOMLCW indicator was amber, signalling that it was just below the maximum threshold of 30 seconds, at which point the figure turns red. However, the low number of total number of domestic calls waiting (green) meant that team managers expected the DOMLCW figure to drop, and therefore ruled out other action such as switching calls from visa to domestic between advisers.

lights flash red, amber or green over sections of the line. However, it is not only the high-tech environment of the call centre where we found colour-coded control systems. As we described in Chapter 3, Retailco stores all utilize a steering wheel to coordinate day-to-day management practice, where each section of the store's operation is coded with red, amber or green lights. Nevertheless, this process of routine monitoring has been accentuated by the advent of more and more powerful forms of computerized control (see Baldry *et al.* 1998), again most evident at the call-centre workplaces. Returning to Telecomco, we found evidence of how targets were recalibrated as staff neared their achievement. A young worker who had recently joined the organization explained:

With the computerization I think... they [Telecomco] expect more all the time. We have performance levels and targets and I think every time we reach them they just put the goal posts that much further and then once you've reached that target they move it along and then expect more.

(Male, full time, no. 8, Telecomco1)

This tendency was not restricted to the workplace: the same technology that allowed work to be performed outside of the workplace has also allowed staff to be monitored in their homes or, in the case of Telecomco engineers, while they were out performing their work. One home worker, who had been at Bankco since 1991, outlined how her performance was evaluated despite working outside of the physical workspace:

I am expected to do a target eleven [telephone calls] an hour, but I could spend forty-five minutes speaking to one customer and then I could spend an hour updating twelve or thirteen accounts.... We are being advised the emphasis is on how you perform... [the] quality of the account. But you do feel under pressure if you have not done your eleven an hour.

(Female, part time, no. 7, Bankco2)

And at Telecomco, call-centre methods of control had been replicated in the organization of the work of engineers. The engineers carried out most of their work outside of the workplace, picking up new jobs through a hand-held computer which was connected to a central clearing system. One of them explained to us how his performance was surveyed, and argued that it was quite an intrusive method:

It's like they'll ring up and say why are you still on that job? They are always watching you, saying 'haven't you finished that yet?' They don't understand that, well they must understand each job can't take the same time. Some jobs might take ten minutes, some might take all day. And then when they look at the figures we're suppose to do three jobs a day. I might do one job all day and someone might do five dead easy ones, finish it for dinner.

(Male, full time, no. 3, Telecomco4)

The increased use of ever more tightly defined statistical forms of monitoring and controls had often been accompanied by the detailed and individualized nature of monitoring. Feedback was given to call-centre staff on their performance at daily, weekly and monthly intervals. This meant staff could individually judge how they were performing. At Telecomco a sales adviser who had only recently joined the organization outlined this:

Because you get your stats every day and that tells you how much you're doing and you're constantly trying to beat yourself.... You should always be making yourself better.

(Female, part time, no. 9, Telecomco3)

At Bankco and Telecomco, therefore, new technology has allowed managers to monitor the quantity and the quality of calls made by staff. Here, the computer serves the same purpose as the intrusive video cameras in fast-food restaurants (Fuller and Smith 1991: 2–3). Staff performance is monitored on a second-by-second and a minute-by-minute basis. This process produces an enormous amount of data and involves a problem of data management. And because senior management often has too little time available to analyse these data, the task is passed down the line where it is commonly seen as a thankless job. For these reasons, across all seven organizations we found that practices of technological performance monitoring complemented other, more personal, processes. Writing about retailing, Du Gay has argued that: 'The regulation of shop floor workers has taken a number of forms mostly involving direct supervision, combined with bureaucratic control technologies and more "anonymous" panoptical surveillance technologies (the labour monitoring facilities of EPOS for example)' (1993: 575). It is this pattern of regulation through combined forms that gives distinctiveness to the modern workplace. At Retailco, electronic data from the checkouts are available to management. However, they are combined with more established forms of regulation. Individual staff appraisal, for example, has been retained as part of the organization's wider method of managing workplace performance. On these occasions the steering wheel was used by managers as a means both of assessing the performance of individual staff and of making them aware of the performance targets of the workplace. In the words of one of the checkout managers:

I have only done a couple [of appraisals] up to now [and] it is interesting with the staff because we have to set... objectives. [Now] we actually discuss the steering wheel.... It is our way of... giving them a clearer understanding. They all know the red, green and amber light, but they don't realize what impact they have on it.... So [we] are using the steering wheel and the appraisal form to set individual objectives based on the different quadrants.

(Female, full time, no. 1, Retailco3)

Telecomco also retained a variety of schemes of individual staff performance. At the telemarketing centre, personal development plans are used to structure staff–manager meetings. A sales manager who had been at the organization since it opened in 1996 highlighted how his coaching performance was regulated through indicators and how this limited scope for individual autonomy:

I believe that coaching is very important but it can be done in a lot of different ways. But what they [senior managers] have done, they have now targeted us on it and bonused us on our coaching and it all has to be done in a certain format so it doesn't give you a lot of time really to do different things with people.

(Male, full time, no. 7, Telecomco3)

And at Mediaco a sales rep who had only been at the organization for just over a year complained about the regulation of their performance through monthly appraisals:

It's really about figures. You'll have your appraisal.... At the end of the day it does come down to figures. We are appraised once a month with the manager. I think they should take into consideration if you are working hard. Because everything comes down to figures, it's difficult to think they look at me as a person.

(Female, full time, no. 6, Mediaco3)

And, as many of the people we talked to were aware, this intensification of performance surveillance has of course taken place alongside the evolution of the 'winner-takes-all' approach to the selection of staff for progression, as we set out in Chapter 6. The increased generation of statistics around staff performance is used for appraisals, which focus more on the already developed capabilities of individual members of staff than on the training that the organization could provide to improve opportunities for future career progression.

In the public sector we also found evidence of staff performance being adjusted and controlled through ever-tighter performance parameters. The wider shift towards a business-like service ethos actually meant staff often spent less time with customers as they had to complete their work according to a tight time schedule, based on a time-based assessment of tasks to be completed. One member of the Community Care Department commented on the growing use of budgets and inspections to increase accountability in the provision of public services:

Whereas before you'd go in and it was like a more friendly basis. You'd go in and you'd do what was required of you and then they [the patients] would want the company, cup of tea, sit down and have a chat. Whereas you can't do that now because time is money, you can't do that.

(Female, part time, no. 4, Councilco2)

Another home-carer agreed that this change had taken place in recent years. She explained how her performance was subject both to external as well as to internal scrutiny:

You are more accountable for what people have, what they are doing, the service that you are providing. There are more inspections and things like that and like the budgets I do, you've got to be aware of the finances.

(Female, full time, no. 6, Councilco2)

At Healthco we observed how the drive to strengthen the auditing of performance tied in with the focus on the customer in the form of the

Patients' Charter, and this was leading to tighter control over the performance of individual employees. This finding was perhaps most obvious among portering services at Healthco, where porters seemed to have to compensate for the extra demands placed on other service areas. One portering manager explained that in the context of pressures to meet external customer targets, porters were placed under increased pressure:

What happens if someone comes in and says I have been here about twelve hours waiting for a bed, the bed's been ready for two hours and we're waiting for a porter. Casualty gets a porter, so the easy way to turn round and get rid of the complaint is to say we've asked the porter and we're just waiting for a porter to get to you.... [But] ... we can only respond when the nurse says, 'right, the bed's there, there's the paperwork, off you go'.

(Male, full time, no. 1, Healthco1)

In sum, despite the growing use of technology to monitor directly the performance of staff, we still found evidence at the workplaces we visited of more traditional methods of controlling how workers performed. Reflecting the diversity of the work performed at our seven organizations and, indeed, the range of occupational groups we interviewed, we found more direct methods still in existence to regulate performance. At Pharmco manufacturing and at the printworks at Mediaco, the operation of the assembly line or the machines still provided the main means of regulating workforce effectiveness, although their role in the wider management structure had been subject to change. Indeed, the two organizations had embraced very different management techniques to maintain (and even increase) workgroup efforts. As we saw in the previous section, Pharmco encouraged increased ownership of the process by the workforce, in a sense seeking to empower workers to regulate their own performance. Mediaco, on the other hand, had adopted a more direct control system, based around a constant implicit threat of plant closure if production targets were not met.

Among call-centre workers, we found extreme examples of the way new technologies had been utilized to exact techniques of performance management as a form of control. However, performance management was not confined to the arena of high-tech workplaces. Many of the low-level staff groups in the public sector organizations had experienced a significant shift in the way their work was monitored, associated with the rise of 'the customer' as a governing force. Importantly, many other professional groups in the public sector spoke of their 'self-exploitation' out of a sense of professional commitment to complete their work tasks, despite a growing workload and sense of work inten-sification. For managers, this operates as an effective, albeit less stra-tegic, approach to controlling labour effort. This approach was most obvious amongst doctors and nurses at Healthco. However, although this strategy was still working—in the sense that both groups continued to work long hours and to work harder while at work—the goodwill and professionalism was being stretched to breaking point. Finally, one group that closely resembles a professional occupation in this sense is the journalists at Mediaco. Here, however, management appeared to undermine the group's sense of professionalism, not because they wanted staff to work any less hard but because the need to maintain a high standard of journalism in order to ensure high sales had declined over time. Writing news features had become much more desk-based, facilitated by the electronic transmission of stories and the growth in the number of press releases issued by private and public sector organizations. The managers were using policies of multi-skilling and flexibility to increase the work intensity of the new recruits, who were less committed to the professional ethos of journalists.

CONCLUSIONS

One of the rationales for the new system of work intensification and job control that we have outlined is its apparent ability to deliver efficiency gains, at least in the short term. The systems can also respond effectively to consumer wants and needs. Of course, these wants are themselves the products of organizational strategies (Harvey 1998). Organizations have to be able to measure and to calibrate what the consumer wants. That they have begun in the last decade to collect this type of data merely adds to the powerful rhetoric of progress in which these changes are embedded. Twenty-four-hour shopping is seen to facilitate a more flexible working life and a more efficient society. What is more, if it is appropriate for buying groceries then it is appropriate for paying your council tax or for visiting your local leisure facility. Similarly, computer banking facilitates customer needs for instant access, while also allow-ing the banks to improve their profits. Everyone gains in this new system; or so it seems.

However, this heightened sensitivity to the needs of the customer, via the organization, has also meant increased pressures for employ-ees, many of whom raise questions about the overall efficacy and sustainability of the new system. In our interviews with them it became clear that we were often speaking to conscripts rather than converts. An emphasis upon 'customer-facing' employment and the need for organizations to care for their customers has been accompanied by a depersonalization of service work. Relationships between people (delivering and receiving a service) is increasingly mediated by machines and regulated by tight rules and pressures of time. In this context, schemes of mock informality become commonplace—they have to be, in order to compensate for the increasingly automated nature of transactions. Strangers are immediately on first-name terms and name badges become de rigueur at work. In all of this there is talk of a new empowerment that accompanies greater responsibilities and array of job tasks. Many of the people we talked to felt that they were being empowered to death, implicated in their own over-empowerment and with little (or no) financial compensation for the performance of extra responsibilities.

Conclusion
Managing Employment Change:
Who's Managing What?

INTRODUCTION

There is no doubt that change is taking place in the UK employment
system. This finding was confirmed at each one of our case study
organizations and at each workplace we visited. The reliance on survey
data in many of the key employment analyses of the 1990s appears to
have underestimated the extent of change in the quality of the
employment relationship. True, unemployment has declined over this
period and jobs may even remain available with a single employer on a
relatively long-term basis. But it is not only the jobs that have changed;
the whole environment within which they are located has been subject
to radical transformation (Heery and Salmon 2000a). This change affects
the ways in which people enter the labour market, their experience of
the work process and their expectations of security in work. Keeping a
job may still be possible, but the personal cost is much greater. As a
Councilco employee put it:

I think it's all boiling down now to: you're expected to do it; you should be glad
of a job; and you are going to take it whether you like it or not.

(Male, full time, no. 11, Councilco4)

It is not just that employees now have to put up with more aggravation
from managers and customers. They also have to put in greater effort
just to keep their jobs, at the same time as finding it more difficult

to keep their own private and family time separate from that offered to their employer (Perrons 1998). Thus the question is not whether changes are taking place, but the nature of these changes, who is controlling or managing them and whose interests they serve.

In much current discourse it is often assumed that the most efficient or effective way to manage the necessary adaptations to major changes in the economic, technological and social environment is to devolve the responsibility for the process of adaptation to the lowest appropriate level. This might be to the enterprise, to the local union branch or to the individual and individual household. The emphasis in recent government publications, from *Our Competitive Future—Building the Knowledge Driven Economy* (DTI 1998) to *Work in the Knowledge Economy* (DTI 1999) has been upon the innovative capacities of business and enterprise, unhampered by state planning and regulation.

In this view it is at the level of the business enterprise and the market place that the need for change is best appreciated and understood. For example, the government has argued that its role is 'to provide the framework in which businesses, communities and individuals can seize these new opportunities with confidence' (Byers 2001: 1). If only, it is argued, the constraint of big bureaucracy could be lifted and discretion and choice returned to individual agents, it would be possible to release the dynamism and innovative capacity needed to respond to current challenges. This belief coincides with the demise of any kind of faith in the possibility of higher-level regulation or indeed planning in the interests of the greater good of the community. The modernist experiment is deemed to have failed. This being the case, it is argued that it is better to free individual agents to make their own plans and adaptations, and to interpret their own needs, than to impose a collective will on everyone. This replacement of the collective by the individual is seen as a positive development and one that recognizes that ideas of the collective have normally been used to serve some out-of-date objective or goal, and one that probably furthered the interests of an elite. In contrast, the individual is understood as a potentially active agent whose creative capacities will be developed once freed from collective constraint. In this way, then, it is argued that the task of managing and of taking responsibility should be passed back to the individual. It is further assumed that through the operation of a decentralized decision-making (market) mechanism we will all be better off. Not only will we be better able to achieve desired outcomes, but we will also enjoy increased satisfaction from these outcomes, as we all share in the responsibility for this development path (see, for example, Hayek 1960).

Of course, the application of this mantra to the public sector involves certain paradoxical tendencies; in order for managers in the public sector to be held accountable for their decision-making, a market or quasi-market system has to be established. However, the introduction of new price and budget-driven controls by the state, justified in the name of increasing local accountability for the quality and cost of service delivery, involves the very same centralized direction and intervention that was seen to be the root of the problem (Hoggett 1996). This process has been called 'concentration without centralisation' (Harrison 1997) and refers to both public sector organizations and private sector corporations.

The abandonment of national policies for the planned and managed growth and development of national economies is regularly justified in terms of globalization and the increasing internationalization of the economy (see Hirst and Thompson 1996). There is now a view that employment generation is achieved by releasing the innovative capacities of firms, which in turn depend on product market deregulation and the minimization of controls over the labour market and the employment relationship. If managers are free to manage, then there should be maximum scope for innovation, creativity and adoption of best practice. In this view, the individual becomes transformed from a dependent employee to an active agent, charged with the responsibility for his or her own employability. This has been associated with a change in the understanding of citizenship, as states have vigorously encouraged the development of private pension provision. Financial institutions have responded by producing more and more products through which individuals can insure themselves against the risks of unemployment or severe ill health.

In this book we have sought to investigate this trend toward decentralization and heightened individual responsibility. We were initially troubled by the fact that the notion of decentralization was based on two assumptions: first, that managers will be able to shape and fashion their organizations to meet their desired ends and, second, that they have clear and creative ideas about the appropriate route they wish their organization to follow. Our findings do not support this view of the world. Indeed, it is clear that although our research has focused on the role of managers in directing and implementing employment change, our use of the term 'managing employment change' is at least partly ironic. The evidence suggests that managers are not at all in control of events, but are buffeted this way and that, dealing with uncertainty and risk by displacing it down the organization—most normally through adjustments of employment policies. The decentralization of managerial authority does not include a parallel responsibility towards employees. Instead, management decisions have often involved a shifting of risk down the organization to the individual employee (Allen and Henry 1996; Beck 1992; Gregg *et al.* 2000). Most notably, this has resulted in a weakening of established notions of job security. In this context previous ideas of what was meant by and contained in a job have been eroded and replaced by others that require the individual worker (not the state or the employer) to take responsibility for their own careers. In this new situation employers have come actively to reconsider their commitments to their employees. This reframing of the employment relationship has been wide-ranging and extends from training to issues of job security and pension provision. The extent and impact of these changes have been the main concern of this book, and our findings provoke questions about the future and the vitality of the established arrangements.

In this concluding chapter we first of all focus on the options available to the key actors (managers, employees and trade unions) in a decentralized and uncoordinated economy to develop their competitive strategies, forge their own careers, or form new and innovative partnerships with individual employers. In practice, we see that the strategies adopted by one group to protect and develop their interests in this unplanned world may transfer or shift the uncertainty onto others.

Through these discussions we raise major doubts over whether any of the active agents (the local managers, the individual workers) are, in fact, able to control the environment in which they are required to manage employment change. We consider how these problems affect each of these three sets of agent. We then turn to the missing part of the managing process—namely, those institutions capable of operating at the national level and providing some form of regulatory or coordinating framework; that is, we argue for the re-establishment of public institutions and public policy.

MANAGING EMPLOYMENT CHANGE—CAN WE TRUST THE MANAGERS?

Government policy in the UK operates to a large degree on the basis that firms can be regarded as a source of dynamism in issues of production, technological innovation, employment change and growth. As part of the neo-liberal agenda, the role of government was seen to involve 'lifting the burden of state regulation' which hampered risk-taking, innovation and change (Jessop *et al.* 1988). So, as the state was 'rolled back', and managers and employees were left at the front line to manage the development of new forms of competition, neo-liberalism was rolled forward. This has meant, in practice, not a reduced role for state intervention, but, rather, an alternative role for the state in managing competition.

Through our case study organizations we have examined the ways in which managers deal with the burden of organizing production, training, recruitment and employee welfare in an increasingly dynamic economy subject to unpredictable swings and change. Management has become increasingly sensitive to risk and recognizes the absence of a safety net in many of their operations. They are working in an ever more uncontrolled environment and they have relatively few levers that they can pull to try to reduce risk for the organization and for themselves. Managing employment change becomes an increasingly important focus of managers' activity, in part because it is one area where they are being told to use their own discretion and initiative. Internal constraints are being blown away by rapid changes in technologies and product markets and by the increased perception among managers that they can afford to face down trade-union opposition and to tear up procedures and policies based on long-established custom and practice. Not only are they being urged to act, but they also increasingly feel able to act, to make radical decisions and to adopt radical strategies in an area where they may previously have felt hemmed in by collective regulations and the pressures of custom and practice.

The pressure to take action comes in two forms. In some of the case studies the motivation to make changes seemed to be associated more with the managers' own perceptions of what they ought to be doing, both in pursuing the interest of the organization, but also frequently in the interest of furthering their own career. The managers we talked to were often conscious of the need to make an impact, to be seen to be innovators and movers and shakers, even if they planned to move on before any possible fall-out from the new innovative strategy was evident. In other contexts the pressures were simply to manage, to make do, to find some way of making sense of incompatible and conflicting pressures (see Mumford 1999). Managers resort to employment change as the means of managing and making do partly because it was one of the few areas where it was felt there was any room for manoeuvre.

This approach was particularly evident in the public sector, as local managers struggled to square the circle of budget cuts and service delivery targets. It was also evident amongst workplace managers in the private sector. Here, head office strategies and policies often gave rise to conflicts and problems at the local level which required further change and adaptation if the production or service system was to function.

Change in some cases appeared to be being made for change's sake—to demonstrate a willingness to be innovative and to think the unthinkable—while in other contexts the changes were intended to help resolve incompatible budget and production pressures. However, whatever the basis for the new policies, the solutions adopted were not necessarily leading towards sustainable, coherent or rational systems of organizing employment. The net impact of both types of change is likely to be felt primarily by those at the receiving end of the employment policies—in the form of increased work intensity, greater insecurity and time pressures. These outcomes may be both intended and unintended. In a context where managers are not necessarily in a position either to control their work environment or to foresee the impact of their policies and programmes, the downward pressure on employment conditions may be a consequence of this uncertain environment and not necessarily the objective of the policies.

This interpretation of developments certainly seems to fit with some areas of the public sector. Here, managers were well aware of the potential long-term damage these short-term cost-reducing policies may inflict on both goodwill and on their ability to recruit able and committed employees. Nevertheless, they still felt unable to develop policies that could serve both their long-term human resource needs and meet current budgetary and service delivery pressures. In a world of 'concentration without centralization' (Harrison 1997) the former pressures had to be given priority. Some private sector managers were also beginning to recognize that their policies may have negative repercussions on long-term organizational performance. For example, Bankco and Pharmco were both taking steps (through the transfer of temporary staff to permanent contracts and other policies) to try to remedy the damage to employment relations inflicted by their more radical downsizing and restructuring phases. However, these remedial measures were still relatively limited and contingent on the avoidance of other crises that might lead to a re-emergence of a harder line approach towards employment security and training and development.

BOUNDARYLESS OR BOUNDED CAREERS?

The decline of traditional internal labour market systems has led to an increasing emphasis on the role of the individual employee in managing his or her career, and, in particular, on managing his or her 'employability' (Arthur and Rousseau 1996; Peck and Theodore 2000; Philpott 1999). If jobs are no longer secure and technological change is rapidly requiring major changes in job content over the course of a working life, the argument is that individuals must necessarily take more responsibility in shaping their own careers and in developing appropriate competencies. Managers, while enjoying greater discretion in the formulation of employment policies, have been busy offloading their responsibilities for managing employment on to individual workers. Gone are the days when employing organizations accepted willingly and openly that in return for taking over the control and direction of people's lives they must assume some responsibility for the future employment and income security of their employees (Supiot 2001).

The employment contract is a relationship between unequal agents. The institutionalizing of a distinctive form of contract in the area of employment—the traditional open-ended employment contract—is, in part, a response to this inherent inequality. The principles of the employment relationship and, indeed, employment contract (at least as understood in some societies) is that in return for the control of citizens' labour time employers should take a higher share of the risks (see Albert 1986; Supiot 2001). The internalizing of employment relations within large organizations protected employees against the risks of job loss and obsolescence of skills associated with unpredictable changes in patterns of demand and technological development. These risks were borne more directly by casual and freelance workers operating outside the protective shell of the organization. The long-term employment contract and the internally structured career also provides a shelter for individuals against the vicissitudes of life, for example, sickness, care responsibilities and old age.

This sharing of risks has been considered to constitute partial recompense, not only for submitting to daily control by the employer, but also for forgoing alternative opportunities to develop skills and pursue careers. Individuals often do have some degree of choice and leverage in the labour market, but once they commit themselves to a particular line of work and a particular organization, many of their options are foreclosed and restricted.

These risks are recognized to have increased, now that organizations are not expected to take responsibility for continuity of employment and now that skills are regarded as more short term and subject to obsolescence through technological and organizational change. Yet the response to these enhanced risks is to pass the burden on to the employee, to require the employee to take responsibility for their continued employability and for managing their own careers. The prospects, however, of being able to take on these responsibilities seem to be reducing in a context in which the risks are not only increasing but are also being passed on to relatively powerless individuals. The employing organizations are themselves no longer able to predict their demands for labour, measured by either skills or by quantity. In this context the task of predicting future trends is passed to the even less knowledgeable individual.

At our case studies we found little evidence of the emergence of the self-managed career. On the one hand, there was clearly reduced scope for upward mobility within organizations for the majority of staff, as a consequence of both flattened hierarchies and downsizing. Yet, at the same time, the emphasis on maintaining employability through training and retraining needs to be treated with scepticism. Most of the training available to the lower-skilled occupational groups has, in fact, been stripped of much of the technical content, and replaced by more personal skills and customer-care skills. These may enhance transferability, but only to similar jobs at similar pay; they do not provide any scope for significant upward career progression. Enhancement of technical skills seems to be increasingly based upon the acquisition of educational credentials and qualifications gained outside the workplace. Opportunities for career development through training provision within the organization appear to be limited, at least for the majority of employees.

Thus, careers are no longer bounded by the organization; however, to use the notion of 'the boundaryless career' is problematic. When used positively and linked to notions of innovation and retraining, it most commonly implies opportunities for upward mobility. However, mobility can also be in the downward direction. Equally, we suspect that the most common experience is one of circulation at a horizontal level among routine jobs that offer little access to serious retraining. These arrangements are commonly justified on the grounds that such employees will not be able to progress across the job divide to the kinds of employment where such high-level technical knowledge can be utilized. The extent to which these findings have been consistent across our seven case study organizations is a matter of concern. All seven companies are major employers of large numbers of people, staffed by experienced and qualified managers. The fact that training provision remains so limited within these kinds of organization suggests that a more comprehensive approach in government policy is required. Numerous government programmes (from Investing in People to the Learning Society, the Skills Task Force and the University of Industry) have emphasized the centrality of training to national economic survival, but they have so far failed to move beyond a voluntary system of participation in training provision.

Women have traditionally dominated many of the occupational areas we have been investigating. As such, a lack of significant opportunities for upward mobility or training could be argued to be nothing new. However, even in traditionally female-dominated occupations, such as banking and telecommunications clerical work or retail work, there has been a decline in opportunities for progression up a career ladder, associated with the flattening of the organizational hierarchies. Yet at the same time that there has been a decline in the share of those workforces that can expect promotion opportunities, barriers to women's upward mobility have weakened, at least in the organizations we have studied. This greater acceptance of women entering supervisory and lower managerial positions has perhaps obscured the overall decline in promotion opportunities. Moreover, the costs of promotion for women seem to have increased, as even lower-level managerial or supervisory jobs are requiring ever longer hours spent at work (see also Simpson 1997).

It is not only women, however, who have been the losers from these changes. Men are also both more likely now to be found in the female-dominated segments—with all the lower terms and conditions that this implies—and to have faced a downgrading in terms and conditions of employment in previously relatively protected male-dominated areas of work. The main examples of the latter experience from our case studies include the printing assistants and drivers at Mediaco, the field engineers at Telecomco and the park wardens at Councilco. These processes of levelling down are continuing. There seems to be a general trend to establish an apparently more gender-neutral flat level of pay for those groups confined to low-level manual and non-manual occupations. These jobs also offer few opportunities for either job or pay progression or even significant overtime opportunities. This is not to argue that gender differences in the labour market overall are disappearing; instead, the differences interact with notions of class so that the main gender divides are now being found around access to higher-level jobs. Although more women are gaining access to these jobs, men are continuing to dominate the top rungs (Halford *et al.* 1997; Savage and Witz 1992; Wajcman 1998). Women may be increasing their presence on the lower rungs of the managerial ladder and, more particularly, are making advances within the relatively low-paying sectors such as the public sector (Crompton 1997; Walby 1997). To the extent that there is convergence of gender differences, it is found among the more disadvantaged workers (Grimshaw and Rubery 2001) and this convergence is based around the norms established not in the male-protected segments but in the low-paid and dead-end jobs typical of feminized segments.

TRADE-UNIONISM—PARTNERSHIP OR WHAT?

One of the most dramatic changes this book picks up on is the changing role of British trade unions. As new systems of governance over the employment relationship have emerged, so trade unions across the industrial sectors have struggled to find themselves a new role (Fairbrother 2000; Heckscher 1988; Kelly 1997; McIlroy 1997). Marginalized at the national level, certainly within the private sector, they are trying to establish a stronger presence at the company and workplace level through new initiatives such as single-employer partnership agreements (Marchington 1998; Marks *et al.* 1998). These agreements, however, suffer from the same limitations as the independent policy initiatives of local managers. In the public sector, the unions, anxious to hang on to their limited but important role in shaping national agreements, seem ready to concede the authority to implement the details of these agreements to local managers. Thus, fragmentation of control applies also to the public sector. Yet it is probably more difficult to develop effective forms of union resistance at the local level as some of the major constraints on the effective implementation of collective agreements relate to statutory policy and the implementation of budgetary controls. The budgetary controls of public sector organizations, such as local authorities and hospital trusts, are determined nationally, and it would seem that this is the appropriate level for collective bargaining over resources. Yet, in practice, there have been real concessions by the trade unions at this level, signing national agreements that are no more than very general frameworks, leaving details to be determined at the local level. This is the basis of Fairbrother's (2000) discussion of the re-emergence of a workplace-based trade-unionism in the public sector. However, as our materials make clear, the workplace can also be the site where vulnerable employees and trade-union organizations can be most easily pressured by a management determined upon a policy of employment change. In many of these instances the national agreement has not been robust enough to provide an effective umbrella under which local negotiations can be meaningfully developed.

Across the private sector we found trade unions struggling to gain a foothold against ongoing management efforts to reshape the employment relationship. Their greatest successes seem to have been at Bankco and Retailco, where new single-employer partnerships have been established. These arrangements applied to working-time flexibility and employment security. The agreement at Bankco led to a major review of human resource policies and a retreat from the use of temporary staff. It also contributed to a less intense division of labour within the new call centres. At Retailco it was more difficult to pinpoint any major changes to HR policies from this new form of agreement. There was a new joint approach to education and training, but we found very little enthusiasm for this in the stores, or evidence that it had made any positive impact upon people's working lives. Retailco changed its policy on temporary contracts, but this seemed to have come about independently of the partnership agreement. Perhaps this suggests that partnership agreements can take on many forms (see Guest and Peccei 2001; Marchington et al. 2001) and may or may not generate significant benefits for unions and workers (Ackers and Payne 1998; Kelly 1996). As general statements of principle, they may facilitate the development of new policies if well argued and pressed for by local trade-union representatives. However, they have been constructed in the context of quite rapid technical and economic change. The speed and the extent of these changes are such that they can easily overwhelm such local responses. National union representatives involved in each partnership appeared to acknowledge the limits to the agreements, but argued that in the context of severe power asymmetries between capital and labour it was the best deal they could currently achieve for workers.

At Telecomco the national trade union attempted to resist some of the degradation in working conditions in the new call centres by balloting for a one-day strike. However (and with dark irony), the union's plan was constrained by the very conditions that it was attempting to change. The question of agency temps had become a persistent source of discontent amongst the union's members. But these agency temps were excluded from the ballot (as employees of the temporary work agency and not of Telecomco) and, as such, were not involved in the decision to strike. In the view of the local trade-union official, this structural split in the labour force was emerging as a major problem for trade-union mobilization.

Meanwhile, at Mediaco, where there had been a traditional trade-union stronghold, we were able to see in stark relief just how far labour's involvement in workplace changes had been eroded. At each of the three workplaces we visited, the trade unions had been unable to arrest substantial (long- and short-term) changes in the conditions of employment at the firm. At the printworks the manager explained to us that 'it has been over ten years since a full-time union rep came on site'. In another example of just how much industrial relations within the organization had changed since the mid-1980s, management had agreed a new deal with the organization's drivers with only minimal involvement of the union.

At Pharmco, the well-organized trade-union branch was unable to resist the major downsizing exercise that took place as part of new 'just-in-time' warehousing and production systems. As we have seen in Chapter 5, the organization soon discovered that this downsizing exercise had been a major mistake and was forced almost immediately to recruit even more new staff than had been made redundant. What this draws attention to is the enormous weakness of the consultation system in the UK, and the absence of detailed discussions of downsizing and redundancy plans between companies and the workers' representatives. This contrasts with the situation in the EU, and in particular in Germany, with its established systems of consultation and works councils. It seems likely that if there had been an obligation to consult on redundancies and to explore alternatives, as in the German system (Bosch 1990), the flaws in these plans might have been revealed before it was too late to prevent the implementation of the restructuring.

Within the public sector organizations trade-union membership has been maintained, but with more active support from management in Councilco than in Healthco. At the hospital, trade unions have become identified as the biggest obstacle to change by the new management after a long history of accepting a process of joint regulation. The assistant HR director argued, in fact, that the 'unions come in and wind staff up'. Despite this hostile climate, management claimed that the unions remained involved in all discussions over changes in terms and conditions. To improve the participation of nurses in the management of the organization (and perhaps also, at least, partially to undermine the unions) a new 'shared governance' structure was introduced. Three councils were formed around separate activities: 'practice and policy', 'education and training' and 'research and development'. Twelve nurses were elected on to each of the three councils. The impetus behind the creation of this new internal system was less about involving staff in employment changes and more about what the deputy director of nursing called 'establishing amongst nurses an understanding of the corporate agenda'. Despite this apparently more open governance structure, the unions were still unable to prevent the conversion of assistant nurses and nurse auxiliaries, covered by national collectively defined terms and conditions, to health care assistants, covered only by local terms and conditions. The unions also remained rather marginalized in ongoing discussions on staffing levels under the proposed PFI, to which the unions, according to management, were becoming increasingly hostile.

At Councilco the relationship with the local unions has continued to be seen as an essential part of the management of the council, particularly as any break with the unions would be unacceptable to the ruling Labour Party group of councillors. At national level, the Local Authority Association developed a close working relationship with the trade unions and after protracted negotiations had agreed a number of national initiatives, of which the single status agreement was the most important. Over a two-year period we observed how the local union branches engaged in the process of trying to establish the basis for the implementation of this agreement. Both parties appeared to be struggling to see how the deal could be introduced and the issue was continually fudged as unions threatened strike action and management sought to avoid it. In other areas management adopted some new policies and strategies that were opposed by the unions. The activation of the previously dormant 'flexibility clause' for community-care workers was a case in point. The unions were attempting to resist the imposition of these changes by taking cases to an employment tribunal. While the staff appreciated these attempts at resistance, they were unconvinced of the long-term ability of the unions to oppose the changes. As an aggrieved member of staff noted wearily:

(A)nd the unions came in then, so the thing's quietened, evened off now. So they [management] are doing it slowly.

(Female, part time, no. 4, Councilco2)

There is no doubting the fact that the trade unions, as active agents within a system of collective bargaining, have been seriously weakened as a result of changes in employment legislation coinciding with a period of radical economic restructuring. Workplaces (such as the Mediaco printworks, Bankco branches and Telecomco offices and call centres) have closed and new ones have opened. Established patterns of work organization (as in banking and telephony) have been transformed by the introduction of new technologies and the creation of new kinds of workplace. Public sector organizations (one of the cornerstones of trade-union membership and commitment) have either been wholly or partially privatized or subjected to significantly different patterns of budgetary constraint and administrative interference (Corby and White 1999; Morgan *et al.* 2000). It is not surprising that in this context we found trade-unionism on the back foot and placed in a far weaker bargaining relationship with the employer than at any time since the Second World War.

This said, it is worth noting that trade-union membership and some forms of collective-bargaining relationships had been maintained in six of our organizations, and in the other, Mediaco, there remained strong areas of trade-union support. Also, in our visits to the different workplaces, many of the workers still expressed the feelings of discontent and identified the same areas of conflict that had been the source of trade-union resistance in the past. To assume that the decline in strike activity indicated contentment would be a mistake. The trade unions are weak not because their members have turned their back on collectivism; rather, they are weak because their members' position in the workplace (and society) has been weakened.

Although workers and unions alike are aware of the extent of the changes that have taken place, it is less clear how either partner should respond to these new realities (Waddington 2000). In the UK and the USA there has been some attention paid to the possibilities of some form of 'trade-union renewal' in the context of the increasingly decentralized 'neo-liberal' economies (Fairbrother 1994, 1996, 2000; Milkman 2000). For example, Fairbrother argues that the devolution and decentralization of management structures in the public sector ought to be accompanied by a similar restructuring of union structures, reflecting the lesser need for national coordinated union action and the greater need for local action, and the opportunities this generates for union renewal. This union renewal thesis centres on the opportunities for increasing the participation of local union members, whether in workplace decision-making structures or in the coordination of local union action in response to management policy. However, others are less optimistic. Gall (1998) points out a number of potential weaknesses with promoting local bargaining as a union strategy: partnership arrangements established locally may be inherently weak; local members may be less informed when they are unable to draw upon the knowledge and support of national officers; and devolution of management structures may be an illusion, conjured up to veil the fundamental management decisions that are still made at corporate level, beyond the involvement of the union. Given the reality of decentralization in many areas of the economy, the proper prescription may be to pursue a two-pronged strategy—for union renewal within the workplace and the restoration of national bargaining (see ibid.). In addition, we can add a third strategy—that is, the introduction of a global framework for labour organizations.

Moreover, a number of studies argue that the fragmentation of the workforce and labour market institutions has been dramatic to the point of crippling any process of trade-union regeneration in its infancy (Gall 1998; Heery and Salmon 2000b). The example of the unsuccessful national action at Telecomco would lend support to this view. It certainly draws attention to the difficult issue of how unions are to represent those on non-standard employment contracts (Delsen 1990; Heery 1998; TUC 1996). More generally, it points to the fact that any alteration in the fortunes of trade union and collective bargaining and consultation arrangements will require a fundamental change in the institutional arrangements that regulate work and employment in this country. The trade unions seem unlikely to achieve this alone.

FROM FRAGMENTATION TO COORDINATION— RE-ESTABLISHING A ROLE FOR THE STATE

The task of designing and implementing managerial policy is becoming ever more complex. In the context of an increasingly uncertain economic environment, combined with both a weakening of national regulatory and collective bodies in the UK and the associated widening of scope for managerial prerogative, the managers in our case-study organizations have, in theory, the opportunity to choose from a range of potential solutions to questions of workforce planning. Moreover, even within a single organization, different employment policies and practices are likely to be adopted as solutions for different groups of workers.

Importantly, this study of changing employment policies and practices suggests that the bundle of solutions implemented within organizations may be generating an unsustainable interaction between conditions internal and external to the organization (see also Streeck 1987). As employers attempt to respond to changing pressures (arising from performance considerations, internal power relations and external labour market dynamics), new policies of hiring and firing, training and working time appear unlikely to meet either the competitive requirements of the organization or the broader needs of society and the economy. The unsustainability of the current situation is all the more pressing in light of the way UK policy-makers persist in identifying the organization as the locus of policy solutions. This characteristic of the UK (and US) decentralized, market-led labour market model is likely to become increasingly associated with poor employment opportunities for a growing proportion of the labour force.

Without new innovation in the management of employment change we are likely to witness a continuing deterioration in the prospects for employer–employee relations within the organization and the economy. As organizations struggle to adapt to new conditions in order even to stay afloat in a sea of uncoordinated and decentralized decision-making, the future prospects for the UK workforce look grim. Past expectations of steady improvement in living standards, coupled with career and skills development, are being eroded and replaced by the knowledge that an expanding layer of work opportunities provides a flat earnings and career profile. For the economy, growing reliance on organizations as the central actors in the reshaping of labour market dynamics is unsustainable. Under this decentralized and uncoordinated approach there is little chance of raising skill levels, bringing about a better balance between work and leisure time or improving access to secure employment.

The long-term viability of the UK economy and society requires the development of a more positive approach to the relationship between employment arrangements (such as opportunities for pay rises, training, career progression and participation) and the performance of organizations. However, this new approach will neither develop spontaneously nor emerge out of decentralized policies and strategies; we need a reassessment of the ability of local, national and pan-national actors (such as EU legislation, the UK government, training agencies, educational institutions and trade unions) to shape the restructuring of employment opportunities.

There are signs of an increasing interest in the need to re-regulate the labour market to meet the new needs of citizens as well as employers. This contrasts with the emphasis on deregulation and flexibility evident in policy debates in the 1980s and 1990s. This increased interest is admittedly more apparent in Continental Europe and the European Union than within the UK. An important catalyst for developing this debate in Europe has been the publication of the so-called Supiot report (2001) on the future of labour law. This report calls for a radical rethinking of the role of labour law and the construction of the employment relationship to take account of the breakdown of the Fordist model, based around male employees in full-time stable jobs and female carers in the household. The proposals of the Supiot report include:

• extending social and legal protection to those engaged in non-standard work and to those engaged in care work by broadening the definition of labour force membership;
• the extension of collective representation to cover excluded groups;
• the development of a comprehensive approach to notions of time at work, and not limited to standard or Fordist full-time work;
• and the more systematic and general pursuit of gender equality through strengthening rights to maternal and parental leave and improving gender representation at work.

This represents a very ambitious and comprehensive agenda for recasting social and legal rights. The agenda that we present here is both more limited—focused more on direct employment—and more parochial, targeted specifically at the UK. Nevertheless, it is intended to contribute to the more general debate on how to move beyond deregulation to re-regulation and the re-institutionalization of the labour market.

Some examples of where such policy intervention is needed can be provided in relation to the specific areas of employment policy that this book has studied as outlined in boxes 10.1–10.5. Three types of policy may help to overcome the problems we have identified:

• policies designed to ensure that the longer-term costs and the consequences for other actors of employment policies are included in the decision-making framework;
• policies designed to change power relations within the labour market, to provide actors, such as employees, citizens or trade unions, with the means to challenge the policies and practices of managers or the state;

- policies designed to encourage, directly or indirectly, the development of new institutions and institutional arrangements aimed at providing new resources for labour market actors, ranging from new professional associations for workers to new supplies of skilled labour for employers.

The policies suggested arise out of our case study analyses. They are not, in any sense, fully developed policy proposals, but are presented here to suggest that we need to move beyond general criticism to a new and more positive phase of policy development and institutional rebuilding. The list, as constructed, may be seen by some as placing undue weight on the potential for legal intervention; for some commentators, such legal intervention may be considered too burdensome on business, while for others legal rights can be considered to be generally ineffective. Both criticisms have some validity if legal rights were

---

Box 10.1. Staffing policies

Policies to change cost structure:

- requirements for employers to provide similar wage levels and benefits to temporary as to permanent staff;
- requirements for organizations to recognize employment responsibilities towards agency temps working under their direction at the workplace.

Policies to provide new rights to employees/citizens/trade unions:

- consultation rights for employees and trade unions on redundancy, redeployment and outsourcing;
- inclusion of temporary staff within employment legislation relating to union representation, strikes, etc. at the workplace level;
- strengthened rights under Transfer of Undertakings legislation to protect against outsourcing decisions primarily motivated by labour cost considerations (for example, rights to query changes in staffing levels if these imply greater work intensity).

Policies to develop new labour market institutions:

- new institutions to assist with retraining and redeployment;
- a government commitment to new public institutions to raise public sector employment.

Box 10.2. Skills and training

Policies to change cost structure:

- all employers to contribute to training costs (for example a requirement to spend a fixed percentage of wage bill on training);
- increased government subsidies for external vocational training to supplement on-the-job training.

Policies to provide new rights to employees/citizens/trade unions:

- rights to training for all staff, including those on non-standard contracts;
- negotiation rights to employees and trade unions over content of training programmes.

Policies to develop new labour market institutions:

- new professional/vocational qualifications to develop and protect occupational/professional labour markets.

Box 10.3. Working time

Policies to change cost structure:

- requirement to base holiday and sick pay provision on actual hours worked not contractual hours.

Policies to provide new rights to employees/citizens/trade unions:

- minimum notice required for variation in hours;
- rights for consultation over scheduling of hours and holidays;
- rights for part-time and full-time leave on a paid basis for care responsibilities;
- increased rights to rest periods/breaks;
- increased rights not to work unsocial hours;
- rights to standard working times for all staff including managerial and supervisory staff (and an end to opt outs under the Working Time Directive);
- improved rights for children with implications for rights to time off for parents, for example, to be accompanied by parent to doctors, hospitals, etc.

Policies to develop new labour market institutions:

- increased role for health and safety executive in areas of working time, to take into account impact of long working hours on stress and health in general.

Box 10.4. Labour costs

Policies to change cost structure:

- establishment of a higher national minimum wage, updated by indexation;
- equal pay comparisons allowed between employers, not just within the same employer;
- requirement not to discriminate in pay between permanent/temporary staff;
- extension of benefits to non-standard staff to be based on actual hours worked, not contractual hours.

Policies to provide new rights to employees/citizens/trade unions:

- right to a transparent pay structure, based on skill and/or performance, not contractual status;
- right to regrading after a maximum period of 'acting-up' in higher positions.

Policies to develop new labour market institutions:

- development of new institutional arrangements for pension provision, etc., to increase security of pension rights, etc., when changing employers;
- development of new institutional mechanisms for pay determination and collective bargaining, which facilitate coordination of pay-setting.

to be enforced mainly through the courts and tribunal systems. However, effectively implemented legal rights are, in practice, introduced through voluntary measures. Under these conditions, the majority of employers take steps to ensure that they are acting within the law, while the majority of trade unions use the legal rights systems to protect individuals and groups at the workplace without having to take a case through the courts. Given the current weakness of the voluntary mechanisms of regulation (Deakin *et al.* 1999), it seems essential to put in place more extensive legal rights, but with the hope and long-term expectation that these would become built into employment policy and practice. Moreover, what we are proposing is a multifaceted approach to re-regulation, but new voluntary and institutional mechanisms are more difficult to predict or suggest than legal rights and responsibilities needed to underpin or push forward this development.

The advanced industrial economies were, at one stage, considered to have all the institutional mechanisms as well as the appropriate economic

Box 10.5. Work intensity

Policies to change cost structure:

- enforcement of improved minimum rest periods, maximum working hours regulations, etc.;
- requirement to pay for overtime hours at premium rates if not possible to take time off in lieu within one month.

Policies to provide new rights to employees/citizens/trade unions:

- right to challenge performance/monitoring standards based on strengthened health and safety legislation;
- right to be protected from undue stress at work and undue disruption to personal/family life;
- rights for trade unions to have access to information on workloads and staffing levels to monitor work intensity levels and to challenge outsourcing decision if based on expected heightened work intensity.

Policies to develop new labour market institutions:

- strengthened health and safety institutions with rights to monitor work intensity/stress, etc.

tools in place to provide for basic human needs in the workplace. These assumptions have been called into question by the process of de-institutionalizing and deregulating labour markets that has persisted over the last two decades (Almond and Rubery 2000). Our case studies leave no doubt over the extent to which the rights of workers have been eroded and the normative structure of workplace relationships recast. People's expectations have been reduced by a remorseless assertion that any job is better than no job (Edwards and Burkitt 2001).

This is the context within which we argue for a serious reassessment of 'flexibility' and the direction being taken by the UK employment system. We are aware that none of these suggestions on their own would be sufficient to reverse these trends. That would require a concerted effort to develop new regulatory policies, new rights and new institutional arrangements across the whole range of labour market and employment fields. The objective would be to try to kick-start the process of reversing the fragmentation of the employment systems, but to do so in a way that reflects the changing nature of labour markets and the new needs of all the stakeholders in the economy. This multilayered and multi-dimensional approach is essential for any renewal of labour market institutions. Without such renewal it will be impossible to reverse the fragmentation and discontinuous reconstruction that has been identified by Sennett (1998) as leading to a 'corrosion of character'. The extent of this problem has been emphasized by organizations such as the International Labour Organization (ILO), which has pointed to the undermining of decent work and the emergence of what it calls a 'decent work deficit' (ILO 2001). In its view, the provision of decent work is fundamental to the well-being of all societies, but to generate and maintain decent work requires a coordinated and integrated policy approach involving the promotion of employment opportunities, employment rights, social protection and social dialogue. These four principles also inform our selection of possible policy approaches as a means of stimulating the debate on the need for some new ways of re-regulating the labour market and rebuilding institutions. This policy framework is needed not to stifle initiative in developing new employment arrangements, but to ensure that initiative and, indeed, innovation and imagination are channelled towards a more productive, coordinated and cooperative outcome.

1

Interviews at the Seven Organizations

	Total	Male, full-time	Male, part-time	Female, full-time	Female, part-time
Bankco					
Senior management	7	4	0	3	0
Staff	46	9	1	26	10
Total	53	13	1	29	10
Councilco					
Senior management	9	5	0	4	0
Staff	54	23	1	16	14
Total	63	28	1	20	14
Healthco					
Senior management	7	6	0	1	0
Staff	21	7	0	12	2
Total	28	13	0	13	2
Mediaco					
Senior management	7	6	0	1	0
Staff	38	26	0	12	0
Total	45	32	0	13	0
Pharmco					
Senior management	7	6	0	1	0
Staff	26	15	0	11	0
Total	33	21	0	12	0
Retailco					
Senior management	4	2	0	2	0
Staff	36	12	2	13	9
Total	40	14	2	15	9
Telecomco					
Senior management	7	3	0	4	0
Staff	33	10	1	17	5
Total	40	13	1	21	5

2

Table A1. Corporate structure in the seven organizations

	Ownership structure	Internal divisional structure
Bankco	A subsidiary wholly owned by a large diversified corporation	Six divisions separated by function, dominated by the Corporate and Commercial and Personal Banking divisions; reduced integration of activities and skills development between divisions
Councilco	A local government authority under state ownership	12 divisions; strengthening of horizontal integration to meet 'corporate objectives'
Healthco	One of around 750 state-owned NHS Trusts	14 directorates; strengthening of horizontal integration to meet 'corporate objectives'
Mediaco	Newspaper offices wholly owned by a national media group, which also has a 50 per cent stake in the printworks	3 divisions at the newspaper offices and 4 at the printworks; relatively high degree of horizontal delineation between departments
Pharmco	Transnational ownership following merger (1998) between one UK-owned and one foreign-owned company	4 divisions split by function with plants spread worldwide; each 'business unit' is responsible for meeting budgeted local profit, but has freedom to allocate resources
Retailco	Wholly owned and the core business of Retailco	Combined functional and regional structure; 6 functional divisions, with retail division subdivided by region
Telecomco	Wholly owned and the core business of Telecomco	Combined functional and regional structure; 3 broad divisions, each organized at a regional level

Table A2. Management structure in the seven organizations

	Degree of centralization of decision-making	Performance targets, accountability and control
Bankco	Relatively strong centralized vision guides business practices across the divisions	Centralized monitoring of performance facilitated by shift from branches to call centres
Councilco	Trend towards greater corporate-led centralization across departments	Annual cost savings required by government; performance judged against published tables comparing national standards of services provision
Healthco	Trend towards greater corporate-led centralization across directorates	Annual cost savings required by government; performance judged against Patient Charter standards
Mediaco	News offices, high degree of autonomy; Printworks, capital investment decisions centralized, but local autonomy to bid for new contracts	Performance pressures shifted from successful print-run and sales growth to advertising revenue and sales
Pharmco	Relatively high level of freedom to adapt system of production within individual plants	Very strict performance/cost targets and strong international competition among business units
Retailco	Centralized decision-making in the key areas of business activity	Highly detailed performance data collected centrally and disseminated to set competitive workplace targets
Telecomco	Centralized decision-making; weak autonomy to adapt services provision or form of work systems at workplace level	Highly detailed performance data collected centrally and disseminated to set competitive workplace targets

REFERENCES

Ackers, P. and Payne, J. (1998). 'British trade unions and social partnership: rhetoric, reality and strategy', *International Journal of Human Resource Management*, 9: 529–50.

——Smith, C. and Smith, P. (eds) (1996). *The New Workplace and Trade Unionism: Critical Perspectives on Work and Organisation*. London: Routledge.

Ackroyd, S. and Fleetwood, S. (eds) (2001). *Realist Perspectives on Management and Organisations*. London: Routledge.

Adnett, N. and Hardy, S. (2001). 'Reviewing the working time directive: rationale, implementation and case law', *Industrial Relations Journal*, 32/2: 114–25.

Aglietta, M. (1979). *A Theory of Capitalist Regulation*. London: Verso.

Albert, M. (1986). *Capitalism Against Capitalism*. London: Whurr Publications.

—— (1993). *Capitalism Against Capitalism*, London: Whurr.

Albrecht, K. and Zemke, R. (1985). *Service America! Doing Business in the New Economy*. Homewood, IL: Dow Jones-Irwin.

Allen, J. and Henry, N. (1996). 'Fragments of industry and employment: contract service work and the shift towards precarious employment', in R. Crompton, D. Gallie, and K. Purcell (eds), *Changing Forms of Employment: Organisations, Skills and Gender*. London: Routledge, pp. 65–82.

Almond, P. and Rubery, J. (2000). 'Deregulation and societal systems', in A. Sorge and M. Maurice (eds), *Embedding Organisations*. Amsterdam: John Benjamin.

Anthony, P. D. (1994). *Managing Culture*. Buckinghamshire: Open University Press.

Applebaum, E. and Batt, R. (1994). *The New American Workplace*. Ithaca, NY: ILR Press.

Archer, M. (1998). 'Introduction: realism in the social sciences', in M. Archer, R. Bhaskar, A. Collier, T. Lawson and A. Norrie (eds), *Critical Realism: Essential Readings*. London: Routledge.

Arrowsmith, J. and Sisson, K. (1999). 'Pay and working time: towards organization-based systems?', *British Journal of Industrial Relations*, 37: 51–76.

Arthur, M. B. (1994). 'The boundaryless career: a new perspective for organisational inquiry', *Journal of Organisational Behaviour*, 15: 295–306.

—— and Rousseau, D. M. (eds) (1996). *The Boundaryless Career: A New Employment Principle for a New Organisational Era*. Oxford: Oxford University Press.

Ashton, D. and Green, F. (1996). *Education, Training and the Global Economy.* Cheltenham: Edward Elgar.

Atkinson, J. (1984). 'Manpower strategies for flexible organisations', *Personnel Management,* 16/8: 28–31.

Audit Commission (1995). *The Doctor's Tale: the Work of Hospital Doctors in England and Wales.* London: HMSO.

Babbage, C. (1835). *On the Economy of Machinery and Manufacturers.* London: Charles Knight, Pall Mall East.

Bailey, R. (1993). 'Annual review article 1993: British public sector industrial relations', *British Journal of Industrial Relations,* 32/1: 113–36.

Baldry, C., Bain, P. and Taylor, P. (1998). ' "Bright satanic offices": intensification, control and team Taylorism', in P. Thompson and C. Warhurst (eds), *Work-places of the Future.* Basingstoke: Macmillan, pp. 163–83.

Baret, C., Gadrey, J. and Gallouj, C. (1999). 'France, Germany, Great Britain: the organization of working time in large retail food stores', *European Journal of Industrial Relations,* 5/1: 27–48.

Barker, K. and Christensen, K. (1998). *Contingent Work: American Employment Relations in Transition.* Ithaca, NY: ILR Press.

Beck, U. (1992). *Risk Society: Towards a New Modernity.* London: Sage.

Beesley, M. and Laidlaw, R. (1997). 'The liberalisation of telephone services in the UK', in M Beesley (ed.), *Privatization, Regulation and Deregulation.* London: Routledge.

Bell, D. (1973). *The Coming of the Post-industrial Age: A Venture in Social Forecasting.* New York: Basic Books.

Best, M. (1990). *The New Competition.* Oxford: Polity.

Beynon, H. (1973). *Working for Ford.* Wakefield: EP Publishing Ltd.

—— (1997). 'The changing practices of work', in R. Brown (ed.), *The Changing Shape of Work.* London: Macmillan.

—— (1999). 'A classless society?', in H. Beynon and P. Glavanis (eds), *Patterns of Social Inequality.* London: Longman.

—— Hudson, R. and Sadler, D. (1994). *A Place Called Teeside: A Locality in a Global Economy.* Edinburgh: Edinburgh University Press.

Bhaskar, R. (1989). *Reclaiming Reality.* London: Verso.

Block, F. (1986). 'Political choice and the multiple logics of capitalism', *Theory and Society,* 15: 175–92.

Bosch, G. (1990). *Retraining not Redundancy.* Geneva: International Institute for Labour Studies.

—— (1995). 'Synthesis report', in *Flexible Working Time: Collective Bargaining and Government Intervention.* Paris: OECD.

—— (1997). 'Annual working hours: an international comparison', in G. Bosch, D. Meulders and F. Michon (eds), *Working Time: New Issues, New Norms, New Measures.* Bruxelles: Editions du Dulbea.

—— (1999). 'Working time: tendencies and emerging issues', *International Labour Review,* 138/2: 131–50.

—— Dawkins, P. and Michon, F. (1994). *Times are Changing: Working Time in 14 Industrialised Countries.* Geneva: International Institute for Labour Studies.

Bowen, D. and Lawler, E. (1992). 'The empowerment of service workers: what, why, how and when', *Sloan Management Review,* 33/1: 31–9.

Boyne, G. (1999). 'Introduction: processes, performance and Best Value in local government', *Local Government Studies*, 25/2: 1–15.

Bradley, H., Erickson, M., Stephenson, C. and Williams, S. (2000). *Myths at Work*. Cambridge: Polity.

Braverman, H. (1974). *Labor and Monopoly Capital: The Segregation of Work in the Twentieth Century*. New York: Monthly Review Press.

Burawoy, M. (1982). *Manufacturing Consent: Changes in the Labour Process Under Monopoly Capitalism*. Chicago: The University of Chicago Press.

Burchell, B., Day, D., Hudson, M., Ladipo, D., Mankelow, R., Nolan, J., Reed, H., Wichert, I. and Wilkinson, F. (1999). *Job Insecurity and Work Intensification: Flexibility and the Changing Boundaries of Work*. York Publishing Services Ltd: Joseph Rowntree Foundation.

Burke, T. and Shackleton, J. R. (1996). 'Trouble in store? UK retailing in the 1990s', *Hobart Papers*. London: The Institute of Economic Affairs.

Byers, S. (1999). 'The Importance of People and Knowledge—Towards a New Industry Policy for the 21st Century'. Speech given at the London Business School, 21 October.

—— (2001). 'Turning change into opportunity: the Next Steps for industrial policy'. Speech given at the Social Market Foundation, 4 May.

Cabinet Office (1999). *Modernising Government*, Cm 4310. London: HMSO.

Callaghan, G. and Thompson, P. (2000). 'Edwards revisited: technical control and call centres'. Paper presented at the 18th Annual International Labour Process Conference, April, University of Strathclyde, Glasgow.

Cappelli, P. (1995). 'Rethinking employment', *British Journal of Industrial Relations*, 33/4: 563–602.

—— (1999). *The New Deal at Work*. Boston: Harvard Business School Press.

Cappelli, P., Bassi, L., Katz, H., Knoke, D., Osterman, P. and Useem, M. (1997). *Change at Work*. Oxford: Oxford University Press.

Casey, B. and Wood, S. (1993). 'Great Britain: firm policy, state policy and the employment and unemployment of older workers', in F. Naschold and B. de Vroom (eds), *Regulating Employment and Welfare*. Berlin: de Gruyter.

Casey, B., Metcalf, H. and Millward, N. (1997). *Employers' Use of Flexible Labour*. London: Policy Studies Institute.

Champy, J. (1995). *Reengineering Management*. London: Harper Collins.

Cochrane, A. (1993). *Whatever Happened to Local Government?* Buckinghamshire: Open University Press.

Colling, T. (1999). 'Tendering and outsourcing: working in the contract state?', in S. Corby and G. White (eds), *Employee Relations in the Public Services*. London: Routledge.

Confederation of British Industry [CBI] (2001). *Employment Trends Survey*. London: CBI.

Cooke, F. L. (2002). 'Maintenance work, maintenance skills: the case of a major water company in the UK', *New Technology, Work and Employment*, 17/1.

Cooke, H. (2000). 'The intensification of nursing work', Mimeograph, Department of Sociology, University of Manchester.

Corby, S. and White, G. (eds) (1999). *Employee Relations in the Public Services: Themes and Issues*. London: Routledge.

Cressey, P. and Scott, P. (1992). 'Employment, technology and industrial rela-
  tions in the UK clearing banks: is the honeymoon over?', *New Technology,
  Work and Employment*, 7/2: 83–96.
Crompton, R. (1997). *Women and Work in Modern Britain*. Oxford: Oxford
  University Press.
Crouch, C. (1997). 'Skills-based full employment: the latest philosopher's stone',
  British Journal of Industrial Relations, 35/3: 367–84.
——Finegold, D. and Sako, M. (1999). *Are Skills the Answer?* Oxford: Oxford
  University Press.
Cully, M., Woodland, S., O'Reilly, A. and Dix, G. (1999). *Britain at Work. As
  Depicted by the 1998 Workplace Employee Relations Survey*.
  London: Routledge.
Cutler, T. and Waine, B. (1994). *Managing the Welfare State: The Politics of Public
  Sector Management*. Oxford: Berg Publishers Ltd.
Daniel, W. W. (1987). *Workplace Industrial Relations and Technical Change*.
  London: Frances Pinter (in association with the Policy Studies Institute).
Darlington, R. (1998). 'Employment trends in the British telecommuni-
  cations industry', CWU Research (4 Feb), London: Communication Workers'
  Union.
Deakin, S. and Wilkinson, F. (1995). *Contracts, Cooperation and Trust: The Role
  of the Institutional Framework*. ESRC Centre for Business Research Working
  Papers 10: University of Cambridge.
Deakin, S., Burchell, B. and Howey, S. (1999). *The Employment Status of Workers
  in Non-Standard Employment*. London: Department of Trade and Industry.
Delbridge, R. (1998). *Life on the Line in Contemporary Manufacturing: The
  Workplace Experience of Lean Production and the 'Japanese' Model*. Oxford:
  Oxford University Press.
Delsen, I. (1990). 'European trade unions and the flexible workforce', *Industrial
  Relations Journal*, 21/4: 260–73.
Department of Trade and Industry [DTI] (1998). *Our Competitive Future—
  Building the Knowledge Driven Economy*. London: HMSO.
—— (1999). *Work in the Knowledge Economy*. London: HMSO.
—— (2001). *Opportunity for All in a World of Change*, Cm 5052. London: HMSO.
Dicken, P. (1998). *Global Shift: Transforming the World Economy*. London: Paul
  Kegan.
DiMaggio, P. and Powell, W. (1983). 'The iron cage revisited: institutional iso-
  morphism and collective rationality in organisational fields', *American
  Sociological Review*, 48: 147–60.
Doeringer, P. B. and Piore, M. J. (1971). *Internal Labour Markets and Manpower
  Analysis*. Lexington: Heath.
Drago, R. (1998). 'New systems of work and new workers', in Barker, K. and
  Christensen, K. (eds), *Contingent Work. American Employment Relations in
  Transition*. Ithaca, NY: ILR Press, pp. 144–69.
Drucker, P. F. (1970). *Technology, Management and Society*. London: Heinemann.
—— (1993). *Post-capitalist Society*. London: Butterworth-Heinemann.
Du Gay, P. (1993). '"Numbers and souls": retailing and de-differentiation of
  economy and culture', *British Journal of Sociology*, 44/4: 563–87.
—— (1996). *Consumption and Identity at Work*. London: Sage.
—— (2000). *In Praise of Bureaucracy*. London: Sage.

Dunleavy, P. and Hood, C. (1994). 'From old public administration to new public management', *Public Money and Management*, 14/3: 34–43.

Edwards, L. and Burkitt, N. (2001). *Wanting More From Work? Expectations and Aspirations of People in Low and Middle Class Jobs.* Research Brief RBX6-01. London: Department for Education and Employment.

Edwards, R. (1979). *Contested Terrain: The Transformation of the Workplace in the Twentieth Century.* New York: Basic Books.

Elger, T. (1990). 'Technical innovation and work reorganisation in British manufacturing in the 1980s', *Work Employment and Society*, 9/special edition: 67–102.

—— (1999). 'Manufacturing myths and miracles: work reorganisation in British manufacturing since 1979', in H. Beynon and P. Glavanis (eds), *Patterns of Social Inequality.* London: Longman.

—— and Smith, C. (eds) (1994). *Global Japanisation?* London: Routledge.

Elliott, L. and Atkinson, D. (1998). *The Age of Insecurity.* London: Verso.

Elliott, R. F. (1995). 'Pay reform and pay dispersion in the public service: a study of three OECD countries', *Public Management Occasional Papers*, 2/1. Paris: OECD.

Fairbrother, P. (1994). *Politics and the State as Employer.* London: Mansell.

—— (1996). 'Workplace trade unionism in the state sector', in P. Ackers, C. Smith and P. Smith (eds), *The New Workplace and Trade Unionism.* London: Routledge.

—— (2000). *Trade Unions at the Crossroads.* London: Mansell.

Felstead, A. and Jewson, N. (eds) (1999). *Global Trends in Flexible Labour.* Basingstoke: Macmillan.

Ferner, A. and Colling, T. (1991). 'Privatisation, regulation and industrial relations', *British Journal of Industrial Relations*, 29/3: 391–409.

Finegold, D. and Soskice, D. (1988). 'The failure of training in Britain: analysis and prescription', *Oxford Review of Economic Policy*, 4/3: 21–53.

Fisher, J. (1997). 'The challenge of change: the positive agenda of the TGWU', *The International Journal of Human Resource Management*, 8/6: 797–806.

Forde, C. and Slater, G. (2001). 'Just a temporary phenomenon? The rise and fall of temporary work in the UK'. Mimeo, Leeds University Business School.

Francis, A. (1986). *New Technology at Work.* Oxford: Clarendon Press.

Freeman, C. and Soete, L. (1996). *Work for all or Mass Unemployment: Computerised Technical Change into the 21st Century.* London: Pinter.

Frenkel, S., Korczynski, M., Shire, K. and Tam, M. (1999). *On the Front Line: Organization of Work in the Information Economy.* Ithaca, NY: ILR Press.

Friedman, A. L. (1977). *Industry and Labour: Class Struggle at Work and Monopoly Capitalism.* London: Macmillan.

Froud, J., Haslam, C., Johal, S. and Williams, K. (2000). 'Restructuring for shareholder value and its implications for labour', *Cambridge Journal of Economics*, 24/6: 771–98.

—— Johal, S., Haslam, C., Shaoul, J. and Williams, K. (1996). 'The right arguments: refocusing the debate of privatisation', International Centre of Labour Studies, *Working Paper 12*, Manchester.

Fuller, L. and Smith, V. (1991). 'Consumers' reports: management by customers in a changing economy', *Work, Employment and Society*, 5/1: 1–16.

Gall, G. (1998). 'The prospects for workplace trade unionism: evaluating Fair-brother's union renewal thesis', *Capital and Class*, 66: 149–57.

Gallie, D., White, M., Cheny, Y. and Tomlinson, M. (1998). *Restructuring the Employment Relationship*. Oxford: Clarendon Press.

Geary, J. (1992). 'Employment, flexibility and human resource management', *Work, Employment and Society*, 6/2: 251–70.

Gennard, J. (1990). *A History of the National Graphical Association*. London: Unwin Hyman.

Gentle, C. (1993). *The Financial Services Industry*. Aldershot: Avebury.

Gershuny, J. (1978). *After the Industrial Society? The Emerging Self-service Economy*. London: Macmillan.

—— (1983). *The New Service Economy: The Transformation of Employment in Industrial Society*. London: Francis Pinter.

Gilroth, R. (ed.) (1998). *Jobs and Economic Development*. London: Sage.

Glynn, S. and Gospel, H. (1993). 'Britain's low skill equilibrium: a problem of demand?', *Industrial Relations Journal*, 24/2: 112–25.

Golden, L. (2001). 'Flexible work schedules: which workers get them?' *American Behavioral Scientist*, 44/7: 1157–78.

Goodhart, D. and Wintour, P. (1986). *Eddie Shah and the Newspaper Revolution*. London: Coronet Books.

Goodrich, C. (1920). *The Frontier of Control: A Study of British Workshop Politics*. London: G. Bell.

Gorz, A. (1976). *The End of the Working Class?* London: Pluto Press.

Graham, L. (1994). 'How does the Japanese model transfer to the US?', in T. Elger and C. Smith (eds), *Global Japanisation?* London: Routledge.

Granovetter, M. (1974). *Getting a Job: A Study of Contracts and Careers*. Cambridge, MA: Harvard University Press.

—— (1985). 'Economic action and social structure', *American Journal of Sociology*, 913: 481–510.

Green, F. (1994). 'Training inequality and inefficiency', in A. Glyn and D. Miliband (eds), *Paying for Inequality: The Economic Cost of Social Injustice*. London: River Oram Press.

—— (2000). 'Why has work effort become more intense? Conjectures and evidence about effort-biased technical change and other stories', University of Kent, Department of Economics Discussion Paper, 00/03.

—— (2001). 'It's been a hard day's night: the concentration and intensification of work in late 20th century Britain', *British Journal of Industrial Relations*, 39/1: 53–80.

—— Felstead, A. and Ashton, D. (2000). 'Are Britain's workplace skills becoming more unequal?' *Cambridge Journal of Economics*, 24/6: 709–28.

—— Felstead, A., Ashton, D. and Burchell, B. (1999). 'Skill trends in Britain: trajectories over the last decade', in F. Coffield (ed.), *Research and Policy Implications of a Learning Society*. Bristol: Policy Press.

Greenbaum, J. (1998). 'The times they are a' changing: dividing and recombining labour through computer systems', in P. Thompson and C. Warhurst (eds), *Workplaces of the Future*. Macmillan Business: Basingstoke.

Gregg, P., Knight, G. and Wadsworth, J. (2000). 'Heaven knows I'm miserable now: job insecurity in the British labour market', in E. Heery and J. Salmon (eds), *The Insecure Workforce*. London: Routledge.

Gregory, A. (1995). 'Patterns of hours in large-scale grocery retailing in Britain and France', in P. Cressey and B. Jones (eds), *Work and Employment in Europe*. London: Routledge.

Grimshaw, D. (1999). 'Changes in skills-mix and pay determination among the nursing workforce in the UK', *Work, Employment and Society*, 13/2: 293–326.

—— and Rubery, J. (1998). 'Integrating the internal and external labour markets', *Cambridge Journal of Economics*, 22/2: 199–220.

—— (2001). *The Gender Pay Gap: A Research Review*, EOC Research Discussion Series, Manchester: Equal Opportunities Commission.

—— Ward, K., Rubery, J. and Beynon, H. (2001). 'Organisations and the transformation of the internal labour market', *Work, Employment and Society*, 15/1: 25–54.

Guest, D. and Peccei, R. (2001). 'Partnerships at work: mutuality and the balance of advantage', *British Journal of Industrial Relations*, 39/2: 207–36.

Gutek, B. (1995). *The Dynamics of Service: Reflections on the Changing Nature of Customer/Provider Interactions*. San Francisco: Jossey-Bass.

Hage, J. and Powers, C. H. (1992). *Postindustrial Lives: Roles and Relationships in the Twenty-First Century*. London: Sage.

Halford, S., Savage, M. and Witz, A. (1997). *Genders, Careers and Organisations*. London: Macmillan.

Hammer, M. (1996). *Beyond Re-engineering*. London: Harper Collins.

Harrison, B. (1997). *Lean and Mean: The Changing Landscape of Corporate Power in the Age of Flexibility*. New York: Basic Books.

Harvey, M. (1998). *Supermarket UK: The Transformation of the Food Commodity*. Mimeo, CRIC.

—— (1999). 'Economies of time: a framework for analysing the restructuring of employment relations', in A. Felstead and N. Jewson (eds), *Global Trends in Flexible Labour*. Basingstoke: London.

Hayek, F. (1960). *The Constitution of Liberty*. London: Routledge and Kegan.

Heckscher, C. (1988). *The New Unionism: Employee Involvement and the Changing Corporation*. New York: Basic Books.

Heery, E. (1998). 'Campaigning for Part-time Workers', *Work, Employment and Society*, 12/2: 351–66.

—— and Salmon, J. (2000a). 'The insecurity thesis', in E. Heery and J. Salmon (eds), *The Insecure Workforce*. London: Routledge.

—— —— (eds) (2000b). *The Insecure Workforce*. London: Routledge.

Herzenberg, S. A., Alic, J. A. and Wial, H. (1998). *New Rules for a New Economy. Employment and Opportunity in Postindustrial America*. Ithaca, NY: ILR Press.

Hicks, J. (1955). 'The economic foundations of wages policy', *Economic Journal*, 259/LXV, September: 389–404.

Hillard, J. and Pollard, E. (1998). *Employability: Developing a Framework for Policy Analysis*. Research Brief No 85. London: Department of Education and Employment.

Hirst, P. and Thompson, G. (1996). *Globalization in Question*. Cambridge: Polity.

HMSO (1991). *The Citizen's Charter: Raising the Standard*, Cmnd 1599. London: HMSO.

Hochschild, A. R. (1983). *The Managed Heart: Commercialisation of Human Feeling*. Berkeley: University of California Press.

—— (1997). *The Time Bind*. New York: Metropolitan.

Hoggett, P. (1996). 'New modes of control in the public service', *Public Administration*, 74: 9–32.

Horrell, S. and Rubery, J. (1991). *Employers' Working Time Policies and Women's Employment*. Equal Opportunities Commission Research Paper: HMSO, 74.

Horsted, J. and Doherty, J. (1995). *Survivors' Syndrome Survey*. Cranfield: Cranfield Human Resources Centre, Working Transitions Paper.

Hutton, W. (1994). *The State We Are In*. London: Vintage.

Hyman, R. (1987). 'Strategy or structure? capital, labour and control', *Work, Employment and Society*, 1/1: 25–55.

IDS (1997). 'Public sector pay', *Income Data Services Report*, 747: 25–8.

Institute of Management (1995). *Survival of the Fittest*. Bristol: Burston Distribution Services.

International Labour Organization [ILO] (2001). *Report of the Director-General: Reducing the Decent Work Deficit—A Global Challenge*. Geneva: ILO.

Jackson, M. P., Leopold, J. W. and Tuck, K. (1993). *Decentralisation of Collective Bargaining: An Analysis of Recent Experience in the UK*. Basingstoke: Macmillan/St Martin's Press.

Jacoby, S. (1984). 'The development of internal labour markets in American manufacturing firms', in P. Osterman (ed.), *Internal Labour Markets*. Cambridge, MA: MIT Press.

Jain, H. C. (1990). 'Human resource management in selected Japanese firms, their foreign subsidiaries and locally owned counterparts', *International Labour Review*, 129/1: 73–89.

Jessop, B., Bonnett, K., Bromley, S. and Ling, T. (1988). *Thatcherism*. Cambridge: Polity Press.

Kalleberg, A. and Epstein, C. F. (2001). 'Introduction: temporal dimensions of employment relations', *American Behavioral Scientist*, 44/7: 1064–75.

Kapstein, E. B. (1996). 'Workers and the world economy', *Foreign Affairs*, May/June: 16–37.

Keep, E. (2000). 'Learning organisations, life-long learning and the mystery of the vanishing employers', Mimeo, ESRC Centre on Skills, Knowledge and Organizational Performance, University of Warwick.

Kelly, J. (1996). 'Union militancy and social partnership', in P. Ackers, C. Smith and P. Smith (eds), *The New Workplace and Trade Unionism*. London: Routledge.

—— (1997). 'Challenges to unions in Britain and Europe', *Work, Employment and Society*, 11/2: 373–6.

—— (1998). *Rethinking Industrial Relations: Mobilisation, Collectivism and Long Waves*. London: Routledge.

Kenney, M. and Florida, R. (1993). *Beyond Mass Production: The System and Its Transfer to the US*. Oxford: Oxford University Press.

Korczynski, M., Shire, K., Frenkel, S. and Tam, M. (2000). 'Service work in consumer capitalism: customers, control and contradictions', *Work, Employment and Society*, 14/4: 669–87.

Krugman, P. (1998). 'America the boastful', *Foreign Affairs*, May–June: 32–45.

Kumar, K. (1987). *Utopia and anti-Utopia in Modern Times*. Oxford: Blackwell.

Lash, S. and Urry, J. (1994). *Economies of Time and Space*. London: Sage.

Lazonick, W. (1991). *Business Organization and the Myth of the Market Economy*. Cambridge: Cambridge University Press.

Leadbeater, C. (1999). *Living on Thin Air*. London: Viking.

Legge, K. (1995a). 'HRM: rhetoric, reality and hidden agendas', in John Storey (ed.), *Human Resource Management*. London: Routledge.

——(1995b). *Human Resource Management: Rhetorics and Realities*. Basingstoke: Macmillan.

Lehndorff, S. (1998). 'From "collective" to "individual" reductions in working time? Trends and experience with working time in the European Union', *Transfer*, 4/4: 598–620.

——(ed.) (1999). *New Working Time Systems, Work Organisation and the Re-distribution of Work*. Gelsenkirchen: Graue Reihe des Instituts Arbeit und Technik.

Leidner, R. (1993). *Fast Food, Fast Talk: Service Work and Routinization of Everyday Life*. Berkeley: University of California Press.

Leyshon, A. and Thrift, N. (1993). 'The restructuring of the financial services industry in the 1990s: a reversal of fortune?', *Journal of Rural Studies*, 9/3: 223–41.

Lipietz, A. (1987). *Mirages and Miracles: The Crises of Global Fordism*. London: Verso.

Littleton, S. M. (1992). *The Wapping Dispute*. Aldershot: Avebury.

McCammon, H. J. and Griffin, L. J. (2000). 'Workers and their customers and clients', *Work and Occupations*, 27/3: 278–96.

MacDonald, C. L. and Sirianni, C. (eds) (1996). *Working in the Service Society*. Philadelphia: Temple University Press.

Machin, S. and Waldfogel, J. (1994). 'The decline of the male breadwinner', Centre for Economic Performance, LSE, Working Paper 601.

McIlroy, J. (1997). 'Still under siege: British trade unions at the turn of the century', *Historical Studies in Industrial Relations*, 1/3: 93–112.

——(1998). 'The enduring alliance? Trade unions and the making of New Labour', *British Journal of Industrial Relations*, 36/4: 537–64.

Marchington, M. (1998). 'Partnership in context: towards a European model?', in P. Sparrow and M. Marchington (eds), *Human Resource Management: The New Agenda*. London: Financial Times/Pitman Publishing.

——Wilkinson, A., Ackers, P. and Dundon, A. (2001). *Management Choice and Employee Voice*. London: CIPD.

Marks, A., Findlay, P., Hine, J., McKinlay, A. and Thompson, P. (1998). 'The politics of partnership? Innovation in employment relations in the Scottish spirits industry', *British Journal of Industrial Relations*, 36/2: 209–26.

Marsden, D. (1995). 'A phoenix from the ashes of apprenticeship? Vocational training in Britain', *International Contributions to Labour Studies*, 5: 87–114.

Marshall, A. (1920). *Principles of Economics*. London: Macmillan.

Martin, S. (1999). 'Picking winners or piloting Best Value? An analysis of English Best Value bids', *Local Government Studies*, 25/2: 53–67.

Martinez Lucio, M. and MacKenzie, R. (1999). 'Quality management: a new form of control?', in S. Corby and G. White (eds), *Employee Relations in the Public Services*. London: Routledge.

Marx, K. (1887). *Capital: Volume 1: A Critical Analysis of Capitalist Production*. New York: International Publishers (1987 edn).

Maurice, M., Sellier, F. and Silvestre, J. J. (1986). *The Social Foundations of Industrial Power: A Comparison of France and Germany*. Cambridge MA: MIT Press.

Milkman, R. (1997). *Farewell to the Factory: Auto Workers in the Late Twentieth Century*. Berkeley: University of California Press.

Millward, N., Bryson, A. and Forth, J. (2000). *All Change at Work: British Employment Relations 1980–1998, as Portrayed by the Workplace Industrial Relations Survey Series*. London: Routledge.

Morgan, P., Allington, N. and Heery, E. (2000). 'Employment insecurity in the public services', in E. Heery and J. Salmon (eds), *The Insecure Workforce*. London: Routledge.

Mumford, E. (1999). *Dangerous Decisions*. Kluwer Academic/Plenum Publishers.

Neathey, F. and Hurstfield, J. (1995). *Flexibility in Practice: Women's Employment and Pay in Retail and Finance*. Manchester: IRS/EOC.

Nichols, T. and Beynon, H. (1978). *Living with Capitalism*. London: Routledge & Kegan Paul.

Nolan, J. P., Wichert, I. C. and Burchell, B. J. (2000). 'Job insecurity, psychological well-being and family life', in E. Heery and J. Salmon (eds), *The Insecure Workforce*. London: Routledge.

Noon, M. (1993). 'Control, technology and management offensive in newspapers', *New Technology, Work and Employment*, 8/2: 102–10.

Nottingham, C. and O'Neill, F. (1998). 'Out of the church and into quick fit: nurses and the secularisation of health policy', in A. Dobson and J. Stanyer (eds), *Contemporary Political Studies*. Nottingham: Political Studies Association.

OECD (1995). *Flexible Working Time*. Paris: OECD.

—— (2000). *OECD Employment Outlook*. Paris: OECD.

Oliver, N. and Wilkinson, B. (1988). *The Japanisation of British Industry*. Oxford: Blackwell.

O'Reilly, J. and Fagan, C. (1998). *Part-time Prospects; Part-Time Employment in Europe, North America and the Pacific Rim*. London: Routledge.

Osterman, P. (1994). 'Internal labour markets: theory and change', in C. Kerr and P. D. Staudohar (eds), *Labour Economics and Industrial Relations: Markets and Institutions*. Cambridge, MA: Harvard University Press.

—— (1996). 'Introduction', in P. Osterman (ed.), *Broken Ladders: Managerial Careers in the New Economy*. Oxford: Oxford University Press.

Oswald, A. and Gardener, J. (2001). 'What has been happening to job satisfaction in Britain?' Press release available from the authors at andrew. oswald@warwick.ac.uk

Peck, J. and Theodore, N. (2000). 'Beyond "employability"', *Cambridge Journal of Economics*, 24/6: 729–49.

Perrons, D. (ed.) (1998). *Flexible Working and the Reconciliation of Work and Family Life: A New Form of Precariousness*. Final Report to Community Action Programme on Equal Opportunities for Women and Men. Brussels: European Commission.

Peters, T. and Waterman, O. H. (1982). *In Search of Excellence: Lessons from America's Best Run Companies*. London: Harper Collins Business.

Philpott, J. (1999). *Beyond the Buzzword: 'Employability'*. London: Employment Policy Institute.

Piore, M. J. and Sabel, F. S. (1984). *The Second Industrial Divide*. New York: Basic Books.

Polanyi, K. (1944). *The Great Transformation: The Political and Economic Origins of Our Time*. New York: The Free Press (1957 edn).

Power, M. (1997). *The Audit Society*. Oxford: Oxford University Press.

Poynter, G. (2000a). *Restructuring in the Service Industries: Management Reform and Workplace Relations in the UK Service Sector*. London: Mansell.

—— (2000b). ' "Thank you for calling": the new ideology of work in the service economy', *Soundings*, spring: 151–60.

Pratt, J. (1998). 'Re-placing money: the evolution of branch banking in Britain', *Environment and Planning A*, 30/8: 2211–26.

Purcell, J. (1987). 'Mapping management style in employee relations', *Journal of Management Studies*, 24/5: 533–48.

—— (1991). 'The rediscovery of the management prerogative: the management of labour relations in the 1980s', *Oxford Review of Economic Policy*, 7/1: 33–43.

Ranade, W. (1994). *A Future for the NHS? Health Care in the 1990s*. Essex: Longman Group.

Rees, G. and Fielder, S. (1992). 'The service economy, subcontracting and the new employment relations: contract catering and cleaning', *Work, Employment and Society*, 6/3: 347–68.

Reich, R. (1991). *The Work of Nations*. New York: Vintage Books.

Rogaly, J. (1998). 'Time for a new David to tackle Goliath', *The Financial Times*, 18 April.

Rosenthal, P., Hill, S. and Peccei, R. (1997). 'Checking out service: evaluating excellence, HRM and TQM in services', *Work, Employment and Society*, 11/3: 481–503.

Rubery, J. (1978). 'Structured labour markets, worker organisation and low pay', *Cambridge Journal of Economics*, 2/1: 17–37.

—— (1994). 'Internal and external labour markets: towards an integrated framework', in J. Rubery and F. Wilkinson (eds), *Employer Strategy and the Labour Market*. Oxford: Oxford University Press.

—— (1998a). 'Working Time in the UK', *Transfer*, 4/4: 657–77.

—— (1998b). 'Part-time work: a threat to labour standards', in J. O'Reilly and C. Fagan (eds), *Part-time Prospects*. London: Routledge.

—— and Grimshaw, D. (forthcoming). 'The employment challenges associated with ICT: the problem of job quality', *International Labour Review*.

—— and Horrell, S. (1993). 'The new competition and working time', *Human Resource Management Journal*, 3/2: 1–13.

—— and Wilkinson, F. (1994). *Employer Strategy and the Labour Market*. ESRC Social Change and Economic Life Initiative. Oxford: Oxford University Press.

Savage, M. and Witz, A. (eds) (1992). *Gender and Bureaucracy*. Oxford: Blackwell.

Sennett, R. (1998). *The Corrosion of Character: The Personal Consequences of Work in the New Capitalism*. London: Norton.

Sharp, M. (1994). 'Innovation in the chemicals industry', in M. Dodgson and R. Rothwell (eds), *The Handbook of Industrial Innovation*. Aldershot: Edward Elgar.

Simpson, R. (1997). 'Presenteeism, power and organisational change: long hours as a career barrier and the impact on the working lives of women managers', *British Journal of Management*, 9 (special issue): 37–52.

Smith, A. (1776). *The Wealth of Nations: Books 1–111*. London: Penguin (1986 edn).

Smith, C. and Elger, T. (2000). 'The societal effects school and transnational transfer: the case of Japanese investment in Britain', in A. Sorge and M. Maurice (eds), *Embedding Organisations*. Amsterdam: John Benjamin.

Sorge, A. and Maurice, M. (2000). *Embedding Organisations*. Amsterdam: John Benjamin.

Stigler, George J. (1991). 'Charles Babbage', *Journal of Economic Literature*, 29: 1149–52.

Storey, J. (ed.) (1995). *Human Resource Management*. London: Routledge.

Streeck, W. (1987). 'The uncertainties of management in the management of uncertainty', *Work, Employment and Society*, 1/3: 281–308.

Sturdy, A., Grugulis, I. and Willmott, H. (eds) (2001). *Customer Service: Empowerment and Entrapment*. Basingstoke: Palgrave.

Supiot, A. (2001). *Beyond Employment: Changes in Work and the Future of Labour Law in Europe*. Oxford: Oxford University Press.

Taylor, P. and Bain, P. (1999). 'An assembly line in the head: work and employee relations in the call centre', *Industrial Relations Journal*, 30/2: 101–17.

Thompson, E. P. (1967). 'Time, work discipline and industrial capitalism', *Past and Present*, December: 56–97.

Thompson, P. (1983). *The Nature of Work*. London: Macmillan.

——and Warhurst, C. (eds) (1998). *Workplaces of the Future*. London: Macmillan.

Tickell, A. (1997). 'Restructuring the British financial sector in the twenty-first century', *Capital and Class*, 62: 13–19.

Touraine, A. (1965). *Workers' Attitudes to Technical Change*. Manpower and Social Affairs Directorate, Social Affairs Division of the OECD. Paris: OECD.

Trade Union Congress [TUC] (1996). *Part of the Union? The Challenge of Recruiting and Organising Part-time Workers*. London: TUC.

—— (1997). *General Council Report: Next Steps for the New Unionism*. London: TUC.

Turnbull, P. J. (1988). 'Leaner and possibly fitter: the management of redundancy in Britain', *Industrial Relations Journal*, 19/3: 201–13.

Turnbull, P. and Wass, V. (2000). 'Redundancy and the paradox of job insecurity', in E. Heery and J. Salmon (eds), *The Insecure Workforce*. London: Routledge.

Ure, A. (1830). *Philosophy of Manufactures*. London: Charles Knight.

Vosko, L. (2000). *Temporary Work. The Gendered Rise of a Precarious Employment Relationship*. Toronto, Canada: Toronto University Press.

Waddington, J. (2000). 'United Kingdom: recovering from the neo-liberal assault', in J. Waddington and R. Hoffmann (eds), *Trade Unions in Europe: Facing Challenges and Searching for Solutions*. Brussels: European Trade Union Institute.

Wajcman, J. (1998). *Managing Like a Man*. Cambridge: Polity Press.

Walby, S. (1997). *Gender Transformations*. London: Routledge.

Walker, B. and Davis, H. (1999). 'Perspectives on contractual relationships and the move towards Best Value in local authorities', *Local Government Studies*, 25/2: 16–37.

Walker, R. (1999). 'Putting capital in its place: globalization and the prospects for labor', *Geoforum*, 31/3: 263–84.

Walsh, T. (1990). 'Flexible utilisation in the private sector', *Work, Employment and Society*, 4/4: 517–30.

Ward, K. G., Grimshaw, D., Rubery, J. and Beynon, H. (2001). 'Dilemmas in the management of temporary work agency staff', *Human Resource Management Journal*, 11/4: 3–21.

Warhurst, C. and Thompson, P. (1998). 'Hands, hearts and minds: changing work and workers at the end of the century', in P. Thompson and C. Warhurst (eds), *Workplaces of the Future*. London: Macmillan.

Webb, J. (1992). 'The mismanagement of innovation', *Sociology*, 26/3: 471–92.

White, G. (1999). 'The remuneration of public servants: fair pay or new pay?', in S. Corby and G. White (eds), *Employee Relations in the Public Services: Themes and Issues*. London: Routledge.

Wilkinson, F. (1983). 'Productive systems', *Cambridge Journal of Economics*, 7/314: 413–30.

Williamson, O. E. (1975). *Markets and Hierarchies: Analysis and Antitrust Implications*. New York: The Free Press.

—— (1985). *The Economic Institutions of Capitalism*. New York: The Free Press.

Willmott, H. (1993). 'Strength is ignorance; slavery is freedom: managing culture in modern organisations', *Journal of Management Studies*, 30/4: 515–52.

Womack, J. P., Jones, D. T. and Roos, D. (1990). *The Machine that Changed the World*. New York: Maxwell Macmillan International.

Wray, D. (1993). 'Changing employment relations in a local labour market: consent after the closure'. Unpublished MA thesis, University of Durham.

Wright Mills, C. (1957). *White Collar*. Oxford: Oxford University Press.

Zemke, R. and Schaaf, D. (1989). *The Service Edge*. New York: New American Library.

INDEX